TRAFALGAR SQUARE

TRAFALGAR SQUARE

Emblem of Empire

Rodney Mace

2005

LAWRENCE AND WISHART
LONDON

First published in 1976, this edition 2005

British Library Cataloguing in Publication Data.
A catalogue record for this book is available from the British Library

Printed in Great Britain by Cambridge University Press

To
Jessica, Joe, Shay, Anisha,
Róisin and Niamh

PREFACE

Like many a schoolchild I was introduced to Trafalgar Square, probably on a day trip to London, by way of feeding pigeons or being photographed against one of the lions at the base of Nelson's Column. Later and much more importantly the Square became a place to hear speeches, to march to or set off from to demonstrate that some hope was left for humanity and justice.

Often on these latter occasions I was struck by an obvious irony. The causes that were so urgently advocated were most often anti-imperialist. Yet the Square in its design is an impenitent and rather vulgar commemorative edifice to men and events that, by force of arms, had helped to extend the hegemony of British capital over large areas of the globe. The present study is an attempt to explore this contradiction and will, I hope, contribute to the debate currently taking place around the bi-centenary of Nelson's death, the battle of Trafalgar and their long aftermath in the popular imagination.

Since this book's first publication in 1976 the Square has continued to be a site of public demonstration, and some of these demonstrations, along with the campaigns they espoused – such as the campaign against the much disliked Tory poll tax – have wrought changes on the government in power. In 2000 the Square was transferred to the Greater London Authority, and there have subsequently been changes made to its century-old layout, which have made it more attractive to the millions of people who pass by or linger there every year, while still retaining its position of being Britain's premier *place politique*.

Many libraries, archives and organisations, along with friends and colleagues, assisted me with the original research for this book. In the intervening thirty years I have often been reminded by those around me that the task I undertook rather lightly in those days of youth has grown more complex with age.

Rodney Mace
Whitbourne, Herefordshire
January 2005

CONTENTS

List of Plates 8
List of Figures 10
Introduction 11

1. Charing Cross 23
2. Hero of Empire 48
3. A Very Select Committee 69
4. Thirty Years in the Making 86
5. Ugly Bronze Images 111
6. Riotous Assembly 134
7. Black Monday and Bloody Sunday 155
8. In the Minister's Gift 204

Appendices 235
Select Bibliography 323
Index 329

LIST OF PLATES

Plates, between pages 234 and 235
(Photographs are by the author unless otherwise credited)

1. Aerial view of Whitehall (Fox Photos)
2. The Duke of York's Column (Fox Photos)
3. Statue of Charles I on site of Charing Cross
4. Imperial Standards of Length, in north wall of Trafalgar Square
5. John Goldicutt's proposal for a London Amphitheatre (R.I.B.A.)
6. St. Martin's Church from Pall Mall East, c. 1825 (G.L.C.)
7. Lowther's Arcade (G.L.C.)
8. Morley's Hotel (G.L.C.)
9. National Gallery and proposed layout for the Square, c. 1838 (Westminster Public Library)
10. Charles Barry's plan for layout of the Square, c. 1840 (Public Record Office)
11. Wyatt's drawing for a Memorial to Nelson (British Library)
12. Nelson's Pillar, Dublin (National Library of Ireland)
13. Wellington Monument, Hyde Park Corner (Science Museum)
14. Nelson Monument, Great Yarmouth (National Monument Record)
15. Goldicutt's design for a National Naval Monument (Westminster Public Library)
16. Bellamy's design for a National Naval Monument (Westminster Public Library)
17. Railton's winning design for Nelson Memorial (British Library)
18. Britton's entry for the Nelson Memorial Competition (Westminster Public Library)
19. Sievier's and Fowler's joint entry (Westminster Public Library)
20. Collmann's entry (Victoria and Albert Museum)
21. Goldicutt's entry (R.I.B.A.)
22. Wetton's entry (Westminster Public Library)
23. M.M.'s entry (British Library)
24. Nelson's Column (G.L.C.)
25. Railton: view of proposed layout for the Square (G.L.C.)
26. One of Railton's designs for layout of the Square (Public Record Office)
27. Nelson's Column under construction (Science Museum)
28. Barry's proposal for a single basin in the Square (Public Record Office)
29. Bas relief "Copenhagen" (National Monument Record)
30. Bas relief "The Nile" (National Monument Record)
31. Bas relief "St. Vincent" (National Monument Record)
32. Bas relief "*Trafalgar*" (National Monument Record)

33. Baily's statue of Nelson (Keystone)
34. Police box in corner of the Square (Fox Photos)
35. Busts of Admirals Cunningham, Jellicoe and Beatty
36. Statue of Major-General Charles Napier
37. Statue of General Sir Henry Havelock
38. A scheme to turn the Square into a garden, 1894 (British Library)
39. Heathcote-Statham's project to redesign the square, 1912 (R.I.B.A.)
40. A suggestion to make Trafalgar Square into Washington Square, 1902 (Harmsworth London Magazine)
41. Suffragette meeting (Radio Times Hulton Picture Library)
42. Launching the "Peace and Joy" Loan, 1919 (Radio Times Hulton Picture Library)
43. Meeting to demand release of Irish prisoners, 1922 (Radio Times Hutton Picture Library)
44. Welcome for Welsh Miners, 1927 (Radio Times Hulton Picture Library)
45. A. J. Cook speaking in the Square, 1927 (Radio Times Hulton Picture Library)
46. Unemployed assembling, 1932 (Keystone)
47. Unemployed in Whitehall, 1932 (Radio Times Hulton Picture Library)
48. Unemployed meeting, 1932 (Radio Times Hutton Picture Library)
49. Unemployed in the Square, 1934 (Radio Times Hutton Picture Library)
50. A placard display (G.L.C.)
51. Second Front Demonstration, 1942 (Keystone)
52. "Wings for Victory Week" (Westminster Public Library)
53. Statue of Charles George Gordon (Radio Times Hulton Picture Library)
54. Meeting to protest against British invasion of Suez, 1956 (Radio Times Hutton Picture Library)
55. A fascist demonstration, 1959 (Keystone)
56. Demonstration during Suez Crisis, 1956 (Fox Photos)
57. C.N.D. rally, 1958 (Camera Press)
58. C.N.D. rally, 1961 (Fox Photos)
59. Committee of 100 sitdown, 1961 (Fox Photos)
60. "Ban the Bomb" demonstration, 1963 (Fox Photos)
61. Vietnam demonstration, 1968 (Keystone)
62. T.U.C. protest demonstration, 1971 (Camera Press)
63. Lapel sticker for students' demonstration, 1972
64. Senora Allende speaking in the Square, 1974 *(Guy* Brett)
65. Protest against ban on meetings on Irish Questions, 1975 (Morning Star)
66. GLC leader Ken Livingstone as Nelson (Rodney Mace)
67. Poll tax riot March 1990 (David Hoffman Picture Library)
68. *Alison Lapper 8 Months Pregnant* 2003 Fourth Plinth competition (Marc Quinn)
69. The Square in 2003 (Hayley Madden, courtesy GLA)

LIST OF FIGURES

Illustrations in text

The Royal Mews at Charing Cross (G.L.C.) 27
Royal Stables at Charing Cross (Westminster Public Library) 28
Temporary barracks at Charing Cross (G.L.C.) 28
Charing Cross and Trafalgar Square 30
John Nash's 1812 proposal (Senate House Library) 32
John Nash's 1826 proposal (Senate House Library) 38
Flaxmann's statue of Britannia (Victoria and Albert Museum) 50
William Woods's proposed National Monument (British Library) 53
Woods's proposed entrance to National Monument (British Library) 54
Construction of Nelson's Column *(Illustrated London News)* 91
Notice prohibiting meetings in the Square, 1848 (Public Record Office) 136
Black Monday, 1886 *(Illustrated London News)* 163
Demonstrators in St. James's Street *(Illustrated London News)* 164
Sleeping out in London *(Illustrated London News)* 173
Handout of bread and soup *(Illustrated London News)* 174
Demonstrations on 23 October 1887 *(Illustrated London News)* 175
Notice prohibiting meetings in the Square, 8 November 1887 *(Illustrated London News)* 178
Police in the Square, 13 November 1887 *(Illustrated London News)* 180
Meeting at Clerkenwell Green, 13 November 1887 *(Illustrated London News)* 181
Demonstrators attacked by police in St. Martin's Lane, 13 November 1887 (Radio Times Hulton Picture Library) 182
Demonstrators crossing Westminster Bridge, 13 November 1887 (Radio Times Hulton Picture Library) 182
Police attack demonstrators in Haymarket, 13 November 1887 *(Illustrated London News)* 183
Police charge in the Square, 13 November 1887 *(Illustrated London News)* 183
Arrival of the Magistrate and Life Guards, 13 November 1887 *(Illustrated London News)* 184
Life Guards parade in the Square, 13 November 1887 *(Illustrated London News)* 185
The Grenadier Guards attack demonstrators, 13 November 1887 (Radio Times Hulton Picture Library) 186
Special constables, 1887 (Radio Times Hulton Picture Library) 186
Notice to prohibit meetings in the Square, 18 November 1887 (Public Record Office) 191
Crane's design for Morris's "Death Song" for Alfred Linnell (British Library) 194
Fifth anniversary of Bloody Sunday (Radio Times Hulton Picture Library) 199
Plan for temporary building in the Square, 1916 (Public Record Office) 211

INTRODUCTION

> … a monument of barbarism, a symbol of brute force and false glory, an affirmation of militarism, a negation of international law, a permanent insult to the conquered by their conquerors …[1]

Most, if not all, capital cities of Western Europe have a place that could be described as their 'front room'. This place, as in a household, attempts to give palpable expression to its host's social, historical and political aspirations. It is most usually a place to be *looked at*, and only occasionally used; somewhere that will impress the neighbours and overawe the country cousins. And death and the memory of death of loved ones are often not far away.

This study argues that in the case of England, for at least the last one hundred and sixty years, Trafalgar Square in the centre of London has been that place. The Square laid out in front of the National Gallery forms the north-eastern corner of an area that is edged by Whitehall to the east, the Palace of Westminster to the south, and Buckingham Palace and Hyde Park Corner to the west, an area that encloses both the symbolic seat of power and the centre of government of the United Kingdom. At almost every turn along the streets and in the parks and open spaces of this square mile stand bronze and stone effigies built to remember past battles and heroic men, most now forgotten. These effigies mark out a history that celebrates those virtues of Britain's national greatness (usually exercised in distant climes) which so enchanted our Victorian and Edwardian forebears – 'strength', 'character', 'courage', 'sacrifice' and 'heroic death'. The equally admired womanly virtues of 'caring' and 'motherhood' are almost totally absent, except for two nurses: a stone statue of Edith Cavell, shot by a German firing squad in 1915, was erected opposite the National Portrait Gallery in 1920; and a large bronze was erected in honour of Florence Nightingale, the 'heroine' of the Crimea, in Waterloo Place in 1915 – five years after her death aged ninety years, and fifty years after the war that made her famous. The reality of war and death for the common soldier, although present all around, is only shown for what it is in Charles Sergeant Jagger's 1925 Royal Artillery Monument at Hyde Park Corner.

What follows is a history of Trafalgar Square written in two interrelated parts; the first part is a detailed examination of how the Square and its monuments came into being in the hundred years from 1840; and the second part shows how, as the national Valhalla, it slowly became transformed into a place synonymous not with heroes of war but with public celebration and demonstration for a better, safer and more just world.

The Square is named after a six hour long sea battle that took place on 21 October 1805 off a small head of land, Cabo de Trafalgar (after Tarf al-Gharb, an Arabic term meaning Cape of Laurels), some thirty miles south along the Costa de la Luz from the Spanish port city of Cadiz.[2] This battle became famous on two counts, firstly because on that windy autumn afternoon the British fleet's commander, the forty-seven-year-old Vice-Admiral Horatio Lord Viscount Nelson, died from a single enemy shot; and secondly, because the combined French and Spanish fleet was routed in the battle, and was never again able to pose any real challenge to British naval domination during the entire period of the ensuing ten years of the war with Napoleon. The coming together of Nelson and Trafalgar as a forecourt to the new National Gallery some forty years after the battle, however, is, as we shall see, more down to chance than to design.

Horatio Nelson's life – from his relatively humble beginnings as the son of a Norfolk parson to his dramatic death aboard the *Victory* – became the subject of legend almost within days of his death. His funeral and burial (in a sarcophagus originally intended for Henry VIII) at St Paul's Cathedral as opposed to Westminster Abbey testified not only to the gratitude of the state but also to the thanks of the City of London's merchants and bankers. Almost to a man they feted his past victories on the high seas – victories which, as it turned out, would keep those very same seas safe for British Empire trade for the next one hundred years. Within a couple of years of his death books about his life and exploits began pouring off the presses; biographies, many hagiographic, were soon written, volumes of his letters were edited, and reminiscences were penned by those who knew him, many detailing his private life – especially his liaison, late on, with Emma Lady Hamilton. Monuments were erected all around the nation and the Empire. But in London – the very centre of Empire – there was no public memorial to Nelson apart from the one in St Paul's Cathedral. As we shall see, it was not until thirty-five years after his death that anyone thought to remedy the situation by mounting a competition to build a public monument in London. Meanwhile, in the years and decades that followed, the Nelson myth grew like Topsy, much stimulated by the many editions of the 1813 biography by the poet laureate Robert Southey (an author not known for his historical accuracy on matters naval, or for that matter on anything else in his hero's life).[3] Widely circulated in English Public Schools and frequently given out on school prize days, this book, and the many ballads and chap-books being read by the newly literate working classes, ensured Nelson's place in the nation's imagination. As the Empire reached its zenith towards the end of Victoria's reign, stories of Nelson's exploits became increasingly anthologised amongst other 'heroic lives' and 'leaders of men', in texts that furthered the myth that Britain's greatness was built solely on muscular, male and Christian values. Alongside all this publishing activity, representations of Nelson's final moments flowed from the brushes of painters and the needles of engravers. The most famous and enduring of these were Benjamin West's famous allegorical painting that portrayed Nelson as a Christ-like figure being born aloft by Neptune and angels with Britannia looking on, and Arthur Devis's iconic painting, *The Death of Vice Admiral Lord Viscount Nelson in the Cockpit of HMS Victory*.

In 2003 BBC Television conducted a poll entitled 'Great Britons', in which Nelson came ninth – one below the singer/songwriter John Lennon but well below Diana Princess of Wales and Winston Churchill. (It is interesting to note that Churchill had Nelson's funeral arrangements in mind when planning his own.) Nelson and Trafalgar are also remembered in town and street names, in pubs and cafes, and – when gravitas is needed – in brands for everything from cigars to insurance. A much restored *Victory*, the ship Nelson commanded at Trafalgar, is the central exhibit at the Royal Naval Museum at Portsmouth and is visited by tens of thousands of people every year. Nelson himself has become part of the heritage and celebrity industry; he is the only British naval officer to have museums solely devoted to his life, and the number of books written about him in recent years is almost an industry in itself. And in the period running up to the bicentenary of his death, there has been a massive increase in all this activity, with new exhibitions, lectures, and television and radio programmes being commissioned, and in particular a major exhibition at the National Maritime Museum at Greenwich.

However, times have changed since the centenary celebrations in 1905, when Britain still believed that it had an Empire and that Nelson and Trafalgar had played an important part in its formation. Among historians at least, Nelson has been pushed off his saintly perch in recent years. Generations of historical writing are now being reappraised, as are the events and personalities involved in his life and exploits; and a more measured view of the man is beginning to emerge. However, it is likely to take some time for this reappraisal to dent the popular imagination's view of Nelson as an archetypal British hero – fearless, vain, high-handed, badly dressed, energetic, humble, disobedient and cunning. Several contemporary commentators might agree with Terry Coleman's description of Nelson as 'a paramount naval genius and a natural born predator', though they might not accept the recent branding of Nelson by some Italian and French academics as a 'war criminal' (because of his treatment of the rebels in Naples in 1794).[4] What all agree is that Nelson was an exceptional and often foolhardy commander, who frequently needlessly risked his own life and the lives of those that served with him; indeed some of his contemporaries suggested that, had Nelson been a bit more careful at Trafalgar, he wouldn't have been such an easy target for a French sniper. But caution and restraint were not his style. When he spoke of the enemy the word 'annihilate' frequently came up – a sentiment not usually found among his peers in the Georgian navy, or given expression on the monuments built to commemorate him.

It is surprising that a figure so deeply embedded in the Victorian imagination should be largely represented in the capital city of the 'nation he so loved' with four rather dull and pedestrian bas-reliefs of his naval victories, and a statue that is out of sight, atop a column placed in an even duller square – none of which warrant more than scant mention in the canons of architectural or sculptural history of the period. Yet despite this Nelson and his monument are perhaps the best-known piece of public sculpture in the imagery of Britain-as-London, as testified by their appearance on tens of thousands of postcards, tourist photographs and trinkets.

The choice of a classical form for Nelson's monument and the Square was probably deliberate, although other forms were initially put forward for consideration, not least those in a 'gothic' style, with their references back to Tudor England (as you will see below in the entries for the Nelson Monument competition: illustrations 15-23 and Appendix 2). However it is not the contention of this book that there is anything more than a very loose congruence, at any particular historical juncture, between, on the one hand, architectural and sculptural forms and, on the other, social and economic forms. It would be too simplistic to argue for a direct correlation between the rise of neo-classicism in England and the emergence of the idea of Empire in a Roman sense. But there is enough evidence to make some general observations. The most blatant examples are to be found towards the end of the period, especially when commemorating military heroes, when direct reference of this kind was both sought and intended.

One particularly interesting example, which predates Nelson's monument, is the Memorial to the Duke of York, one-time Commander-in-Chief of the British Army, that stands in Waterloo Place, not more than a stone's throw from Trafalgar Square.[5] In 1829 the Duke of York Memorial Committee (which counted among its members the Duke's successor as C-in-C and later prime minister, the Duke of Wellington, as well as Lord Palmerston, Lord Shaftesbury and Sir Robert Peel) decided on Benjamin Wyatt's edifice for the memorial, which was modelled almost exactly on the Emperor Trajan's Column in Rome. This was a quite deliberate choice. Trajan's Column, it will be remembered, was erected to illustrate two successful military campaigns, which in themselves marked the moment when the Roman Empire had reached its greatest extent. (The absence on the London column of a bas-relief similar to Trajan's resulted from the constraints of economy rather than design.) Several other suggestions for this Memorial had been equally 'imperial' in their choice of forms. The architect C. R. Cockerell thought a 'Temple of Military Virtue' appropriate. Someone else put forward a column surmounted by a Roman Eagle. Short shrift was given to one sculptor's suggestion that 'at the feet of the statue' a group of children should stand 'pointing to the Prince under whose benevolent attention and parental care they had been fortunate enough to have lived'. A memorial to a drunken womaniser and military incompetent seemed gross to many – but personal virtue was usually of scant importance in the matter of public statuary, as we shall see.

Similar allusions to a Roman military commander were undoubtedly in the minds of a similar group of men in choosing in 1839 a design for Nelson's monument (the group again included Wellington – himself already a military hero – and also Peel, twice prime minister, later to meet a rather inglorious death through falling off his horse). They chose William Railton's design for the Memorial, in which the classical reference was a little less direct but no less potent. Railton's Memorial was directly modelled – especially in its Corinthian capital – on a column in the temple of Mars Ultor (Mars the Avenger) in the Forum of Augustus in Rome. Ronald Syme describes the Forum and the Temple – which together formed the culmination of the whole building programme of Augustus – as the 'shrine and setting where the Senate debated on war and peace, where generals offered prayers before going to their armies or thanksgiving when returning from successful wars':

> … Around the Forum stood the mailed statues of military men with the inscribed record of their *res gestae*, from Aeneas and Romulus in the beginning, down to recent worthies who had held triumphs or received the *ornamenta triumphalia* in lieu of distinction. In the temple itself three deities were housed in concord: Mars, Venus Genetrix and Divus Julius …

> The Temple of Mars the Avenger had been vowed by Caesar's son at Philippi when he fought against the assassins of his parents, the enemies of the Fatherland.[6]

To a romantic classicist like Railton, the similarities between the events and people depicted in the Forum of Augustus and those of England's wars with France (and particularly with Napoleon) must have been overwhelming.

The fact that the Square's principal feature is a pale reflection of Imperial Roman greatness may have incensed many people, but it has not yet resulted in any concerted attempts by the populace to physically destroy it. The ruling class, on the other hand, to judge by their considerable protectiveness towards the column and the Square in 1848 and 1887 and many times subsequently, has perceived these emblems of Empire as properties of immense importance. In the monument's early days threats to its fabric by a popular uprising were often on the minds of police and government, and in the 1870s they had before them the example of the Paris Commune's treatment of the Napoleon column in the *Place Vendôme* in May 1871. The Commune, it may be recalled, demolished what Theophile Gautier described as the 'great exclamation mark set at the close of the sonorous phrase the First Empire', because of its 'Caesarian' Bonapartist associations.[7]

Almost exactly one hundred years after Railton's Nelson monument was begun, a man whose imperial ambitions were to put in the shade those of Napoleon or Nelson got quite close to destroying it as a feature of the London landscape. Adolf Hitler's plan was not to bomb the column, but to remove it, after a successful German invasion of England (code-named Operation Sea Lion) in September 1940. The plan, drawn up by the Nazis' Department III of the Security Service (the SS) and dated 26 August 1940, was as follows:

> There is no symbol of British Victory in the World War corresponding to the French monument near Compiegne … On the other hand, ever since the battle of Trafalgar, the Nelson Column represents for England a symbol of British Naval might and world domination. It would be an impressive way of underlining the German Victory if the Nelson Column were to be transferred to Berlin.[8]

The column's re-erection in the capital of the Thousand Year Reich would have undoubtedly been ably stage-managed by Hitler's architect, that exemplary latter-day Roman revivalist Albert Speer. Instead of looking down on Britain's Imperial focus – Whitehall and the Palace of Westminster – Nelson would have looked with an equally stony and disdainful one-eyed gaze on Germany's: the Reichstag and the Fuhrer's Chancellery. It is interesting to speculate whether the SS would have also removed the bronze replicas of Britain's Standard Imperial Measures which are let into the wall of the North Terrace, and replaced them with metric ones in iron.[9]

Many writers have remarked on how the classical column, with its Roman references, developed a fetish-like significance for nineteenth-century capitalism; it appeared on buildings large and small, singly and in groups, particularly in cemeteries and war memorials. In 1890 Ignatius Donnelly (pseudonym for Edward Bois-Gilbert, a leading figure in the American Populist Party) wrote a utopian novel entitled *Caesar's Column*, a book that unremittingly assailed the graft and corruption of the capitalism of his day. The novel's hero, Gabriel Welstein, arrives in New York from East Africa in 1898 to find that latter-day capitalism has developed into a system of unprecedented selfishness on the part of the rich minority, built on an equally unprecedented brutalisation of the 'working masses'. The story culminates with a very bloody unplanned worldwide insurrection, and a total massacre of the rich, with the workers, under the leadership of a sinister Brotherhood of Destruction, achieving the destruction of capitalism. Not surprisingly after a massacre on that scale, the streets of New York lay thick with the corpses of the rich. To dispose of these, the Brotherhood's leader, Caesar Lomellini, commanded that they be laid in layers, feet to the centre, and covered with concrete, to form an enormous column in 'commemoration of the death and burial of modem civilization'. A civilization, the column's inscription says, that was dominated by giant corporations who 'plunder the poor … (have) hearts harder than nether mill-stone … and degrade humanity and outrage God'.[10] By making the ruling class become the column instead of surmounting it, Donnelly succeeds, albeit somewhat crudely, in defiling a near sacred form.

Trafalgar Square and its several monuments, of course, speak the language of the ruling class. To the mass of ordinary people, whose exploitation and death through nearly three centuries had enabled the ideal of Empire to be realised, the Square offers no bronze or granite memorial; yet it is they and their descendants who in the course of time by the use of the site as a public forum have given it its real significance.

Among the most oppressed in the cause of Empire were the armed forces themselves. Sadly, few among them put words to their conditions of life. Those that did, however, spoke with poignancy more than equal to that found in the work of their more fortunate contemporaries. A soldier after being flogged with a cat-o'-nine-tails for a minor offence in 1832 recalled:

> … Only fifty (lashes) had been inflicted and the time since they began was like a long period of life; I felt as if I had lived all the time of my real life in pain and torture, and the time when existence had pleasure in it was a dream, long, long gone by.[11]

Flogging, a punishment often meted out in great measure by Nelson, was still common practice in the British Navy well into the twentieth century. It was officially abolished in 1939.

In 1797, when Nelson was near the height of his fame and fortune, an anonymous sailor fighting desperately for a better life for those who served below decks during the Nore Mutiny wrote:

> Whilst Landsmen wander tho' control'd
> And boast the rites of freedom,
> Oh! view the tender's loathsome hole
> Where droop your injured seamen.
> Dragged by Oppression's savage grasp
> From every dear connection,
> Midst putrid air, oh! see them gasp,
> Oh! mark their deep dejection.
>   Blush then, O! blush, ye pension host,
>   Who wallow in profusion,
>   For our foul cell proves all your boast
>   To be but mere delusion.
>
> If Liberty be ours, O! say
> Why are not all protected?
> Why is the hand of ruffian sway
> 'Gainst seamen thus directed?
> Is thus your proof of British rights?
> Is this rewarding bravery?
> Oh! shame to boast your tars' exploits,
> Then doom these tars to slavery.
>   Blush then, &c
>
> Hark then, ye minions of a court
> Who prate at Freedom's blessing,
> Who every hell-born war support

And vindicate impressing,
A time will come when things like you,
Mere baubles of creation,
No more will make mankind pursue
The work of devastation.
Blush then, &c' …[12]

Conditions a hundred and fifty years later for those still being forced to live below decks under admirals like Cunningham, the last 'hero' commemorated in the Square, were hardly different from those under Nelson. In 1946 one of them wrote:

> … I had no bunk. I slept where I could, when I could. The mess deck was a den indeed. We continuously shipped seas, our ventilators took in large quantities of water. For days on end, sometimes weeks, there was water to the depth of two or three inches about our living quarters, water that mingled with fuel-oil and vomit … We lived like felons. Tired men coming off watch, weak with vomiting, tried to clear up the filth, but only added to it. The stench was horrible. I was always wet. There was no means of drying our clothes. The ablutions were primitive. Two or three ordinary kitchen bowls served as baths. There was only one bath in the ship – for officers.[13]

It is only left to echo in this respect the poet John Masefield's famous words: 'Our naval glory was built up by the blood and agony of thousands of barbarously maltreated men.'[14]

The Navy didn't have it all its own way in the Square, for between 1856 and 1886 three 'soldier heroes' of the British Army made their appearance in bronze. Two of them, Charles Napier and Henry Havelock, are almost completely unknown today, while the third, Charles Gordon, now relegated to Embankment Gardens, is probably only known for his appearance as the hero in the big budget Hollywood movie *Khartoum*.[15] All three were well known in the nineteenth century as soldiers who, as ruthlessly as Nelson, championed the British Empire abroad, Napier and Havelock in India, Gordon in China and Sudan.[16]

In the original design for the Square the plinths at the corners of the north terrace were to be surmounted by equestrian figures, but this never happened – or not in the way the original design intended. George IV, who occupies the plinth on the north east side opposite South Africa House, is there by mistake; and what has come to be known as the 'Fourth Plinth' has, until recently, remained conspicuously empty. However this all began to change in 1996 when Pru Leith, Chair of the Royal Society of Arts, began a campaign for the empty plinth to become the site for contemporary sculpture. After three successful trial runs to test public reaction, which included a naked Christ figure with a crown of barbed wire and an inverted plinth in transparent resin, a limited competition, with a jury chaired by the director of the National Gallery, was held in 2003. Of the six entries, the joint winners were Marc Quinn's *Alison Lapper 8 Months Pregnant* and Thomas Schutte's *Hotel for Birds* (see illustration 68). Marc Quinn's entry caused a considerable stir as his subject was not only pregnant but also disabled; it brought forth the usual chorus of derisory comments about modern art, and anyway wouldn't a statue of the Queen Mother be better. Both the jury and Quinn himself defended the figure, pointing out that Nelson himself was without part of a limb and had limited sight in one eye. But also to the point is that Quinn's proposal is a woman, the first to be remembered in the Square ever, and the third in the whole Westminster area. However, and rather sadly, *Alison Lapper 8 Months Pregnant* is not to be permanent, as it is intended that the Fourth Plinth should become a site for a changing exhibition over the years.[17]

The last three chapters of this book are devoted not to an analysis of the architectural and sculptural elements that make up the Square, but to its use as a public forum, almost as soon as it was built, by working-class organisations, trade unions, peace groups and the like in their struggle for a more just and safe world.

After one particularly turbulent time in the 1880s the designer and socialist William Morris wrote *News from Nowhere*, a vision of a future England transformed from capitalism to socialism. In the famous Chapter Seventeen, 'How the Change Came', Morris details the precipitating event that brought about this revolution: the 'massacre of Trafalgar Square'. This was an event of such gravity that the worker's consciousness was changed from a mere trade union one to a higher and more political one, thereby producing a qualitative change in the relations between the classes.[18]

It is arguable that most of the events that have taken place in the Square over its lifetime have contributed only on the margins to the sort of change wished for by Morris and the early socialists. But one event, the 'anti-poll tax riot' of March 1990, did much to unseat Margaret Thatcher as leader of the Tory Party a little later. Uncannily these 'anti-poll tax riots' in the Square seemed to mirror the events of the riot of November 1887 (see illustrations 25, 29), including the riding down of a demonstrator by a police horse, but this time in full view of the press and television cameras.

In the late 1990s a change did come, though not of quite the sort that

Morris had imagined, when institutional responsibility for the Square changed. Along with Parliament Square, it was handed over from central government to the newly created Greater London Authority.

Some might have seen this as a poisoned chalice for new Mayor of London Ken Livingstone, at the time much derided by New Labour and Tories alike. However, the opposite turned out to be the case. Within months of coming to power the GLA set in train plans that were to transform the Square from a traffic island into a truly popular esplanade. In July 2003 the project was completed with a grand flight of steps connecting a traffic free concourse in front of the National Gallery down into the main body of the Square. Traffic was re-routed, a cafe and public lavatories were set into the north wall, heritage wardens were appointed and serious attempts were made to rid the Square of the pigeon infestation – with Ken Livingstone describing pigeons as 'flying rats'. In 2004 the National Gallery opened a new street-level entrance giving direct access to the concourse, which completed the transformation of the Square, and was much welcomed by the Square's neighbours and everyone who uses it, including demonstrators.

But what has really made the difference is the way the Square has been reclaimed by the people of London, ably assisted by the GLA, for it is no longer the sole preserve of the state and its dead, with the population let in on sufferance, but truly a place that is both popular and yet still political.

In summary, the object of this book is simple. It sets out to show that, as in any drama, the stage and all that is on it form an integral and indissoluble historical link with the narrative.

NOTES

1. The French revolutionary, Felix Pyat, on Napoleon's Column in the Place Vendome, quoted in Stewart Edwards, *The Paris Commune 1871* (Newton Abbot 1972, pp.301-2).
2. By coincidence a laurel wreath indicating honour and glory was placed on Nelson's coffin next to his cocked hat and viscount coronet at his state funeral in St Paul's Cathedral. No women were invited to the funeral, not even his wife Francis Lady Nelson.
3. Robert Southey, *Life of Nelson* (London 1813). More than fifty editions of this book had appeared by 1914, and a further fifty by 2000.
4. For a full discussion of these issues, see Terry Coleman, *Nelson: The man and the legend* (London 2002).
5. For correspondence relating to this monument see PRO WORKS 20/5/1 and PRO WORKS 20/6/1.

6. Ronald Syme, *The Roman Revolution* (Oxford 1966) pp.470-1. See also, Alex Boetius and J. B. Ward Perkins, *Etruscan and Roman Architecture* (Harmondsworth 1970), p.190.
7. Quoted in Frank Jellinck, *The Paris Commune of 1871* (London 1937), p.283.
8. Quoted in Norman Logmate, *If Britain had Fallen* (London 1972), p.135. For details of this whole invasion plan see David Lampe, *The Last Ditch* (London 1968); and R.R.A. Wheatley, *Operation Sea Lion* (London 1958).
9. For the correspondence relating to the placing of these standards see PRO WORKS 20/2-3.
10. Ignatius Donnelly, *Caesar's Column* (Chicago 1890), pp.329-30. For an interesting discussion of this novel see A. L. Morton, *The English Utopia* (London 1971), pp.229-232.
11. Quoted in the writer and poet John Masefield's extraordinary book first published in 1905, entitled *Sea Life in Nelson's Time* (London 1971), p.74.
12. PRO ADMIRALITY 1/727, Nore Mutiny, papers of the Repulse No 2 1797.
13. Quoted in Hannan Swaffer, *What would Nelson Do?* (London 1946), pp.27-8.
14. Masefield op. cit., pix.
15. Basil Dearden's ponderous 1966 film featured an all-star cast, with Charlton Heston playing Gordon, and Laurence Olivier a blacked-up Mahdi.
16. For a particularly good analysis of the making of male heroes in the nineteenth century, see Graham Dawson, *Soldier Heroes: British Adventure, Empire and the Imagining of Masculinities* (London 1994).
17. Artists during the trial period were Marc Wallinger, Bill Woodrow and Rachel Whiteread. The other artists in the competition were Chris Burden, Sokari Douglas Camp, Stefan Gec and Sarah Lucas.
18. For some of the circumstances surrounding the writing of *News from Nowhere*, see Fiona MacCarthy, *William Morris* (London 1994), pp.583-8; and E. P. Thompson, *William Morris: Romantic to Revolutionary* (London 1955), pp.692-8.

1

CHARING CROSS

"Where all that pass *inter nos*
May be proclaimed at Charing Cross"
Pope

THE APPROACH TO WHITEHALL

Until about 1820 Charing Cross was the effective northern "gate" to Whitehall and the Royal Park of St. James. Trafalgar Square was an enlargement of the forecourt, as it were, in front of this "gate". It is not possible within the scope of this book to do more than hint at some of the events that for three hundred years made Charing Cross the site for a continuing sparring match between the State and the people.

Firstly, however, a brief word to clear up some of the confusion that surrounds the name Charing Cross. This, by the way, does *not* refer to the nineteenth-century monument by E. M. Barry in front of the Southern Region railway station. The village of Charing existed long before the planting *c.* 1293 of the commemorative cross to Eleanor of Castille by her bereaved husband Edward. In an article in *Notes and Queries*, the philologist, Walter Skeat, suggests that Charing does not derive, however appealingly, from a corruption of *chère reine* (Eleanor); instead, as in other places, from the Anglo-Saxon *cerr*, Old High German *cher*, meaning a turning or bend (in the Thames), the most pronounced one between Chelsea and Wapping.[1]

Incidentally Eleanor's Cross was pulled down by order of the Long Parliament in 1647. Its Caen stone was used to improve some of the paving in Whitehall, its Dorset marble to make knife handles. One verse writer bemoaned that "Now Charing Cross is down" that lawyers would be "undone" and unable to find their way to Westminster.

To return to events. To approach Whitehall Palace from anywhere except by boat meant to approach it via Charing Cross. During the sixteenth and seventeenth centuries the river Thames was, of course, the most important entrance to the centre of government; it was not, however, the route that armies returning successful from battle, dissidents intent on overthrowing the crown, or large corteges of noblemen on horseback would take to present themselves to the Palace. Being on foot or horse, they most often came through the City, much of which had spread westwards along Fleet Street and the Strand, behind the large houses and palaces on the river front. Charing Cross was, as it were, "without" the Palace of Whitehall walls, a place where the "State" and "People" could and did demonstrate their often mutual distaste and disapproval of each other, and sometimes their pleasure and rejoicing.

The State had, by the erection of gates, mounting of guards and the enacting of legislation, quite successfully prevented any sacking or assassination within the Palace walls. *Wriothesley's Chronicle* tells how in 1542 Henry VIII had forbidden anyone to come before him wearing a sword, so afraid was he for his life;[2] also how in 1554 Sir Thomas Wyatt, angered at Queen Mary's intention to marry Philip of Spain, marched on London, and at Charing Cross he temporarily defeated the troops of Sir John Gage; but in a later encounter,[3]

> "the Earl of Pembroke's men cut off his trayne and slue divers of the rebells; but Wyatt himself with divers others came in at Temple Barre and so throwowe Fleet Street to the Bell Savage, crying 'A Wyatt, a Wyatt! God save Queen Marie!'"

During this period several men, both Spanish and English, were hanged at Charing Cross for murder in pursuance of their causes.[4] In 1640 Prynne, Burton and Bastwick presented themselves at Charing Cross to plead their case; Prynne was attended by hundreds of horses and carriages and many on foot having joined his cause along the way. After the Battle of Edgehill in 1643 the City was fortified; Charing Cross as in later times was itself not closed, but left free for the movement of troops, between the Palaces and the artillery forts built at Hyde Park Corner and Constitution Hill.[5]

During the Civil War Charing Cross was the place of countless beheadings, hangings, drawings and quarterings. The majority of regicides were put to death there. At the execution of John Cook and Hugh Peters, Oliver Cromwell's chaplain, in 1660, the head of Harrison, who had been executed three days earlier,[6]

> "was placed on the sledge which carried Cook, with the face uncovered and directed towards him".

These displays of brutality had a considerable effect on the public, arousing substantial sympathy for the victims. So much so that the Government ordered that in future all such events should take place at

Tyburn, Charing Cross being too close to the centre of power for such an assembly of large often anti-government crowds.

Not all the dissent was expressed or suppressed in such a violent way. During the seventeenth and eighteenth centuries, Charing Cross was the site of many taverns and coffee houses; the places of so much intrigue and plotting against the Crown. During the reign of William III, the "Blue Posts" in Spring Gardens was "a great resort of Jacobites"; Thomas Macaulay says Channock breakfasted there on the day he ambushed the King at Turnham Green.[7] There too, Tobias Smollett is said, after having walked through the obvious rejoicings and bonfires in the streets celebrating Cumberland's cruel success at Culloden, to have read the first six stanzas of his poem "The Tears of Scotland" to some friends. The friends urged prudence, but Smollett would have nothing of it and wrote the seventh there and then.

On 11 June 1731, the *Daily Advertiser* gives a clear and somewhat grim description of another activity that was seemingly a common sight at Charing Cross during the first half of the eighteenth century: the practice of branding, nose splitting and ear lopping.[8]

> "Joseph Crook alias Sir Peter Stranger, stood on the pillory for one hour, after which he was seated in an elbow chair. . . . The common hangman cut off his ears with an incision knife and showed them to the spectators . . . slit, both his nostrils with a pair of scissors and seared them with a hot iron. . . ."

Sir Christopher Wren, aware some forty years earlier of the possible threats to the security of Whitehall Palace, wrote in September 1689:[9]

> "Whereas information hath been given to this board (their Majesties Works) that there is a great and numerous concourse of Papists and other persons disaffected with the Government that resort to the Coffee House of one Bromfield . . . there is a Door lately opened out of that court (Buckingham Court) into the lower part of the Spring Gardens that leads to St. James Park, which the said Papists and disaffected persons meet and consult which may be of dangerous consequence . . . the said Door to be forthwith bricked or otherwise so closed up as you shall judge most fit for the security of their Majesties' Palace of Whitehall, and the said Park and the avenues of the same."

ROYAL PREROGATIVE AND COMMON RIGHTS

Disputes over the right of the Crown to curtail, prevent or change what were seen as common rights were not only events of the nineteenth and twentieth centuries. After the dissolution of the monasteries by Henry VIII the right of commoning on Charing Cross Field was given to the parishioners of St. Margaret's (Westminster) and St. Martin's-in-the-Fields, incidentally both "Royal" churches, this right existing up until the beginning of Elizabeth's reign. Elizabeth, wanting to increase her revenues, leased a greater part of the area to a man called Dawson. Dawson immediately divided and enclosed it, depriving the parishioners of these common rights. Angered by this, the parishioners assembled with picks and spades, destroyed all the fences, filled up the ditches and generally returned the ground to its original condition. Representations were made to the Queen and after an investigation it was found that the revenue from Dawson was so small that the common rights were restored and Dawson's lease terminated.[10]

Other than James Gibbs' St. Martin's-in-the-Fields (1722–6) the statue of Charles I is the only other item on the landscape of Charing Cross and Trafalgar Square that was there before 1800 and has survived more or less unscathed to the present day. Hubert le Soeur began work on it in 1633 and completed it in 1638 (though it was not finally put in place until 1676), and it is supposed to be the first equestrian statue of its kind in England. The pedestal is probably by Joshua Marshall, a carver employed by Grinling Gibbons. The statue itself has had a chequered history; it survives today only by good luck, pieces having been stolen and the vandalisms of one sort or another to which most public statues fall victim having put it in constant need of repair. The *Annual Register* reported that on 14 April 1810, the sword buckles and straps fell off. It has acted not only as a coach stop, a sedan chair stand, and an obstacle to traffic, but also as a place where the unemployed gathered and until 1837, when it was abolished, the site of a public pillory. It was some hundred and thirty-five years earlier, in 1703 Daniel Defoe had stood in the pillory on 29, 30 and 31 July; he, however, was not stoned to death, but garlanded with flowers, while his "Hymn to the Pillory" was sold in large numbers as a broadsheet to the crowd.

During the whole of the period just discussed almost all of the area just north of Charing Cross, bounded on the east by the (then) lower end of St. Martin's Lane, on the west by Whitcombe Street and on the north by Green Street had been occupied by the Royal (King's) Mews. A Royal mews of sorts had existed from at least the fourteenth century; Geoffrey Chaucer the poet, being a clerk of works there during the reign of Richard II.

Major reconstructions and extensions had gone on during the reigns of

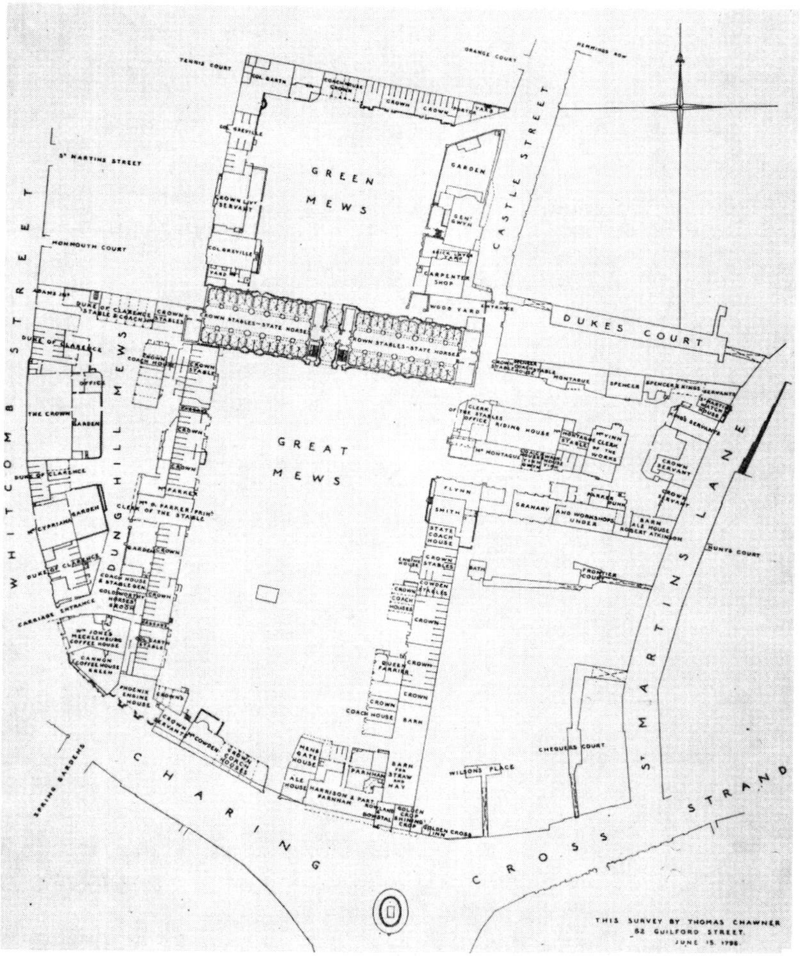

1. The Royal Mews at Charing Cross (1796)

2. William Kent's Royal Stables at Charing Cross (1749)

3. Temporary barracks, east side of the Great Mews at Charing Cross (1815)

Edward VI and Mary. George II had the architect William Kent rebuild the "Crown Stables", a building that divided the Great Mews (the lower' from the Green Mews (the upper) in 1732. Within seventy years, however, through neglect and mismanagement the mostly timber buildings, as well as Kent's more substantial one, had fallen into disrepair. Concomitant with this, most of the leases had little time to run and some were already being put to other uses, including a temporary barracks. These factors undoubtedly influenced John Nash to include the area as one for development in his 1812 report to H.M. Commissioners for Wood Forests and Land Revenues;[11] more of this below.

By 1820 the King, in the knowledge that he was to get new stables in Pimlico, approved the newly established New Street Commissioners' proposals for a road to connect Pall Mall East to St. Martin's. All, as usual, was not going to be straightforward. The Master of Horse, the gentleman responsible for the mews, was rather unwilling to release his property until his demands in relation to alternative accommodation had been met – demands, which the Treasury thought far outstripped the budget. Nash was particularly exasperated and in June 1821 wrote to Alexander Milne, the Secretary of the New Street Commissioners, that "the keeper of the mews having himself refused to give any information (on the subject of the state of buildings) and (had) interfered so as to prevent it being obtained otherwise". It was not until March 1825 that the Master of Horse finally passed over the last of the buildings in his charge.[12]

It is not clear when the temporary barracks came to occupy the eastern part of the mews, but in 1820 the New Street Commissioners were left in no doubt by the Treasury of their importance to the "Public Service" and were instructed that they should remain. By all accounts these barrack buildings were unsatisfactory and in 1825 new accommodation was constructed for the 800 men on the site of the old Green Mews. The Green Mews was more suitable as the Master of Fortifications put it "as it gave free access from the back of the barracks to all the North Parts of the Town".[13] So by 1826 both the east and west sides of Great Mews were demolished leaving an uncluttered view from the top of Whitehall of Kent's rather fine building. Its contents had, however, been removed and in their place came "Mr. Cross's Menagerie" and box upon box of government records from Westminster Hall. It was finally demolished in 1835.

However, before we move on to consider Nash's first report in detail one important influence in the area needs some mention. While the State itself and some of its most powerful figures occupied offices and houses on

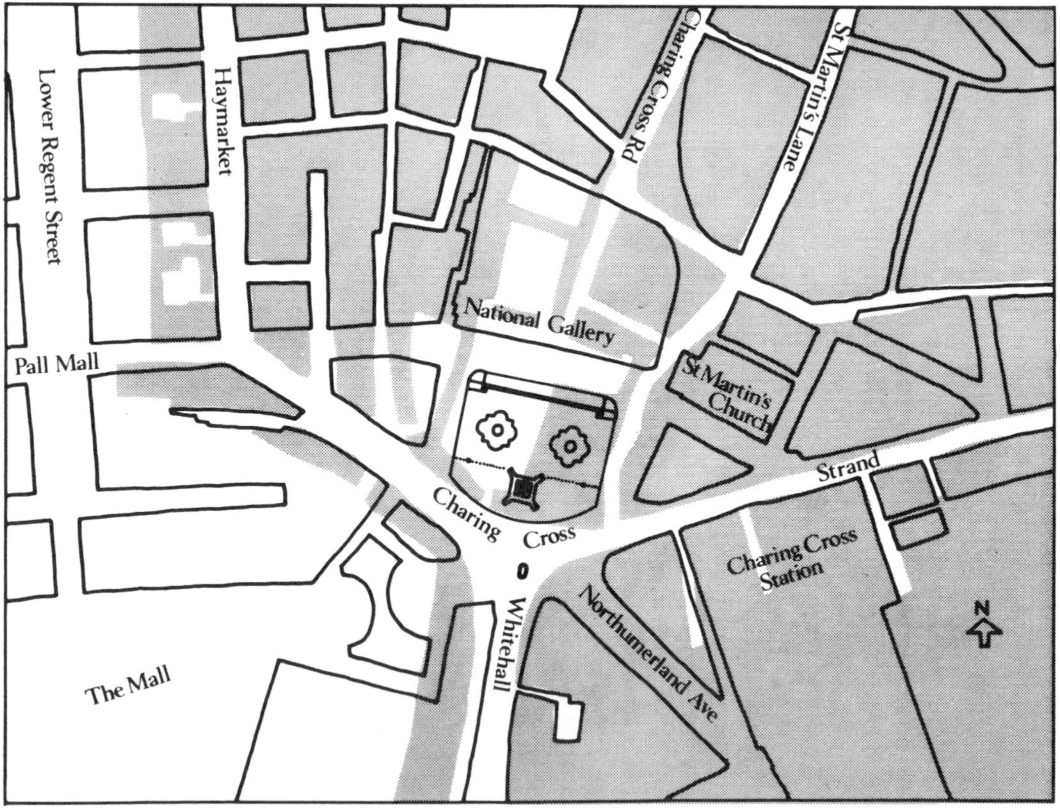

4. Charing Cross and Trafalgar Square. The black outline indicates their

the south and south-west sides, and a considerable part of the area just north-west of Charing Cross, some of the city's poorest and most destitute people occupied the north and eastern parts, around St. Martin's Church. In the eighteenth century and for a considerable part of the nineteenth St. Martin's Lane was the only road directly north from Charing Cross, passing as it did through the rookeries of Porridge Island, Seven Dials and that bogy of the upper classes, St. Giles'. It was not until the late 1870s that the building of Charing Cross Road with its attendant reconstruction was to change this.

The increasing presence on the edge of Bloomsbury and St. James throughout this period of large numbers of the very poor were to lead those in power to devise ways and means which at least prevented the sight of this growing number from offending their eyes, let alone live in conditions where trouble could be fermented or even revolution. Sadly, for the most part the people of these areas were far too busy trying to scrape together enough, even a few pence, to keep their families from complete and utter starvation.

The "Gordon Riots" in 1780 had caused widespread fears among the London upper classes, the rioters' primary aim apparently being the destruction of property, and not the securing of loot! To add to their anxiety, the mob violence was informed as George Rudé has pointed out, in a much more general way "by a groping desire to settle accounts with the rich if only for a day".[14] The military were called upon to suppress the mob – a decision which both C. J. Fox and Edmund Burke deplored. The Whig Government, with its libertarian leanings, did not like it either, but, to avoid anything of the kind occurring again, built barracks in Knightsbridge beside Hyde Park.

THE PROJECT OF JOHN NASH

John Nash in 1812 in (his) the First Report of H.M. Woods, Forests and Land Revenues, wrote:[15]

> "Every length of street would be terminated by a façade of beautiful architecture . . . and to add to the beauty of the approach from Westminster to Charing Cross, a Square or Crescent, open to and looking down Parliament Street, might be built round the Equestrian Statue at Charing Cross, which at the same time that it would enlarge that space, from whence, as before observed, the greatest part of the population of the Metropolis meet and diverge, it could afford a magnificent and beautiful termination of the street from Westminster. The lofty situation of Charing Cross and gradual ascent to it are peculiarly calculated to produce a grand and striking effect. Such a

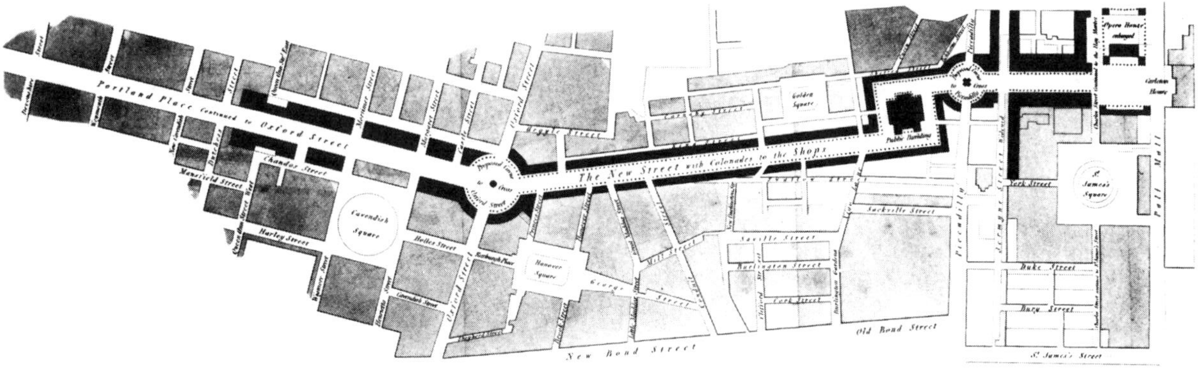

5. John Nash's 1812 proposal for a "New Street from Charing Cross to Portland Place". In the event only the part south of Piccadilly was built to this plan. The remainder was realigned to its present position during the 1820s

building might be appropriated to additional Offices for the Government . . . or Royal Society, Royal Academy and Antiquarian Society might be placed there."

This, as Sir John Summerson rightly points out in his biography of Nash, is "the germ of the project which later developed into Trafalgar Square".[16] Unlike some germs, which die for lack of sustenance, the life of this one was assured by an Act of Parliament, which received Royal Assent on 10 June 1813,[17]

> "An Act making a more convenient communication from Mary le bone Park and the Northern parts of the Metropolis . . . to Charing Cross . . . and for making a more convenient sewage for the same";

for in paragraph one it stated:

> ". . . and for widening Cockspur Street from the South end of the Haymarket to Charing Cross; and forming an open Square in the Kings Mews opposite Charing Cross."

Nash's views on the *social purpose* of his new streets (Regent Street and the proposed one leading to Bloomsbury) are significant; views which even Summerson mildly censures. Nash saw the new streets as, and designed them in such a way as to provide,

> ". . . a boundary and complete separation between the Streets and Squares occupied by the Nobility and Gentry"

to the west, and the

> ". . . narrow Streets and meaner houses occupied by mechanics and the trading part of the community"

on the east side. Nash is more specific elsewhere:

> "It will be seen by the Plan that there would be no opening on the East side of the New Street all the way from the Opera House to Piccadilly . . . and the inferior houses and the traffic from the Haymarket would be cut off from any communication with the New Street,"

adding that

> ". . . the Line of Separation between the inhabitants of the first classes of society, and those of the inferior classes is Swallow Street. . . ."

Not content with separating the classes, Nash intended to see to it that many of the lower classes would not penetrate his new street or Park while going about their daily business, and the legislation duly stated that the street and Park

> "shall be open at all times to all His Majesties Subjects to pass and repass along the same (. . . except . . . Waggons, Carts, Drays or other Vehicles for the carriage of goods, merchandise, manure soil, or other articles, or Oxen, Cows, Horses or Sheep in any drove or droves)."

This regulation in a modified form still pertains to Regent's Park, and of course the other parks in the vicinity of the Royal Palaces.

Not content with destroying their homes through his plan, Nash seemed bent on destroying the very livelihood of many working-class people. Two markets, St. James's and the Hay Market, and shops that existed to the east of Leicester Square were over the period 1815–30 either totally run down or relocated.

Although granted a Select Committee in 1816, some of the inhabitants of St. James's Market failed to persuade the Government that they should have access to the New Street in order to benefit from any possible increase in trade. Nash's response to their claim was both irritable and short: "No, it would spoil the beauty of the plan entirely," he wrote, "for people *riding* up and down might see offal or something of that kind"[18] (my italics—R.M.)

Shortly after the completion of the southern end of the New Street one trader complained that his Saturday takings had dropped from £20 to £2.

In 1817 the Duke of Leeds, owner of the market, sold his leasehold rights back to the Crown for £22,000. By then most of the weekly and monthly tenants had left leaving only a few yearly ones to be paid compensation.[19]

Five years later four hundred and fifty inhabitants of the parishes of St. Martin's and St. Anne's Soho signed a petition complaining of the closure of "the passage through the Royal Mews recently shut in the interests of the Public Service" (the army—R.M.).[20] A passage it would seem much used for getting from Westminster and Pimlico to Soho. The closure had put several traders and small shopkeepers out of business. The Haymarket was moved to Cumberland Market, Regent's Park after considerable pressure from the inhabitants of Piccadilly and St. James's that it was causing a nuisance.

The net effect, therefore, and perhaps the underlying purpose of much of Nash's plan, was to substantially eradicate the cheap traders in food and household necessities and replace them with those more able to serve the needs of the better off: a pattern we can still observe in every high street.

Nash's appointment, in 1813, by direct command of the Prince Regent on the death of James Wyatt, to Surveyor-General only lasted until the reorganisation of 1815. Nash became one of the "three attached architects" under a political head who assumed the title of Surveyor-General. Although his status changed, he continued to be the personal architect to the Prince Regent, and in 1821 was given orders to carry out the more or less complete rebuilding of Buckingham Palace.

NASH, ARBUTHNOT AND THE PUBLIC FUNDS

The extravagant expenditure on Buckingham Palace caused considerable public outcry, much to Sir John Soane's joy, as he was the person supposed to be responsible for the Royal Palaces. Nash's popularity waned with the King's, but there were some powerful people who still gave him the support he needed. One of these was Charles Arbuthnot.

In 1822 Charles Arbuthnot had left the Treasury, because of bad health, where he had been since 1809, succeeding the Duke of Wellington's younger brother Henry as a Joint Secretary. Appointed to the post of a Commissioner of Woods, Forests and Land Revenues in the same year, an office about which at that time Lord Liverpool had remarked[21]

> "that it (the O.W.F.L.R.) had become one of peculiar delicacy from the connections which must exist between the discharges of the duties of the state and the administration of the King's private affairs."

So successful was Arbuthnot at the latter that, when he was on the verge in 1823 of being sent to a debtors' prison, George IV made him a gift of £15,000 (borrowed it seems from the Rothschilds).

Despite the scandals and alleged malpractices, by 1825 Regent Street (as revised to its present line) seemed a success, sufficiently so for the Commissioners to ask Nash to revise his plan for a square at the top of Whitehall. As they put it in their report:[22]

> "When the line of Communications between Pall Mall and Portland Place had been completed and as soon as we are in possession of the Site of the Lower Mews at Charing Cross, we took measures for proceeding to execute that part of the Improvements, which had its object the continuation of Pall Mall into St. Martin's Lane, terminating at the Portico of St. Martin's Church, and forming an open area in front of the Kings Mews; and it having appeared to us, after mature consideration, that the unequal lengths of the two sides of the

open Area, proposed by the original plan, would be a deformity, peculiarly striking, in the approach from Whitehall; that a much larger Space, than was first designed, ought to be left open, and the West end of the Strand considerably widened; and that the design was, in other respects, susceptible of great improvement; we directed Mr Nash carefully to reconsider the subject, with the view of getting rid of this, and of other objections which had occurred – We at the same time desired that he would suggest what might appear to him the best mode of improving the Communication through the Western parts of the Metropolis."

The Commissioners also requested Nash to devise a

> "more commodious access from the Houses of Parliament . . . to the British Musuem and the numerous and respectably occupied new Buildings in the part of the Metropolis, in which that great National Repository is now being permanently established";

but at the end of their report they give a clear indication that only the area around St. Martin's seems likely, for the time being, to be carried out:

> ". . . Having submitted these several Plans to the Lords of the Treasury, with our opinion that they were well entitled to their Lordships serious attention, we were directed to call for more detailed Plans, and to prepare the best Estimates we could of so much of the originally proposed Plan as related to the alterations in the neighbourhood of Charing Cross and St Martin's Church, and the West end of the Strand, with a view to the early execution of these Improvements; but their Lordships, as they intimated to us, deemed it to be advisable, that the consideration of the remaining part of the proposed Improvements should for the present be postponed. . . . Although the execution of a great part of what was proposed has been thus deferred for the present, the whole would so promote the Convenience, Ornament and Health of the Metropolis as to induce us to hope that they may hereafter be reconsidered and ultimately adopted."

Two months earlier, Charles Arbuthnot asked in the House of Commons for leave to bring in a bill "for making several improvements in the neighbourhood of Charing Cross and the Strand. . . ."; but before making any statements about the improvements themselves,[23]

> "he felt it necessary to state, that those which he should propose would be carried into effect by the same architect whose designs in the formation of Regent Street had received such deserved commendation from the public; he meant Mr. Nash."

Although not in possession of any plans, Arbuthnot then went on to expound in some considerable detail the proposals for these improvements. He began by stating, that should the House consent to the project in question, it was intended

> ". . . to purchase that tract of ground which joined to the present Kings Mews at Charing Cross, and extended to St. Martin's Lane . . . also . . . to purchase the whole of that tract on the East side of St. Martin's Lane, which was bounded on the North side by Chandos Street on the South side by the Strand. . . ."

The effect of this alteration

> ". . . would not merely be to embellish and adorn the Metropolis, but to create a more convenient communication between the East and West ends of town."

Assuming that such purchases would be made (which they were),

> "It was contemplated, that a large splendid quadrangle should be erected, the West side of which would be formed by the College of Physicians and the Union Club House; the East side would correspond with that already existing; namely the grand portico of St. Martin's Church; and on the Northern side a new line of buildings would be erected;"

the purpose of all this being,

> ". . . to throw open to those in Pall Mall a full view of the magnificent portico of the Church" (St. Martin's).

Nash's published plan showed a building in the centre of the open space, a Royal Academy. This was an idea very current at the time, of which John Goldicutt's is a surviving example. Arbuthnot, however, held that

> "It was the general opinion that it would be preferable to leave it an open Space. . . . He mentioned this, as the point was yet undecided and would be left to the consideration of the House."

The clearing away of the buildings on the east side would also enlarge the passage between Charing Cross and Bedford Street, "this narrow gut", as Arbuthnot called it. Stoppages at this point caused considerable delays to the east–west traffic. A new street was to be formed across the south side of St. Martin's churchyard, (the church being offered an alternative graveyard to the north of the Euston Road) a street later to be named after Lord Duncannon, who in 1832 became Chief Commissioner of the Office of Woods, Forests, Land Revenues, Works and Public Buildings.

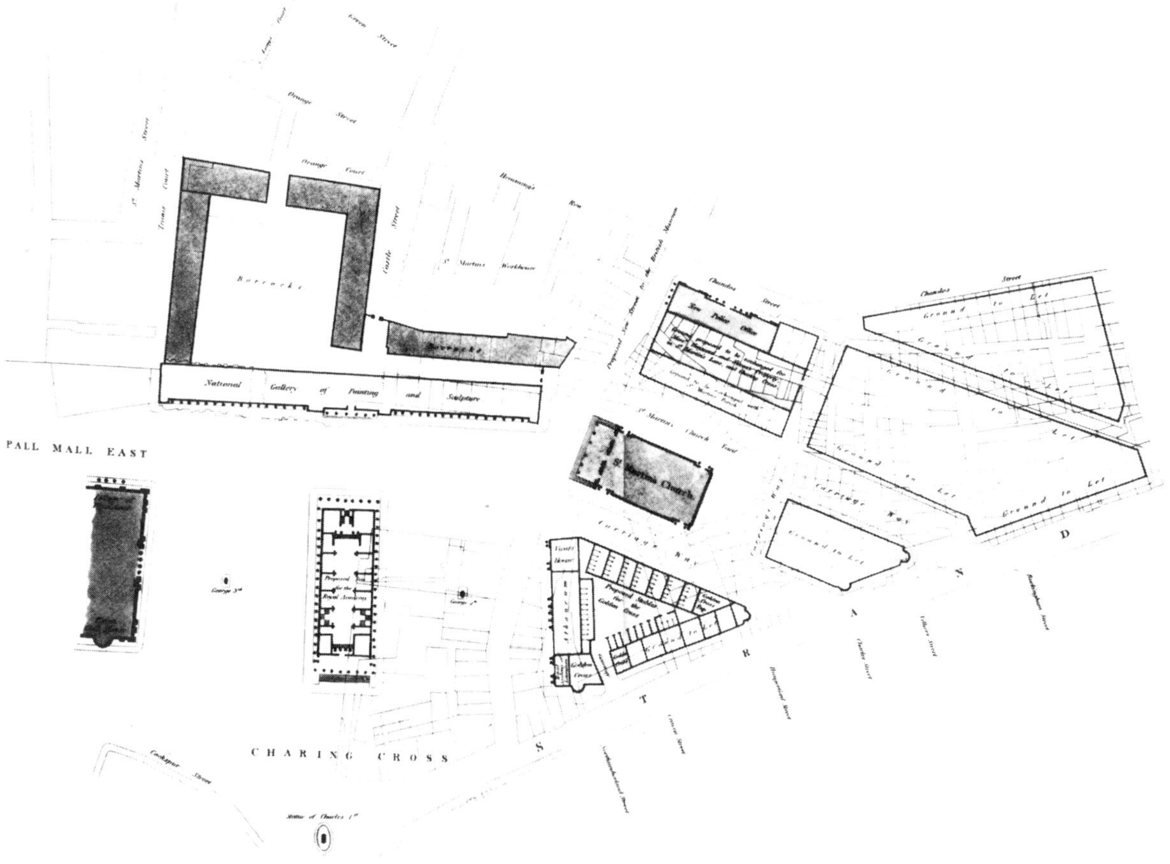

6. John Nash's 1826 proposal for improving Charing Cross, St. Martin's Lane and the entrance to the Strand. The plan clearly shows how these improvements were intended to sweep away the innumerable

All these changes would not only, in Arbuthnot's opinion, offer

> "a great benefit to the Metropolis in the way of free communication from one end to the other" (for carriages, that is; Arbuthnot never described any other sort of traffic) "but would also have the advantage of getting rid of vast numbers of bad and unsightly houses (and their occupants – R.M.) which at present crowded together in the vicinity of St. Martin's Church, which would add considerably to the beauty of that part of the Metropolis."

As to the expense of it all, Arbuthnot thought it sufficient to state:

> ". . . by the exchange of Crown lands in some instances, and the sale of others . . . the department with which he was connected would be enabled to meet the greatest part of the expense."

Should this not prove sufficient, a continuation of the Act of 1813 would enable sufficient mortgages to be raised. He anticipated little objection to the plan, and repeated his view that it was

> "highly desirable to get rid of the unsightly appearance which would be presented, by allowing some of the houses in the neighbourhood of Charing Cross to remain as they stood."

For he felt that, like Regent Street, which was constructed in a time of war,

> "and such as it now was, he did not believe that it was regretted by one man in the country."

In 1829 he was to regret this remark, for Colonel Davies, member for Worcester, was to accuse Nash of malversation and fraud in connection with its building. Baring, one of the Committee, voiced what seemed to be a general feeling, when he said of Nash, that[25]

> ". . . as a manager of public money and as an exhibitor of taste, he was sorry the public ever had anything to do with him."

Nash's reply to this was to issue a "Statement" defending his actions, claiming that he had assumed the role of speculator solely to ensure that his own designs were carried out.[25]

Winding up his speech, Arbuthnot said that he thought the $2\frac{3}{4}$ per cent return expected compared well with the 3 per cent derived from Regent's Park, and that, like there, the

> ". . . open space . . . would be of great benefit, by contributing to the health of the inhabitants in the vicinity."

Little objection was raised to the Bill. Sir M. W. Ridley asked about the

Exeter Change; Arbuthnot saw no difficulties – it was, after all, the private property of the Marquis of Exeter. Mr Hume raised an objection to the continuing existence of St. George's Barracks; they were, he said, "a downright nuisance". On 28 April 1826 the bill received its third reading, at which Arbuthnot was able to confirm that

> "he had had communications with the Marquis of Exeter and the Duke of Bedford, and both these noblemen expressed their anxiety to lend their aid towards the accomplishment of the proposed improvement."

The Bill received royal assent a month later.[26]

There were thirty-four leaseholders whose property was in question and by the end of June the conveyance of the first of these, two houses in Burleigh Street owned by Mr. John Flashman, had been completed. The Enrolment Books show that the majority of the leases to be conveyed had only short periods to run, very few having been originally for terms of more than twenty-one years. Soon sums of money ranging between £200 and £6,000 were changing hands for the hundred and fifty or so properties. There were of course a few exceptions well beyond this: the proprietor of the Golden Cross Hotel, William Howard, received £30,000, the previously mentioned Marquis of Exeter received almost £50,000 for his property and the Duke of Bedford £30,000 all but a few pounds.[27]

We may recall that Charles Arbuthnot had suggested, when speaking in the House of Commons, that expenditure could be reduced by "the exchange of properties". In the event only a few such transactions took place. In 1827 the Bethlehem Hospital exchanged its properties in Wilson's Court, St. Martin's Lane and Vine Street for properties in Duke Street, St. James's, Piccadilly and Jermyn Street; a little later in the same year Mr. Prendergast exchanged his six properties in Vine Street and Old Round Court for three in Frith Street, Soho. In 1828 the Duke of Northumberland exchanged the five houses and the hotel in St. Martin's Lane he leased for eighty-six feet of extra Thames river frontage adjacent to the garden of his Charing Cross house. A year later George Richards, the vicar of St. Martin's-in-the-Fields, exchanged eight properties on the east side of Charing Cross for five properties on the north side of his churchyard, along with six on the east side of St. Martin's Lane.[28]

Such exchanges of property may not have cost money in Arbuthnot's terms, but when added up the cost of assigning the other leases totalled £711,095.[29] The Commissioners suffered no legal trammels in raising loans to cover such an enormous amount, but would need to look to two different sources both of whom were to charge usurious rates of interest.

Nash's project and estimate of costs had been drawn up during the height of the speculative boom of 1824–5. With its crash in late 1825, early 1826 severe restrictions were imposed among other things on the issuing of Exchequer Bills on loans for Crown projects. Section 49 of 7 Geo IV, c. 77 specifically ordered an upper limit to the mortgage for the Improvements of £400,000, just over half the sum required. Three separate loans, two of £150,000 and one of £100,000 were raised during 1827 and early 1828; against the security one hundred and forty eight properties in Regent Street and Regent's Park, and seventeen in Waterloo Place. The rate of interest was to be in "annual instalments of £2 10s 0d per cent altogether with interest thereon at the rate of £4 per cent per annum until the same shall be payed off". Seven years later it appears that £323,750 of the loan still remained to be paid off.[30]

The outstanding £300,000 to make up the original sum was not required until 1829 and the Commissioners turned to that group of money lenders, the assurance companies, who had supplied finance for the Regent Street scheme twelve years before. Tenders were invited from ten companies, seven accepted, but only three of them for the whole amount; Royal Exchange at £4 10s 0d per cent (they had lent £600,000 in 1817 for the Regent Street scheme), London Assurance at £3 15s 9d per cent and the Equitable Society at £3 10s 0d per cent. The Equitable Society's offer was accepted.[31]

Provisions of 7 Geo. IV, c. 77 were as specific as those of that mentioned at the beginning of this chapter (53 Geo. III, c. 121) about who and what could make use of the space:

> ". . . to appoint fit and convenient Places in such Streets, Squares, Ways, Passages and Places to be made and improved . . . for the stands for Hackney Coaches, Hackney Chariots and Cabriolets.
>
> "And be it further enacted, that if any Waggon, Cart or other Carriage shall be left to stand or remain in any of the Streets, Squares, Ways, Passages and Places to be made . . . with or without Horses; for any longer time than shall be necessary for loading and unloading thereof; or if any Hackney Coach, Hackney Chariot, Cabriolet, Stage Coach, Post Chaise or other Carriage let to him shall be left to stand or remain in any such Streets . . . other than such Situations as shall be appointed for Stands of such Carriages . . . for loading or unloading their baggage . . . then and in any case the Owner or Driver of every such Carriage shall for every such Offence forfeit and pay any sum not exceeding 40 shillings."

The visual appearance of the buildings was also provided for; the approval accorded to the items in the first and second paragraphs here quoted is in notable contrast to the tone used in the third (in the original the last paragraph comes first):

> ". . . authorize and permit the building of Porticoes, Arcades and other covered ways . . . be built of Brick, Stone or Metal or Stucco or Cement laid on Brick or Stone. . . .
>
> ". . . authorize and permit the erecting or making, the Fronts of any Houses or Buildings . . . in such Manner as that some Fronts may recede behind or advance before others, and with Bow Windows or other Projections, and with Virandas, Alcoves, Balconies, Pilasters, Columns, and Shop Windows. . . .
>
> ". . . to take down, take away, remove, alter or regulate, in such manner as they shall from time to time judge proper, all Signs or other Emblems, used to denote Trade, Occupation or Calling of any Person or Persons, and all Sign Irons, Sign Posts and other Posts, Sheds, Penthouses, Spouts, Butters, Steps, Stairs, Bow and other projecting Windows, Window Shutters, Palisades and other Encroachments, Projections and Annoyances, . . . which do and shall in their Judgement obstruct the commodious Passage along the Carriage or Footways. . . ." (fine of 20 shillings/day should above be there).

Provision was also made to move St. Martin's Workhouse, the Parochial School, Library and Free School, but as the Act says, "not until they (the Crown) have provided proper sites elsewhere".[32] For the Workhouse this was not to be until 1864.

There seem to be two claims to the origins of the naming of "the quadrangle Charing Cross"; one, by William IV, the other by an architect at the Admiralty, George Ledwell Taylor. Taylor's claim, like the King's is impossible to substantiate: in the autobiography he wrote at the end of his life he gives this account of a conversation in the late part of 1830:[33]

> "I had laid out the buildings in flats, and my first tenant, Mr Barton, was very pressing to know how to have his cards printed, so I resolved to go to His Majesty with my plan of the Square, and suggest the opportunity of recording the victory at which Nelson fell a sacrifice; so I repaired to St. James's where I found officers waiting for audience, and among them Sir Thomas Hardy. 'Ah, Taylor, what are you here for?' 'A private matter, Sir Thomas!' However, while we were waiting a thought struck me; if I could get Sir Thomas to moot this subject, in whose arms Nelson died! So I addressed Sir Thomas, and told him my object, adding 'If he would be so kind as to make the suggestion to His Majesty'. 'What,' said he 'what do you take me for? To ask the King, who has consented to its being called after his own name? Are you mad? I wish you well through it. I will have nothing to do with it!' Notwithstanding this unpropitious opinion I awaited my time, and was before the King. I had some

difficulty in opening my case, but His Majesty took most kindly my arguments and said 'I like the idea, LET IT BE CALLED TRAFALGAR SQUARE. Go and tell Lord Duncannon so from me!' Here was an awkward situation. I said, 'Your Majesty, I am but a humble man, unauthorised to convey such an order.' 'I see,' said His Majesty, 'give me your plan – pen and ink.' He wrote TRAFALGAR SQUARE, WILLIAM REX. 'There, take that to Lord Duncannon!'

Lord Duncannon being in Dublin, I took the plan with the King's signature to Mr. Mylne, the Secretary to the 'Woods and Forests'. 'Very irregular,' said he, 'I will have nothing to do with it!' 'Well, then,' said I, 'I must go to Dublin, and place it in Lord Duncannon's hands! You know you wished the alteration to be made, and it would not have been done but for me!' After consideration Mr. Mylne said, 'Leave the plan with me.' The result was: 'TRAFALGAR SQUARE'."

The buildings he refers to are those that later became Morley's Hotel. He became bankrupt soon after its completion.

THE NATIONAL GALLERY

By 1830 it must have appeared to John Nash that there was little hope of the project of 1826 for a National Gallery of Painting and Sculpture or Royal Academy on the site of the "old State Stables" being built. Although the recently established (1824) National Gallery was outgrowing its premises in Pall Mall, continuing procrastination by the Treasury, by the Gallery trustees and most importantly the Prime Minister had delayed any firm decision for its new location. The Treasury and the Prime Minister feared the expense, the trustees had their eyes on a portion of St James's Palace. However, as we noted earlier, Kent's Royal Mews, the "old State Stables" were still standing and it was at the suggestion of William Wilkins of converting this building that thoughts returned to Nash's original project. Nash, meanwhile, never to lose an opportunity had been making "Plans and Elevations for a Building on the North Side of the Square at Charing Cross with an offer from Mr. Nurse for building the same."[34] William Nurse was a local butcher and landowner with whom it seems Nash had been doing "business" since mid 1831. The change of heart brought on by Wilkins's suggestion and the cause being taken up by Sir Robert Peel, a Gallery trustee the detractors in the Goverment declared, to many people's surprise, in favour of a new building.

Three designs were to be considered: a modified one by Nash, one combining a row of shops at street level by C. R. Cockerell and, submitted at the last minute, one by Wilkins. The committee set up to consider the whole issue of the need for a gallery favoured Wilkins's and finally after some argument over whether it be built of brick or stone the Commons voted on 23 July 1832, £15,000 on account towards the new building. A building which was to house the Royal Academy, the Public Records and the considerably enlarged collection of paintings from 99 Pall Mall.

Wilkins's proposal was for a long low building in the Neo-Classical style; a central temple form surmounted by a small dome flanked on either side by wings terminated with small campaniles. The main portico incorporated columns from the recently (1826) demolished Carlton House – the rest of the materials having been sold off to help pay for Buckingham Palace – and the west wing an archway giving access to the barracks behind plus some provision for a "soldiers kitchen" on the ground floor.[35] Considerable debate was to surround his design, fashion rudely described as "Wilkins' Greek Job" or the "National Cruet Stand", the latter alluding to "mustard pot cupola" and "pepper caster" campaniles. Most criticisms were made from the aspect of the composition as viewed from Whitehall. More recently John Betjeman has suggested that Wilkins designed it to be seen from Pall Mall East; as a left hand flat to St. Martin's-in-the-Fields.

That Wilkins did not design it to be seen from Whitehall is a reasonable assumption; but his abhorrence of St. Martin's portico, which only under public pressure did he move the line of his building back to reveal, seems totally unfounded. However the most important feature of his final executed design was the raising of the whole building twelve feet above street level, giving as some people have suggested an importance "its own height did not have".

In early 1837, with building nearly completed, the Office of Woods prompted by Wilkins suggested to the Treasury that[36]

> "The advanced state of the building erected for the National Gallery and Royal Academy, having drawn the attention of this Board to the necessity of forthwith completing the line of street in front of that building, as well as the laying out and ornamenting in an appropriate manner the area of Trafalgar-square, we considered it proper to consult Mr. Wilkins, the architect to the above-mentioned important structure upon these subjects; and we beg leave to transmit herewith, for your Lordships' consideration and information, a copy of the plan, report, and estimate furnished by Mr Wilkins for the proposed works."

Wilkins's report besides considering the "principal object" also devoted a paragraph to the area beyond "the foot pavement in front of the new building on the opposite side of the continued line of Pall Mall East". This area Wilkins suggested should be "about 21 feet in front of the present palisading of the new building" and "be made inaccessible to the public by means of a slight fence". It should also be paved and kept up at the expense of the Office of Woods. The total cost for the works was to be seven thousand six hundred pounds.[37]

The Treasury moved slowly, and in May the Office of Woods, Forests and Land Revenues, prompted again by Wilkins, wrote to them again. Wilkins had shown considerable irritation at the interference of several senior government ministers; an irritation that was to be shared by several of his successors, for he had written that it was[38]

> "With a firm conviction that my plan for enclosing the area of Trafalgar-square was the only one calculated to give a considerable degree of importance to the new buildings, and afforded the only means of obviating the discord of horizontal lines, cut by others in an oblique direction; with this conviction, which perhaps is not apparent to eyes less interested than my own. . . ."

The less interested eyes were those of the Chancellor of the Exchequer, most of the Cabinet, Lord Lansdowne and Earl Grey. It was only after Wilkins had at some length managed to convince Earl Grey as to the efficiency of his plan that the others had agreed. Nevertheless, the Treasury procrastinated again and in eighteen months Wilkins was dead; the project unstarted, his gallery more or less completed.

Charles Barry was finally (and publicly) commissioned for the works in April 1840 and in June of that year produced his estimates – four thousand pounds more than Wilkins's – and the designs. The plan remained more or less unchanged and was built; the estimate also remained largely the same, with some minor modifications and extras.[39]

The Office of Woods, Forests and Land Revenues wrote to the Treasury within a day assuring them that

> "The Commissioners of Woods, etc., have adhered to the principle of Mr. Wilkins. . . ."

and so, it seemed, had Charles Barry.

Alfred Barry, Charles Barry's son and biographer, puts it slightly differently:[40]

> "A plan was already under consideration, which contemplated the raising the whole square to the level of the pavement in front of the new building, and

finishing it with a terrace and balustrade towards Cockspur Street. To this he had a strong objection. In common with the world at large, he considered the National Gallery to be already greatly deficient in importance and unworthy of its magnificent site. Such a terrace as was proposed, seen in the foreground on approaching from Whitehall, would throw it back into utter insignificance. He advised, therefore, that the level of the square should be kept down to that of Cockspur Street, instead of being raised to that of the base of the building, and the terrace thrown back so as to make it appear a part of the building, thus increasing instead of diminishing its height. This plan was adopted, but greatly injured by the erection of the Nelson Column, against which Mr. Barry protested in vain."

The Treasury had, however, decided to further delay the plan until work on the Square's principal feature, the Nelson Monument, was more advanced, several ideas for which had preceded that for Trafalgar Square.

Notes to Chapter 1

1. *Notes and Queries*, 7th Series vol. 9, p. 132.
2. *Wriosthesley's Chronicle*, vol. 2 (London 1575–7).
3. *ibid.*, p. 112.
4. *ibid.*, pp. 125–8.
5. J. H. Macmichael, *The Story of Charing Cross* (London 1906), p. 9.
6. *Memoirs of Lieutenant-General Ludlow* (London 1690), vol. 3, p. 75.
7. T. B. Macaulay, *History of England* (London 1849), vol. 4, pp. 664–5.
8. Quoted by Macmichael, *op. cit.*, p. 48.
9. Letter Book in the Lord Steward's Office. Quoted in Peter Cunningham's *A Handbook for London* (London 1849), vol. 1, p. 126.
10. W. E. Harland-Oxley, Memories of Westminster, *Westminster and Pimlico News*, 30.9.1904.
11. *First Report to His Majesty's Commissioners for Woods, Forests and Land Revenues* (London 1812).
12. *P.R.O. CREST 26/178.*
13. *ibid.*
14. George Rudé, "The Gordon Riots", *Transactions of the Royal Historical Society*, 5th series, vol. 6 (1956), pp. 93–114.
15. First Report, etc., p. 90.
16. John Summerson, *John Nash – Architect to George IV* (London 1949), p. 126.
17. 53 Geo. III, c. 121.
18. Report from the Committee on the Petition of the Tradesmen and Inhabitants of Norris Street and Market Terrace. P.P. 1817 (79) iii. 83.
19. *PRO L.R. 1/255.*
20. *PRO CREST 26/188.*
21. A. Aspinall, *The Correspondence of Charles Arbuthnot* (London 1941), p. ix.

22. *Fifth Report to His Majesty's Commissioners of Works, Forests and Land Revenues* (London 1826).
23. *Hansard* 2nd series, vol. XV c. 62 *et seq.*
24. Report from the Select Committee on Crown leases, *Reports and Committees, 1829 III.*
25. H. M. Colvin, *Biographical Dictionary of English Architects, 1660–1840* (London 1954), p. 405.
26. 7 Geo. IV, c. 77.
27. *PRO L.R. 1/255 et seq.*
28. *PRO CREST 40/83; CREST 26/152; L.R. 1/268–9.*
29. *ibid.*
30. *PRO CREST 26/181b.*
31. *PRO CREST 26/53.*
32. 7 Geo. IV, c. 77.
33. G. L. Taylor, *Auto-Biography* (London 1870), pp. 177–8. See also Taylor's alternative suggestion two years later that it be called "Kings Square". *CREST 26/75.*
34. *PRO CREST 26/54.*
35. *PRO CREST 26/187.*
36. *PRO WORKS 2/2*, Treasury Letter Book No. 2, 1835–40.
37. *PRO WORKS 20/2–1.*
38. *ibid.*
39. *ibid.*
40. Alfred Barry, *The Life and Work of Sir Charles Barry* (London 1867), pp. 122–3.

2

HERO OF EMPIRE

A man amongst the few who appear, at
different periods to have been created
to promote the Grandeur, and add to
the Security of Nations. . . .

The Lord Mayor, Alderman, and
Common Council, of the City of London,
Have caused this monument to be erected
Not in the presumptuous hope of
Sustaining the departed Heroes memory
But to manifest their estimation of the Man,
And their admiration of his deeds,
This testimony of their Gratitude,
They trust will remain
As their own renowned City shall exist

The period to
NELSON'S FAME
Can only be
THE END OF TIME[1]

IS THE SPOT MARKED BY NO COLOSSAL BUST?

During the first fifty years of the nineteenth century, just as economic power moved from the landed aristocracy to the bourgeoisie, so did the patronage of the arts. This change, which was a very gradual one, was accompanied inevitably by a change in the nature and content of the objects patronised. This was especially true in the case of sculpture devoted to the memory of the dead.[2]

Throughout the eighteenth century the aristocracy had adorned their private chapels, estates and even their houses with scuptural memorials to the recent dead. An only too familiar sight in many mediaeval churches is the eighteenth century addition of a vulgar crowd of cherubs and senatorial figures adorning nave walls and chantries. Westminster Abbey comes to mind as a notable example of these excesses (as does the much later St. Paul's Cathedral which was to become during the Napoleonic

Wars – as power moved from the land to the City of London – the new national shrine for heroes).

Very few of these memorials except where they were on the outside of buildings found their way into the public street or square; their intention was largely private, for the moral edification of the dead person's relatives, friends and acquaintances. That they might be seen also by some small section of the masses was incidental to this main purpose.

Two events, the French Revolution and the wars which Britain was to have with Napoleon between 1793 and 1815 were to change all this. During this period sculpture (especially memorials to the dead) declined from being a private indulgence of the ruling class admired by a small band of connoisseurs to an object of more public display, often financed by the Government,[3] with a direct didactic purpose.

In the early 1790s the British army and navy had suffered a series of devastating defeats at the hands of the French in both Europe and the Caribbean. These defeats were very expensive in both men (40,000 were lost in Pitt's adventure in the West Indies in 1793–6) and money, The financing of wars by British private capital was of course only worthwhile so long as their object was achieved: namely, the expansion and control of trade. French capitalists undoubtedly had similar ambitions.

During 1797 and 1798 Napoleon had gained control of the Mediterranean and with his army had sailed into the ports of the Nile delta – taking Malta, Britain's main naval base in the area, on the way. All seemed set therefore, to the horror of the British, for an unlimited French advance eastwards to Constantinople and eventually perhaps, India.

Nelson and the British Fleet went in pursuit. After a surprise encounter at Aboukir in the mouth of the Nile, the French fleet was defeated leaving Napoleon and his army locked up in Eygpt. At home the victory was greeted with jubilation. Nelson was the hero of the day. His ascent as the brightest star of what was to be the beginning of the second major expansion of the British Empire seemed assured.

In London within three months of the Aboukir engagement, a committee under the Duke of Clarence (later to be William IV), was formed "for raising a Naval Pillar or monument" to commemorate the victory.[4] It was almost as though the ruling class were wanting to express their gratitude to the navy for saving their face. It also undoubtedly had the other function of confirming the same class's victory over the mutineers of Spithead and the Nore two years earlier.

Although in the event no monument or pillar was raised, one of the more famous proposals for one, that of John Flaxman is worth mention-

7. John Flaxman's Statue of Britannia to be placed at Greenwich (1799). Drawing by William Blake

ing. Flaxman proposed placing a colossal statue, 200 feet high, of Britannia accompanied by crouching lions at her feet on the summit of Greenwich Hill. This site for Flaxman had a double importance. Firstly, one of direct association; it would be adjacent to the Naval Hospital. Its second association would be less direct and in the context of the present work the more interesting symbolically, For in Flaxman's own words the statue would be near to "the Kent Road" which formed "the egress to London from Europe, Asia and Africa". Furthermore, it was "the place from whence the longitude is taken" and would "like the first milestone in the city of Rome be the point from which the world is measured".[5] Zero longitude was established, it will be remembered, at Greenwich Observatory during Britain's first period of colonial expansion in the seventeenth century. At Greenwich also were kept the standard imperial linear measures, replicas of which, as was noted above, were to be put at the height of Britain's imperial fervour in the late nineteenth century, in Trafalgar Square.

Five years later, on 21 October 1805, saw the last sea battle of Britain's war with France (and as it turned out the last with a European power for a hundred years), the Battle of Trafalgar. The British fleet's victory finally established Britain as Europe's number one sea power. The subsequent exercise of this sea power enabled the British ruling class an unfettered expansion of their economic and therefore political power over large sections of the globe. For the remainder of the century many nations, from small islands to great continents, had their economies and cultures pillaged to keep the "workshop of the world" in business.

Trafalgar was of course also the occasion of Horatio Nelson's death. This event, "heroic" in manner and "victorious" in timing, might have been tailor made to form the central prop to the whole panoply of bellicose patriotism that for fifteen years had characterised Britain's anti-Jacobin ruling class.

Within days of 5 November, the day that the news of Nelson's death reached England, and in some cases before his actual corpse arrived, plans were being drawn up, subscriptions gathered and actual monuments were being made in many places throughout the country. The first monument in this rash of devotional fervour was actually erected in Ireland, at the small town of Castletownend in County Cork on 10 November 1805. Its form was a rude stone arch standing on a hill overlooking the sea. Its "designer" was a Captain Joshua Rowley Watson, R.N. He built it with the help of the twelve hundred Sea Fencibles under his command and the assistance of eight masons, completing the task in five hours.[6]

It was in Ireland, too, that three years later what was to become perhaps the second most famous memorial to Nelson was also erected: The Pillar in Sackville (now O'Connell) Street, Dublin. The Pillar was designed by William Wilkins and the Irish architect Francis Johnston. The statue of Nelson on the top – it was nearly a Roman Galley – being by the Irish sculptor Thomas Kirk. Unlike Wilkins's later and very similar column at Great Yarmouth the Dublin Pillar contained a staircase leading to a viewing gallery at the top, from which the sea could be seen. (The entrance fee to the staircase was 10 pence per person in 1809!)

The Pillar, as W. B. Yeats was to comment in 1923, "represents the feeling of Protestant Ireland for a man who had helped break the power of Napoleon". Its building coming nine years after the Act of Union was seen by others at the time a little more critically,[7]

> "The statue of Lord Nelson has been placed on the column in Sackville Street dedicated to his memory. We never remember an exhibition that has excited less notice, or was marked with more indifference on the part of the Irish public, or at least that part who pay the taxes and enjoy none of the plunder. This latter description can have little interest and consequently less feeling in the triumphs of a Nelson or a Wellesley. English domination and trade may be extended, and English glory perpetuated, but an Irish mind has no substantial reasons for thinking from the history of our connexion that our prosperity or our independence will be more attended to, by our masters than if we were

actually impeding the victories, which our valor have personally effected. In short the most indifferent capacity in the country take little pride in combats in which our country will never be considered only as an outwork or a depot. We have changed our gentry for soldiers, and our independence has been wrested from us, not by the arms of France, but by the gold of England. The statue of Nelson records the glory of a mistress and the transformation of our senate into a discount office."

Similar sentiments undoubtedly lay behind the action of the group of Republicans who with great skill removed with explosives the statue of Nelson from the top of the pillar on the fiftieth anniversary of the Easter Rising in 1966. (It was left to the Irish Army to demolish the pillar itself, and half the windows in O'Connell Street, a couple of days later.)

MEMENTO MORI

Before we move on to look at some other monuments devoted to the memory of Nelson it seems worth giving a mention to a contemporary tract that in part lends further substance to the discussion on the changed didactic nature of sculpture in this period.

In 1808 a William Wood published *An essay on National and Sepulchral Monuments.*[8] It was partly directed, undoubtedly, at the Committee for National Monuments – the "Committee of Taste" as the *Gentleman's Magazine* called it – who had since 1802 been responsible directly to the Government for allocating money and selecting designs for many monuments. Although the committee allocated considerable sums of money (£40,000 was voted by Parliament between 1802 and 1812) no large scale pieces of outdoor sculpture had in fact been commissioned. This failing, interwoven with sentiments of nearly overbearing chauvinism, was at the centre of Wood's argument.

"The ordinary feelings of men are not adequate to the present crisis. They must be sublimed from the domestic apathy in which they *now* contemplate the approaching storm, to a state of active patriotism and manifest their *love* for their country by a gigantic effort to *preserve* it."

After conceding that England had "proudly stemmed the torrent of revolutionary frenzy" and had extended "the power of its arms and the unrivalled produce of its manufacturers to every corner of the globe", Wood pointed out that it had sadly neglected to record "its public triumphs". Parallels with the actions of the "ancients" were of course invoked:

"We should cultivate that spirit of national devotion which united the Greeks in *victory* at Marathon and in *death* at Thermopylae."

There was also a sideways jibe at the Romantics,

"The Shepherd's pipe, and the carol of the lark may be sufficient to excite the response of domestic virtue; but not to awaken a sense of public glory."

For Wood, and he may have been right for a tiny minority of Englishmen who fought in the Napoleonic wars,

"It is the thirst for posthumous fame; the wreath of immortality; and the tears of national gratitude; which induce men to forego private comfort and resist the temporary allurements of individual benefits."

Wood's remedy to all this was the building of an enormous pyramidal tomb, 250 feet square "to raise the mind above the contemplation of private interests and strengthen national devotion". The tomb would be guarded by four lions, one at each corner. The use of lions, a motif that was to occur again and again in similar memorials in the next thirty years, was not without special significance. The lion, Wood emphasised, had long been the "classical representation of British courage and generosity", combining as it did "grandeur of form and the idea of protection and safety" which "is inseparable from friendly power"!

The tomb, which was to be dedicated to Nelson and the increasing number of lesser dead heroes of the wars, had an inscription which (should

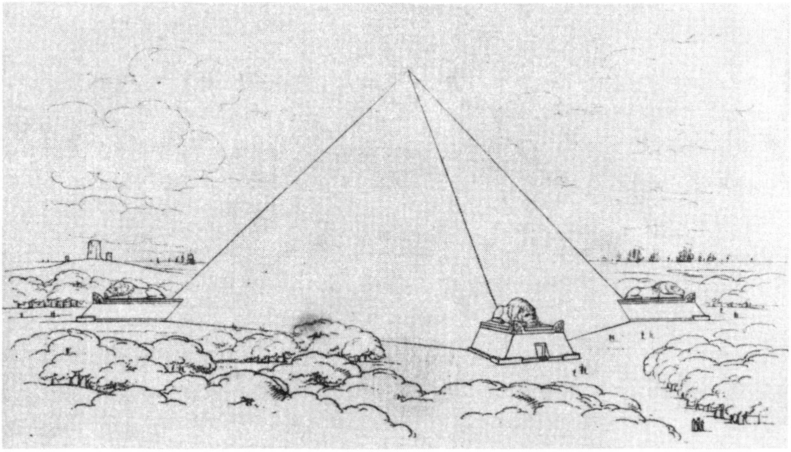

8. William Woods. Proposed National Monument (1808)

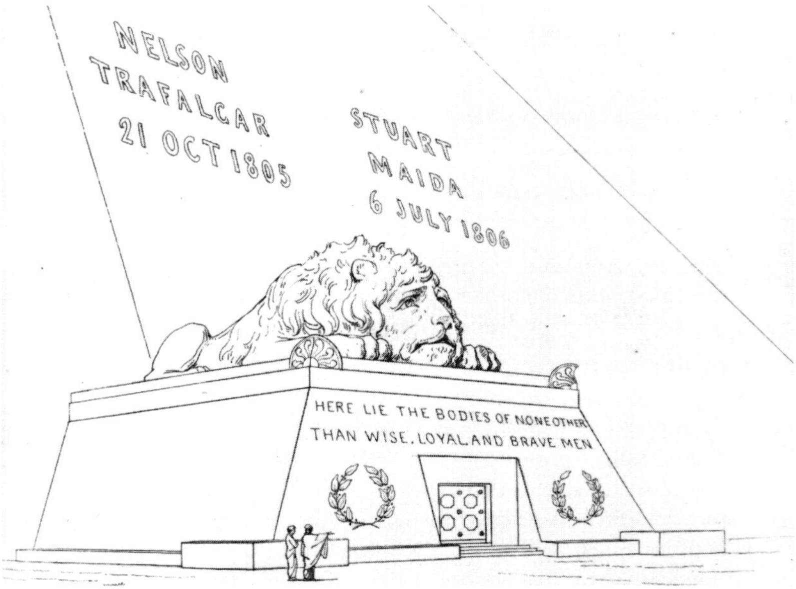

9. William Woods. Entrance to proposed National Monument (1808)

the architectural symbolism pass anyone by) would press home the point of the whole edifice,

> "By bravery and discipline the Roman Legions defeated their enemies; until subdued themslves by loss of virtue."

Wood rounded off his essay by obliquely pointing a finger at anyone who entertained Jacobin thoughts, for it was obvious to him that nobody

> "who loves his Religion, his King, his Country, and its law; can be insensible to the present awful crisis; a juncture in which not only our own existence as a nation, but the continuance of rational liberty on the earth is about to be decided."

Rousing sentiments, indeed. Fortunately for posterity, however, the economics of wartime prevented their being given concrete expression.

In the same year as Wood published his essay the young sculptor and decorator Matthew Coates Wyatt published his *Prospectus of a Model devoted to the Memory of Lord Nelson.*[9] M. C. Wyatt was the seventh son of the architect James Wyatt and was in 1813 with Sir Richard Westmacott to make his first public commission, the Nelson Monument in Liverpool. Considerably disliked by his fellow sculptors it was often said of him that it was only "thanks to the Royal and influential patronage that he enjoyed any reputation at all. In 1836 he completed the statue of George III "the pig tailed abomination of Cockspur Street";[10] an important project for which no competition was held, Wyatt having received the commission directly from a committee under Lord Liverpool.

However, let us return to the "Model" of 1808. Wyatt admitted to having been guided by two principles in his design. The first was aesthetic; for he had "endeavoured to appropriate the design exclusively to the hero . . . by minute and circumstantial allusions to his leading exploits and by embodying as far as possible his dying thoughts". The second was commercial (it was, after all, to be sold for 25 guineas); "its dimensions in their complete form to most entance halls, large libraries, etc., in private houses . . . public buildings, naval and military academies." The last two being important for it was there that "it may tend equally to honour the departed and encourage those who are entering the same career".

The principal figures that make up Wyatt's composition are the ones that recur time and time again in similar sculpture of the period. Besides Nelson, apparently naked "with an eye steadfast and upraised to victory", there is Victory herself handing down a fourth naval crown, and Death skulking beneath a flag lying "in ambush for his victim". All this for Wyatt is intended to intimate that Nelson "received the reward of Victory and the stroke of Death at the same moment". The other figure that looks on is apparently an "enraged British seaman" representing the zeal of the navy that is bent on wreaking vengeance on an enemy who had "robbed it of its most gallant leader". Britannia makes her usual appearance; but this time rather precariously for according to Wyatt she is leaning, laurels in hand, on her spear. This leaning posture Wyatt emphasised was intended to describe that the country's feelings were "fluctuating between pride and anguish".

British capitalists, as we have seen before, had always been jubilant over Nelson's various victories, and on his death it is not surprising that there was the wish to pay some form of tribute to his memory. However, money was tight and the City of London's competition for a memorial to be put in the Guildhall failed to attract many of the great sculptural talents of the day. Accompanied by the usual claims of unfairness, nepotism and the like that inevitably seem to surround these events the project was finally given to one of John Flaxman's former assistants

James Smith. Suffice it to say here that the form of the monument was not exceptional; it contained many of the same allegorical elements as Wyatt's model set against the background of a pyramid.

Although in the ten years between Trafalgar and Waterloo half a dozen similiar monuments, including John Flaxman's in St. Paul's Cathedral (1808–18), had been or were being erected by one body or another to Nelson's memory no national tribute as such in stone or bronze had been made. In 1816 it suddenly looked as though the situation was to be remedied, for a resolution was made in the House of Commons to the effect,[11]

> "that an humble address be presented to his Royal Highness the Prince Regent, humbly to represent that this House, being desirous of commemorating the splendid achievements of the British Navy throughout the late wars, by erecting a national monument to its most signal and decisive victory, have humbly to request that his Royal Highness will be graciously pleased to give directions that a national Monument be erected in honour of the ever-memorable victory of Trafalgar, by which the maritime power of his Majesty's enemies was humbled and subdued; and to commemorate the fame of Vice-Admiral Lord Viscount Nelson, and the other officers, seamen and marines, who died gloriously in their country's cause on that occasion, and in the maintenance of our national independence."

Although Lord George Beresford was able to report that the King was in agreement, little was done, as nobody seemed prepared to raise the money – a state of affairs that was to continue for another twenty-two years.

THE NELSON MEMORIAL COMMITTEE

What was it, then, that in the late 1830s renewed interest in the project? Nelson had, after all, been dead for nearly thirty-five years. There seem to be several reasons, which when taken together may give some clue to the change of mind.

Trafalgar Square had for some years been the possible site (for sculptors and architects touting for work anyway) of a naval monument, at the centre of which, as in Thomas Bellamy's and John Goldicutt's schemes, sat or stood the figure of William IV. In June 1837 William IV died and therefore the possibility, through flattery, of gaining a much needed commission disappeared. The new nineteen year old Queen, Victoria, didn't somehow present the same opportunity.

Much more important than the impecunious state of artists was growing economic crisis, which Lord Melbourne's Whig government seemed unable to control. The Whigs were deeply divided over what to do with the Corn Laws but united, more or less, with what to do with the infant Chartist movement and the burgeoning trade unions.

Under such circumstances, as we have seen so often since, the British ruling class makes chauvinistic appeals in an attempt to stay the erosion of its hegemony. The arts, especially painting and sculpture were again, needless to say, to play their small part in invoking these necessary sentiments. It was nearly inevitable, therefore, that people's minds should return, well sugared with nostalgia, to the country's triumphs over Jacobinism; the wars with Napoleon and their heroes Nelson and Wellington.

Early in 1837 the City of London commissioned Sir Francis Chantrey to complete an equestrian statue of Wellington for a site outside the Mansion House. A year later a Wellington Memorial Committee under the Chairmanship of the Duke of Rutland was formed and appointed Matthew Coates Wyatt to complete another figure of the Duke, this time to be placed on top of the arch opposite Wellington's Apsely House at Hyde Park Corner. (Wellington was of course still very much alive and leading the Opposition in the House of Lords.) Wyatt's statue, which has been described by at least one critic as the "greatest sculptural fiasco of the nineteenth century", depicted the Duke astride his horse Copenhagen on the eve of Waterloo, 18 June 1815.[12] Interestingly, it did not depict any of Wellington's then more recent achievements like being Prime Minister 1828–30, duelling with the Earl of Winchilsea in 1829, or walking in Hyde Park with Mrs. Harriet Arbuthnot.

For the Nelson Memorial Committee (N.M.C.) which held its first meeting on 22 February 1838 at the Thatched House Tavern in St. James' Street the task appeared a little easier, for at least their subject was dead.

The resolution (proposed by Admiral Sir Pulteney Malcolm and seconded by the man who was with Nelson when he died, Vice Admiral Sir Thomas M. Hardy),[13]

> "That at this meeting, impressed by and with the deepest veneration for the Memory of Lord Nelson, propose that a General Subscription be raised for the purpose of erecting a National Monument in a conspicuous part of this Metropolis in commemoration of his glorious achievements."

and passed by this first meeting is interesting in two respects. Firstly London is unequivocally seen as the site for a "National Monument". Secondly, the subtle change of emphasis from the 1816 resolution quoted above, for no mention is made of "the other officers, seamen and mariners" of whom 993 were killed and 2,834 injured in the four battles depicted in Railton's final design.[14]

A temporary committee was formed for the purpose of

> "receiving subscriptions and communicating with Noblemen and Gentlemen with the view of forming a Permanent Committee".

At the meeting was Charles Davison Scott, son of Nelson's late secretary John Scott (killed at Trafalgar), who the meeting unanimously agreed should be appointed the Secretary – a job he was later to regret having taken on. A circular letter was drawn up by Scott to be sent to the "Noblemen and Gentlemen", and eighteen banks[15] were asked to receive subscriptions, plus the Army and Navy agents. The statement was also published in the *Times, Chronicle, Strand* and the *Globe* newspapers.

By 12 March the Secretary was able to report that agreement had been received from the Prime Minister, Lord Melbourne and Thomas Spring Rice, Chancellor of the Exchequer, for the forming of a permanent committee and also to serve on it. Eighteen other "Noblemen and Gentlemen" also agreed. Twelve days later, a much larger meeting was held, mostly of Captains and Admirals, at which the Duke of Buccleuch, absent at the time, was suggested as Chairman and Nelson's old friend Admiral Sir George Cockburn as his deputy; Trustees were also solicited. It was at the fourth meeting that a first mention was made of Trafalgar Square; the minutes record:[16]

> ". . . (that) this meeting most earnestly request the committee (N.M.C.) to make every possible endeavour to obtain a space of ground in Trafalgar Square as the site of the proposed Monument, and they cannot but express their hope that the Government will not refuse so appropriate a situation."

Approaches were to be made to the Chancellor of the Exchequer and the Office of Woods, Forests and Land Revenues by the Deputy Chairman. To an attentive audience, Scott then read a letter that he had received from a George Sheddon, Esq., the contents of which surprised everyone present; for the letter referred to a Fund, seemingly unspent, for erecting a Monument to Nelson, and it was being offered to them. It read:

> "A subscription for a Public Monument to the Memory of the Ever to be lamented Vice Admiral Lord Viscount Nelson was commenced towards the close of the Year 1805 by the late Mr. Angerstein and the late Mr. Sheddon (the writer's father) and Members of the Patriotic Fund Committee, but only as much was collected as enabled the Trustees, Mr. Angerstein, Mr. Sheddon

and Mr. Hope to purchase in their joint names on the 12 November in that year £1330 at 3 per cent reduced."

The most important part of the letter, further on, reads as follows:

"The dividends have since been regularly received and added to the Principal, so that the original sum has been quadrupled as £5,369 19s 5d. Reduced 3 per cent was at the end of 1836 standing in the names of the present trustees, namely
George Sheddon
Abel Smith
George Robert Smith
William George Sheddon
The amount of the accumulated stock is now (March 1838) £5,545 19s 0d."

The Committee graciously accepted this sum, and asked the one-time Captain of the Channel Fleet, Sir Thomas Troubridge, to resign as a Trustee, appointing Abel Smith in his place.

The next meeting was even larger and the Duke of Wellington made this his first of many attendances. However, the Duke of Buccleuch, writing from his home in Scotland, said he did not mind being Chairman, but wished to point out that he was not in London very often. Nobody appeared to raise any objection to this. Scott had received a reply from the Chancellor of the Exchequer about using Trafalgar Square. Spring Rice, wishing them the greatest success in their venture, assured them that as

"His Majesty's Government have for a considerable length of time been desirous that the site should be appropriate for the Nelson Monument, there will be therefore every willingness that a suitable site should be appropriated for this purpose, provided that the plans and designs be first approved by His Majesty's Government."

COMPETITION AND PRIZES

Accordingly, with the site assured (more or less) and the subscriptions coming in, the Committee decided to ask "Artists, Architects and Sculptors to submit plans and designs" before the end of June 1838. An advertisement was drawn up to be published in all the papers as soon as was possible. Headed in bold type "Nelson Monument", it read:

"The Committee for erecting a Monument to the Memory of Lord Nelson hereby give notice that they are desirous of receiving from Architects, Artists or other persons, Designs for such a Monument in Trafalgar Square.

The Committee cannot in the present state of the subscriptions fix definitely

> the sum to be expended, but they recommend that the estimated cost of the several Designs should be confined with the sums of £20,000 and £30,000. This condition and that of the intended site are the only restrictions to which the artists are limited.
>
> The Committee is not bound to adopt any of the offered Designs; but rewards of £200, £150 and £100 will be given to 1st, 2nd and 3rd places. . . . The Designs, sealed and marked within and without with the Designers name or any mark . . . . and an Estimate of the cost as accurate as he may be able to make."

All this in three months! The shortage of time brought several letters of complaint; Patrick Park, writing from Rome, asked for the time to be extended to enable him and his fellow sculptors in Rome to send in their entries, and another letter signed with an "anchor" said at least six months were needed.

Subsequent events were to make the points raised in a letter from the architect (and Fellow of the newly formed Royal Institute of British Architects) Ambrose Poynter of more than passing interest, however. He put the following queries:

> "1. . . . . whether the decision of the majority of the Nelson Memorial Committee is to be final or whether the Commissioners of H.M.W.F.L.R. have waived their usual right to control all Designs placed upon sites granted by them on any terms.
>
> 2. . . . whether it is intended that the artists whose design is adopted shall execute the work.
>
> 3. . . . whether any means will be taken to ascertain that the designs can be executed for the sum limited or whether all designs will at once be laid aside which exceed it.
>
> 4. . . . whether the Designs will be open to Public inspection before or after the Decision."

and finally,

> "5. . . . whether any of the Committee are permitted to offer designs of their own."

Competitions of this sort were notorious for the inequality of their judgements, and the bias – it would be too strong to term it corruptness – of many of the judges.[17]

Taking into account the pleas for more time, and making no recorded comment on Poynter's remarks, the Committee postponed the entry date until 31 January 1839. The same conditions were re-advertised, in Scotland and Ireland as well as England, and it is this readvertisement which has given rise to the belief that there were in fact two separate competitions. Many people did "submit twice", this usually meaning that they added further to their models and designs after the first closing date. (Many were to do so again as we shall see below when the time was extended once more three months later.) The Committee did not meet again until a month after the final closing date, when the Secretary had several important items to report.

Another circular letter had been sent out about the subscriptions, with special mention of places abroad such as the Supreme Council at Calcutta and the similar one at Madras. The Duke of Wellington, who had taken the chair at this meeting, reported on a meeting that he had attended of Bankers, Merchants and Traders in the City of London. Support from the City was definitely good for the funds and the tone of that meeting's fourth resolution added the confidence needed. It read, Wellington reported;[18]

> "The Bankers, Merchants and Traders in the City of London present . . . pledge . . . to use individually and collectively every exertion to procure subscriptions, for the erection such a monument as shall be worthy of the glory of Lord Nelson and the Country which he so long and successfully served and in the course of which he died in the Arms of Victory."

Although at the second meeting, a year or so before, it had been moved that the state of the accounts should be read out at each meeting, this seems to be the first at which it was done. £14,293 3s 5d was the sum so far collected; this included the £5,545 19s 0d from the Patriotic Fund, and to most this seemed good progress indeed for a year's work.

The response to the competition had been enormous; the secretary reported that he had received 40 models and 124 designs, all causing a considerable problem of storage at his New Bridge Street office. It had been clear for some time that if the competition provoked a high response, then the hiring of a large space somewhere would be required – however, some difficulty had been encountered in this, mostly because Scott did not want to waste valuable money on rent. It looked, fortunately, as though the situation had been saved by the offer of a Mr. Alexander Rainy of the gallery at his house, no. 14 Regent Street. No. 14 Regent Street had in fact been the house Nash built for himself in 1824 and where he lived until he leased it to Rainy in 1830.[19] Rainy's letter does not make clear which of the two galleries he was offering, but it is likely to have been the "Gallery of Architecture".

Now that the Committee had a suitable venue for showing the models and designs, a small sub-committee had to be set up to assess them.

Fourteen members were appointed, and the Duke of Wellington was elected as Chairman; the members included the Duke of Northumberland (after all, his house would have a direct view of the winner), the Earls of Aberdeen, Cadogan and Minto, Sir Robert Peel, Thomas Spring Rice the Chancellor of the Exchequer, Admiral Sir George Cockburn the deputy chairman of the Committee, and Sir R. H. Inglis (later to be on the Select Committee on Trafalgar Square). It was agreed that they should meet at Mr. Rainy's Gallery, at one o'clock on 11 February.

Eight of the fourteen Sub-committee members turned up, including Peel, Spring Rice, and Inglis. (Both Davison Scott and Wellington had before the meeting received another letter from Patrick Park, recently returned from Rome, accusing the sculptor Baily of ". . . doing things to his model after the closing date . . .". Angered by this, Scott had called Park to his office to make the allegation in front of Baily; the allegations were found to be groundless.) As not all members of the Sub-committee could be present, Wellington suggested, and it was agreed, that a decision on the winners should be deferred until a more suitable day. Five days later, thirteen members attended Rainy's Gallery and selected three entries for recommendation to the General Committee that was to meet a week later. They were:

"1st Prize	–	No. 81 Mr. Railton
2nd Prize	–	No. 10 Mr. Baily
3rd Prize	–	No. 37 Messrs. Fowler and Sievier"

An extended description of these and many of the other competion entries is contained in Appendices 1 and 2.

NELSON FAILS TO GET OFF THE GROUND

Scott himself spoke on behalf of the Sub-Committee, Wellington (and Peel) being absent, and explained Railton's scheme. He reported that the Sub-Committee, although agreeing that Railton's scheme should take first prize, had this reservation about the column; that

> ". . . at such a height (174′ 0″) the features and character of the Statue could not be satisfactorily distinguished, and as the sub-scribers would be naturally desirous of transmitting to Posterity a closer Resemblance of the Great Man . . ."

that the Sub-committee proposed,

> ". . . a life size marble statue of Nelson be placed in the National Gallery or a like place if funds allowed."

A member moved a resolution that, as not everyone was present, a decision on the sub-committee's recommendations should be adjourned. This was agreed, another meeting fixed for 9 March, and meanwhile the models and designs would be on display for the General Committee to see.

Throughout February the press, particularly the new and influential bi-monthly magazine *Art Union*, cast a cynical eye over the whole proceedings. Its editors felt quite assuredly that the display at Rainy's gallery "did not exhibit a single spark of genius".[20] The provisional winner, as Railton still was, of course, came in for particular abuse. His design, the *Art Union*, said "was no design at all" and even the "figures and landscape (were) by an artist whom it would not be difficult to name". Malevolent remarks were also directed at the selection committee itself for "the off-hand manner in which the chosen drawing was determined on solely by one noble member of the Committee" (Wellington).

Letters of complaint from competitors continued to be received and at the 9 March meeting a letter from a "committee of artists" caused quite a stir. Wellington from the chair suggested that Sir Hussey Vivian (like Inglis, also to become a member of the Select Committee on Trafalgar Square) should see the artists concerned. Scott read out the letter; the second resolution very pointedly went:[21]

> ". . . that this meeting is convinced that a first and second visit to the Exhibition of 160 designs can only lead to a superficial and therefore inefficient and injurious conclusion, and that under present Regulations but few will see them more than once . . . also that it should be open longer, and that every artist in London should have a free ticket."

Unmoved by this, the Committee passed a resolution that the prizes should stand as per the Sub-Committee, but did add a rider that,

> ". . . further consideration of the Report should be adjourned till the first Saturday of June and that Models and Designs may be again sent or fresh ones produced by any artists on or before the last Saturday of May."

In the interval the *Art Union* was again voicing protest about the conduct of the competition. Artists as a body, for instance, they claimed, "feel offended" that the first prize was awarded hastily and "without competent advice". A situation that could be remedied by appointing a committee of judges made up of four Royal Academicians, and three members of the Institute of Architects. They were also censorious of the fact that many of the designs, including those of the three winners, had protrayed Nelson in "his usual attire with cocked hat and small clothes". "Surely," they said, "it is not necessary to hand down specimens of the bad taste of a nation ... marble should perpetuate character, not costume, (it) should exhibit the attributes of the mind not the decoration of the body."[22]

Few of the competitors it would seem took equal advantage of this interval; many did make minor adjustments, Railton for instance changed his lions from Egyptian to African ones,[23] but most undoubtedly felt a final decision on the outcome of the competition had already been reached.

In an attempt to cool the atmosphere at the meeting on 1 June, two members proposed that[24]

> "each member should enter three names of three designs . . . and that a ballot should take place on Wednesday the 19th June when a final decision will be taken . . ."

After some hesitation, perhaps aided by Wellington's absence, the proposition was passed, with the change that it should be on 22 not 19 June. So at the Committee's thirteenth meeting the ballot was taken, but not before a petition from eighteen artists[25] had been read out stating in no uncertain terms,

> ". . . that a partial exhibition encourages partial statements in the Public Journals unchecked by Public Opinions."

Little was done to meet the many objections of the "artistic community" and their demands for openness. Some concessions were made in the issuing of tickets to friends of the Committee – but that was all.

The results were published at the next meeting and the Sub-Committee's original order was confirmed. This decision marked the end of the General Committee's work, but not, as we shall see, for several of its members. A Sub-Committee was set up to administer the project, with Admiral Sir George Cockburn as chairman, and having among its members Wellington, Spring Rice, Northumberland and Inglis. Spring Rice attended only one meeting; Wellington only a few.

Railton's designs were in a sense ambiguous as to the exact location of his column, since the plans for Trafalgar Square were so uncertain; but Sir George Cockburn was able to report some advance at the first meeting of the Sub-Committee.[26] The Office of Woods, Forests and Land Revenues had replied to their earlier letter saying that there were no fixed plans for Trafalgar Square,

"... so that any plan which may be suggested by the Committee ... will be quite open for consideration."

It seemed, therefore, up to the Committee to make some form of recommendation. This it did, but not without some considerable discussion. Finally a motion by John Wilson Croker was passed unanimously, which said:

"... that the column should be erected as near to the Southern Boundary as possible" (of Trafalgar Square).

Poor old Railton was not even consulted. He was, however, called in to give his estimates for erecting the column. These he presented in two parts: £16,500 for the column and its scaffolding, £1,000 for the capital and mouldings, £4,000 for the four lions, £5,000 for the Nelson statue in bronze, and £4,000 for the four bas-reliefs also in bronze.

Railton was then dismissed, and the meeting went on to give the first mention of something that was, by 1860, to turn out to be among their most regrettable decisions. It was that,

"... it deemed it expedient that portions of the work should be executed by different artists."

Edmund Hodges Baily, the runner-up, was to be asked to make the Statue of Nelson, and the sculptor John Graham Lough to make the lions. A decision about the four bas-reliefs was referred to the next meeting.[27]

The meetings now moved from Thatched House in St. James' to the "Boardroom" of the National Gallery, where they continued to be held until the Committee was to wind up on 20 July 1844. The Treasury had been sent a copy of Railton's scheme and estimates, and Cockburn was able to report that they had approved the design, but that no action could be taken until the Office of Woods, etc.

"... have determined whether the Square shall be levelled and how it shall be enclosed."

Delay in the laying out of the complete Square did not seem to deter the Sub-committee in the least, for they resolved at the end of the meeting that "... immediate measures should be taken to commence the column and the statue ..." and that "... the issue of the lions and the bas reliefs should be postponed ...".

By 15 August, as a result of approaches by Railton, the engineer Tierney Clark was able to report to the next meeting of the Sub-Committee about the "state of the ground on the proposed site". Tierney

Clark reported that the soil was "of good load-bearing qualities, being Brown London Clay, and not soluble in water" and quite suitable for the weight of the column. He also said that in his opinion a hollow column would also be quite possible and feasible, but did have some general reservations about the overall stability of such a column in high winds. The public and the Government had all expressed doubts about its stability; it was, after all, going to be the highest single Corinthian column in the world. Spring Rice was of the opinion that both the Treasury, the Office of Woods, Forests and Land Revenues and the public would be reassured if,[28]

> ". . . men of eminence were asked to make a declaration as to its stability . . ."

Sir Robert Smirke and Mr. T. Walker were approached by the Treasury, and they reported two months later,[29] that although there are

> "no examples among the work of ancient or of modern times in which similar proportions have been adopted for a monumental structure rising to an equal height"

this did not raise in their minds

> "any strong doubts in regard to the safety of the intended work. For they believed that if the work be well executed with regard to the security of the foundations, the quality of the materials, and the perfect connexion of every part of it, there would be little reason to doubt its stability, or its power to resist the effects of high wind."

At the time, however, they thought it right to add,

> "that these important objects will be attained with greater certainty, and in a very satisfactory manner, if some diminution were made in the height of the column."

The last sentence is the most important, as it cast sufficient doubt to make the Treasury ask Railton to meet Smirke and Walker to discuss a reduction in height. The meeting was arranged and Railton (it is not known whether under protest or not), agreed.

A second report then sent by Smith and Walker to the Treasury and Office of Woods, etc., read that:[30]

> "in order to remove all doubts concerning its stability and its power of resisting the effect of high winds, we beg leave to recommend that the height of the monument be reduced not less than 30 feet, of which reduction not less than 20 feet should be made in the shaft of the column; that the shaft be of

> solid stone, and (with its pedestal) of granite; that the lower diameter of the shaft be made larger in proportion to its height; that the flutings upon it be made elliptical instead of semicircular, and that the capital be made of bronze.
>
> With these alterations, and the work properly executed upon a good foundation, we should feel perfect confidence in the stability of the proposed monument."

A copy of the report was also sent to the Sub-Committee, who in their reply to the Treasury on 11 December, rather grudgingly complied.

On the same day Scott wrote to the Office of Woods, etc., requesting a "quick decision on the fixing of the levels in Trafalgar Square" and asking that Railton be permitted to ask for tenders. These were not the only problems. John Lough had made an estimate for the lions; in granite, for the size that Railton required, the cost would be £4,000 and the weight 141 tons each! The subscriptions had advanced little since the result of the competition, so Lough was asked to be patient as no decision could yet be made.

This lack of progress of the subscription plus the need to get firm tenders for the work delayed the next meeting of the Sub-Committee until four months later, April 1840. But it was in the intevening time that the Office[31]

> "delivered over the proposed site . . . and" (declared themselves) "willing to cooperate with the Committee in everything except the Architectural Decoration of the Square (if any such decoration shall hereafter be considered)."

The tenders received were thought reasonable and the lowest, £17,868 by Grissell and Peto, was accepted.[32]

All seemed set to start; but in July the opponents of the scheme sought by means of a Select Committee of the Houses of Parliament to halt, or at least seriously delay, any further progress.

Notes to Chapter 2

1. Anonymous, *To Horatio Viscount and Baron Nelson etc.* Pamphlet written for the occasion of the placing of the memorial to Nelson in the Guildhall (London 1810).
2. Margaret Whinney, *Sculpture in Britain 1530 to 1830* (London 1964), p. 197.
3. In 1816 the Government voted £300,000 for memorials to Waterloo and Trafalgar, see H. M. Colvin and J. M. Crooke, *The History of the King's Works*, vol. VI, *1782–1851* (London 1973), p. 294.

4. John Physick, *Design for English Sculpture, 1680–1860* (London 1969), p. 169.
5. *ibid.*
6. *The First Monument erected to the memory of Lord Nelson, being an account of an arch built to his memory at Castletownend*, Cork Historical and Architectural Society Journal, Series 2, vol. III, pp. 228–9 (1897).
7. Quoted by Patrick Henchy, *Nelson's Pillar*, Dublin Historical Record, vol. x, p. 59 (1948).
8. William Wood, *An Essay on National and Sepulchural Monuments* (London 1808).
9. M. C. Wyatt, *Prospectus of a Model to the Memory of Lord Nelson* (London 1808).
10. *Art Union*, July 1840, p. 111.
11. *P.P. 1844. 484 XXXIII 630*, Treasury Minute.
12. John Physick, *The Wellington Monument* (London 1970), p. 2.
13. *PRO WORKS 6. 119, Nelson Memorial Committee Minute Book, 1838–1844.*
14. See William James' *Naval History of Great Britain* (London 1902): Battles of Copenhagen, vol. III, p. 57; Trafalgar, vol. III, p. 443; Cape St. Vincent, vol. III, p. 49; The Nile, vol. II, p. 197.
15. These banks are listed in *Statement of Subscriptions to the Memorial of the Achievements of the late Admiral Lord Viscount Nelson* (London 1841).
16. *PRO WORKS 6. 119.*
17. H. S. Goodhart-Rendell, Victorian Public Buildings in *Victorian Architecture*, ed. Peter Farraday (London 1963), pp. 87–90.
18. *PRO WORKS 6. 119.*
19. *PRO L.R.R.O. 37–42.*
20. *Art Union*, February 1839, p. 18.
21. Letter containing resolution of this meeting dated 4 March 1839, copied in *PRO WORKS 6. 119.*
22. *Art Union*, April 1839, p. 46.
23. *Art Union*, July 1839, p. 100.
24. *PRO WORKS 6. 119.*
25. The artists were George Foggo, James Nixon, H. Coffee, F. Parkinson, Raphael Brandon, W. Groves, S. Manning, C. A. Reeves, J. Tarring, W. Granville, Samuel Nixson, W. Beattie, Thomas Hopper, Thomas Moule, R. G. Wetton, Alfred Beaumont, Peter Hollins and W. P. Griffiths.
26. 8 July 1939, see *PRO WORKS 6. 119.*
27. *ibid.*
28. *ibid.*, 15 August 1839.
29. *ibid.*, 11 December 1839, also *PRO WORKS 20/2–1.*
30. *ibid.*
31. *ibid.*, 11 January 1840.
32. The other tenders were: John Malcott, £27,422, Thomas Jackson, £18,200, George Baker & Sons £17,945, Robert Hicks & Sons, £20,400; and Thomas Harvey, £19,707.

3

A VERY SELECT COMMITTEE

NELSON'S THREAT TO THE NATIONAL GALLERY

On 3 July 1840 Parliament resolved that

> ". . . a Select Committee[1] be appointed to inquire into the plan sanctioned by the Commissioners of Woods Forests and Land Revenues for the laying out of the vacant space in Trafalgar Square in front of the National Gallery."

Two days later, the Committee of fifteen MPs was nominated; (they were Mr. Galley Knight, Sir James Graham, Mr. Lock, Mr. Greene, Mr. Pendaroes, Sir Hussey Vivian, Sir Robert Inglis, Mr. Tufnell, Mr. H. T. Hope, Mr. Stanley, Mr. Protheroe, Sir C. Lemon, Sir S. Canning, Mr. Reddington, Sir C. Douglas), and empowered to report to the House of Commons. It was more or less equally divided between Whigs and Tories, the Chairman's party giving it a bias to the latter. Galley Knight as Chairman was the oldest member of the Committee, both in age and term of service in Parliament; he was the elected member for Aldborough in 1812 (and was to die in 1846). None of the members represented any of the London constituencies – in fact, they tended to be from distant ones in Cornwall, the North Midlands, Carlisle and Scotland. Sir Robert Inglis, M.P. for Oxford University, was the only one not from beyond the "Styx".

The Committee reported on 27 July 1840. In the very first paragraph the limits of their report were already apparent; the point at issue was not Trafalgar Square at all, but the Nelson Monument:

> "Your Committee must begin by observing, that the nature of the projected works in Trafalgar Square not having come under their consideration till after those works were begun, they found themselves in a position less advantageous for the performance of the task which was placed in their hands than had the field of enquiry been completely disembarrassed. They endeavoured, however, to free their minds from all extraneous circumstances, and only to consider what would most contribute to the embellishment of that part of town."

The last phrase was a direct reference to the Nelson Memorial, which in the second paragraph, they emphasised again, was in

> ". . . a situation which is indisputably one of the noblest in the Metropolis; an

area which has been obtained at great cost, and the final decoration of which must have so large a share in determining the character of that conspicuous part of the capital."

They went on to explain that Barry's plan and estimate for the laying out of Trafalgar Square had been accepted.

At this point there was also an indication that Sir Robert Inglis, and some of the other members (notably Sir Hussey Vivian and Mr. Tufnell) had not in all instances concurred with the final report. Protheroe had in fact supported all Inglis' amendments (marked *). The report went:

"The chief features of Mr. Barry's plan are, the levelling of the area from front to back and the construction of a terrace 15 feet high on the South side of the street in front of the National Gallery; *the effect of this terrace will be greatly to improve the appearance of the National Gallery, by giving it the elevation, for want of which it has been chiefly censured.* Mr Barry . . . gave it as his opinion that the appearance of National Gallery might be further improved, by continuing the order of pilasters through the whole length of the front and relieving the *baldness of the cupola by encircling it with pillars and giving it a bolder cornice."

In the next paragraph, Sir Robert Inglis disagreed with the Committee that Barry's plan

". . . under all circumstances of the case (was) well adapted to reconcile the various difficulties of the spot and attain the desired end. . . ."

but had obviously concurred that it should

". . . enquire what effect the column . . . would have on the National Gallery; (and) how far a column of such dimensions would be seen to advantage in such a position; and how far it would contribute to the embellishment of that part of the Metropolis."

The Committee also reported the results of the opinions they had sounded from

"several architects of acknowledged merit . . . (and of) eminent sculptors and men of taste . . ."

This part of the report, as we shall see below, does not fully agree with the sentiments expressed by the witnesses; a view shared by Sir Robert Inglis, to judge from his dissensions in the following excerpts (again marked*). The Committee gave it as their opinion:

"*that such a column so situated would have an injurious effect on the

National Gallery, by depressing its apparent altitude, and interrupting that point of view which should be least interfered with* . . .

that a column of such dimensions will render the surrounding buildings less important, and, so situated, will not group well with anything in its neighbourhood . . .

that as approached from Whitehall, as seen at the termination of this grand avenue . . . the National Gallery will be much injured by the column. In this point of view the column will cut the National Gallery through the centre, and the pedestal of the column alone will nearly conceal both the portico and the cupola . . .

that the site selected is not a favourable position for the column itself . . .

that the statue of King Charles is not in a line with the column; nor could this defect, from the proximity of the two objects fail to catch the eye. So long as there is no column in the proposed situation, the statue of King Charles, where it now stands is a fortunate circumstance, offering a subordinate object, in front of the National Gallery which serves as a scale, without obstructing the view."

Finally, they expressed themselves

> *"unable to avoid arriving at the conclusions, that it is undesirable that the Nelson Column should be placed in the situation which is at present selected. If it is desirable in a great city to suggest the idea of space, and having obtained space, not to block it up again; if the general architectural effect of Trafalgar Square or of the buildings around it, is to be considered; or if, at any time, an equally conspicuous position should be desired for any other monument, the situation at present selected for Nelson Column is most unfortunate.*"

So strong was the Committee's belief that it would be possible to prevent the column going ahead, that they had investigated how much money had already been spent on it, and how much compensation would be needed to be paid to the contractors should the work be terminated.

Not content with arming itself with the opinions of a section of the professional establishment, the Committee wished to bring discredit on the Nelson Memorial Committee itself, and William Railton, claiming that although the

> "Lords of the Treasury . . . entertained the fullest confidence that funds would be provided for carrying out the work in conformity to the plans and drawings . . . they (Select Committee) should be wanting in their duty if they failed to direct the attention of the House to the fact that, according to the evidence, the subscription is at present deficient for the purpose, to the amount of some thousands of pounds. Mr. Railton informed the Committee that his estimate of

the Column amounts to £28,000 whilst the sum subscribed does not exceed £18,000, nor does it appear that any well grounded hope exists of any considerable addition."

It also maintained that

> ". . . a perishable statue of Portland Stone is most objectionable; and supposing the terms of the contracts are fulfilled to the letter (which in works of such magnitude is seldom the case) the remaining £3,000 is wholly inadequate to meet the expenses of casting the capital, of obtaining such a statue as ought to crown the summit, and of providing the bronze bas reliefs for the sides of the pedestal, and the lions at the corners of the base. Even if the fund should prove sufficient to complete the masonry, no statue can be raised but one of Portland Stone, and the column without its bas reliefs will remain a denuded mass, which however gigantic will have a mean effect."

Harsh words; but then the four days of the taking of evidence was marked by a distinct air of acrimony from both sides. On the first day (10 July), when Railton was examined, the Chairman asked about costs. Before Railton could answer, Inglis moved that

> "the question having reference to the mode in which certain individuals have employed funds raised by them by private subscription for carrying into effect a plan . . . should not be put."

The motion was defeated by seven votes to two, but it succeeded in changing for the time being the line of questioning. The Chairman then asked Railton the height of his column; "170 feet", Railton replied.

> " – Was that the original height?
> – It was not, it was 203 feet originally.
> – Was it 203 feet at the time of the competition?
> – Yes it was; it was reduced after that.
> – By what authority was it reduced?
> – By order of the Government.
> – Of the Government?
> – Yes.
> – Not by order of the Nelson Committee?
> – It was sanctioned by both.
> – At whose instigation; do you know at all?
> – I am not aware."

Did Railton know that his column exceeded the height of any other column of the Corinthian order in existence? He did. Did this fact not expose the column to problems of stability? Railton replied that the report of Smirke and Walker, although suggesting that it be lowered, expressed no doubts as to its stability. "What I want to know," asked Tufnell, "is whether you consider the Commissioners of Woods, Forests and Land Revenues and the Treasury have approved your plan on comparison with the others or after it had been selected in the competition." Railton's increasing irritation was becoming obvious; when asked whether he knew of Mr. Barry's plan for the Square, he replied rather sharply "No, he did not", as he had, after his design was approved, sent to the Office of Woods, Forest and Land Revenues several designs for the Square of his own.

Neither did he think he would have changed his designs had he known of the details of Barry's plan. At this stage, Railton admitted that he had changed his designs between the two competition submissions. He had changed the pedestal and base, lowering the former by 4′ 6″. It was not, however, until halfway through Railton's interview that the first question about the effect of his design on the National Gallery was put. (" . . . The Gallery is a very long line and requires to be broken. . . .") Did Railton, asked Vivian, referring to the moving of the Column to the southern edge of the site, think it was less of an impediment? " – it has never been an impediment." By this time Railton was clearly getting angry, and the Chairman tactfully changed the line of attack again to a discussion about Railton's schemes for laying out the Square.

Two of Railton's schemes were, as he outlined them, similar to Barry's; the third would have placed his column at the southern end of an "inclined plane", changing slightly therefore the height in relation to the National Gallery. He admitted, however, that the overall effect on the National Gallery would have been the same. Railton, however, was at pains to emphasise, like some of the "expert witnesses" to the Committee, the full effect of his column, as seen from all points around and not merely from a given point in Whitehall. "It is better seen," as he said, "from the Strand and Cockspur Street and from different places"; and he added, that in relation to the National Gallery,

> "it obstructs the view of the Gallery and all the buildings in the Square less . . . and by putting it in the centre, you have a better view of the National Gallery from every point than by putting it in a different situation."

Once again, he defended the height of his column, this time by comparing it with the height of the spire of St. Martin's. This, being 192 feet in height, was higher than his column (170 feet); and,

> "St. Martin's Church is considerably (higher and) meaner than the National Gallery . . . and if it does not injure it, I do not see how my column can."

Next, as though to press his argument home. Railton suggested that in any case,

> "You never could have erected anything in Statuary of sufficient consequence for the magnitude of the Square for so small a sum of £30,000."

Did this, Railton was asked, not imply an architectural monument? He thought not; it implied any monument suited to the site.

The next person to appear before the Committee was the rather cautious Scot, Alexander Milne, Second Commissioner of Woods and Works. Throughout these proceedings and the subsequent time that he was in office, Milne, nearly alone, showed an impartial but firm regard for what was becoming a very disputed issue. He carefully related the Office of Woods, etc.'s involvement in the Charing Cross Improvements, and gave a detailed account of the various costs in Barry's scheme, including that part of the £11,000 which would be used to improve Green Park. Tufnell then asked, had there been any conditions annexed to the permission granted for erecting the column that related it specifically to Barry's plan? Milne replied firmly that no conditions had been so annexed, as Barry's plan had not been ready until 1 June 1840. (In reading the evidence of the Select Committee, it often seems that several of the M.P.s had not really done their homework and consequently often asked rather ill-informed questions.) As far as Milne knew, Barry had no objections to Railton's design, but he added that so far Barry and Railton had not met to discuss the issue. The Chairman suggested that this be done as quickly as possible, and Milne agreed to arrange it. Was Barry's lack of objection to the Column based on the fact that he believed it to be a "settled thing", asked the Chairman. Milne admitted that he thought this was probably the case. (Barry's own evidence given on the next day shows no ambiguity on this point.)

To end the first day, Sir Francis Chantrey, C. R. Cockerell, Philip Hardwick, Decimus Burton and Edward Blore, "as practical and professional men and also men of taste", were called in and asked to give an answer within a few days to the following questions:

> "1. What effect, in your opinion, will a column of which the pedestal including the steps is 43 feet high and the height altogether 170 feet have upon the National Gallery?

2. What effect, in your opinion, will the said column have as an ornamental object in combination with the surrounding buildings?
3. What effect will the column have on the National Gallery as you approach it from Whitehall?
4. How far do you consider that position a favourable position for the column itself?"

Their answers, "whether written or spoken", were to be made public.

THE NATIONAL GALLERY DEFENDED

On the next day of the proceedings (13 July), Sir Richard Westmacott, Sydney Smirke, Joseph Gwilt, Thomas Donaldson and John P. Deering were asked to answer the same questions, the Chariman this time adding that

> " . . . we do not ask for an opinion about the architectural merits of the column itself."

The whole of the remainder of that day was devoted to Charles Barry's evidence, and because of its importance, both with regard to his laying out of the Square and his opinions of Railton's scheme, it will be quoted at some length. The Chariman first asked Barry to explain his scheme, which he did in some detail:

> "The area is proposed to be level; on the north side in front of the National Gallery is proposed a terrace 165 feet long and 32 feet wide, with a flight of steps at each end to the area before the same width (each step being two feet wide and five inches high) with ample landings in the circular corners of the Square. The terrace is proposed to have at each end two large oblong pedestals for groups of sculpture, and circular pedestals for candelabra are proposed to be placed at the foot of each of the flights of steps, as well as at the angles of the Square towards Cockspur Street, and the Strand. The Terrace flanking walls of the steps are to be surmounted by a balustrade. The terrace wall and balustrade will be 14 feet high. The front or south side of the Square, and the north side of the terrace towards the road in front of the National Gallery, are proposed to be enclosed by ornamental stone posts so placed as to be a barrier against carriages and horses. The area is proposed to be covered with asphaltum. The terrace is to be paved and the whole of the masonry in the terrace and retaining wall, the steps, landings, the pedestals, balustrades and lateral parapets as well as the posts on the south side of the Square and on the terrace are proposed to be wholly Aberdeen Granite."

The Chairman's second question again referred to the relation of the Column to the National Gallery as seen from Whitehall. The detail of

Barry's reply would indicate that he had either, for some other reason, worked it out beforehand, which is likely, or had some foreknowledge of the question:

> "When viewed from Craigs Court, the stylobate will conceal the entire centre, extending to the columns in front of the gateways in breadth and nearly the whole height of the podium . . . the die of the pedestal will conceal one half of the portico in breadth and up to within 3 feet of the springing of the dome in height. . . . From Whitehall Chapel the stylobate will conceal the whole of the portico."

When asked for his opinion "as to the propriety of placing the Column in Trafalgar Square", Barry replied:

> "The area is in my opinion, too small and confined for a column of the height and magnitude proposed: the effect of it would be to reduce the apparent size of the Square, and render the surrounding buildings insignificant. The National Gallery, being small in its parts, and low in elevation, will suffer materially in this respect, more especially when viewed from Whitehall and Charing Cross. . . .
>
> . . . the irregularity in the form of the area, the variations in the levels of the surrounding streets, and the direction of the several lines of approach, are not calculated to afford a favourable view of the column except from Charing Cross and Whitehall. . . . From all points of view the unsymmetrical position of the column, in respect of the surrounding objects, will be striking and unsatisfactory. The view of the proposed column from the ends of Duncannon Street and Pall Mall East, as well as from the road in front of the Gallery, would be unfavourable, in consequence of the points of sight being from eleven feet to fourteen feet above the base of the stylobate on which the column rests."

To the question, would he change his design if the column was removed (obviously still a hope of the Committee), Barry said that he would make no changes in principle, and that

> "it would in my opinion be desirable that the area should be left wholly free from all insulated objects of art, which in consequence of the irregular form of the Square . . . unfavourably seen from many points of view. The four pedestals might be surrounded by groups of sculpture, say man and horse, exhibiting the characters, varieties of the human and brute forms of each quarter of the globe; in the centre of the terrace wall might be a fountain, composed of sea-horses, naiads, and tritons, surmounted by a semi-colossal figure of Neptune, which for the sake of the composition and obtaining an effective view of it both from the Square and the terrace, might be placed at the level of the balustrade. The four circular pedestals, two of which are proposed

to be placed at the foot of the steps from the terrace, and the other at the angles of the square towards Cockspur Street and the Strand might be surmounted with candelabra, supported by a group of figures and containing each a Bude or Drummond light which should be illumined by night."

Barry then moved on to describe his motives for this modest scheme. It would afford, he said, an opportunity

" . . . of giving scope and encouragement to sculptural art of a high class, and of giving that distinctive and artistic character to the square, which is so needed in public areas and squares of London, to excite among all classes that respect and admiration for art, so essentially necessary to the formation of a pure and well grounded national taste."

Sentiments such as these were to be the target of bitter satire in an issue of *Punch* a few years later, when these words appeared describing a cartoon entitled "Substance and Shadow":[2]

"There are many silly, dissatisfied people in this country, who are continually urging upon Ministers the propriety of considering the wants of the pauper population, under the impression that it is as laudable to feed men as to shelter horses.

"To meet the views of such unreasonable people, the Government would have to put its hand into the Treasury money-box. We would ask how the Chancellor of the Exchequer can be required to commit such an act of folly, knowing, as we do that the balance of the budget was trifling against him, and that he has such righteous and paramount claims upon him as the Duke of Cumberland's income, the Duchess of Mecklenburg Strelitz's pin-money, and the builder's little account for the Royal stables.

"We conceive that Ministers have adopted the very best means to silence this unwarrantable outcry. They have considerately determined that as they cannot afford to give hungry nakedness the substance which it covets, at least it shall have the shadow.

"The poor asked for bread, and the philanthropy of the State accords – an exhibition."

The Committee, obviously thinking that Barry was on their side, then asked if he could suggest an alternative site for the column. Yes, he most certainly could: how about St. James's Square, or the Crescent at the top of Regent Street (Park Crescent), or the Circus at the junction of Regent Street and Oxford Street (Oxford Circus), or for that matter, "out of London (altogether), perhaps the best and most appropriate site would be in conjunction with Greenwich Hospital?"

His opinion on Railton's scheme seemed quite clear to the Committee, but as architect to the Square he had to admit that although he had been asked (but never officially), his views were only known "incidentally". Barry must have known that his evidence would be made public, but probably felt that his reputation was better safeguarded if it was made known through the report of a Parliamentary Committee. He was never, however, drawn to make the "official complaint" that the Select Committee spent so long trying to persuade him to make.

His experience with the Office of Woods, Forests and Land Revenues (it was four years since he had won the competition for the Houses of Parliament) seemed to make him more sceptical of the Select Committee's powers to put a stop to Railton's scheme, for again he confirmed his belief that,

> "I assumed it as a thing (the column) settled and determined . . . and under the circumstances I made my plan in the best manner I could."

Barry had thus to cope with two "elements" in his composition, for both of which he had very little regard, as he made clear in his answers to questions from Sir James Graham:

> " – Will the erection of so high a column have the effect of making more prominent the defects of the National Gallery?
> – No doubt of it.
> – Will not the National Gallery look much worse than it does? (after Barry's terrace had been made)
> – I would not say it would look worse."

It should be recalled here that Barry could hardly have been said to have "got on" with Wilkins; Wilkins had, after all, made him the object of some very severe public criticism after he won the competition for the new Houses of Parliament.[3]

So concerned were the Committee with the view of the National Gallery from Whitehall, that they suggested that a mock-up of the pedestal should be made up from scaffold poles and canvas. Towards the end of his evidence Barry talked a little about what he saw as the injurious effect of the Nelson Column on St. Martin's Church:

> "it (the injurious effect) would apply more to the body of the church than to the spire; the column of the portico would suffer most by contrast."

As is suggested by his earlier evidence, it seems Barry would have preferred that his design should have been carried out unencumbered, for the

> "area is not large enough for monuments of a proper size for effect."

Barry's unwillingness to jeopardise his relations with the Office of Woods, etc. (which was, after all, to be his employer for the next twenty years) caused the Committee to find themselves at the end of the second day of evidence seemingly very far from achieving their hopes.

CROSS-EXAMINATION OF WITNESSES

The whole of the following day of the Committee's sitting (16 July) was spent examining Charles Davison Scott, the Secretary of the Nelson Memorial Committee. Scott was to come in for somewhat harsh questioning which at times verged on an interrogation. Many of the questions put to him concerned the state of subscriptions. Mr. Hope first asked, was not a certain large sum of money from a previous subscription (Patriotic Fund) included in the statement and if this was so, was not the figure of £18,000 being claimed an incorrect one; should it not be nearer £12,500? Scott, in his reply, declared himself unable to see that the two were separate, and added that subscriptions were still coming in. He did, however, hint that subscriptions were not coming in as fast as they had in the beginning, mentioning as a probable cause the lack of progress in getting on with the project. He was able to report that the contract had been placed, and that they had done this believing that they had the full support of the Office and that the subscriptions would be sufficient to cover the ultimate cost. Allegations were then levelled at an indignant Scott that he had altered a letter from the Chancellor of the Exchequer, Thomas Spring Rice, dated 7 April 1838. Scott retorted that it had been done by the Chancellor himself at one of the meetings of his Committee after it had been sent; of this he was quite sure.

Again, the issue of the difference between the original estimate and the present state of the subscriptions was raised, and Scott was asked whether his Committee had ever entertained the thought of a grant from the Government. His reply was evasive.

> "Any hopes the Committee have had or entertained, can have been the subject rather of discussion only by the Committee at Committee meetings. I am not authorized to discuss what was passed at any Committee."

Pressed further, he denied that he had not had any direct or indirect assurances from the Government at all. That the contract had been placed considerably annoyed Galley Knight, the Chairman, who in response to Scott's earlier remarks said:

"Then the effect of my addressing you a letter on 5th July, to propose that the works should be suspended till the Committee had reported, was to induce you to order them (the contractors) to accelerate the works",

to which Scott replied,

"I did not understand your letter; I could give no order in the absence of the authority from the Nelson Memorial Committee, to stop the works."

In any case, the Committee wished

"if possible to have the foundation finished by the 1st August, because it was the Anniversary of the Battle of the Nile, and we had every hope that Her Majesty or her Royal Consort would lay the first stone on that day."

(This hope was not to be fulfilled.) Scott's final words that day were to reiterate, in response to a question by Douglas, his affirmation that Spring Rice had made the alteration in the letter before mentioned, and not he. To end the day Galley Knight read out the answers to the four questions that had been asked of the "architects, artists and men of taste".

Six – Blore, Burton, Cockerell, Donaldson, Hardwick and Smirke – were architects. Two – Chantrey and Westmacott – were sculptors. The remaining two – Gwilt and Deering – constituted the "men of taste". Gwilt was a prolific writer on architectural theory; Deering although once an architect (he had assisted Wilkins on the design of University College London) had retired some twelve years before to pursue the life of a country gentleman.

As a group they could not all be said to be disinterested in the outcome of the Select Committee, for Cockerell, Donaldson and Smirke among the six architects, and Westmacott (Chantrey hardly if ever competed) of the sculptors had as we have seen submitted designs, unsuccessfully, in the competition. However, this interest was likely to be somewhat tempered by the acrimonious debate in the press that was surrounding the whole project. All ten men were by any measure extremely successful and unlikely to risk their reputations by getting involved in a project however prestigious it might appear. Patronage they all knew could be fickle indeed. In fact, as the *Art Union* put it:[4]

"The majority of these gentlemen it seems almost certain will dislike on principle to report anything which would have the effect of interfering with the decision already arrived at. . . ."

With the exception of Blore and Donaldson, who practised almost wholly in revivals of Gothic or Tudor styles, all the others were unashamed practitioners of the Graeco-Roman style. Burton although much younger than the others, he was only just forty, had established a national reputation with his Athenaeum Club in Waterloo Place (1827–30), the Screen at Hyde Park (1825) and the massive, now demolished Colosseum in Regent's Park (1823–7). C. R. Cockerell had on Wilkins' death in 1839 become Professor of Architecture in that bastion of Neo-Classicism, the Royal Academy. During one of his famous lectures he had unabashedly admitted that "in the present day all styles (are) in request, but of all of them, the Roman (is) the most practicable for us".[5]

Donaldson, besides practising as an architect, his output was quite small, was a Select Committee witness undoubtedly because of his position as Secretary in the then recently (1835) founded Institute of Architects (now the Royal Institute of British Architects). Donaldson has been described as the "embodiment of the new architectural professionalism",[6] the Institute being founded with the sole aim of gaining for architects some professional respectability, a respectability that people like Nash had done so much to lose. Hardwick's position in some ways must have been doubly difficult, for besides sharing the other witnesses' reticence for a change in the *status quo*, he was personal architect to the Duke of Wellington. The Duke of Wellington, it will be remembered, was probably the person largely responsible for the selection of Railton's design. A year before Hardwick had completed his uncompromising Greek Propylaeum at Euston Station (the Euston Arch), an edifice that had brought him much acclaim from the critics. Sydney Smirke, the much younger brother of Sir Robert, was perhaps the least distinguished among the architect witnesses. His choice may well have been determined by the fact that he had been for a couple of years (1830–2) the Clerk of Works of the King's Mews at Charing Cross.[7]

The two "artists" Sir Francis Chantrey and Sir Richard Westmacott were the old men among the witnesses; Chantrey was just on sixty, Westmacott sixty-five. Both men had made a lucrative career out of memorials of one sort or another including many of Nelson. (Chantrey's financial success can be gauged by noting that on his death he left an estate worth £150,000 having started life as the son of a small tenant farmer in a village near Sheffield.) Not long after Nelson's death Chantrey had made a design (unexecuted) to stand on a pier "projecting far into the sea" at Great Yarmouth for a colossal statue to the memory of Nelson.[8] It was to be one hundred and thirty feet high, the pedestal was to be made from the bows of vessels taken from the enemy and the whole edifice was to be illuminated at night.

Westmacott, on the other hand, could count no such grandiose devotions among his works. In the late 1820s he undertook to do the frieze depicting Nelson's life that was to adorn one of the long sides of the Marble Arch. Twenty years earlier, in 1809 he had completed a statue of Nelson for the city of Birmingham. The statue, unlike Chantrey's, was a modest life size; so modest in fact that someone said it was little more than "sorrowful". In 1815 he had completed with M. C. Wyatt a Nelson memorial in Liverpool and a couple of years later one in Bridgetown, Barbados.[9]

Besides all this the choice of the witnesses was obviously determined by their known attitudes to the most prominent and controversial buildings in the Square; the National Gallery and the Church of St. Martin's-in-the-Fields. Although built in the 1720s, the latter, James Gibbs' church, reflecting as it did the considerable influence of Sir Christopher Wren, was still in the 1840s the subject of considerable adverse criticism, especially from the purists of the Graeco-Roman school. The vitriol that continuously poured on poor Wilkins's National Gallery we have already mentioned.

MUCH ADO ABOUT NOTHING

The Select Committee in its choice of witnesses would seem to have tried to steer a course that would enable an apparent balance of opinions to emerge while not allowing the influential anti-National Gallery faction to gain the upper hand (a faction that was undoubtedly of the opinion that the National Gallery was an unmitigated disaster and any monument occupying the Square would be an improvement).

With the exception of Cockerell and Deering who answered the questions with rather fulsome letters, the remaining eight answered as requested each question separately, and to the point. (Burton's answers never went beyond one sentence.)[10]

Their opinions were equally divided on questions one and three that referred to the column's effect on the National Gallery. Blore, Burton, Chantrey, Donaldson and Cockerell all suggested that the column might diminish the apparent size of the National Gallery but would not "injure it". The others, Gwilt, Hardwick, Smirke, Westmacott and Deering all thought more or less the exact opposite.

The second question which was intended to elicit a more general statement about "architectural composition" gave several witnesses, notably Chantrey, Gwilt and Cockerell the opportunity in their answers to give a display of historical scholarship. Obviously throughout the debate the interpretation of precedents, especially classical ones, was of utmost importance. Cockerell, for instance, anticipating the criticism that Trafalgar Square was too small a space for such a large edifice as Railton's column, referred the Committee to the example of the Columns of Trojan and Antoninus, and the "colossal statues of Jupiter and of Minerva which occupied the entire nave of their temples" – none of which, Cockerell thought, "can be said to deteriorate from the architecture in connexion with which they are seen". However, he was quick to point out that the placing of "colossal objects in extensive areas", as had happened in Rome, Paris and St. Petersburg, "is a wholly modern practice and a departure from the principle of effect on which they were originally founded by the ancients".

Donaldson, in a supplementary letter to the Committee (published with the evidence) made a roundabout plea dear to the hearts of many sculptors and architects during what was to be a lean period in terms of work for many of them, that

> "the enrichments of sculpture and a due decoration in the subordinate parts are essential to convey all those impressions which it is necessary to produce when erecting a monument. . . ."

He hoped in fact

> "that the erection of the Nelson column may not become an instance of miserable national parsimony on such a noble occasion".

The witnesses having disagreed on the first three questions were unanimous in their approval, except for Gwilt, when it came to answering the fourth question, was the Trafalgar Square " . . . a favourable position for the column itself"? Donaldson went as far as to say that as it

> "compels an effort on the part of the beholder in order to see all its parts . . . being obliged to raise their heads and use some exertion in order to see the full height of the column (it) will create an impression of dignity upon the mind".

On 22 July, Railton was to appear again before the Committee, having been asked to present a list of the "Committee of Gentlemen" who had chosen his scheme. After some explanation of the several competitions, Sir Robert Inglis asked Railton,

> "if any other interruption should take place in the progress of the work as now

advanced, and supposing (a) fresh competition necessary, do you consider such interruption would have any, and what effect, in deterring other professional men engaging in the same?"

Railton replied in no uncertain terms:

"I should think no professional man would venture to compete again; it would deter the profession completely, it would be a complete breach of faith."

The Chairman went on to ask:

"did any first rate artists compete the last time?"

Several, indicated Railton.

"Sir Francis Chantrey?"

Railton's reply was sharp and to the point.

"He never competes, except it is with one or two. . . ."

Would Railton have designed the column on another site? No, he was very firm, it had been designed specifically for Trafalgar Square.

Railton was the last witness that day, and that day the last for examining witnesses. The Chairman's concluding remarks must have seemed truly hypocritical to Railton:

"You will understand that the Committee have not asked any questions of Mr. Barry or any other professional gentlemen, respecting the merits of your column as a work of art, but merely with respect to its position."

Why the recommendations of the Select Committee did not, when published, have an effect in delaying, postponing, let along stopping altogether Railton's scheme from going ahead is not clear. At the time there was much speculation and it seems likely that besides not wishing to change the *status quo*, the Government was not willing to induce the ailing Wellington's wrath for fear of killing him off.

Notes to Chapter 3

1. *Report from Select Committee on Trafalgar Square, together with Minutes of Evidence taken before them*, and Appendix 27.7.1840 in *P.P. 1840 (548), XII, 387.*
2. *Punch*, vol. XIV (1848), pp. 22–3.
3. Wilkins had written a pamphlet entitled *An Apology for the Design of the New House of Parliament marked Phil. Archimedes* that attacked Barry's project. See also *PRO WORKS 20/2–1.*

4. *Art Union*, August 1840, p. 128.
5. *The Builder*, vol. III, 31, p. 85.
6. N. Pevsner, *Some Architectural Writers in the Nineteenth Century* (London 1972), p. 83.
7. H. M. Colvin and J. M. Crook, *The History of the King's Works*, vol. VI, 1782–1851 (London 1973), p. 676.
8. See Chantrey entry in Rupert Gunnis, *Dictionary of British Sculptors* (London 1953).
9. Margaret Whinney, *Sculpture in Britain, 1530–1830* (London 1964), p. 203.
10. Appendix to the *Select Committee.*

4

THIRTY YEARS IN THE MAKING

"They would have made us slaves nay worse; but then
We struck to show that we still were men.
And all who value worth and manliness
Have sympathised with us, except the Press –
The Press! that engine to enlarge the slave
Can it refuse when truth and justice crave?
Alas! Oppression sways the venal pen –
Corruption backs the master – not the men!
But time will come when these things will no be –
When heaven will give success to honesty.
And those who worked at Nelson's Monument,
At Woolwich too – by slavery unbent,
Shall with their brethren raise a noble name
That tyranny shall daunt and treachery shame.
Oh may the members of the Houses be
As were the builders foes to tyranny."[1]

MOBS AND FOUNTAINS

Ever since the demolition of the King's Mews the shopkeepers around Charing Cross had constantly complained in the press or directly to the Office of Woods, Forests and Land Revenues that the constant building work on or around the Square was causing them to lose trade.[2] Complaints of a more aesthetic nature were not infrequent either. The Royal College of Physicians, for example, complained that Barry's new "building" would considerably detract from the appearance of their recently completed building (Sir Robert Smirke, 1825). As was frequently the case, architects of renown were asked to give opinions on the matter; in this case, Decimus Burton, writing to J. Mackenzie, the College's President, in 1841:[3]

> " . . . in my opinion the appearance of the Club House will not be improved thereby and although by increasing the depth of the area the tendency will be to darken the North windows of East Front area.
>
> I recommend that the Committee should offer no opposition."

He was, of course, referring to the new incline and retaining walls of the road on the West side of the Square.

Concern with light was also the subject of a meeting that Barry had had with the local Paving Board, who objected in no uncertain terms to Barry's whole scheme, as (Barry reporting to the Office):[4]

> " . . . the proposed plan of covering the area with either paving asphalt or gravel on account of the annoyance and inconvenience that would be felt by the residents of the immediate neighbourhood from the glare of light and the reflection of heat that such an extent of surface would entail . . . (also) the accumulation of dust from the surrounding streets that would be likely to cover it. . . ."

The report added that

> " . . . a strong desire was expressed for the addition of the two fountains as it was considered . . . they would not only have a striking effect in conjunction with the column, and the surrounding works, but would tend materially to change and refresh the air."

Barry rejected their other proposal, that trees should be planted, on the grounds that the foliage would be harmed by the smoky atmosphere, but did concur with their view about the fountains.

> "In my opinion, the best mode of obviating to a considerable extent the evils apprehended, that the Basins of the proposed should be of considerable size, say 80 feet to 100 feet square, so as to occupy a very large portion of the entire area. . . . If . . . the fountains were of bronze of a massive character similar in taste to those which have lately been erected in the Place Louis Quinze in Paris . . . in conjunction with the column and the architectural decoration of the Square they could produce a reasonably striking effect."

In a long letter from the First Commissioner of Woods, Forests and Land Revenues to the Treasury, in which he asked that the expected costs of construction should be included in the next year's estimates, the first hint appears that disquiet of a different nature than either cost or "design" was present in the official mind:[5]

> " . . . It appears to us, we confess, that the other evils of a generally objectionable character may be anticipated from leaving open so large a space in this particular quarter of the Metropolis."

"The other evils of a generally objectionable character" were of course the fear of the "urban mob" which was as we shall see causing so much trouble to the authorities throughout the country, and seemed to take advantage of large public open spaces. To meet these fears, Barry proposed an alternative to his two fountains scheme; in it, the top half of the Square beneath the terrace, and stretching the whole width between the staircases, was to be filled with a single basin containing two fountains.[6] In the event, it was rejected, because the thought was already in most people's minds that[7]

> "the well which would form the source water of the proposed supply, like others of the same description, may ultimately prove a failure. . . ."

Barry's fountains' water supply did in fact fail, the water table fell in the two wells bored by the engineers Easton and Amos during the next thirty years, and by the 1880s was nothing much more than an "overflow from a beer bottle."[8]

Barry's fountains were not to meet the approval of either the public or the professionals. *The Builder*, in an article in 1845, used these words:[9]

> " . . . the fountains are nothing more nor less in design than might have been purchased, dolphins and all, ready made, at any artificial stone shop in the Paddington Road."

This disaffection with the fountains seemed to persist, for in the 1930s they were to be remodelled by Sir Edwin Lutyens to commemorate Lords Jellicoe and Beatty, Naval heroes of the First World War.[10] The originals now stand in front of the Parliament Building in Ottawa.

The construction of the Square itself went on during 1842 and 1843, and encountered very few problems with either the contractor, Grissell and Peto, or the various subcontractors. One item, however, apart from the water supply already mentioned, did cause constant problems, and this was the lighting; more specifically the light fitting itself. Street lighting, like hard paving and "Macadam roads" had only then just begun to be used in any organised way in the Metropolis.[11] With the advent of a police force to replace the traditional watch box system[12] run by the vestries, the need to illuminate the "Peeler's" beat was paramount. The presence of the police at night had to be seen as well as heard, now that with the improved pavements people could walk the streets with greater ease. As Trafalgar Square was to remain "open", unlike the gardens and London Squares that were always fenced, and gated, adequate lighting was needed not only to prevent footpads from lurking in the shadows, but also to make it more difficult for the homeless to rest there unseen. In 1839 the London Gas Company had asked for permission to lay a 12-inch main from Whitehall to Trafalgar Square to provide gas for the lighting, and the work was finally completed in 1844.[13]

The light fittings themselves were designed by the Bude Light Company, but the actual burner was to the design of Boccius and Company. Both these companies claimed great benefits would be bestowed on the Square by using their designs; the Bude Light Company claiming that[14]

> "the light in the House of Commons and Lobbies had given great satisfaction when used in 1842 and it was hoped to use it in the New Houses of Parliament."

The Bude Company lanterns still survive, but sadly Mr. Boccius' burner was within the year to prove totally inadequate. After several attempts in the following years, the mantles were finally replaced in 1850 by ones to the design of "Mr. Leslie's Patent". This was not the end of the matter, for Mr. Boccius kept up a continuous correspondence with everyone concerned, including Barry, complaining that his reputation had been irretrievably damaged by the publicity its failure had received.[15]

At the end of Chapter 3 it was shown that the Select Committee did not succeed in persuading Parliament to stop the works on Nelson's Monument. This was in July 1840. One month earlier, the Nelson Memorial Committee agreed to pay the sculptor Baily £500 to complete the statue of Nelson; they also contracted Messrs. Bramah, Presage and Ball to cast the bronze capital, including the four figures of Victory, plus the abacus and bronze weathering, and C. H. Smith & Co. of Birmingham to model all the parts of the capital from Railton's drawings for £250. They also instructed Railton to employ a Clerk-of-Works at a salary "not exceeding £2 12s 6d per week".[16]

A WEIGHTY MATTER

In December came reports of the first of the many practical difficulties that were to be encountered in constructing the column, when Scott wrote that Baily was having no success in obtaining a piece of Portland Stone of sufficient size to make the statue of Nelson in one peice. Baily had suggested that the Duke of Buccleuch might be able to help in the matter, (the Duke, besides being the Chairman of the Memorial Committee, was the owner of a considerable stone quarry at Granton, near Edinburgh). Unless a large peice could be found, Baily feared that, if it was to be made in three or four pieces, it would be unsafe, and stated that he "certainly would not be responsible for the result". Scott had approached the Duke, who, fortunately had replied saying that he was informed that such a piece (12 feet by 6 feet) was available, and that he was willing to supply it "without profit", as Scott had suggested.

Within a few days of receipt of this letter, Scott received one from the Duke's agent stressing the difficulty of shipping such a large piece, so much so, he said, that he had not been able to find a vessel willing to take it. This letter was followed the next day by another, this time from the quarry contractors saying that while the promised stone was being removed from its place in the quarry it had broken along a fault. But all would not be lost, they suggested, if Baily would allow the masons at the quarry to "roughen out" another piece of a slightly smaller size. Not only would this reduce the weight of 40 tons, but it would perhaps also make the shipping problem easier, for, in the words of the shipping agents approached by Scott:[17]

> "the first question is, how will it be got aboard the vessel; St. Katherine's docks had once done 40T but unwillingly . . . 30T perhaps . . ."

And even if that stage of the removal could be accomplished, there would still remain the problem of

> "how that can be raised to the top of a column 170 feet high . . . (it) cannot be done by block and tackle and nothing but a second tower of Babel can accomplish it."

In an attempt to resolve the problem of weight, Baily at the end of November dispatched his foreman to the quarry to reduce the size of the stone. But even this, a reduction of 17 tons, did not placate the shippers, who still refused to carry it; and so, late in December, Baily conceded, and the stone was finally shipped in two pieces.

Three years later, in 1843, the *Illustrated London News* was to write an article describing how the final statue was hauled into position on 3 November, starting at the very early (and dark) time of 5.20 a.m. Containing as it does some interesting material about contemporary construction methods (and other things besides), it is quoted at some length:[18]

> "There is one feature in the mode of carrying into execution buildings of great magnitude, in the present day, in which a wider departure from the practice that existed down to the commencement of the present century, is observable, than could; perhaps, be found in the varying circumstances of many ages, in almost any other respect. We allude to the altered mode of constructing the

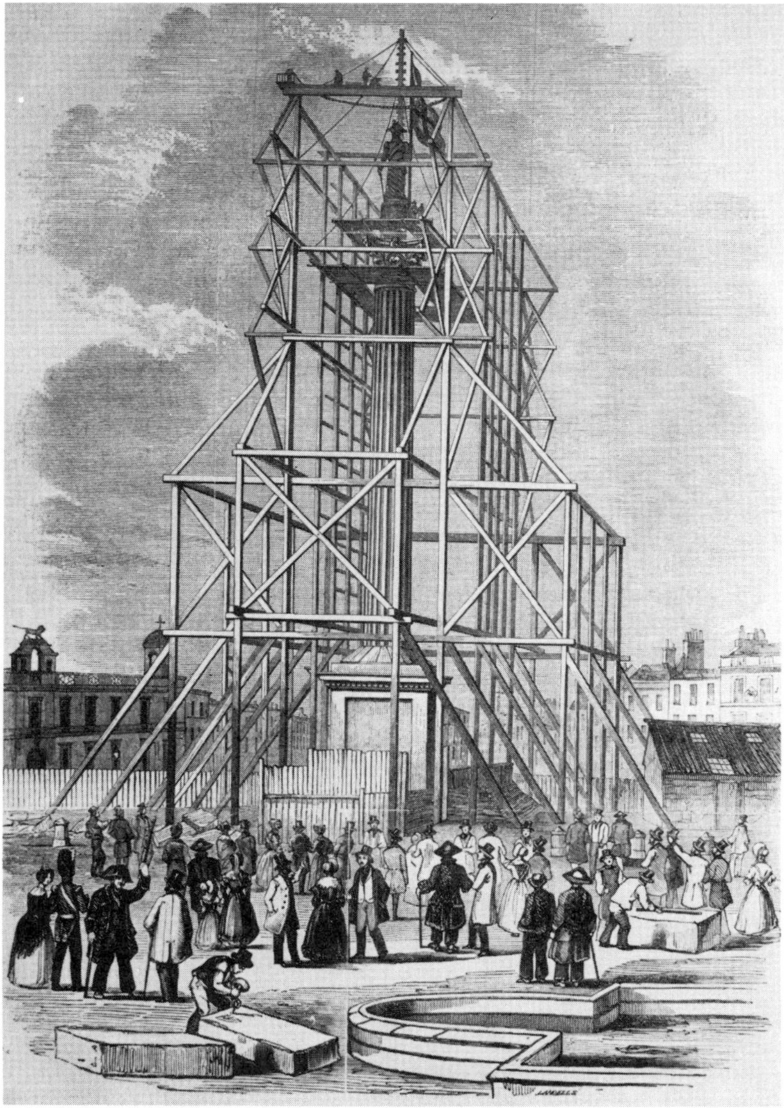

10. The construction of Nelson's Column, November 1843

scaffolding, in which the forest of small round poles (slight in themselves, and most difficult of connection, either for increase of strength or height, and often almost wholly dependent for support on the building to which they were attached), thus communicating to the green and newly formed wall the oscillation caused by every gust and often giving rise to lasting inclinations and contortions – has rapidly given way to substantially erected platforms. These have been exemplified in many larger buildings recently erected in this country, as well as many now in progress in the metropolis. Among them the Royal Exchange affords a very fine instance, and Trafalgar-square exhibits, perhaps, the loftiest and most skilful ever attempted.

The timbers preserve the square and rugged proportions in which they floated down their native streams, and are secured to each other in the simplest and strongest manner. There are five grand uprights on standards on the east side, and a corresponding number on the west, in six stages, or stories, marked by the horizontal beams and curbs, which occur at nearly equal intervals; the base being greatly extended, and the sides strengthened by diagonal and raking braces.

On the upper part is placed a very powerful engine, moving on a railway; and this is again supported by a travelling platform of great strength, capable of being moved at right angles, so that before or after receiving its load, the engine can be readily brought over any required spot; and the stone with which it is charged is deposited in the exact position in which it is to remain. Thus, blocks of from six to ten tons weight were, at a rate of progression scarcely more perceptible than the motion of a clock weight (being only thirty feet in the hour), raised to a great elevation, and set down with less muscular exertion than would be expended on a lamp-post.

The lower block of the figure, hoisted on the 3rd of November, was adjusted on the ground at 5hr. 20m. a.m.

Reached	the first stage	6	45
,,	the second	8	08
,,	the third	9	25
,,	the fourth	10	23
,,	top	11	20

Two minutes were sufficient for the transit of the stone from the verge of the scaffolding to the centre, and the setting was completed at a quarter before twelve. The upper and lighter block was hoisted on the following day. These blocks were the largest that the quarry had produced; and a prodigious amount of labour and perseverance was required to raise, convey to the seaside, and ship them; a dock was also to be excavated for the reception of the vessel, which had been expressly dispatched with the necessary tackling. Our engraving represents the figure completed, and the union flag unfurled above it; but this has given place to the veritable ensign under which the gallant hero fell. Long may it be preserved, and may the great memorial on the summit of which it now so proudly waves, be as a pharos to the public spirit in all-coming time."

At the beginning of 1841 it was becoming increasingly obvious that, unless something was done, the subscription for the Memorial was not going to meet the costs for completing it. On 1 January, the Memorial Committee published a small edition showing who had subscribed and how much.[19] It makes very interesting reading, for it does seem that many of the "gentlemen" who made up the original committee either did not bother to subscribe or else, given their stations in life, gave very paltry amounts. Perhaps the purpose of the publication was to shame the detractors into paying up. (At several earlier Committee meetings remarks had been passed about promises not being met.)

There were approximately fifteen hundred subscriptions, varying in amounts from two shillings and sixpence (Mrs. Beeby), to five hundred guineas (the Queen). Next highest to the Queen's, came the subscription from His Imperial Highness the Grand Duke Alexander of Russia, who gave £300. The Queen Dowager, the Duke of Buccleuch, and the Duke of Wellington gave two hundred pounds each. Five Marquises gave £375, twelve Earls £764, and five Viscounts, including Nelson's one-time commanding officer, St. Vincent, gave £150. Many institutions, like the Bank of England, and the East India Company, each gave one hundred guineas. But these large amounts were few in number and most, like Railton, the Bishop of Ripon (one of Railton's most important clients) and Sir Hussey Vivian, gave sums nearer ten guineas each.

Considerable chauvinism was expressed by many subscribers, such as this one, from the Black Horse public house in Bedfordbury (a street just North of Charing Cross):

> ". . . from a few True Britons who admire judgement and nautical knowledge displayed by the late Admiral Lord Viscount Nelson; and who feel grateful for the service he rendered to his Country at a most critical period of our History; and the moral influence which his gallant conduct effected in highly advancing the Character of the British Navy." (£2 5s. 0d.)

It was only to be expected that sailors contributed; and like A. D. Turnbull, an East India Company engineer, they contributed one day's pay. By April 1841 the state of subscriptions had not improved much, and it was suggested that a Ball be held as an attempt to raise more money.

However, the Committee at its next meeting evidently felt this effort would be fruitless, as a resolution described them to be[20]

> "of the opinion that considering the circumstances of the season the question relating to the Ball be adjourned."

The "circumstances of the season" are not explained, but perhaps the much sought-after patronage of the Queen was not forthcoming, a patronage deemed so vital to the success of such a venture.

At the next meeting, the last of that year,[21] a letter was read from Railton, enclosing the first of many requests from the contractors claiming that their work costs were far outstripping their estimates. It appears that the first part of the contract provided for incremented payments of £2,000, amounting to £8,000 when the cornice of the pedestal was completed. Grissell and Peto were now saying that they had already completed £8,000 worth of work, and this was before the second instalment was due. The Committee declined Railton's advice to pay up and stuck resolutely to the contract. By so doing they began what was to become a continuing feud between them and the contractors, with poor Railton in the middle.

INDISCIPLINE ON THE QUARTER DECK

Starting in the autumn of 1841 and continuing through a bitter winter until May 1842, Grissell and Peto were to be involved in a feud of a very different kind. Thomas Grissell and Samuel Morton Peto had made a considerable fortune, along with many other building contractors,[22] out of the railway and speculative building boom of the late 1830s. This fortune was not, of course, made without the thorough degradation through ruthless exploitation of innumerable building workers. The case of the railway navvies is notorious. The very mobility of their job, whether they were labourer or craftsman, often mitigated against any trade union organisation, making them easy prey to an unscrupulous employer.

In the towns and cities the same employers were frequently faced with a very different situation especially with any masons they employed. The Operative Stonemasons Union in 1834 was the only building craft union in the 1830s and 1840s to survive in any strength. In 1838 with a membership of nearly 5,000 it was the country's most powerful union. It was also among the building craft unions the only one that could act nationally; others like the bricklayers or plumbers union tended to act in each town separately.

Unionised workers were naturally not popular with the contractors, but during periods of relative full employment as in London during the 1830s they were often forced to engage them. However, so as to ensure a minimal amount of trouble on a site they frequently engaged a tough bully as a foreman.

In May 1840 Grissell and Peto were awarded by the Government the first of a series of contracts for the completion of Barry's new Houses of Parliament. Although the work proceeded reasonably smoothly, interrupted only by the occasional stoppage over a grievance, a deep resentment was building up among the masons towards one of the foremen, George Allen. Allen, often known as the "Black Prince", was "a man who damns, blasts and curses at every turn" daily threatening and bullying men on the slightest pretext. Allen's job was, in Grissell's words, "to maintain (on the site) the discipline of the quarter deck".[23]

The masons declared that in pursuit of this discipline Allen had "committed acts of tyranny and oppression" and they would strike until such time as Grissell and Peto replaced him. Grissell and Peto refused their demands and on 13 September the 468 masons on the job came out to a man. Even then Grissell did not budge; wasn't after all the strike the work of a few agitators and the men would soon see sense and return to work? They had not, however, calculated on Thomas Shortt, the General Secretary of the Masons' Union, who saw the strike as not being over pay and hours (which were negotiable), but over the more important issue that "the employers not only expected to purchase the labour of a man but also his soul". Shortt saw that the masons were fighting for a cause; a cause that would engage the whole working class whose collective action in support of the masons would "ensure that this fundamental principle was settled once and for all time".

Shortt, naïvely perhaps, petitioned the Lord Lincoln, First Commissioner of Woods, etc., to intervene on their behalf. Lincoln, who had given Grissell and Peto a day or so earlier the Commissioner's full support in "maintaining that authority and control over your workmen . . . for employers must be protected from the union of workmen", not unexpectedly declined.

In an attempt to break the strike Grissell and Peto – aided and abetted by the Lords Commissioners – tried recruiting masons from other districts to blackleg. The union's national organisation through its many branches was quick to counter this move, giving Grissell's agents short shrift in many of the towns that they visited. Grissell's next step was to launch an extensive press campaign to discredit the strikers at the same time giving further financial inducements to masons as far afield as Ireland to blackleg. The union retaliated by organising defence committees whose job was to raise money for the strikers and launch a counter campaign. However, the joint power of the Government and the employer began to take its toll, some masons began to take jobs on other sites. Picketing of the site too was to weaken as the strikers had to face twice daily the large police escort that would accompany any blackleg through their line.

Throughout the early days of the strike, other of Grissell and Peto's sites in London had lent their financial support, but as the situation at Westminster worsened, they decided to take more militant action. Masons at two sites, Nelson's Monument and Woolwich Dockyard, downed tools in sympathy. With two prestigious jobs in the centre of the capital, both already surrounded by controversy, at a standstill, the Lords Commissioners increased their help to Grissell and Peto. Pressure was brought to bear on the quarry workers who were supplying the stone for Nelson's Column to call off their strike of sympathy, others were sacked for refusing to supply material for "black" work.

Grissell himself called a meeting with the masons in Trafalgar Square, but they stood firm in their solidarity for their brothers' demands that Allen should be dismissed. It is interesting to note here that under a clause in the contract for the work at Westminster, Charles Barry had the right to dismiss the contractor's foremen if he thought them "improper in any way". During the eight months of the whole dispute there is no evidence that he ever thought of exercising this right with regard to Allen.

For the union, with several other strikes on its hands in the country, the London disputes were quickly developing into a very costly affair. Monies had to be paid not only to the masons but in many cases potential blacklegs were given a financial inducement not to break a picket line. Despite innumerable fund-raising activities and a large contribution from the Scottish masons, Shortt's depleted resources were forcing masons on all three sites to seek work elsewhere. Grissell and Peto (and the Commissioners) were delighted by the masons' weakening position and brought in more blacklegs; on Nelson's Column, as the *Art Union* rather coyly described it,[24]

> "... measures have been adopted by the contractors to supply their places by men unconnected with unions so as to expedite the work without further delay."

Suitably enough, as has been commented on before by other writers, the most famous monument to the British Empire was to be built by scab labour.

By July 1842 Railton was able to report that apart from continuous claims by the contractor for more money, the work was proceeding well, and the masons reported that they expected to finish the shaft as high as the capital by May 1843.[25]

SUBSCRIPTIONS SOLICITED, ARTISTS REPLACED

The making of the capital was to run into some difficulties at about this time when the senior partner in Bramah's died and the firm dissolved. The work was transferred to George Clark & Sons, and within two weeks George Clark collapsed and died in a Birmingham chemist's shop. All, however, was not lost, for Clark's son continued the work, but not, as we shall see, without further interruptions.

It is popularly thought that the capital was cast from guns salvaged from the *Royal George*, one of Nelson's flag ships; but there is nothing in fact to suggest that this is the case. It is true that the Queen did give a "grant of ordinance", but it was not entirely free. The Committee had to pay the Government £200 (which included 800 days' labour of convicts – £40) for $2\frac{1}{2}$ tons of gun metal. They also had to pay £400 for further gun metal from the "Wellington City Committee as well as other metal in Mr. Railton's possession".

Railton's original design for the capital had contained four figures of Victory, and at the next meeting the first mention is made of these when, after discussion, this interesting resolution was passed:[26]

> " . . . the four figures of Victory intended to have been placed as part of the capital of the Monument and considering that such a description of Ornament is not sanctioned by any Authority have decided that they should be omitted . . ."

It is not clear from the minutes whether Railton or someone in the Committee had suggested the change, but Railton was instructed to ask Clark what deduction he would make for the change. Clark did reduce his costs, under some protest, but only by £100, which was, it seems, less than the Committee would have liked.

It was to be nine months before the Committee met again,[27] and by this time Railton was able to report that the fluted shaft, the bell of the capital, the abacus and the pedestal of the Nelson statue were ready, and that "the stone for the figure (Nelson) has been for some months under the chisel of Mr. Baily in Trafalgar Square and may be hoped to be completed by the end of July."

(It was not in fact erected into position, as we have seen, until November although it was hoped to do it on 21 October, Trafalgar Day.) The meeting ended with an extended discussion as to whether the capital should be gilded or not – a discussion so heated, that the chairman saw fit to ask for a vote, which resulted, not unexpectedly, in eight to three against such action. The rejection was not on the grounds that it would incur further costs, but that it would offend good taste in these matters.

It became increasingly clear during the subsequent year that the very little that had been added to the subscriptions was not going to be sufficient to meet even the current costs – the Committee had debts of £1,685 – let alone the sum of £12,000 which would be needed for completion. The bas reliefs and the lions had not yet even been commissioned, and it was the general opinion that without them the column would be a "denuded mass".

Finally, therefore, four years after the Select Committee (who it will be remembered had cast grave doubts on the financing of the project), the Committee had to admit defeat and was forced to approach the Government for financial aid. At a meeting on 16 May 1844 the Committee resolved that a letter should be sent to Sir Robert Peel (who was after all on the original selection committee),[28]

"setting forth the inability of the Committee to obtain the full amount of funds requisite for completing the Memorial according to the original Designs."

The letter began with a tinge of bitterness

" . . . the committee have erected the Nelson Column and have in doing so desired to perform a duty which perhaps the nation ought to have discharged not less than 30 years ago in honour of its greatest naval hero."

And although many examples of columns and statues to Nelson existed elsewhere, Sir George Cockburn pointed out

"nothing, until the efforts of this committee, had before been done in the metropolis of the empire."

The Treasury took nearly two months to reply, during which time many opinions were canvassed, and the Lords generally agreed

" . . . that it would not be consistent with what My Lords feel to be due to the memory of such a man, if they were to permit the monument to remain in its present and unsightly state."

The Treasury therefore recommended, and this was the catch, that the monument could be completed as long as it was "in such a manner as after full consideration may be approved of by their Lordships".[29]

The state of the subscription was, however, to improve very slightly, much to the Treasury's pleasure, whose responsibility the affair was, for at the next meeting of the Committee the Duke of Wellington reported on a letter he had received from Count Orloff, written while staying at Buckingham Palace. The letter, which had been written (possibly at the Queen's suggestion) at the command of His Imperial Majesty the Emperor of Russia, read:[30]

> *Monsieur le Duc,*
>
> *. . . Majesté l'Empereur, désirant contributer à l'érection d'un monument que la reconnaissance nationale a élevé à la gloire de L'Amiral Nelson m'a chargé de recourir à votre obligeante intervention pour ajouter en son nom à la soucription déjà ouvert la somme cijointe de £500.*
>
> *L'Empereur a jugé que pour réaliser cette pensée, il ne pouvait mieux faire que de s'adresser directement à celui dont le nom est inséparable des souvenirs les plus glorieux de l'Angleterre . . .*
>
> ["... His Majesty the Emperor, wishing to contribute to the erection of a monument which national recognition has raised to the glory of Admiral Nelson, has instructed me to respond to your obliging suggestion by forwarding in his name to the subscription already opened the accompanying sum of £500.
>
> The Emperor is of opinion that to realise his intentions he cannot do better than address himself directly to him whose name is inseparably linked with England's most glorious memories . . ."]

It was of little help to the Committee. A month later, without even recalling a meeting of the full Committee, but having received an assurance that the Government would pay to complete the works, it disbanded.[31]

Railton's client was now the Office of Woods, Forests and Land Revenues, the First Commissioner of which was Lord Lincoln. Within a month of the change Railton was being asked to make alterations in his design. To start with, Lincoln attacked the project as a whole, saying the column was inappropriate. Railton defended himself by quoting the custom of the "ancients" of providing "public buildings with courtyards and erecting columns". On 2 December, with the support of Sir Robert

Peel and the Treasury but against the advice of Barry, Lincoln insisted that the steps at the base of the pedestal be omitted. Railton, not being in a strong position to argue, conceded without a fight.[32]

Lincoln's reasons for making the change, although supposedly aesthetic, have had the practical effect that a speaker now requires a ladder to get to what in Railton's original design had been an easily accessible platform.

During the year 1845 work was to proceed at a very slow rate. The shortage of granite, and the difficulties involved in working such large pieces, all contributed to a general irritation on the part of the Office of Woods and Forests, and a barrage of criticism about slowness from the press. Railton, too, was becoming impatient as to what was happening and in November wrote asking, rather plaintively, when the bas reliefs and the lions were due to start. The Office of Woods, jolted seemingly out of its inactivity by this, requested a meeting of the four artists of bas reliefs. Lincoln was not content only with altering Railton's design, he also wanted to change the sculptors of the reliefs. After seeking the advice of Charles Eastlake, only Woodington of the original four (Sievier, Campbell, Westmacott and Woodington) was retained. To replace Westmacott, Eastlake recommended John Edward Carew, one of Westmacott's one-time assistants. A former and very temperamental pupil of Sievier, Musgrave Lethwaite Watson was to take his former master's place. Campbell's place was to be taken by the relatively minor sculptor John Ternouth.

The meeting was held at Railton's office on 13 December and it was agreed that "the principal figures" should not be less than 6 feet 6 inches high; that the relief including the ground was not to exceed fifteen inches; that "the costume of the period" was to be observed; and although all were to be battle scenes "the introduction of smoke is to be avoided". The Office of Woods had thought this meeting necessary before they issued their official conditions, which concluded that £1,000 would be paid for each design. The conditions said nothing about workmanship, it being evidently supposed that as all concerned were "gentlemen", the work would be carried out to the highest standards.[33]

Charles Eastlake, however, was more cautious, for he wrote suggesting that all metal to be used should be provided by the Government "so as to avoid the artists being tempted to make casts extremely thin".[34] This, as we shall see, was a vain hope indeed. He also suggested that *all* the artists should use Thomas Cubitt's Yard on the Thames Embankment to make their moulds and the casts.

The Office of Woods did not heed this advice either. (But more of this later.)

Many people objected to the Nelson figure when it had been unveiled, saying that its legs were encumbered – which Baily had said was to provide stability – and that it would have been better done totally in bronze. Although the stone figure was completed, Lord Lincoln on several occasions gave official weight to the oft-expressed hope that a bronze figure would replace the stone one in the "not too distant future". In addition to this change, he also expressed the desire for a more important one:

> " . . . I should hope more, viz, that an architect might be consulted as to the possibility of altering the character of the flutes of the column so as to suit a Doric capital . . ."

These remarks were written within brackets; as Lincoln himself put it, "I think of it as a dream."[35] A dream it was to remain, as the present column shows. Nevertheless, it was a feeling shared by many people, that the "feminine" references of the Corinthian Order were totally unsuitable to support the very masculine figure of Nelson – especially if it was a reference to Lady Hamilton.[36] Fortunately for everyone, Lord Lincoln's office was to be terminated at the end of November 1847 with the change of government, and his successor, Lord Morpeth, had greater respect for Railton, or was too concerned with other things to interfere.

FOUR FAMOUS BATTLES

It seems that Carew, Woodington, Ternouth and Watson had chosen which of the four themes they each personally desired to do, the themes themselves having been originally chosen by Railton. These were to be based on Nelson's four most famous battles: St. Vincent (1797) – Watson; The Nile (1798) – Woodington; Copenhagen (1801) – Ternouth; and finally the one at which he met his death from a sniper's musket ball, Trafalgar (1805) – Carew. Having chosen the themes, the artists were faced with several problems: firstly, which incident in the battle to depict; secondly, whose account to read;[37] and thirdly, it would seem from their letters, what in fact a "man of war" looked like.

It would seem that only Ternouth asked "if he were tied to any particular moment of the attack on Copenhagen" (his subject), and it seems that neither Railton, Eastlake, nor the Office of Woods had any particular incident in mind for him, or for any of the other three. The aspects of the bas reliefs reflected very much the importance of the events. On the South side, facing Whitehall and looking in the same direction that Nelson does, was to be placed Carew's "Death of Nelson" relief (which was in fact to turn out larger than the others – some even say the largest bronze casting of its kind in Europe). On the north side was Woodington's "Battle of the Nile" (Aboukir); on the east, Ternouth's "Bombardment of Copenhagen", and finally on the west side, Watson's "Battle of St. Vincent". Two of the reliefs show Nelson as the wounded hero (north and south), and two as the triumphant conqueror (east and west).

This equal division between death and conquest, both, it should be emphasised, central neo-classical themes, is very much on a par with the many paintings on the subject of Nelson's victories, both contemporary with the reliefs and earlier, that exist. Devis' "A picture of Nelson's death-bed in the cockpit of the Victory" is perhaps the most famous of these.[38]

An explanation of the events that the bas reliefs portray would perhaps be helpful here. On 1 August 1798 the English fleet was engaged with the French fleet of the Bay of Aboukir, west of Alexandria. Nelson was on the quarter deck, looking, it is traditionally reported, at Hallowell's sketch of the bay, when he was struck on the head by a piece of *langridge*, a form of scrap shot used by the French for destroying rigging and sails. The wound was just above his "bright eye", and it bled profusely, blinding him, as Nelson himself thought, finally. As was Nelson's practice, he did not allow it to be generally known that he was wounded, and asked that the Principal Surgeon should not be told. This practice was normal, as the maintenance of "order" on the ship depended to a very large extent on the rigid hierarchy and personal power maintained by the captain. The bas relief suggests Nelson was acting benevolently towards his fellow sailors; it is more likely, however, that his motives were to ensure that his authority and that of his officers would not be challenged.

The bombardment of Copenhagen seemed to present difficulties to Ternouth, for as a "battle" it had apparently no heroic moments worthy of portrayal. The battle was not received in London with such acclaim as was given to Nelson's success at Aboukir, perhaps because the English did not see a success over the Armed Neutrality Alliance of Denmark, Russia and Sweden in the same light as they saw a victory over their traditional enemy, France. The Alliance had to be broken, however, so as to maintain the fight with the French, for Copenhagen was the gateway to the much-needed Baltic timber trade.[39] Ternouth's work depicts the sealing of a cannon by Nelson after his successful bombardment of the city; the sealing of the cannon is an event of so little significance that many works on Nelson do not even mention it. But it should be admitted that the signing of an Armistice around a table does not make the ideal subject for a relief sculptor.

Watson's relief subject presented far less difficulty, for in the Battle of St. Vincent Nelson had committed a rather stupid, some would say heroic, act in leading a boarding party on to a Spanish "Eighty", *San Nicholas*. It is reliably reported that Nelson, mindful as ever of posterity, charged blindly through the smoke to the quarter deck, uttering the immortal words: "Westminster Abbey, or Glorious Victory!"[40] (in the event Nelson was to be buried in St. Paul's); only to find that the Spaniards had already surrendered, and that the ship's Flag Captain, falling immediately to his knees, wished to present him with the sword of his Admiral Don Francisco Xavier Winthuysen, who was dying from wounds below. Nelson himself admitted that the ship had not surrendered as a result of his boarding party, and it was "good fortune" that the Admiral had been on board.[41] But popular sentiment in England tended to blur the reality of the event, a victory much needed at the time, and it was this sentiment that persisted and was capitalised on by Watson.

Of all the reliefs the one that depicted Nelson's death at Trafalgar was the most charged with myth. Although, of all the incidents in Nelson's career, it was probably the best documented, and had occupied the most column inches in all his biographies, the portrayals by both painters and sculptors had studiously avoided the "true" state of affairs. Oman describes Nelson's fatal wounding as follows:[42]

> "At about 1.35 p.m. . . . Hardy saw the Admiral on his knees with the finger tips of his left hand just touching the deck. The single arm gave way, and Nelson fell on his left side . . . Sergeant Major Seeker of the Marines and two seamen were there in a moment, raising him. As Hardy bent, he saw a smile and heard the words, "Hardy, I believe they have done it at last . . .". The shuffling party carrying an officer with a fractured spine descended as quickly and as quietly as possible from the light of day. . . . As the party prepared to negotiate the last ladder leading to the cockpit, already thickly bloodstained and very slippery,[43] they encountered a parting clergyman. The chaplain of the Victory had been so overcome by horror and nausea as to be unable to continue his ministration to the dying."

It is clear from this account that the battle was still raging, which explains why Nelson's body had to be taken below as soon as possible. Officers and men would not have congregated around his fallen figure on the deck, as this would have presented a good target for further sniping and encouraged the enemy had they thought Nelson hit.

Nelson did not in fact die until 4.30 p.m., by which time the battle was almost over. In the introduction something has been said of the conditions of seamen at the end of the eighteenth century and the beginning of the nineteenth century, but I would like to re-emphasise the point that the conditions of naval war were hardly understood or known of outside the navy. As most of the battles took place many miles from home, the wounded either died or were sufficiently healed on the way home for the full picture of the horror to have faded. It was not until the First World War, when the wounded were transported home in field dressings by the boat and train load, that the civilian population in this country had the full gruesome effects of war thrust upon them again after a gap of more than two hundred years. Neither Carew nor the other artists can be blamed for their misrepresentations, for an accurate account was not what they were being asked for. What *was* being asked for, was a representation of the facts that would confirm the growing imperialistic ambitions of the ruling class as personified in people such as Peel and Palmerston. It was important that these ambitions should not be seen to have been overly tainted with blood.

The work on the bas reliefs proceeded during the early part of 1848, during which time occasional complaints were received at the Office of Woods from the four artists, most of them technical, but some, like Ternouth's, of an "artistic" nature. His question was: did Nelson wear decorations as he sealed up the cannon at Copenhagen? Lord Morpeth replied that he should decide this for himself, as it was, after all, an "artistic question".

By June all the reliefs had been made in plaster, and the four were starting to obtain tenders for the bronze work. The tenders came in at prices ranging from £385 from Christy Adams and Hill for Ternouth's, to £400 from the Regent Canal Iron Company for Carew's.[44] Each artist received at least three tenders; but, for reasons which are difficult to explain, the normal practice of taking the lowest was not followed. Sir Richard Westmacott, who with Charles Eastlake was acting as adviser, had suggested that the casting should all be done at the Royal Arsenal at Woolwich, Cubitt's having been unable to find space in the time.[45] But the artists went ahead against this advice and used the firms who had tendered to them to do it.

Late in August Watson died, and his incomplete work was "taken over by his friend Woodington".

The arrangements for the transportation to the founders and the casting itself were to take another year, and it was not until September of 1849 that two of them were ready for erection. The third and fourth – Watson's, which Woodington was still completing, and Woodington's own – were still at the Yard of Moore, Fressage and Moore. At this point Railton suggested that the Office of Woods should provide a "superintendent during the fixing of the sculptured objects", and Sir Richard Westmacott was asked and agreed to do it. Carew, who throughout the proceedings had acted rather aggressively towards any interference by the Office, wrote complaining about Westmacott's supervision, saying:[46]

> "if this is the position in which it is to remain (the bas relief) it will entirely frustrate my intentions as the figures will have the appearance of falling out of the panel . . ."

and,

> " . . . I cannot believe Her Majesty's Commissioners will sanction this unfavourable appearance of my work and subject me to public ridicule."

This effect of "falling out of the panel" was attributable to Carew's panel not being square, a fault he blamed on the founders who in turn blamed it on him. The Office of Woods, however, pointed out that the lack of squareness[47]

> "meant no more, than that the panel was somewhat narrower at the top than at the bottom; that as the pedestal followed the inclination of the column."

They added that any action against the founders would be of no effect, as ". . . the affairs of Messrs. Christie being at present depending on the Bankruptcy Court . . ." On top of this, Carew's final account for the casting was £605, nearly double the original figure tendered. When all the accounts were finally received, this was not to be the only one. Woodington was in ill health, and his work proceeded slowly. Two years were to elapse before the last of his two reliefs were stated to be ready.

BRAZEN FRAUD EXPOSED

In August 1852 the Office received an anonymous letter alleging that Moore, Fressage & Moore had acted fraudulently in respect of the amount of metal used in their cast of both Woodington's designs. The letter, it was later discovered, came from two of the company's own workers, and the information appeared convincing. The Office sent an inspector, a Mr. Fincham, to the foundry to investigate. Within a week they received his report and it said in no uncertain terms that the allegations were true, as the casting contained "10 cwt. 1 qtr. of cast iron and plaster" and was therefore not all bronze. This "loading" was confirmed by Moore, and Fincham reports him as saying:[48]

> "I cannot deceive you, you have found us out, I therefore candidly tell you that it is loaded, and unless we did that we would lose money . . ."

Some consternation was expressed at this news, as one of the reliefs cast by Messrs. Moore was in place (The Battle of Aboukir) and was probably of suspect workmanship also. Messrs. Moore admitted as much, and said they had used tin weights to resemble real ones at the final weighing of the bronze (as the bronze had been supplied by the Government, all surplus had to be returned after the final cast, and surplus metal had been weighed together with the cast itself).

Another inspector, John Percy, was dispatched to Trafalgar Square to survey the relief in question, and he reported that the casting was bad, there were holes in the garments and that lead had been used for repairs, and that in his view "the castings in their present condition will not be durable".

This evidence, together with the earlier report, prompted the Treasury Solicitor to advise the Attorney General to press an action for fraud and breach of contract against the foundry. This he agreed to do, and on 13 December a draft of an indictment was drawn up. Five days later Messrs. Moore, Fressage & Moore appeared before Mr. Justice Earle and were committed to the Queen's Bench Prison until £200 bail could be found. The trial was fixed for 11 January 1853.

In the interval Moore, Fressage & Moore pleaded with Sir William Molesworth, the First Commissioner of Woods, Forests and Land Revenues, not to put them on public trial, as [49]

> "It is believed that the chief witness in support of the indictment is a man formerly in our employ who has seduced and gone away with the wife of Petre Antoine Fressage, and is now living in adultery with her, and he is mainly actuated by feelings of malevolence against us";

adding that

> "John Moore and James Moore have wives and increasing families besides an aged mother depending on them for support . . ."

The trail was delayed until July, as several difficulties arose out of settling who should take over the work, and no space could be found in the Court's calendar. At the end of January, without waiting for the trial, the two informants and Fressage's wife left the country on the *Prince Arthur* bound for Australia.

The Court sat at the Guildhall on 7 July, and after hearing the evidence, sentenced John Moore and Petre Fressage to three months', and James Moore to one month's imprisonment in the Queen's Bench Prison.[50]

It took nearly another year to sort out Moore, Fressage & Moore's affairs; their creditors had to be paid off, new founders obtained, and it was not until 19 May 1854 that the St. Vincent relief was finally put in place. The designing, making and erection of the four reliefs had taken nine years and cost half as much again as was originally intended.

It is interesting to note that there is little evidence that Woodington was ever seriously called to task over what was essentially his responsibility. It may have caused him to lose work, but unlike the foundry involved, he neither went bankrupt nor to prison for his part in what was, after all, a somewhat fraudulent enterprise from start to finish.

A TALE OF FOUR LIONS

The career of Railton's four lions was to be equally erratic. In 1846 John Lough seemingly tired of the endless delay and Railton's insistence that the lions "be purely architectonic in character",[51] resigned saying that any further association with the project "would be bad for my reputation".

The *Art Journal*, which had always thought little of Lough's abilities as a sculptor of human beings let alone animals (of which it seems he had little or no experience), was overjoyed with his departure. The Government's next choice was the sculptor Thomas Milnes, a minor figure by all accounts. Milnes' lions were a disaster; they were returned to him and now stand at Saltaire in Yorkshire. In July 1858 as though in desperation (some cynics said the intention was to create yet further controversy), the Office of Woods approached Sir Edwin Landseer, asking him if he was willing to complete the lions, but this time in bronze.[52] Landseer was an odd choice, for although he was an able if sentimental animal painter he had no experience of large-scale animal sculpture. Despite what would have seemed to many artists of his skill and experience a daunting if not impossible task, he accepted the commission. He did so, however, on the understanding that he could not actually start for nine months as he was already busy on other work.

His appointment brought howls of protest from sculptors but the

Government closed its ears and stuck to its decision. Landseer's start was to be further delayed, for in May 1859 he wrote to the Office requesting to see certain casts of a real lion that were, he believed, in the Albertin Academie in Turin. He did not want to go there himself, but suggested that casts could be made of the casts and brought to England. The Foreign Office approved the request, and two weeks later a telegram was sent to Turin. One month later the answer came, and proved to be rather disappointing. It appeared that a cast had indeed been made, of the head, limbs and, after dissection, much of the anatomy, of a real lion (once in the possession of the King of Sardinia), but that the original moulds had subsequently been destroyed. The telegram went on to say that for fear of damage to the original casts, the Academie did not think it possible to make further moulds from which new casts could be made. However, a way was found, and a year later the Foreign Office reported that casts were being made, and they would be sent to England as soon as possible. They were shipped in May, six months later, and arrived at Baron Marochetti's, Landseer's founder, studio in August.

Marochetti's choice as Landseer's founder was not without controversy either. Since his design for Napoleon's tomb in Les Invalides in 1841, a design which the *Art Union* said was a direct crib of Goldicutt's design for the Nelson Monument, British critics had disliked and distrusted him. His success in Royal circles at first in France (he fled to England in 1848) and later with Queen Victoria led to a great antipathy towards him among his fellow sculptors.

Ill health dogged Landseer and his progress on the models was very slow indeed. It was not until June 1863 that the Office of Woods and Forests was at last able to contract Landseer for the final figures. All this delay was causing a continuous stream of jokes in the press about the lions, the most recurrent one being that the lion on Northumberland House was frightening the others away. It took four years for Landseer to finish all four lions, during which time his arguments with Baron Marochetti reached the level of a public debate. Marochetti was in fact paid nearly £11,000 for his work (half of which was paid out for the bronze); this, plus Landseer's fee of £6,000, brought the final cost of the lions to £17,183. Railton, it will be remembered, had estimated for £3,000 in 1840.

The lions were put in place without ceremony in February 1867. It was nearly thirty years after the first meeting of the Nelson Memorial Committee, most of the members of which were now dead. Railton was sixty-eight and living in Brighton, and did not even bother to attend.

So relieved was everyone that the Memorial was now completed, that two years later, when Messrs. Robinson & Cotter were asked to report on the "state of the Founders work", they said:[53]

> "The castings are rough and spongy in parts. . . . The finishing or chasing is very imperfectly done, and we consider they would be much improved if rechased in parts and entirely re-bronzed. . . . Lumps of metal are left on in places and the joints show too plainly . . ."

nobody wished to act, for fear of bringing on themselves further scorn and derision.

No final account exists for the Monument but it is possible that by 1870 at least £50,000 had been spent altogether.

Notes to Chapter 4

1. Quoted in W. S. Hilton, *Foes to Tyranny* (London 1963), p. 82.
2. *The Times*, 15 June 1830.
3. *PRO WORKS 20/2–1*, 6 April 1841.
4. *ibid.*, 18 September 1841.
5. *ibid.*, 21 September 1841.
6. *ibid.*, 20 October 1841.
7. *ibid.*, 21 September 1841.
8. This well, like many others in central London, was to fail completely by 1900. For details see S. Buchan, *The Water Supply of the County of London* (London 1938); and for the Orange Street Well in particular see *Memoirs of Geological Survey*, vol. II, 1889, p. 142.
9. *The Builder*, 8 March 1845, p. 119.
10. See chapter 6.
11. See 5 Geo. IV, c. 100: "An Act for effectively paving, lighting, watching, etc. New street from Regents Park to Pall Mall"; also: 6 Geo. IV, c. 38, "Further work to 5 Geol IV, and Pall Mall East"; also: 7 Geo. IV, c. 78 . . . "authorise the conversion of the pavements in several parts of the metropolis into broken stone roads".
12. See under watch boxes in 10 Geo. IV, c. 44.
13. *PRO WORKS 20/2–1*, plan dated 11 June 1839.
14. *ibid.*, "Bude Light Company Prospectus".
15. *ibid.*, 18 August 1845 to 2 July 1851.
16. *PRO WORKS 6. 119*, 17 June 1840.
17. *ibid.*, 24 November 1840.
18. *Illustrated London News*, vol. IV, p. 331.
19. *ibid., Statement of Subscriptions, etc.*
20. *PRO WORKS 6. 119.*, 5 May 1841.
21. *ibid.*, 2 August 1841.
22. Terry Coleman, *The Railway Navvies* (London 1965).
23. W. S. Hilton, *op. cit.*, pp. 74–85.

24. *Art Union*, November 1841, p. 186.
25. *PRO WORKS 6. 119*, 2 July 1842.
26. *ibid.*, 29 July 1842.
27. *ibid.*, 26 May 1843.
28. *ibid.*, 16 May 1844.
29. *ibid.*, 5 July 1844.
30. *ibid.*, 10 June 1844.
31. Last meeting of Nelson Memorial Committee, 20 July 1844.
32. *PRO WORKS 20/2–1.*
33. *PRO WORKS 20/3–1*, 27 January 1846.
34. *ibid.*, 1 January 1846.
35. *ibid.*, 15 January 1846.
36. For an interesting explanation to the origins of the Corinthian Order see Joseph Rykwert's The Corinthian Order, *Arena*, June 1966.
37. By 1840 there were about twenty biographies and accounts of Nelson's exploits already published, most of them differing widely in their facts.
38. In the National Maritime Museum, Greenwich.
39. George P. B. Naish, *Nelson and Bronte* (London 1958), p. 15.
40. Carola Oman, *Nelson* (London 1947), p. 182.
41. *ibid.*, p. 185.
42. *ibid.*, pp. 611–12.
43. It was the custom to paint the middle and lower decks red so as to make the presence of blood less conspicuous. The *Victory* now at Portsmouth has been restored to show this.
44. *PRO WORKS 20/3–1*, 30 June 1848, 8 August 1848.
45. *ibid.*, 18 May 1849.
46. *ibid.*, 16 October 1849.
47. *ibid.*, 6 February 1850.
48. *ibid.*, 30 August 1852.
49. *ibid.*, 1 January 1853.
50. *ibid.*, 8 July 1853.
51. *PRO WORKS 20/3–2*, 14 February 1846.
52. *ibid.*, 6 May 1859.
53. *ibid.*, 4 March 1869.

5

UGLY BRONZE IMAGES

> "The Anglo Saxon thinks that everything which unnecessarily interferes with his freedom is wrong: he thinks and acts on the principle that all men have equal rights – self-government is *natural* to him. Not so the Oriental. *He insists on being governed* and considers being compelled to govern himself as the greatest oppression and tyranny. He expects to be ruled and to be *ruled well.*"[1]

GEORGE IV

It is said that George IV, then Prince of Wales, was overcome with grief on hearing of Nelson's death. The Prince claimed to have "loved him as a friend", vaunting him "the greatest character England could ever boast of".[2] But the feeling was far from mutual. For Nelson, the Prince was little more than an "unprincipaled liar" (the Prince had intimated several times in public "how Lady Hamilton had struck his fancy").[3] Neither could have known that after their deaths their principal commemorative statues would chance to share the same home – Trafalgar Square – nor that the sovereign's pose would cause him to gaze fixedly up at the backside of the commoner.

Although Charles Barry's original design of 1840 for the Square had provided pedestals at its north-west and north-east corners for equestrian statues of George IV and William IV, financial stringency at the time had prevented their being commissioned. Despite this, the east pedestal was not to remain bare for very long.

In July 1829 George IV had personally directed Sir Francis Chantrey to complete a massive bronze equestrian statue of himself to be placed on top of John Nash's Marble Arch (the Arch was intended to stand as a triumphal gateway, commemorating British victories, in front of the reconstructed and considerably enlarged Buckingham Palace). Within a year, George IV died, and with the succession of his brother William the appropriateness of such an edifice (especially the statue part) was brought into question. It was decided not to cancel the commission altogether, and Chantrey continued with the work. Chantrey was a very busy man, and work on the piece proceeded very slowly indeed. It was not until February 1836 that casting the bronze actually got under way. In his original contract with the Office of Woods, Forests and Land Revenues, Chantrey had expected to be paid in three equal instalments; one at the beginning, one on completion of the model before casting, and a last one when the project was finally completed. The second instalment was of particular importance, for as Chantrey pointed out to the Office, the amount of bronze for "the undertaking is large and the outlay great".[4]

The Office, aware, perhaps, that Chantrey was hardly on the breadline, took nearly a year to pay up, during which time neither Chantrey nor any of his innumerable assistants seemed to have touched the work at all. The work was only just completed in November 1841, when Chantrey suddenly died of a heart attack. Although his death occasioned considerable mourning among people in "high places", it was not until his executors claimed the third instalment of his fee three months later (it took six months for that to be paid) that it dawned on the Office of Works that the statue was in fact their responsibility. A home, even a temporary one, had to be found for it. After some consultation the Chief Commissioner at the Office of Woods, etc., directed Charles Barry to place it *temporarily* on one of the pedestals in Trafalgar Square. Barry was delighted, and with considerable difficulty he had the massive object wheeled the two miles from Chantrey's Belgravia Place Studio, and hoisted into position in November 1843.

Fifteen years later, in 1858, someone wryly suggested that it be removed from this temporary home, and placed it where it was originally intended to be: on the top of Marble Arch. The Arch meanwhile had found a permanent and relegated home at Cumberland Gate, Hyde Park. It seemed just as easy to leave the statue where it was. Some fifty years later someone else wrote to the Office of Works suggesting again that it be moved. This time, however, a rather disrespectful reason was given: nobody knew who the man on the horse was. The Office of Works (which by then had superseded "Woods, Forests and Land Revenues") responded quickly by issuing instructions that the inscription GEORGE IV (in Roman type, of course) be put in large bronze letters on the pedestal:[5] the squatter had come to stay. The other pedestal has remained empty (except as an occasional resting place for pigeons) to this day.

While the merits and demerits of Nelson's column were being picked over by the "artistic" establishment, and the Government was wondering what to do with a bronze effigy of a deceased and by then discredited monarch, the person whose memorial was to next inhabit the Square was busy putting down Chartists in the north of England.

MAJOR-GENERAL NAPIER

In February 1839, the ageing, yet still spritely, Major-General Charles James Napier was appointed to the command of the troops in the Northern District of England. The District was comprised of eleven counties: Cumberland, Cheshire, Denbigh, Derbyshire, Durham, Flint, Lancashire, Northumberland, Nottinghamshire, Westmorland and Yorkshire.

The choice by the Tory Lord Hill of an avowed Radical such as Napier was a clever but not altogether surprising one. Napier combined several important qualities, most of which were undoubtedly known to Hill as C.-in-C. of the Army, and to his Home Office advisers. Firstly, Napier was known to be in agreement with many of the aims of Chartism, but abhorred even the thought of the use of violence as a means of achieving them. It is often said that the near pathological fear of *civil* war in Napier's mind (for that is what he saw the outcome to be if the Chartists really did take up arms) stemmed from his having lived through the horrors of the 1798 rebellion in Ireland. Secondly, Napier had published two years before in 1837 (and by 1839 it was being widely read), a treatise on military law.[6] Among the many areas the treatise touched upon, two were of immediate importance to the government. The first part dealt at length with the relationship between military and civil law, and consequently with the role of military in dealing with riots. The second, and much longer, part looked in some detail at the ways and means of improving the conditions of the ordinary soldier.

In considering the first question, Napier outlined a position for the military that would, if anything, strengthen (not weaken, as tradition might have dictated) the authority of the civil magistrate: a position which he himself was to adopt with considerable success in the Northern District. In Napier's view, the past indiscriminate use of military force by magistrates, as in Britstol in 1831, to quell a civil disturbance, had been demonstrably counter-productive. Civil Law had become weakened, and as often as not, both the magistrate and the soldier made into a laughing stock.

In the second area, of soldiers' conditions, Napier was fully aware that the ever-present danger of disaffection (always a problem when troops are used to aid the civil power) is exacerbated by poor conditions of service. Napier's view was that a well-fed, well-housed soldier is less likely to be persuaded out of his responsibilities than one who is not. He also laid great stress on the extent to which billeting in private houses, which was the rule outside big towns, also exposed soldiers to possible bad influences. To remedy this, he suggested a national system of barracks, where exposure to such influence could be eliminated, or at least controlled.

Despite all his radicalism, Napier could not escape the essential characteristics of his class. He was motivated by a deep sense of patriotism; an unshakable belief that the established order could only be changed at a pace slower even than the snail's; and a conviction that Britain's destiny was to maintain and expand its "imperial greatness". In the words of one of his many nineteenth-century biographers, he wanted, like Cromwell,[7]

> ". . . that the people should govern themselves; but like Cromwell, he was so anxious for their well being that if they ignorantly misused their power, he would have driven them perforce into more excellent ways . . . (in fact) nature had formed him to enact the benevolent despot".

Throughout the two years that Napier commanded the Northern District, he did so with unabashed firmness, which was by no means all directed at the Chartists. The local bourgeoisie, who were for ever clamouring for the Army to protect their "lives and property", would receive the sharp end of Napier's tongue no less than a troop of dragoons. In his view the bourgeoisie, by and large, had privilege enough. By 1841 the ever-present danger of a large-scale armed confrontation between the Chartists and the military had been diverted, mainly due to Napier's skill in handling both sides.[8]

Chartism did not come out unscathed; many of its leaders were imprisoned or transported, and much of the rank and file disillusioned. But for Napier his success certainly did not spell Chartism's defeat. He believed, as he put it, that "the Chartist spirit is not broken, it has only been made more cautious, and therefore perhaps stronger".[9]

However, Britain's mid-Victorian ruling class were not in the habit of erecting statues in important public places to men, who, in one moment of their lives, had *desisted* from riding down their adversaries, cutlass in hand. Blood and conquest, not appeasement, were the essential prerequisites for immortalisation in stone or bronze. For Napier such glories were to be found in India.

In April 1841 Napier was offered and accepted an appointment to be general in command of Poonah, a small city about 75 miles south-east of Bombay. In December when he took up the command, he found he had arrived at a critical time for the British in India; they had just lost Afghanistan and it looked as though the Amirs (rulers) of the adjacent

Upper and Lower Sind were going to follow this example and drive the British out. Sind had only been under extensive British influence (the first treaties having been signed in 1832) since 1836, when Lord Auckland attempted to get the Amirs on the British side against the invading Runjeet Singh, Maharajah of the Punjab. The maintenance of British control of Sind's principal river, the Indus, was of course fundamental to the East India Company's expansion of trade from Karachi to the mountains of Kashmir.

The difficulty for an indigenous population in signing treaties with an invading imperial power like Britain was that the invader was always finding excuses for extending rather than reducing its influence. The second article of the 1832 treaty between the British and the Amirs had said[10]

> "that the contracting Powers bind themselves never to look with the eye of covetousness on the possessions of each other".

An open hypocrisy. The British were not in India to take the waters or the sun; they were there to take all they could lay their hands on. (In 1845, the only legal tender in Sind were coins bearing the Queen's head!)[11]

The failure of the Afghan affair, besides being a considerable territorial loss for the Empire, was also a personal blow to the new and ambitious Governor General of India, Edward Law, first Earl of Ellenborough. Spurred on by a need "for some glory more positive than the subdued credit of a victorious defeat"[12] Ellenborough used the excuse that the Amirs were breaking the treaty to issue armed threats against them.

Napier, now over sixty and probably on his last (and only) command of a fighting army, longed for glory too. Having taken Ellenborough's charges against the Amirs at face value, he dictated a treaty that would have forced the Amirs to cede their most important territories to Britain. It would have lost them their national independence and reduced them to a state of vassalage. The Amirs were uncowed by the provocation, and held their ground. Angered by this, and egged on by the sentiment of Ellenborough's instruction (of a few months before) "to exact a penalty (on the Amirs) which shall be a warning to every Chief in India",[13] Napier marched on Hyderabad, the Amir's capital.

Napier seemed ready, even anxious, to fight, although intelligence reports had told him that he would be outnumbered ten to one when he finally met a part of the Amirs' army. The odds, in some curious way, appeared to stimulate him.

The two armies met at a dry river bed near the small town of Miari just south of the capital. The battle was fierce, but the Amirs' force, armed only with sword and musket, were no match, despite their superior numbers, for the bayonet and cannon. At the end of the day, the battle was over. The Amir surrendered; 5,000 of their men were killed. The British casualties were 256. Undoubtedly Napier felt it had been a good day (he received £70,000 bounty for his success) and that history would be on his side. Was it not a law of nature "that barbarous peoples should be absorbed by their civilised neighbours"?[14] Within a few months the few remaining Amirs were crushed. By the middle of August 1843 Sind was formally annexed to the rest of British India.

Napier was soon promoted to the post of Governor of the new territory, which he ruled in "rude and vigorous manner" for four years. In 1847 he returned to England, and after one more brief visit to India in 1849–50 he settled down on a small estate at Oaklands near Portsmouth. During the last years of his life he wrote two short but influential pieces on military matters. The first, published in February 1852, was *A letter on the Defence of England by Corps of Volunteers and Militia* which was partly responsible for stimulating the "volunteer movement" seven years later. The "volunteer movement" was chiefly made up of men from the upper and middle classes, who saw it as being their job to defend the country "in the event of invasion or rebellion".[15] The "movement" also occasioned a nauseous rhyme by Tennyson in which this exhortation features:[16]

"Let your reforms for a moment go!
Look at your butts and take good aim!
Better a rotten borough or so
Than a rotten fleet or a city in flames.
Form, form, Riflemen, form
Ready, be ready against the storm!
Rifleman, Rifleman, Rifleman, form!

The second piece, published soon after his death (29 August 1853) on the *Defects, Civil and Military, in the Indian Government*, contained several hints as to the troubles in that country which were, several years later, to make "two heroes in one"[17] of Henry Havelock, the man whose statue was next to be placed in Trafalgar Square.

Within three years of Napier's death two statues both by George G. Adams, one in marble and one in bronze, had been raised to his memory. Finding a site for the marble one (it now stands in St. Paul's Cathedral) was an easy task; but the colossal bronze presented considerable difficulties. Despite the fact that the statue's subscription committee contained many distinguished names, and was chaired by Napier's one-time master, Lord Ellenborough, the Office of Works seemed loath to agree to its being erected in a central position. Lord Ellenborough wanted Waterloo Place, just off Pall Mall. "Would not a site in one of the Squares in Chelsea Hospital suit?"[18] wondered the Office of Works in reply. Relegation indeed for the man who had helped restore Ellenborough's reputation those many years before! Some months later, when it became known that Waterloo Place was to be the site of the "projected opening of a new entrance into the park"[19] (St. James'), Ellenborough tentatively suggested Trafalgar Square as an alternative. The Office of Works, to his surprise, agreed (somewhat reluctantly, it seemed) and in the late summer of 1856, "perhaps the worst piece of sculpture in England"[20] was placed on its pedestal.

GENERAL SIR HENRY HAVELOCK

That Napier and George IV should have found themselves neighbours in Trafalgar Square is probably only a little more than chance. But this is certainly not the case with Henry Havelock. His statue was, right from the outset, in 1858, intended to stand in the position it holds today. What, then, was so important, so different, about this man Havelock (who until two years before his death in 1857 was hidden in the obscurity of the Indian Army) that should have led the ruling class to elevate him to the level of a national hero nearly on a par with Nelson?

His death, reported *The Times*, "has fallen upon the British public with the suddenness of a thunderclap". "Never," mourned another paper, "since the death of Nelson, has the removal of any commander been so deeply and so universally deplored."[21] The desire to commemorate this man in bronze, marble and eulogistic prose stemmed, of course, from the part he had played in suppressing the "Indian Mutiny" that had started in the spring of 1857.

In his *Defects, Civil, etc.* Napier had said:[22]

> "The ablest and most experienced of the East India Company consider mutiny as one of the greatest, if not the greatest danger threatening India."

It is important to remember that British rule in India was maintained by a *small* army of British regular soldiers commanding a *large* army of enlisted Indian soldiers (*sepoys* or *native soldiers* as they were most often called. At Lord Dalhousie's departure from India in 1856 there were 45,322 British as against 233,000 Indian troops.) Strict discipline was enforced and the penalty for mutiny – death – was resolutely carried out whenever the British saw fit.

Since the early 1840s there had been several "mutinies", rebellions or uprisings, all of which the British had more or less successfully suppressed. What was new in the mutiny of 1857 was the enormity of its extent. Although it "began as a military mutiny, the uprising quickly assumed the proportions of a popular rebellion". There were several important reasons for this: reasons which, despite the wealth of scholarly research, are ignored by many historians who still hold that its *prime* cause was bullets greased with animal fat (a convenient and suitable explanation that still carries weight with those who hold that Indians are – or were – an irrational, emotional, and therefore inferior race). Briefly, the general causes which affected Indians both inside and outside the army would be summed up under the following headings. Lord Dalhousie's policy of annexation, especially of Oudh in 1856, accompanied as it was by the feudal policy of excheat, that is, the forfeiture to Britain of lands on the death of the owner; the projected removal by the British of the descendants of the Great Mogul from their ancestral seat; rising unemployment among previous employees of dispossessed princes; and the zealousness with which the British attempted to convert everyone, especially those in their employ, to Christianity – these represent a more accurate anatomy of the causes of the 1857 mutiny than those more usually proferred.

In the army itself, pay and conditions were often appalling. The Indian soldier was often in a near-*Catch 22* position: a position that Napier had identified five years before as an obvious source of discontent. It went like this. If an Indian soldier was fighting, as he often was, in a foreign state, he would receive a supplement to his pay. But should he win, and the State become part of the Empire, his pay would be reduced; for he was no longer "abroad".[23]

In 1857 England was of course not only at war in India. Wars were being fought in the Crimea, in Persia and in China, all of which put an enormous strain on Britain's military resources, and required some withdrawal of regiments from India. The Indian soldiers and civilians who came together in 1857 were very well aware of this. This is not to say that the "mutiny" as a whole was preplanned. It was not. But certainly many of its smaller actions, particularly in the beginning, were not simply spontaneous eruptions. They expressed a continuing and growing desire among the people to get rid of their conquerors.

One of the early risings of 1857, that of Barrackpore and Berhampore in Bengal, was quickly suppressed and the culprits summarily punished (Barrackpore had been the site of an earlier mutiny in 1824 which was only "quelled after the mutinous regiments had been fired on by the British Artillery and the parade grounds made a shambles").[24] In 1844 when Gough was putting down a mutiny among his own troops, Henry Havelock had instanced the guiding principle of the 1824 actions of Sir Edward Paget at Barrackpore as one to be followed: in short, the offenders must be executed.

Havelock's response to the Bengal mutinies thirteen years later was equally harsh:[25]

> "It is clear that no regular Native Infantry regiment can now be trusted. All are in heart implicated in treason if not in act. . . . Every other act (of mutiny) must be visited with prompt attack and bloody overthrow."

In fact, he continued:

> "Mutineers must be attacked and annihilated: and if they are few in any regiment, and not immediately denounced to be shot or hanged, the whole regiment must be deemed guilty and given up to prompt military execution."

Within a month of the failure of the revolt in Bengal, three regiments of Indian troops successfully broke out of Meerut and made their way to unoccupied (by the British, that is) Delhi, several miles to the south-west. They proceeded to proclaim the Mogul dynasty. The swiftness of their action was only matched by that of its retribution. So severe was the loss of Delhi to the prestige of the British Empire that plans for its immediate recapture became the key to British policy for crushing the revolt.

This was not easy. In mid-June the British had lost nearly all control over the area of what is now the state of Uttar Pradesh. When Delhi was finally recaptured in September, the brutality of the British troops knew no bounds. As the *Bombay Telegraph* reported:

> "All the city people (residents – R.M.) found within the walls when our troops entered were bayoneted on the spot; and the number was considerable, as you may suppose, when I tell you that in some houses forty or fifty persons were hiding."

During that summer, as the British army marched to "relieve" besieged forts, indiscriminate murder followed in its wake. Even in areas unconnected with the revolt the British took the opportunity to show the iron hand. A Deputy Commissioner in one such district, one Frederick Cooper, saw fit to execute 250 people on the afternoon of 30 July.[27]

In Benares a Colonel Neill put to death all mutineers who were captured, and even "suspects and disorderly boys were executed by infuriated officers and unofficial British Residents who volunteered to serve as hangmen".[28] The same Colonel, on his way from "relieving" Allahabad in June was so indiscriminate in his executions that one of his officers had to remonstrate with him "that if he depopulated the country he could get no supplies for the men".[29]

The British desire for vengeance ("the slaying of natives", the "peppering away at niggers") was strengthened further still with the massacre of 125 women and children at Cawnpore by the rebels, as a reprisal for the British atrocities at Benares and Allahabad. Havelock, too, even before his discovery of the Cawnpore massacre, had been indiscriminate (prodigal?) with his executions.[30]

> "In two days forty-two men were hanged on the roadside, and a batch of twelve were executed because their heads were 'turned the wrong way' when they were met on the march. All the villages in his front were burned when he halted."

From the time of Cawnpore until Havelock's relief of the besieged residency at Lucknow, there was truly a season of "indiscriminate massacre".[31]

> ". . . the unfortunate who fell into the hands of our troops was made short work of – Sepoy, or Oude villager, it mattered not – no questions were asked; his skin was black and did not that suffice? A piece of rope and the branch of a tree or rifle bullet through his brain soon terminated his existence.
>
> "It was taken for granted that every Sepoy had murdered (British) women and children".

In Havelock's mind – and by no means only in his – the murder and plunder were for:[32]

> "a righteous cause, the cause of justice, humanity, truth and good government in India"

– all, of course, with the blessing of the Almighty.

Havelock's brutality alone, however, would not have been sufficient in itself for him to make any particular claim on mid-nineteenth century British colonial history. As has been noted, competition was keen among his brother officers. What made Havelock, and several others, so prominent during the "mutiny" period was the concrete expression they offered of the much cherished ideal of the British "Christian soldier".

The British had for a considerable part of the early nineteenth century believed that the whole of India could and would be converted to Christianity. Needless to say, by the 1840s, in a country with such strong religious traditions as India had, the conviction had worn very thin indeed; the original sentiments, like those of the unrequited lover, had quickly turned sour. The "mutiny" not only challenged Britain's (and the East India Company's) political and economic control, but its religious one too. The Indian rebels showed that, after all those years of proselytising by their conquerors, they were impressed neither by Christian theory nor Christian practice. In British eyes this rejection was translated into an admission by India of being "the incarnation of Satanic evil". Such evil could not, at any cost, be allowed to destroy the "Providential Design" which in its unfolding required Britain to rule over India through "divine right".[33]

In the mind of a man like Havelock, therefore, nearly all actions against the rebels were justifiable, on the simple grounds of Christian duty. Was not God fighting side by side with every Englishman? The "Providential Design" was, in reality, territorial gain: Divine Right, the monopoly of the East India Company. But then, Havelock was not to know that.

Back in England, where, for the most part, the mass of the population were in near total ignorance about Indian affairs, news of the "mutiny" came as a rude awakening. The newspaper reports painted India as a place of indescribable depravity and unmitigated violence (confirming what the missionaries, the only source of information for most people, had been saying for a long time). Lurid tales were told in the greatest detail of the murder of women and children, such as at Cawnpore, and the violation of white women by black men.

Enormous detail was also given of the punishments meted out by the British; such as the case of the forty rebels blown at once from the mouth of a cannon at Peshawar. A punishment which the anonymous writer of one pamphlet (dedicated to Havelock and sold to raise money for the orphans of India) had the following to say:[34]

> "It may appear horrible, but it is expedient – the deep thinker will tell you MERCIFUL. The Brahmin has a horror of dying mutilated; he believes its effects in his Heaven will be terrible. . . ."

Although this form of punishment was thus seen to be a deterrent, it also showed the British officers' total contempt for a religion that was not his own. The British Officer, steeped as he was in a public school Christianity that put *healthiness* and *manliness* before godliness, found many an

Indian's devotion to asceticism, celibacy or piety nearly intolerable. To "an officer and a gentleman" such virtues were nothing less than the worst excesses of effeminacy, not to say sensuality. "Those niggers are such a confounded sensual lazy set, cramming themselves with ghee and sweetmeats. . . ."[35]

The rise of Havelock to the position of *beau-ideal* of Victorian chivalry is thus perhaps understandable, because he was both a Christian and a soldier. He feared God, honoured the Queen, and proved himself in the[36]

> "contest between the barbarism and fanaticism of Asiatic hordes and civilised authority of Christian rulers . . ."

That these hordes had been, and were being held back, would enable those of the middle class to see India as a refuge where it was possible to acquire more than just a semblance of aristocracy. India, for the aristocracy, presented itself as a fully-fledged bureaucratic state where the ruler was in no way answerable to the ruled – a position they were fast losing at home.

Within a month of the news of Havelock's death reaching England, many of these aristocrats and members of the middle class were clamouring for a memorial to their dead hero. The sculptor, Behnes, was quickly commissioned and a subscription list opened. All went well, until Lord Dover, the Chairman of the subscriptions committee, suggested a quotation from Havelock himself to go on the south side of the pedestal. It read:[37]

> "Soldiers! Your labours, your privations, your sufferings and your valour will not be forgotten by a grateful country. You will be acknowledged to have been the stay and prop of British India in the time of her severest trial."

The reply came back from the Office of Works with the (mildly censorious) suggestion, that:

> "those who will read the inscription may require rather to remember that justice, truth and mercy, qualities of which Sir Henry Havelock himself was a conspicuous example, should be relied upon as well as military force for the maintenance of British influence in India."

It was all right, in other words, to be a "muscular Christian", as long as you kept your frock-coat on in public.

GORDON

It was not long before another "muscular Christian" was to find himself commemorated in bronze in the Square. This time it was no obscure

Indian Army General, but a man whose exploits over many years had made him the apotheosis of the late Victorian imperial ideal: Charles George Gordon, "Chinese Gordon" as he is often known.

During the three decades that elapsed between Havelock's death in 1857 and Gordon's in 1885, Britain continued to expand her Empire, largely by the use of force. Vast tracts of land and their peoples in Asia and Africa became subject to the sharpness of the Christian sword or bayonet. Such gains were not made, of course, without wars, and Victorian war always produced its crop of heroes – noble and high-minded. Gordon (like Havelock) has often been characterised as being the next thing to a Saint: a position the mercenary, especially in the nineteenth century, has often occupied. A contemporary, writing a few years after his death, described Gordon as:[38]

> "a man of average height – about 5′ 9″, with brown curly hair and luminous blue eyes, eyes that look you through and through, and summed you up at a glance; eyes that told you of a stronger will than yours; eyes that seemed to read your very soul and wring from you the truth."

It need hardly be said, that such sternness was tempered with

> "a sweetness of disposition which made him beloved wherever he went; a wrath so terrible it made him feared."

A veritable late Victorian Charlton Heston!

Public imagination, which was already well inflamed with the growing chauvinism of the popular press, was first fired by Gordon for his part in Elgin's sacking and pillaging of the Summer Palace in Peking in 1860, and the suppression of the Taiping Rebellion three years later. The "opening up" of China in the 1890s – that is, the legalising of the exploitation that the East India Company had been indulging in for many years – became necessary as China itself became more important to Western Europe as a potential market. For many years, despite several decrees by China's rulers, Britain had supplied enormous quantities of Bengali opium to the Chinese. Remembering that one seventh of the total revenue of the British Government in India was derived from this trade, it is not surprising that Britain was engaged in three "Opium Wars" with China between 1840 and 1860.[39]

The capture of Peking in 1860 was the culmination of twenty years of aggressive Western diplomacy (and of course war) that finally succeeded in getting the Chinese to sign treaties not altogether in their own favour. No sooner had the Treaties been signed, than the two former adversaries (the allies, France, England and China) joined forces to fight the enemy within.

Since about 1850 Taiping ("the Great Peace"), a revolutionary movement, had been taking shape in the south of China. The movement, guided and partially inspired by Christian ideals, promoted several causes, many of which were inimical to their rulers, whether Chinese, French or British. Taiping fought for a more equitable system of taxation, the treating of women as equal with men, the abolition of foot binding, and the forbidding of opium. They also killed many of the infamous landlords and their supporters, burnt title deeds and divided up much of the land among the poorest peasants. Besides all this, and here was the rub as far as the British, French and to a certain extent the Americans (who enjoyed "favoured nation" status) were concerned, there was the Taiping policy of trading with external powers. In short, the movement aimed at breaking the European monopoly which had been created by the 1860 treaty. The external powers' response to this threat was to supplement the Chinese Imperial Army that had been fighting Taiping for some years, with a large mixed force of Western mercenaries. (The expenses of the force were met by several prominent Shanghai merchants.)

The use of British military might was justified to the British public in similar terms as at the time of the events in India:[40]

> "The Taiping rebellion was of so barbarous a nature that its suppression had become necessary in the interests of civilisation."

So, on 24 March 1863, "in the interests of civilisation" Gordon took command of the force – "The Ever Victorious Army", as it was often called – which within eighteen months with its superior arms decimated the rebels. To the Emperor of China, Gordon was a hero, to the Shanghai merchants Gordon was a hero, and to the British public he was a hero. Twice in six years the barbarians had been repulsed.

Over the next twenty years, apart from making the news on the odd occasion, Gordon was engaged in the quiet and selfless pursuit of his Christian ideals: putting down the slave trade in Egypt, being Governor of the Equatorial Provinces of Africa, and later Commandant of the forces in the Cape. In January 1884 he was regretfully unable to take up, at the behest of the Belgian King, a senior military position in the (new) Belgian Congo, as the War Office refused to sanction his appointment. The War Office refusal was not one of principle, but of opportunity. They required Gordon to go and evacuate some Egyptian detachments in the Sudan. The mission failed. Almost exactly a year later Gordon's head was ceremoniously carried into the Mahdi's camp just outside the walls of the fallen Khartoum. It was to be thirteen years before the British gained supremacy in the Sudan again, when Kitchener at the head of an Anglo-Egyptian army destroyed the Mahdist states on the plains of Karari on 2 September 1898 (an event that has been described as a great landmark in British Imperial History – Gordon avenged, the Sudanese saved, the Nile waters secured, the British Empire extended).[41]

When the news, and especially the manner, of Gordon's death reached England in the first week of February 1885, the outcry in the Tory popular press was unparalleled. The death of their standard bearer – the man who had so valiantly carried the flag of truth to the Sudanese slave traders and had his head chopped off for his pains – was laid at the Liberals' door. It was, as one writer put it, as though:[42]

> "Gordon's head was construed as a symbol of British interests, and the traditions of mission and of course, were held cheap by the Liberals, and as a sign in their hands the honour and security of the country was not safe."

To make amends, perhaps, the Government declared a day of national mourning for Friday, 13 March. Memorial services attended by the royal family, members of Parliament and the Lords, were held in Westminster Abbey and St. Paul's. Local dignitaries attended similar services all over the country. By July the Government had voted £20,000 to his relatives and the Treasury had agreed to pay nearly £4,000 for a commemorative statue.[43]

At first it was suggested that the statue, a 10 feet 6 inches high figure, by Hammo Thornycroft, should stand in Waterloo Place between the Athenaeum and the United Services Club, and opposite to the Crimean Monument. But it was thought that a single figure (and that is all the Treasury were willing to pay for – there was no public subscription) was not "important enough" for the site, so the Office of Works looked elsewhere. The *Morning Post*[44] suggested that as the memory of Napier had dimmed in the public imagination Gordon should replace him – a suggestion that brought a flood of objections from Napier's relatives.[45]

Although the statue was completed in early 1886, it was not until May 1888 that the Office of Works finally decided that it should stand, complete with 18 foot pedestal, on the site of the large gas lamp between the fountains in Trafalgar Square. The *Graphic* described the completed statue:[46]

> "Gordon is represented as a Staff Officer wearing a patrol jacket. His head is

> slightly inclined forward, resting his chin on his right hand; his Bible he firmly grasps with his left. He carries no sword or weapon, only his short rattan cane, often called during his China campaign his 'Wand of Victory'. Standing firmly on his right foot his left is raised on a broken cannon. *This action is intended to symbolise his moral attitude as a soldier. Although he hated war and bloodshed, he seemed bound by fate to be ever fighting.*" (My italics – R.M.)

It was unveiled without ceremony on 16 October 1888. In 1943 it was temporarily removed to Lord Rosebery's house to make way for a Lancaster bomber on show during Wings for Victory Week. In 1953 the Ministry of Works, under some pressure that the Square was no longer an appropriate place for military heroes, re-erected it in the Embankment Gardens outside the Ministry of Defence where it still stands today.

ADMIRALS JELLICOE AND BEATTY

While the nation was in mourning for Gordon, the two men whose commemoration in the late 1940s was to make the biggest physical change to Charles Barry's design for the Square were both in sailor suits. The eldest, John Rushworth Jellicoe, was a gunnery lieutenant on a clapped out "old three decker" the *Excellent*: one of the Navy's gunnery schools at Portsmouth. The other, David Beatty, at the tender age of twelve, had just become a Naval Cadet on the masted trainer *Britannia* at Dartmouth.

It should be remembered that even in the early 1880s, although ostensibly guardian of an expanding Empire, the Navy was still dominated by the traditions and methods of the old wooden fleets of Napoleonic days. Most battleships, although steam powered, were still heavily rigged, and had large sail power. The disposition of their arms had changed little; muzzle loaded guns in broadside, boarding pikes, cutlasses and tomahawks were still valued weapons.[47] This, however, was to change rapidly as Britain's ascendancy as Europe's number one imperial power became increasingly challenged by the growing economic and military power of her European neighbours.

It was during one of the conflicts that attempted to resolve this challenge, World War I, that David Beatty and John Jellicoe arrived, in the popular imagination, as great heroes. Some mention should first be made, however, of these two heroes' involvement in one of the many inevitable colonial skirmishes which at the end of the nineteenth century the Navy engaged in.

When China was ignominiously beaten in war by the Japanese in 1895, it became abundantly clear to the other imperial powers that, without great cost to themselves, gradualist policies towards China should be turned into aggressive ones: that is, that policies of encroachment should be transformed into a major scramble for concessions, leading eventually to partition. Such imperiousness, whether by the Dual (France and Russia) or the Triple (Germany, Austria and Italy) Alliances, or by Britain which stood alone, only intensified an already open hatred of foreigners by many Chinese.

By 1899 the frequent guerilla attacks in north-east China on European traders, Christian churches and the like had grown into a fully-fledged uprising. (The uprising, which in the West is more usually – and wrongly – termed the "Boxer Rebellion", was in fact a revolutionary peasant movement directed against the Manchu government as well as the foreign imperialist.)[48]

The Boxers' declared aims were to "wipe out foreigners" so as to protect their country; to kill Christians as "the heresy (Christianity) has no respect for either Gods or Buddha".[49] The eight imperial powers, long aware that their presence in China often put their officials at risk, tended to live jointly in semi-stockaded quarters on the outskirts of the cities or big towns. It is not therefore surprising that the Boxers should soon march upon two of the most important ones; Tientsin, a major treaty port, and Peking itself.

The Allies' response was to send two motley expeditions of sailors and soldiers to "relieve" both settlements. Beatty was severely wounded in the arm in an ambush on his way to Tientsin on 19 June.[50] Two days later Jellicoe received a bullet in his left lung on his way to Peking.[51] Both men retired hurt. Beatty's actions so commended him to Admiral Sir Edward Seymour that within five months he was at the exceptionally young age of twenty-nine promoted to Captain (a rank already held by Jellicoe, twelve years his senior). This extraordinarily rapid promotion, although applauded by the popular press, was received with some understandable distaste by the nearly four hundred lieutenants senior to him. When, ten years later in 1910 he was promoted to Rear Admiral, parallels with Nelson became more and more frequent. No such comparisons were drawn when Jellicoe became a Vice-Admiral commanding the Atlantic Fleet twelve months later.

Beatty was further to incur the displeasure of his fellow officers when, much against their advice in 1912, Winston Churchill, then First Lord of the Admiralty, chose Beatty as his naval secretary. Beatty's naval reputation was smudged once again a year later when he was appointed by Churchill "over the heads of all" to command a battle-cruiser squadron in Jellicoe's fleet.

Throughout this period Britain's overseas monopoly was becoming increasingly threatened by Germany. Germany's fleet (like Britain's) was being greatly expanded – at a rate faster than Britain's, due to its greater organisation in iron and steel production. New alliances began to be struck to prevent German expansion – Dual and Triple *entente* with France and Russia were established. France (it would be better or more accurate to say, the French industrial magnates) was particularly aggrieved, as Lorraine, which formed much of the basis of Germany's prosperity, once belonged to them.

In Europe the "arms race" was on, and war was just a matter of time. In 1914 (on the excuse of an assassination during a dispute between Austria and Serbia) the Great Powers declared war; Britain, France and Russia on one side, Germany, Austria, Hungary, Bulgaria and Turkey on the other. In four years the war killed millions, toppled the thrones of the Romanovs, Habsburgs and the Hohenzollerns, and kept the British Navy busy.

Although Jellicoe and Beatty had unswervingly served the British capitalist class with skill and tenacity, this same class was not above kicking them in the teeth if the political moment required it. This was especially the case for Jellicoe, who never became the public's darling that Beatty had been. In 1917 Jellicoe was forced into premature retirement when he was dismissed by the first Lord of the Admiralty, Sir Eric Geddes (the Railway King).[52] Before he died in 1935 this retirement was interrupted by four years as Governor General of New Zealand, President of the British Empire Service League, the President of the British Legion, and as a "special" guarding a gas works for the ten days of the 1926 General Strike.[53]

Beatty retired in 1927 and seemingly spent most of the rest of his life hunting on his country estate (not, it should be mentioned, bought with a naval pension – in 1901 he had married the daughter of the Chicago millionaire, Marshall Field, and had been able to live "independent of the navy". He had also received a windfall in 1919 from the Government of £100,000 "for services rendered" when he was created an Earl. Jellicoe, it is interesting to note, received only half that amount when he was made a Viscount at about the same time.) Four months after Jellicoe's death, Beatty too was dead. Both men, after funerals on a grand scale, were buried near to Nelson in St. Paul's Cathedral in the City of London.

Within a month of Jellicoe's death, the Cabinet gave its formal approval for the erection of a national monument. However, as it was their recommendation that the State pay for it, a debate and vote in the House was necessary. Most of the members who spoke in the debate thought, like Viscount Halifax, that Jellicoe's death "had deprived the country of a great public servant", and saw Jellicoe in Viscount Mersey's words, as "a tough, wiry, resourceful . . . and religious man", in fact, "a really great Englishman".[54] Only Winston Churchill seemed of a different opinion when he said of Jellicoe in a reference to Jutland: "He was the only man on either side who could lose the war in an afternoon." Stanley Baldwin, who had moved the resolution, curtly replied that the House should "leave history to judge"; Jellicoe had, he thought, like Haig, "played his part".

The resolution was carried. Four months later the Cabinet agreed, after Beatty's death, that it would be appropriate for the two men to have a joint memorial. Finding a site for such a memorial was again to present some difficulty, but more important than that was what sort of memorial should it be. At first, the Office of Works thought[55] in the traditional terms of statues, and it was not long before the north side between the Gordon statue and the wall of Trafalgar Square was suggested (a place, incidentally, at one time strongly canvassed for a statue of that imperial monster, Cecil Rhodes). However, the Royal Fine Arts Commission objected. The next proposal was that Napier and Havelock and even George IV be removed, so as to make the Square solely a "Naval Piazza". This too was rejected.

While investigations into possible sites were going on, a similar exercise was launched to find a suitable sculptor. Various authorities were approached for their views. One of them, Eric McLagan of the Victorian and Albert Museum felt that as[56]

> "the statue will obviously have to be naturalistic representations with correct uniforms and so forth, I suspect that you will have to offer the job to established academic sculptors. The result will almost certainly not be interesting, but will probably pass with those principally concerned."

This was not without difficulty, he went on to point out, as so many of these "academic sculptors" were old men.

For several months the situation seemed to have reached an impasse. Without a site no sculptor could be commissioned. Another attempt was made to find an alternative site for George IV. Perhaps, it was suggested, he could move to beside the temple he had erected on the island in Virginia Water. The First Commissioner replied dryly that the best site at Virginia Water for the equestrian statue "would be at the bottom of the lake".

When in the middle of 1937 the President of the Royal Academy suggested that the site difficulties could be resolved by redesigning the existing fountains in Trafalgar Square, naval opinion was enraged. The opinion was shared by the Royal Fine Arts Commission, who felt that "emblematic groups as centre pieces of the great basins . . . would not be appreciated in this country". The Chief Commissioner, however, persisted (without taking up the advice of the Royal Academy President to employ C. H. James and Charles Voysey) and invited Sir Edwin Lutyens to do the work.

Needless to say, naval opinion was not to be appeased by the change of designer, and there were continuing complaints at what was seen to be a demeaning of their heroes. In the end, the Office of Works was won over to this view, and it was finally decided (or so it was thought) that[57]

> "Trafalgar Square should be a Naval Piazza, and that the military heroes (such as they were) should be removed."

Besides Lutyens as the architect for the project, two sculptors, William McMillan and Charles Wheeler were appointed. Having found an appropriate site and three apparently satisfactory artists, the Office of Works thought the project would start without further delay.

One detail, however, had been overlooked. The Office of Works either ignored, or chose to discount as unimportant, the dislike Beatty and Jellicoe had had for each other when they were alive. Lady Jellicoe had not forgotten: and she lost no time in writing to the Office to remind them. Frankly, she wrote, she did not approve of the idea of her late husband sharing a public position with someone who was, after all, of "lesser rank". The Office of Works apparently unruffled, after writing a placatory letter explaining that no designs had yet been made, went on to ignore her remonstrations and invite Lutyens to produce his design.

The first design produced featured, at the centre of each fountain, a thirty-foot-high cenotaph surmounted with coronets "as on Nelson's Monument in St. Paul's". At the base was a series of nautical emblems, some of which were, in Lutyens words, to be made as[58]

> ". . . Nautilus shells (which) are sheer beauty in their shape. I had a pair made in Delhi pointed from a real one, by an Indian. They pour beautifully and are God's own good shape."

McMillan and Wheeler prepared a bust for each Admiral to go separately in the surround of the two fountains. The scheme met with the disapproval of the Royal Fine Arts Commission, who suggested the theme depicted should have a more baroque flavour. Such a style, they believed, would be justified, given the site which was in "need of variety and liveliness". In any case, the baroque style would be "more appropriate to the personalities of the Admirals". The ensuing delay and, some held, the unjust interference by the Royal Fine Arts Commission, caused sufficient rumours for a question to be asked in the House of Commons as to when the project was expected to start. It was now two and a half years since the Cabinet's first decision.

The delay gave Lady Jellicoe another opportunity to complain about the jointness of the proposed memorial. Writing from Droitwich, she contended again "that her husband should have recognition different from, and higher in kind than that of Lord Beatty". Haig, she argued had a memorial to himself; so why not her late husband? While a resolution to the whole problem was being sought, the Office of Works received a suggestion from Frank Pick of London Transport. Pick's idea was to place separate busts of the Admirals somewhere along the north wall of the Square, similar to the arrangement arrived at by the sculptors who produced the "Reformers Wall" in Geneva.

Armed with this alternative idea, the sculptors and Lutyens went ahead with their second and final design, plus the flower-beds, and the intention of completing the whole project by July 1939. The issue of seniority between Jellicoe and Beatty raised its head once again: the question now being, on which side of Nelson should they respectively be placed? The Office of Works advocated that Jellicoe, as the senior officer, should stand to the right, the fountains, as it were, being neutral. The Admiralty readily agreed.

But now there was to be a new obstacle. Capitalism was about to engage in yet another war in Europe. The project was forced to remain incomplete for nearly ten years.

In 1966 the bust of a naval hero of this latter conflict, Earl Cunningham of Hyndhope – the only one, in fact, so commemorated[59] – was placed, with due ceremony, on a vacant pier to the left of his one-time superior officers.

Notes to Chapter 5

1. John Jacob, *Remarks on the Native Troopers of the Indian Army* (Bombay 1854), p. 2.
2. Christopher Hibbert, *George IV Prince of Wales, 1762–1811* (Newton Abbot 1973), p. 250.

3. Carola Oman, *Nelson* (London 1950), p. 522.
4. *PRO WORKS 20/27.*
5. *ibid.*
6. Charles Napier, *Remarks on Military Law and the Punishment of Flogging* (London 1837).
7. T. R. E. Holmes, *Four Famous Soldiers* (London 1889), p. 28.
8. F. C. Matthew in *Chartist Studies* (ed.) Asa Briggs (London 1959), p. 380.
9. Pricilla Napier, *Revolution and the Napier Brothers, 1820–1840* (London 1973), p. 277.
10. *The Cambridge History of India* (1929), vol. v, p. 523.
11. *ibid.*, p. 531. The conquest of Sind enabled the East India Company to raise its price for opium three hundred per cent, see Charles Napier, *Defects, Civil and Military of the Indian Government* (London 1853), pp. 436–7.
12. V. A. Smith, *The Oxford History of India* (London 1970), p. 608.
13. *The Cambridge History of India*, p. 539.
14. Holmes, *op. cit.*, p. 85.
15. H. A. R. May, *Memoirs of the Artists Rifles* (London 1929), p. 6.
16. *The Times*, 9 May 1859.
17. W. H. Aylen, *The Soldier and the Saint or Two Heroes in One* (London 1858), p. 2.
18. *PRO WORKS 20/32.*
19. *ibid.*
20. *Art Union* (1868), p. 98.
21. W. C. Pollock, *Way to Glory* (London 1957), p. 1.
22. Charles Napier, *Defects, etc.*, p. 12.
23. *ibid.*, p. 11.
24. R. C. Majumdar *et al.*, *An Advanced History of India* (London 1960), p. 733.
25. Pollock, *op. cit.*, p. 150.
26. Quoted in Majumdar, *op. cit.*, p. 777.
27. E. J. Thompson, *The Other Side of the Medal* (London 1925), p. 58.
28. Majumdar, *op. cit.*, p. 776.
29. J. F. Horrabin, *A Short History of the British Empire* (London 1946), p. 39.
30. *ibid.*
31. Thompson, *op. cit.*, p. 75.
32. Pollock, *op. cit.*, p. 170.
33. Francis G. Hutchins, *The Illusion of Permanence* (Princeton 1967), p. 81.
34. Anonymous, *Who and What is Havelock?* (London 1857), p. 8.
35. W. H. Russell, *My Indian Mutiny Diary* (London 1957), p. 8. "Ghee" is clarified butter made from buffaloes' milk.
36. *Edinburgh review*, vol. CVI, p. 593.
37. *PRO WORKS 20/34.*
38. A. C. Hake, *Events in the Taiping Rebellion* (London 1891), p. 1.
39. Karl Marx, *On China* (London 1968), p. 8.
40. *Dictionary of National Biography*, vol. 22, p. 170. Entry for Charles George Gordon.
41. R. O. Collins, *Egypt and the Sudan* in *The Historiography of the British Empire Commonwealth* (Durham N.C. 1966), p. 270.

42. A. P. Thornton, *The Imperial Idea and its Enemies – A Study in British Power* (London 1959), p. 61.
43. *PRO WORKS 20/50.*
44. 1 December 1885.
45. *PRO WORKS 20/50.*
46. 30 October 1888.
47. Geoffrey Rawson, *Beatty* (London 1936), p. 9.
48. Hu Shêng, *Imperialism and Chinese Politics* (Peking 1955), pp. 109–67.
49. V. Purcell, *The Boxer Rebellion* (Cambridge 1963), pp. 224–5.
50. Rawson, *op. cit.*, p. 42.
51. Reginald Bacon, *The Life of John Rushworth, Earl Jellicoe* (London 1936), p. 112.
52. *ibid.*, p. 374, p. 390.
53. *ibid.*, p. 496.
54. *The Times*, 12 December 1935.
55. *PRO WORKS 20/229.*
56. *ibid.*
57. *ibid.*
58. *ibid.*
59. Oliver M. W. Warner, *Cunningham of Hyndhope* (London 1967), p. 266.

6

RIOTOUS ASSEMBLY

*"THE NELSON COLUMN EMEUTE**

Recitative

O'er Nelson's Column, by a hoard concealed
All London cried to have the base revealed;
Those dismal hoards have shut it in for years,
Washed by two ginger-beer-like fountains' tears.

Air

'Twas in Trafalgar Square
We saw the blackguards there:
Each scamp was busy then.
A frothy noodle spoke
They turned his words to joke,
Both the boys and the men.
To'ards NELSON's Column rolled the wave,
Three cheers the little blackguards gave,
A roar devoid of beauty;
To Scotland Yard the signal ran,
For MAYNE expects that every man
This day will be on duty.

And now the urchins roar
More wildly than before;
Young SNOBKIN led the way
His hand a stone has aimed,
And a policeman, maimed,
Is useless for the day.
That broken head was dearly bought,
For SNOBKIN from a truncheon caught
A crack that spoiled his beauty;
He roared, as from the scene he ran,
"I'm a poor boy, and that 'ere man
Has been and done his duty!"

* A popular rising or disturbance.

The base of NELSON's shaft
A flight of stones received;
Good taste was on the side
Of those who push'd and shied
And thundering brickbats heav'd
The sticks and stones flew thick and fast;
The ugly hoarding fell at last:
'Twas void of use or beauty;
It tumbled with a crash and bang;
The Square with the confession rang –
"The scamps have done their duty!"

6 MARCH 1848

It was the year 1848; immediately below these verses a *Punch* cartoonist had drawn the statue of Nelson dancing with excitement at "finding his hoarding" removed.[1] *The Times*, in reporting the same incident, adopted a graver view – very hostile to the crowd that had assembled on the 6 March. They were there to hear C. Cochrane speak against the raising of income tax from 3 per cent to 5 per cent to pay for national defences that had been introduced in the Budget two weeks before (18 February):

> ". . . at noon the large area of Trafalgar Square was filled with a mob, among whom, judging from appearances, not a dozen probably were subject to tax . . ."

This was not surprising; neither was the fact that the

> "8,000 to 10,000 persons assembled in the Square, (were) belonging entirely to the working classes, and the great mass of them apparently out of employment."

Cochrane, although he had been egged on earlier by an associate to hold a meeting "to defend and help the people of England and clear them from the accursed taxes",[3] at the last moment deferred to the police's advice that it was illegal and did not speak. However, G. W. M. Reynolds, the young Chartist leader, was not so deterred. Holding high a placard proclaiming "A Republic for France – The Charter for England", he cautioned the[4]

> "glorious French Republic, the tyrannical Louis Philippe and the Parisian people . . . not to take the leading articles of the aristocratic newspapers nor

NOTICE.

WHEREAS large bodies of Persons assembled yesterday, in the Forenoon and throughout the Day, and part of the Night, in TRAFALGAR SQUARE, and in the Neighbourhood, and committed many acts of Violence and Rioting, and serious Breaches of the Peace.

And whereas large bodies of Persons are at this time there assembled, whereby the Public Peace is greatly disturbed, and the peaceable Inhabitants of the Neighbourhood are interrupted in their lawful Business, and alarmed:

NOTICE IS HEREBY GIVEN,

That all such Meetings and Assemblies are

CONTRARY TO LAW.

And orders have been given to the Police to prevent such unlawful Meetings, and to apprehend and take into their Custody all Offenders, that they may be dealt with according to Law.

And all Persons are hereby cautioned and strictly enjoined not to attend, or join, or be present at any such Meeting.

And all well disposed Persons are hereby called upon and required to aid the Police in the discharge of their duties, and to assist, as far as they may be able, in protection of the public Peace.

WHITEHALL, *March 7th*, 1848,
Two o'Clock.

Printed by W. CLOWES and SONS, 14, Charing Cross.

11. Notice prohibiting meetings in the Square. 7 March 1848

the opinions of the West End oligarchy as an expression of what the English nation thought of them."

At the mention of Louis Philippe someone from the crowd asked Reynolds what would he do with him if he had the French king in his grasp? Would he kill him for instance? Reynolds replied with characteristic wit "that he certainly would not," instead "he would put him in Woombles Menagerie and exhibit him at sixpence per head".[5]

Before Reynolds could go any further, the police, two inspectors and thirty constables appeared wielding their batons and "in doing so several (demonstrators) received injuries" (sufficiently bad in fact to be later taken to hospital). Incensed by the attack, the crowd took stones from the building work around the base of Nelson's Column and pelted both the police and the column itself with them. When this supply of stones ran out, they tore down the "palisades around Nelson's Column" to replenish their arsenal and set fire to the contractors' sheds. At the height of the affray, a cry went up: "To the Palace! Bread and Revolution!", and a large section of the crowd moved off towards St. James' Park, smashing street lamps and the windows of the Reform Club on the way. The police had effectively sealed off all the entrances to the Park and only a small number of the crowd managed to get through; the remainder returned to Trafalgar Square, where they then occupied[6]

"the steps that form the basement of the Nelson Column (and) continued their disturbance of the public peace."

Three days later, *The Times* leader adopted a more muted, if rather smug, tone in commenting on these events, referring, for instance, to the damaged shop windows in Regent Street (where some of the crowd had gone when the meeting finally dispersed) as[7]

"the only memorials left of the late impotent and contemptible attempts on the public peace."

The article further said that,

"We trust . . . that this senseless, and in a political sense, ridiculous movement (Chartism) is now entirely at an end, and that there may be no necessity for applying the fountains of Trafalgar Square for a purpose more than once suggested during the early part of the week.

"These fountains have generally ceased to be ornamental, but it still remains to be seen whether they might not be made useful, in whether a hose attached to them might not enable the authorities effectually to throw cold water upon a Chartist emeute in the Square."

This change of tone had been stimulated by the Government, who wished to play down the whole affair. Sir George Grey, the Home Secretary, in answering a question in the House about the disturbances and the role of police had said two days before, that he had[8]

> "not been aware that any graver consequences had ensued than the breaking of some lamps and windows in a disturbance which the police had most effectually and, he believed, most temperately repressed."

In fact between 6 and 8 March the police made 103 arrests in or around Trafalgar Square. Of this number 73 were convicted, the remainder being unconditionally discharged. It is perhaps interesting to note that the majority of those arrested were aged about twenty.[9]

A week later, however, the Government was to express clearly the underlying fears and forebodings it felt about such activities when it published a cautionary notice, headed "Kennington Common"[10] (now Kennington Park):

> "Whereas a meeting is called to assemble on Kennington Common on Monday next the 13th inst. and information has been received that larger bodies of persons intended to proceed there from place to place, whereby the peaceable subjects of Her Majesty are likely to be alarmed and the public peace endangered, notice is hereby given that persons will not be permitted to march or move in procession through the streets in large bodies at any unseasonable hour . . . (and) that all necessary measures will be adopted to prevent persons from marching or moving about in large bodies, and effectually to protect the public peace. . . ."

The Times' comment on this, after applauding this caution, was to report

> "that gunsmiths have agreed to unscrew the barrels of all the firearms in their possession . . . so as to render them harmless in the event of seizure by the rabble."

Perhaps more significant is the note that follows:

> "it is satisfactory to know that the respectable classes are thoroughly aware to the necessity of preserving public order, and that for the last few days vast numbers (100,000 in London, 170,000 over the whole country – R.M.) of the same tendered their services and cooperation for that purpose."

But before proceeding further, it is necessary at this point to go back in time a little in order to put such actions and the sentiments they aroused in some perspective.

AGITATIONS AND THEIR SUPPRESSION

Throughout the eighteenth century there were riots of many different sorts with a host of different causes. Besides those associated with religious feelings, public executions, and elections, by far the most common and persistent cause was that of "current grievances", such as bread and food prices, enclosures, press gangs, and sometimes new turnpikes.[11] 1795, a year of European famine and extreme scarcity, was the high point of the disturbances associated with food prices; and, coming as they did in a climate of growing fear of the spread of the French Revolution to England, these caused the Government to react, often ferociously. But as often as not the Government were caught unawares, and the riot was over before sufficient militia could be brought in to prevent the "looting and burning of unpopular citizens' houses and shops."[12] The disturbances were more common in areas of severe unemployment, most often the fast growing conurbations.

Organised riots and demonstrations began to happen with increasing frequency in the early years of the 1800s, especially between 1811 and 1820. Stimulated by events abroad, by books like Paine's *Rights of Man* (by then in wide circulation), and the appalling conditions of increasing industrialisation, the urban and rural poor, often combining with middle-class dissension, took to the streets in an organised way. The machine-breaking of the Luddites (1810–12), the Spa Field Riot (1816) and the March of the Blanketeers from Manchester to London in 1817, plus many more minor disturbances, caused considerable fears among the upper classes. Although Waterloo had been won two years before, and the fear of Revolution spreading from the continent was declining, a new fear, that of English radicalism, was quickly taking its place.

Lord Sidmouth had become Home Secretary in 1812, and being an energetic legislator responded well to the needs and fears of the Government and class he served. In order to suppress "agitations", he suspended the Habeas Corpus Act between 1817 and 1818, and in 1817 introduced what was popularly called "Sidmouth's Gagging Bill" (57 Geo. III, c. 19). Passed on 31 March, it was entitled "An Act for more effectually preventing seditious Meetings and Assemblies", and contained forty paragraphs. As an Act, it was to be in force for a substantial part of the period with which this book is concerned, and because of its fundamental importance will be quoted extensively in the following pages.

The opening paragraph leaves little doubt as to its overall intentions:

> "whereas Assemblies of diverse Persons, collected for the Purpose or under the Pretext of deliberating on public Grievances, and of agreeing on Petitions, Complaints, Remonstrances, Declarations or other Addresses to His Royal Highness The Prince Regent, or to both Houses or either House of Parliament, have of late been made use of to serve the Ends of factious and seditious Persons, to the great Danger and Disturbance of the Public Peace, have produced Acts of Riot, Tumult and Disorder, and may become the Means of producing Confusion and Calamities in the Nation; Be it therefore enacted
>
> ....
>
> that no meeting of any description of Persons exceeding the Number of Fifty Persons . . ."

(except Meetings of Corporations, Assizes, and the like)

> "shall be holden for the Purpose or on the Pretext of considering of or preparing any Petition, Complaint, Remonstrance or Declaration, or other Address to The King, or to His Royal Highness The Prince Regent, or to both Houses or either House of Parliament, for Alteration of Matters established in Church or State, or for both the Purpose or on the Pretext of deliberating upon any Grievance in Church or State, unless Notice of the Intention to hold such Meeting, and of the time and Place when and where the same shall be proposed to be holden, and of the Purpose for which the same shall be proposed to be holden, shall be given, in the Names of Seven Persons at the least, being Householders resident within the County City or Place where such Meeting shall be proposed to be holden, whose Places of Abode and Descriptions shall be inserted in such Notice, and which Notice shall be given by public Advertisement in some public Newspaper usually circulated in the County and Division where such Meeting shall be holden, Five Days at the least before such Meeting shall be holden. . . ."

As was so often the case, by using the property qualification as a precondition, the Act immediately denied to a large percentage of the population the possibility of doing other than breaking the law. The fear of punishment, on this fact alone, was seen by the State as the first line of deterrent effect. Should a participant, however, be lucky enough to be a householder,[13] the Act asked him to identify himself both to the State and to the public via published and named notices in the press before any meeting. And just in case something in the event itself caused the authorities displeasure, the clause requiring him to keep a copy of his intention to hold the meeting for two weeks after the meeting had taken place, provided the State with further evidence of the individual's complicity. It was not possible to adjourn the meeting to another day without going through the same statutory procedures all over again.

Having thus established who can and who cannot hold meetings, the Act goes on to explain that it really means business:

> "And be it further enacted, That if any persons exceeding the Number of Fifty shall be assembled contrary to the Provisons hereinbefore contained, it shall and may be lawful for any One or more Justice or Justices of the Peace, or the Sheriff of the County in which such Assembly shall be, by Proclamation to be made in the King's Name, in the Form hereinafter directed, and he and they are hereby required to make or cause to be made Proclamation in the King's Name, to command all Persons there assembled to disperse themselves, and peaceably to depart to their Habitations, or to their lawful Business; and if any such Persons shall, to the Number of Twelve or more, notwithstanding such Proclamation made, remain or continue together by the Space of One Hour after such Proclamation made, that then such continuing together to the Number of Twelve or more shall be adjudged Felony without Benefit of Clergy, and the Offenders therein shall be adjudged Felons, and shall suffer Death as in cases of Felony without Benefit of Clergy.
>
> "And be it further enacted, That the Order and Form of the Proclamation to be made as aforesaid, shall be as hereafter followeth; (that is to say), the Justice of the Peace, or other Person, or One of the Justices of the Peace, or One of the other Persons authorized by this Act to make the said Proclamation, shall, among the said Persons assembled, or as near to them as he can safely come, with a loud Voice, command or cause to be commanded Silence to be while Proclamation is making and after that shall openly and with loud Voice make or cause to be made Proclamation in these Words, or like in Effect:
>
> > "Our Sovereign Lord the King chargeth and commandeth all Persons here assembled immediately to disperse themselves, and peaceably to depart to their Habitations or to their lawful Business, upon Pain of Death.
> >
> > GOD SAVE THE KING."

The meeting may have been legal to begin with, but it was important that the discussion,

> "shall not express or purport that any matter or things by law established may be altered otherwise than by the authority of the King . . . or any matter therein contained, shall tend to incite or stir up the People to Hatred or Contempt of the Person of His Majesty. . . ."

As with illegal meetings, the penalty for non-dispersal of the participants was to "suffer Death . . . without Benefit of Clergy".

In the first instance it was hoped that the meeting (mob, crowd, rabble) would disperse, after the threat of death had been duly announced by a magistrate; however, provision was made to call in "Constables and other Officers of the Peace" to assist. Should things get out of hand, the Constables and other officers were to be well protected, by the clause in paragraph X:

> ". . . if the Persons so assembled, or any of them, shall happen to be killed, maimed, or hurt, in the dispersing, seizing, or apprehending, or endeavouring to disperse, seize or apprehend them, by reason of their resisting the Persons so dispersing, seizing or apprehending, or endeavouring to disperse, seize or apprehend them, that every such Justice of the Peace, Sheriff, Under Sheriff, Mayor, Head Officer, Magistrate, High or Petty Constable or other Peace Officer, and all and singular Persons being aiding and assisting to them or any of them, shall be free, discharged and indemnified, as well against The King's Majesty, His Heirs and Successors, as against all and every other Person and Persons, of, for or concerning the killing, maiming or hurting of any such Person or Persons so continuing together as aforesaid that shall happen to be so killed, maimed or hurt as aforesaid."

Two years later such a clause was to enable the Government actually to congratulate those responsible for the death of eleven people and the injury of many hundreds at "The Massacre of Peterloo" in Manchester, on 13 August.[14]

Besides making provision against the actions of the dissenters themselves, the Act also provided by heavy fines against any person who let his "House, Room, Field or Place" be used for any such events, whether he be the "Owner or Occupier thereof". This was to cause a little difficulty in the case of Trafalgar Square, as it was (and still is) the property of the State; but more of this later. To enable such proceedings and fines to be imposed, magistrates were empowered to enter premises that were under suspicion and make arrests whether the licence (to hold any meeting a licence was required) had been granted or not.

So far, the Act had made no special reference to location (except that certain provisions were to be enacted slightly differently in Scotland and Wales); but in paragraph XXIII it singled out London, and more specifically, the City of Westminster, for particular attention.

> "And Whereas it is highly inexpedient that Public Meetings or Assemblies should be held near the Houses of Parliament, or near His Majesty's Courts of Justice in Westminster Hall, on such Days as are hereinafter mentioned; Be it therefore enacted, and it is hereby enacted, That it shall not be lawful for any person or Persons to convene or call together, or to give any Notice for

Persons to convene or call together, or to give any Notice for convening or calling together, any Meeting of Persons consisting of more than Fifty Persons, or for any Number of Persons exceeding Fifty to meet in any Street, Square, or open Place in the City of Liberties of Westminster, or County of Middlesex, within the Distance of One Mile from the Gate of Westminster Hall, save and except such Parts of the Parish of Saint Paul's Covent Garden as are within the said Distance, for the Purpose or on the Pretext of considering of or preparing any Petition, Complaint, Remonstrance, Declaration, or other Address to The King, or to His Royal Highness the Prince Regent, or to both Houses or either House of Parliament, for Alteration of Matters in Church or State, on any Day on which the Two Houses or either House of Parliament shall meet and sit, or shall be summoned or adjourned or prorogued to meet or sit, nor on any Day on which His Majesty's Courts of Chancery, King's Bench, Common Pleas and Exchequer, or any of them, or any Judge of any of them, shall sit in Westminster Hall, any thing hereinbefore contained to the contrary notwithstanding; and that if any Meeting or Assembly, for the Furposes or on the Pretexts aforesaid, of any Persons, shall be assembled or holden on any such Day, contrary to the Intent and Meaning of this Enactment, such Meeting or Assembly, shall be deemed and taken to be an unlawful Assembly, by whomsoever or in consequence of what Notice soever such Meeting or Assembly shall have been holden: Provided that nothing in this Enactment contained shall be any Construction whatever be deemed or taken to apply to or effect any Meeting convened, called or holden for the Election of Members of Parliament, or any Persons attending such Meeting, or to any Persons attending upon the Business of either House of Parliament or any of the said Courts."

This, of course, included Charing Cross and the King's Mews – the site twenty years later of Trafalgar Square. Fears for the safety of the officers of the Government and Civil Service had been provided for, in Nash's developments of 1813, in the carefully laid out "safe and commodious" routes from the places of residence of these persons to the palaces and the centre of Government.

Throughout the eighteenth century and particularly after the Gordon Riots of 1780, those whose property had been damaged or destroyed had pressed for further legislation that would give them better compensation for their losses.[15] This Act not only gave them their desire, but also provided that this compensation should come out of the local taxes in the area where the damage had been done. The last paragraph but two of the Acts reads as follows:

"And be it further enacted, That in every case where any House, Shop or other Building whatever, or any part thereof, shall be destroyed, or shall be in any manner damaged or injured, or where any Fixtures thereto attached, or any Furniture, Goods or Commodities whatever which shall be therein, shall be destroyed, taken away, or damaged by the Act or Acts of any riotous or tumultuous Assembly, the Inhabitants of the City or Town in which such House, Shop or Building shall be situate, if such City or Town be a County of itself, or is not within any Hundred in which such Damage shall be done, shall be liable to yield full Compensation in Damages to the Person or Persons injured and Damnified by such Destruction, taking away, or Damage. . . ."

This provision is obviously intended to bring pressure to bear locally by the use of financial sanctions. It was, however, to backfire seriously, for as cities became more divided in areas for the rich and areas for the poor, disturbances tended more to occur in the vicinity of those of the rich.

It cannot be overemphasised, that the conditions of the majority of the English population were very poor indeed, and economic conditions over the next several years were hardly to improve their lot. The very extensive literature and scholarship on the subject leave no doubt about this. Writing in 1859, Samuel Bamford recalled the period after the introduction of the Corn Law in 1815 in these terms:[16]

"In London and Westminster, riots ensued and were continued for several days . . . at Bridport there were riots on the account of the high price of bread; at Bideford there were similar disturbances to prevent the exportation of grain; at Bury . . . the unemployed . . . destroy machinery; at Ely . . . (the riot) was not suppressed without bloodshed; . . . at Nottingham . . . at Newcastle . . . at Birmingham . . . at Dundee . . ."

As the Act did nothing to get at the root causes of the discontent, like the Corn Laws, or the enormous increase in the rural poor migrating to the cities, it proved insufficient, and in 1819 the notorious "Six Acts" passed through Parliament between 11 and 30 December.[17] These Acts, in addition to reinforcing those of the Act of 1817, added somewhat to its scope with reference to what was to be permitted debate. It read,

". . . that no meeting of any description of persons exceeding the number of fifty persons . . . shall be holden for the pretext of deliberating upon any public grievance, or"

(and this is the extension)

". . . upon any matter or thing relating to trade, manufacture, business or profession or upon any matter of Church or State. Unless . . ."

The "unless" was as before – requiring seven people with property qualifications. It should be remembered here that property qualifications were an integral part of franchise and franchise was, until the first Reform Act of 1832, a very exclusive affair.

It has been estimated that on the eve of the passing of that Act, only 435,000 people out of a total population of 14 million had the right to vote, and these were drawn exclusively from the middle and upper classes alone.[18] This meant that from the point of view of the working classes, 53 Geo. III, c. 19 and the "Six Acts" represented a cruelly repressive legislation compounding their already severely limited human rights.

REFORM – AND THE HUNGRY FORTIES

Repressive as the legislation was, the fight for the first Reform Bill in 1830–31 was accompanied by outbreaks of organised disturbances, and those in Bristol in October 1831 seemed to many to herald revolution.

The Duke of Wellington's view on the Reform Bill was that it would[19]

> "render the ordinary operations of Government difficult and the protection of the institutions of the County and its property by the Government as nearly impracticable. . . ."

A year after its stormy passage through the Lords and Commons he was to say of it:[20]

> "The revolution is made, that is to say, that power is transferred from one class of society, the gentlemen of England, professing the faith of the Church of England, to another class of society, the shopkeepers, being dissenters from the Church, many of them Socinians, others atheists."

Suffice it to say that Wellington's "revolution" was of a very different kind from the one that the working class had fought so hard for, and lost; for as G. D. H. Cole has put it:[21]

> "The middle class reformers, though they were ready enough to use demonstrations of force (the Bristol riots, the burning of Nottingham Castle, etc) as arguments for the Bill, were in no mind to see their hopes of a *bourgeois* Parliament drowned in a Red Revolution."

They had to wait until the second Reform Bill (1867) for the franchise to be extended to a fraction of their number, for even then only one person in eleven had the right to vote.

Disorder after the Reform Bill can be grouped into three more or less distinct phases. The first was from the spring of 1837 to the end of January

1840; the second, the summer months of 1842; and the third, from November 1842 until October 1843:[22]

> ". . . violence, the most important fact in the Gordon Riots, was the least important fact in Chartist demonstrations; that unlike the mob, drawn by a strong passion . . . the men and women who kept the Chartist movement alive had a steady and responsible quarrel with the conditions of their lives."

There were one or two exceptions to this; at Todmorden in Lancashire a crowd, enraged by the New Poor Law, burnt houses and destroyed belongings of prominent mill owners. On 15 July 1839 another angry crowd, upset by a local magistrate's suppression of local Chartist meetings, destroyed by burning several shops and warehouses in the Bull Ring area of Birmingham. To suppress the riot, the same magistrate called in the police and the dragoons to prevent what he saw as "another possible Bristol".

Besides calling in the dragoons, the local magistrates had police reinforcements sent from London on the "New Railway". This is not the place to say more than to note that the coming of the railways considerably eased the movement of troops and police (especially Metropolitan police) to areas of disorder. The use of police and soldiers from other areas had the additional important advantage, besides that of reinforcement, of considerably reducing fraternisation, a danger always present when local men were used. A month later, crowds attempted to set fire to Bolton Town Hall. By late in 1839 Chartism's initial success had dwindled, internal dissension and an increasing number of prosecutions against its leaders had blunted its impact. However, it took only until July 1840, when the National Chartist Association was launched in Manchester, for its fortunes, this time based more on moral than physical force, to pick up again.

This change to "moral force" has been suggested by some as a reason why the period 1840–1 was relatively free from the sort of disturbances that had been so prevalent in the preceding five years. During the second period of disturbances, throughout the summer of 1842, the whole of the North and Midlands, and at times Scotland, were affected. In response to both the demands in the Charter, and the general (and just) claim for higher wages, workers held widespread strikes, marching in large crowds from factory to factory, picketing. These disturbances, often called the Plug Plot Riots (plugs were removed from boilers, to prevent them from working), caused a fierce reaction from the authorities, and again troops were dispatched from the Metropolis to quell them. Major-General Charles Napier, at this time Commander of the Northern District, was constantly critical of Whigs and Tories alike for being the 'real authors of these troubles' and did much, as was noted above, to prevent any bloody clashes between his forces and those of the Chartists developing. Queen Victoria, seemingly much influenced by Lord Melbourne, reacted strongly against these disturbances, as she was to do a little time later to the Welsh Rebecca Riots.[23] Again, the authorities successfully prosecuted the leaders, and a lull ensued. But not for long.

The third period covers the time of the "Rebecca Riots", so called because some of the rioters dressed up as women; their leader, also in woman's dress, was known as Rebecca. (This naming and dressing up was in fulfilment of a text from the *24th Chapter of Genesis*:

> "And they blessed Rebekah and said unto her Thou art our sister, be thou the mother of thousands of millions, and let thy seed possess the gate of those which hate them.")

Their hatred expressed itself in rick burning, the destruction of toll gates and houses, and an attack on Carmarthen workhouse. Subsequent research seems to show that there was little connection between these disturbances and the aims of Chartism, although at the time the authorities were convinced that they were all one and the same.[24]

The middle years of the "Hungry Forties" were quiet. The "Rebecca Riots" had been finally suppressed by the beginning of 1844, and Chartism was once again divided by internal quarrels and preoccupied by Fergus O'Connor's Land Scheme, and no longer was acclaimed as a major rallying force for the oppressed. It was not until the trade depression in 1847 and O'Connor's election to Parliament accompanied by the revolutionary fervour in Europe that the Chartists were stimulated again to attempt to bring about their "six points"; but this time using public agitation as one of their tools.

Not only the ruling classes were to see strong connections between the ideals of Chartism and the revolutionary events in Europe. In March 1848 several shop-keepers in Kensington wrote to the *St. James Gazette*:

> ". . . the Metropolis and Provincial towns are swarming with French Revolutionary Propagandists present at Chartist meetings . . ."

and a letter to Sir George Grey, the Home Secretary, from Swansea, spoke of[25]

> ". . . a certain class of persons designating themselves as Chartists, taking advantage of the present state of nations on the continent to endeavour to

> excite the lower classes of this Kingdom to deeds of lawless violence and aggression. . . ."

adding that they were "factious Demagogues".

These fears of the European Revolution (Louis Philippe had surrendered to the insurgents on 25 February) were compounded by the complete closure of the European markets to English goods and the consequent failure of many manufacturing firms resulting in an even steeper rise in unemployment. The unemployed, as so often before and since that time, took action, action against those they saw to be responsible, namely the Government and the owners of the means of production, the bourgeoisie. On 5 March a serious riot took place in Glasgow; the "mob" armed with weapons attacked the city, looted shops, in particular, and interestingly, those of gunsmiths and jewellers. The attack took the city by surprise, and it was not until the following day that the military checked the rioters by firing upon them, killing some and injuring many more. As though to confirm their victory the authorities paraded a regiment of cavalry in the city in the ensuing days.

KENNINGTON COMMON

It is in this context, therefore, that the events in Trafalgar Square with which this Chapter began should be seen. At last it seemed to both sides that the time had arrived for the final decisive battle, and each of them set about making the necessary preparations. Ways and means were accordingly adopted by the Government, the police and the Army for preventing a "breakdown of public order in public places". Compared with the State's preparations, those of the Chartists and later groups were uninformed, not to say naive, in their not fully realising the power the State had (and still has) at its disposal to prevent (and manipulate) their activities.

The Kennington Common meeting of 13 March had done little except to add to the fear throughout the Metropolis, and when a massive march was announced for 10 April, the alarm rose to near hysteria. Private citizens in their scores wrote to Sir George Grey offering their yards, their halls and their gardens as stations for the troops[26] – less, one suspects, with the public good in mind, than in fear for the safety of their personal property and lives. The Royal Family left London and took refuge at Osborne House; many middle class families followed suit and fled to the country. The Press had played down the Glasgow riots and took a rather timid line in dismissing the possible events of 10 April. The *Morning Chronicle* wrote:[27]

> "In the present disposition of the London householders, we are by no means sure that the police are not likely to be called in to protect the Chartists from them, than them from the Chartists."

The Duke of Wellington, however, still Commander-in-Chief of the Army, by no means shared this view; after reading in *The Times* that "200,000 Chartists are to assemble in or about London on April 10th" and that the Government had not taken sufficient measures, he said that he looked[28]

> "to the precautions and other arrangements to be adopted (by him) with a view to the defence and military protection of the Tower, the Royal Palaces, and the Government of the Country";

adding,

> "I do not know whence they will come, or what is their avowed or their real or their supposed object".

His own object, however, he saw clearly:

> "to secure a communication among the troops stationed in their several Barrackes and Cantonments . . ."

In his opinion, he concluded, it was

> "absolutely necessary to keep the Parks . . . clear from Mobs as well as the Street from Trafalgar Square to the Houses of Parliament . . . all park gates to be shut before 11.00 in the morning . . . no heavy carriage to be allowed to circulate Trafalgar Square. . . ."

To protect Whitehall and Trafalgar Square he positioned a regiment of Infantry at St. George's Barracks behind the National Gallery and a body of Cavalry in Lord Fitzharding's stables in Spring Gardens.

All in all, Wellington deployed 890 cavalry, eleven pieces of artillery, including three 12 lb howitzers, nine brigades of Infantry (that is 5,000 men) and 12,000 enrolled pensioners. Besides St. George's Barracks and the stables, he planned and did use Hyde Park, Bethlehem Hospital, the Royal Mews, the Tower of London and the grounds of the Royal Palaces to station troops in the centre of the Metropolis. Not since the Civil War had London been so "fortified".

In using troops Wellington was cautious enough to state that,

> "If (the troops are) not required, it would be best not to show them, and in the meantime their position will preserve in security all the essential points in the Town; the great communications between each of the Military Stations; and with Headquarters and the Government and with Parliament."

He also requisitioned Thames steamers to enable the river to be used for ferrying reinforcements, should they be needed.

Sir George Grey, writing to the Lord Mayor of the Government's preparations for 10 April, gives the key as to why the demonstration, in one sense, was to be a failure. He says he is writing to him so that,[29]

> "most sufficient arrangements may be made for opposing an adequate Civil Power to any attempt to oppose the passage of the proposed Procession over Blackfriars Bridge, Waterloo Bridge, Hungerford Bridge, Westminster Bridge and Vauxhall Bridge will be occupied (by) the Metropolitan Police."

The Home Office were to issue a Memorandum on the same day stating that the assembly *would not* be prevented from taking place. However, provision was made to prevent the people assembled[30]

> "an hour after the Petition had gone forward . . . (from passing over) any bridges except Westminster Bridge."

On the day, the demonstration, in perfect order, set out from starting points mostly *north* of the river and marched (on routes indicated by the police) over the bridges to Kennington. The meeting attended by 150,000 people had hardly begun when the Chartist leader O'Connor was asked to speak to the Commissioner of Police Mayne; this he did. Mayne explained that although he would allow the assembly to continue, the leaders who were taking the Petition to Westminster (a petition supported by many signatures for the six-point Charter) could not be accompanied in procession by the crowd. Any attempts to do so, he said, would be prevented by the police and troops stationed at the bridges. So the Chartists, by accepting the Government's concession to allow their assembly to take place *south* of the river, had been outwitted by the most elementary military manœuvre. O'Connor and the crowd, therefore, had no choice but to concur so as to prevent what could possibly have caused the useless shedding of blood.

The meeting, after appeals by both Ernest Jones and O'Connor not to be provoked by the sight of armed soldiers and police, dispersed without even a brawl. In the evening, as though to add to their humiliation, the Chartists were to hear and see a jubilant middle class crowd walking the wet streets of the West End singing "God Save the Queen". "'God Save our Shops' is what they ought to be singing",[31] some Chartists were heard to say as they made their despondent way home.

The next day Charles Arbuthnot, by now Wellington's confidant, wrote to his son,[32]

> "Never was anything more successful than yesterday's result. The Duke had made the most perfect arrangements. Not a soldier was seen; but everyman was close at hand if the mob had been too much for the police. Guizot is in admiration and astonishment. He could not have believed it possible. It will have a great effect on the continent. . . ."

Lord Palmerston, the Foreign Secretary, writing to the British Ambassador in Paris, similarly gloated[33]

> "Yesterday was a glorious day. The Waterloo of peace and order. . . ."

In the long term, however, it was the sentiments of people like the Marquis of Lansdowne that belied the truth when he declared in the House of Lords a couple of days later[34]

> "If there was anything which had imparted to Her Majesty's Government that degree of confidence which was necessary to enable them to act as they had done, it was the certainty which they had acquired in the last eight and forty hours that, if they had occasion to call on any part of the community for support, it would have been readily afforded."

The Marquess of Northampton in the same debate put his finger more accurately on it, when he said:[35]

> "The spirit of order and attachment to the English Constitution – of religion and morality exhibited by the middle classes – would long be remembered."

That is the 100,000 or so special constables. The scale of this rally to "the defence of law and property" was a lesson not easily forgotten by the aristocracy and the bourgeoisie.

The failure of both the Petition and the demonstration to have the slightest effect caused Chartism as a force for change to disintegrate almost completely within a year. It was, however, to give the ruling class one more scare. It was rumoured that the Chartists had regrouped, this time with arms (which, in some areas, was the case), and that another series of demonstrations was planned for Whit Sunday, 12 June, in and around the centre of the Metropolis.

The Inspector General of Fortifications, Major-General Sir John F. Burgoyne, quickly responded with a memorandum to Wellington with a copy going to the Commissioner of Police (reprinted complete as Appendix 3). Wellington concurred with much of Burgoyne's advice for as he saw it[36]

> ". . . we must be prepared in all quarters to give support to the police and to resist the opponents."

Once again, he required that the Royal Parks be shut, and the approaches to the centre of Government well guarded. The Strand was also

> "to be reconnoitred and a note taken of all houses with bay windows – of houses forming corners of streets or out of regular line which would give a command of fire along the streets . . . (also) the Commissioner of Police is to take care to keep clear the Communication from Trafalgar Square to Parliament House throughout the day."

So seriously did Wellington regard the threat, that he not only increased the number of troop stations (extending them to outer edges of the city to places like Bethnal Green and Victoria Park), but also the weight of heavy armour. Besides that employed in April, he added three 24 lb howitzers, big guns indeed to use in the confines of a city, which were to be placed in Carlton Mews and used to protect the Royal Palaces (although the Royal Family were still in the Isle of Wight).

Five days before the planned demonstration three prominent London Chartists were arrested for seditious speeches ten days before at a meeting on Clerkenwell Green. On the day of the demonstration itself Ernest Jones was arrested and brought to London (Jones and the others were later sentenced to two years' hard labour).

Unlike in April (but as in March) the police issued a proclamation declaring demonstrations in general, and Chartist ones in particular, illegal.

Wellington's and Burgoyne's instructions were carried out, nearly to the letter; 10,000 troops were secreted in the centre of London, special constables manned streets, and many public buildings were fortified (often with nothing more substantial than bound copies of *The Times*). The Police were busy occupying the places in advance where the meetings were to be held, ensuring that when the marchers did arrive they had to disperse. In some places, often provoked by the police, the frustrated marchers rioted, leading to the inevitable crop of arrests. In the ensuing days, more people (nearly five hundred) were arrested and were to follow Ernest Jones and the other Chartist leaders in spending the next two years or more in prison doing "hard labour".

Chartism was suppressed; it was a blow from which the mass working-class movement in England was to take a long time to recover. However, one immediate achievement which the Chartists had not expected to gain was that over the period of their activities, especially in the later years, they had provided the State with ample opportunity to develop, almost without any bloodshed, its police and military skill to maintain "law and order" in the streets.

During the next thirty years or so, outbreaks of public disorder in the country as a whole and especially in London became very infrequent indeed. It seems generally agreed that the upswing in the economy after 1850 had slightly raised the standard of living of the population, although there is enough evidence to suggest that the differentials that had preceded it persisted unchanged. The considerable increase in the police force, especially in London, as an effective civil power, also, obviously, contributed in no small way.

Whatever the facts of the case may be in this aspect of the matter, the outcome of any battle – and battle it certainly was – is in many instances decided, or at least considerably influenced, by the physical disposition of the battlefield itself. In London during the whole of the nineteenth century (and, many would have it, since that time too) a considerable number of so-called "improvements" were actually the efforts of one small section of community to arrange the battlefield physically to their advantage, not only socially and politically, but also militarily.

This argument will be pursued in the next chapter.

Notes to Chapter 6

1. *Punch*, vol. XIV, p. 110 (1848).
2. *The Times*, 7 March 1848.
3. *PRO MEPOL. 2/64.*
4. *The Times, op. cit.*
5. *PRO MEPOL. 2/64, op. cit.*
6. The Times, op. cit.
7. *ibid.*, 10 March 1848.
8. *ibid.*, 8 March 1848.
9. *PRO MEPOL. 2/64, op. cit.*
10. *The Times*, 13 March 1848. In 1848 Kennington Common was "managed" by the Duchy of Cornwall Estate.
11. For an extensive survey of these, especially food riots, see E. P. Thompson's *Making of the English Working Class* (London 1963), Chapter 3.
12. *ibid.*, p. 81.

13. No clear statistics exist as to property ownership, but overcrowding figures, assuming there was little co-ownership, gives some guide. See *London County Council Statistics*, XII, Chapter X.
14. For a full account of this event see D. Reed's *Peterloo*, (Manchester 1958).
15. Compensation was already available under 1 Geo. I, c. 5 (The Riot Act).
16. Samuel Bamford, *Life of a Radical* (London 1859).
17. See *Statues at Large*, XVIII, pp. 1–8.
18. G. D. H. Cole, *British Working Class Politics, 1832–1914* (London 1946), p. 4.
19. Dennis Holman (ed.), *Earlier Nineteenth Century Portraits and Documents* (London 1965), p. 96.
20. D. L. J. Jennings (ed.), *The Croker Papers* (London 1944), pp. 205–6.
21. G. D. H. Cole and Raymond Postgate, *The Common People, 1746–1946* (London 1971), pp. 254.
22. J. L. and B. Hammond. *The Bleak Age* (London 1934), p. 14.
23. See Lord Melbourne to Queen Victoria 17.8.1842 and 22.6.43, in A. C. Benson and Viscount Esher, *Letters of Queen Victoria, 1837–61* (London 1908), vol. 1, pp. 425 and 483.
24. David Williams, *The Rebecca Riots: A Study in Agrarian Discontent* (Cardiff 1955).
25. *PRO HO 40/59.*
26. *ibid., also PRO HO 41/26.*
27. The *Morning Chronicle*, 8 April 1848.
28. *PRO WO 30/81, 28–1.* Memoranda by the Duke of Wellington with statement showing distribution of troops.
29. *PRO HO 41/26*, *op. cit.*
30. *ibid.*
31. Elie Halevy, *Victorian Years (1841–1895)* (London 1951), p. 246.
32. A. Aspinal (ed.), *The Correspondence of Charles Arbuthnot* (London 1941), p. 268.
33. Quoted in Th. Rothstein *From Chartism to Labourism* (London 1929), p. 344.
34. *ibid.*
35. *ibid.*
36. *PRO WO 30/81.*

7

BLACK MONDAY AND BLOODY SUNDAY

"That the said Place of Square called Trafalgar Square, and all the ornamental commemoration of Victories gained over the French Revolution, will witness the revenge of the revolution and the destruction of English feudalism. It means the Army is better able to cope with the mob than a foreign foe and is confident that, the people having renounced the fetish of legality, the despotism of wealth now relying solely on force, will speedily disappear."[1]

IN THE QUEEN'S POSSESSION

On 6 August 1844 an Act of Parliament was passed which provided,[2]

"That the said Place or Square called Trafalgar Square, and all the ornamental and other Works, Matters and Things now being or which may hereafter be placed or erected in, upon, about, or around the same, shall be and the same are by this Act vested in the Queen's most Excellent Majesty, Her Heirs and Successors, as Part and Parcel of the Hereditary Possessions and Revenues of Her Majesty in right of Her Crown, within the ordering and Survey of the Court of Exchequer.

II. And be it enacted, That the Care, Control, Management, and Regulation of the said Place or Square, and of all ornamental and other Works, Matters and Things now being or which may hereafter placed or erected in, or upon, or about or around the same, shall be and the same are by this Act vested in the Commissioners for the Time being of Her Majesty's Woods, Forests, Land Revenues, Works, and Buildings; and the said Commissioners shall and they are hereby required, by and out of such Monies as may from Time to Time be placed at Her Majesty's Disposal for that Purpose by Authority of Parliament, to well and sufficiently pave, light, cleanse, water, repair, and keep in good Order and Condition the said Place or Square, and all ornamental and other Works, Matters, and Things now being or which may hereafter be placed or erected in, upon, about, or around the same, any Law, Statute, Custom or Usage to the contrary in anywise notwithstanding.

III. And be it enacted, That all the Clauses and Provisions of an Act passed in the Tenth Year of the Reign of His late Majesty George the Fourth, intituled An Act for improving the Police in and near the Metropolis, and of another Act passed in the Second and Third Year of the Reign of Her present Majesty, intituled An Act for further improving the Police in and near the Metropolis, shall extend and apply to this Act, and to the said Place or Square, and to the

> Works, Matters, or Things for the Time being in, upon, about or around the same, so far as such Clauses and Provisions are not repugnant to or inconsistent with the Provisions of this Act."

It will be noted how Clause I brings Trafalgar Square firmly into the realm of the Queen's possession (interestingly, the only one in the Metropolis which is any other sense a public place). The Queen's possessions normally are confined to parks and places directly associated with the royal places.

Public order in places such as Parliament Square, or for that matter anywhere else except those mentioned above, were the direct responsibility of the Home Office, via its agents, the (Metropolitan) Police. But, as is indicated in Clause 11, the 'Care, Control, Management, and Regulation' of Trafalgar Square is the responsibility of the Office of Works. This involvement of another powerful government department was to be of importance in the events of 1886 and 1887, as was the inclusion of the two Police Acts[3] mentioned in Clause III.

These points, with several others, will be discussed later on. In the meantime, it is necessary to look at some of the Metropolitan "disturbances" that occurred after 1848 not only in Trafalgar Square, but also in their other principal location, Hyde Park.

The hardening of the ban on public assembly in Trafalgar Square as a direct result of 1848 had the effect of moving the centre of such assemblies to Hyde Park. Although the authorities disliked the use of either place, Hyde Park represented, as a *place*, less of a threat to the centre of Government than did Trafalgar Square. Sensitive to problems of banning meetings altogether, the authorities allowed on 24 June 1855 a protest meeting against the Sunday Trading Bill to take place. Hyde Park, it should be noted, is more than one mile from Westminster Hall, so any meeting there does not contravene Clause XXIII of 57 Geo. III, c. 19, and by 1855 the parts of this Act concerning the content of meetings was not being vigorously enforced. (The meeting, after all, was to be a protest by shopkeepers and the like; were not these part of the respectable classes?)

The meeting, however, did get out of hand, and when it was reported that another was to take place the following week, the Metropolitian Police, sanctioned by the Home Office, issued a notice to proscribe it.[4] The legality of this notice was doubted by many, and this, combined with the strength of feeling, encouraged a vast crowd to assemble. A notice prohibiting the meeting and urging the crowd to disperse was read out repeatedly, but the crowd did not respond. Eventually, the police had to use force and, as always at such a point, the real trouble began. Many arrests were made for assaulting the police or obstructing them in the course of their duty. For the Government, it was not that the police had arrested so many that was to cause difficulties, it was that the public was enraged by the manner in which the arrests were made.

In the subsequent Royal Commission[5] set up to investigate the affair, so great was the number of complaints that only two points will be mentioned here. The first is that, as in 1848, some of the blame for the affair is put on the people who came bent on causing disturbance, and these people are repeatedly identified with the "lower classes". The Commission alludes to it as follows:[6]

> "The multitude assembled consisted of varied classes. A vast number of persons of all ranks were there, simply for the ordinary purpose of exercise and recreation to which the Park is specially dedicated; others came with a view of expressing by their presence their disapproval of the Sunday Trading Bill; a large number also, chiefly lads and young men, with a view of giving expression to their disapprobation by shouts, cries and noise along the Drive. There was also a mixture of thieves, pickpockets and other reckless and disorderly persons, bent on plunder and mischief, and seeking to effect their purposes under the shield of popular excitement."

The use of the word "plunder" is of course associated with the other emotive words like "mob", "rabble" and so on, that were the usual vocabulary of such reportage. The complaints of police violence were largely directed at a Superintendent Hughes, the officer in charge, who had, so it was alleged, used improper language, used his horsewhip too freely, and ordered his men to use their staves without giving warning or time for the innocent to disperse. The Commission upheld the complaint against Hughes; but it did not recognise the right, claimed by many, for freedom to hold public assemblies in the Park. The police, so it was thought, had the right, and should maintain the right, to disperse crowds as they saw fit.

It was not until ten years later and the coming of the Second Reform Bill that this ruling was to be challenged. As before, the Home Office concurred with the Metropolitan Police's decision to ban a meeting on 23 July 1866; and, as before, those organising the meeting decided to defy "the law".[7] John Bright, in a letter to the Secretary of the Reform League, wrote, on hearing of the ban:[8]

> "It appears from this that the people may meet in the parks for every purpose but that which is most important and most dear to them. To meet in the streets

is inconvenient, to meet in the Parks is unlawful – this is the theory of the police authorities of the metropolis."

Meetings in the street, besides being inconvenient, were also unlawful in that the police had powers, under the obstruction clauses of the 1839 *et seq.* Police (Metropolitan) Acts to prevent any group of people from assembling on the public highway for any reason whatsoever.

The meeting was prevented from taking place and was transferred by the organisers to Trafalgar Square. However, a small group did succeed in gaining entry to the Park and the ensuing controversy that surrounded their actions (and the actions of the Police) led the Government a year later to allow another meeting, called by the Reform League, to take place. This withdrawal from the position of 1866 by the Home Office showed a lack of confidence in the authority of the police, and sufficient pressure was brought to bear to make the Home Secretary resign. Added to this, the Home Office's actions were interpreted by many as a recognition of the right of holding meetings in the Park. An attempt was made in 1872, in the passing of the Royal Parks and Gardens Acts, to clear up the ambiguity of the legislation, which to a certain degree it did; but as is obvious, meetings have continued to happen (with restriction) in increasing number.

Meetings in Trafalgar Square during the same period had been marked by their moderation, and consequently, although the Seditious Meetings Act still applied, the legal status of Trafalgar Square was in many senses, like that of Hyde Park before 1872, still rather unclear.

Moderate they may have been, with the exception of those mentioned above, but the military continued to see their role very much in the Duke of Wellington's terms. In 1865 a War Office memorandum on the siting of Barracks in London stated that the principal duties of troops in London were to form Guards of Honour, provide security of the Palaces, protect Government and Public property, and " . . . to aid in the suppression of riots when called upon". For, the memorandum continues,[9]

"It is obvious, and indisputable that in the case of disturbances the power of the Mob can be kept in comparative subjection so long as the body of the Multitude can be confined to the streets and can be prevented from forming masses in the Parks. Hence it is necessary that the Barracks should be so situated as to enable the troops to form in and command the open spaces, closing all approaches to them, while the troops themselves shall have open communication with all the principal points to be defended."

When, eight years later, the issue of moving Knightsbridge Barracks to Millbank was discussed, a Sir E. Ellice in a memorandum writes, again on "the question of sites for cavalry barracks in London":[10]

> "the first essential point to bear in mind is the selection of tactical sites, in order to enable the cavalry and troops quartered in the Metropolis to act efficiently in case of emergency."

To give authority to his argument, he quotes all of Wellington's 1848 Memorandum, mentioned in the last chapter, and underlines St. George's Barracks (i.e. the one behind the National Gallery) as important. Not content with invoking Wellington, he also quotes at length from the Inspector-General of Fortifications Sir John Burgoyne's *Military Opinions*:[11]

> "Parks and other open spaces afford valuable lines of communication in towns. Thus in London the Parks form in connection with the river, a valuable strategical line, and, by taking advantage of their circumstances, nearly all the great Public Establishments could be combined into one system of mutual concentrated support."

He goes on to reaffirm that, as in 1848, bridges can be used to divide insurrectionists and the Parks used to station cavalry, infantry and artillery. For he sees

> "these troops would be employed not only to support powerfully any points that might be threatened or attacked, but could debouch from any part of the circuit occupied by them, in order to attack the rioters in front or flank."

Summing up, Sir E. Ellice thought then, as did the Duke of Wellington before him, the watchword was, "Deny the Parks and Open Spaces to the Mob".

The outcome of the discussion on barrack siting was that Knightsbridge Barracks were to be rebuilt on the same site, and that the objections that the Houses of Parliament were inaccessible to cavalry coming from there and the west (to complete the circuit) would be overcome by the building of Millbank and Victoria Street in the 1870s. The building of Millbank more than that of Victoria Street had a strategic importance, for it isolated the Houses of Parliament and provided a protected route, with gardens (parks) on one side, the length of the Government sector, besides the Thames.[12]

Thirty-five years later, speaking of the 1870s and the early 1880s, Winston Churchill said:[13]

> "It was the end of an epoch. The long dominion of the middle classes, which had begun in 1832, had come to its close. . . . Slaves were free. Conscience was free. Trade was free. But hunger and squalor and cold were also free and the people demanded something more than liberty."

It was these demands which in turn led to the "rediscovery of poverty",[14] and opened up an urgent public debate on an issue that until then had been a relatively private discussion. This debate amongst the middle classes, stimulated by the depressing economic conditions they themselves were facing, as in 1848, was a reaction more inspired by fear than charity. People like Samuel Smith were writing:[15]

> "I am deeply convinced that the time is approaching when this seething mass of human misery will shake the social fabric . . . unless we teach it the same virtues which have elevated the other classes of society."

The education he speaks of is, of course, liberalism and the economics of *laissez-faire*, for which many still held out hope. There was, however, another form of education, that of socialism, which was going to transform much in this period. England had managed to resist socialism in all its forms, although by the 1880s many trade unions had become established. Karl Marx, whose ideas were so successful in helping form working-class parties on the continent during the seventies, had had little direct success in the country where he had lived for so many years.

SOCIALISTS AND UNEMPLOYED

G. D. H. Cole distinguishes three groups of socialists in the 1880s.[16] The first group contended that the achievement of revolution was paramount, and that socialists should have no truck with parliamentary elections. The second group, headed by William Morris, did not reject parliamentary elections altogether, but held that participation should wait on an increased consciousness on the part of the working class. This increased consciousness would be achieved by education, and – importantly, in the context of the present study – by agitation. The third group, strongly supported by the Fabians, held that Socialists should permeate all parties, rather than create a separate Socialist Party. (The make-up of these groups, the movement of people from one group to another, and the substance of their policies, are far too complex to discuss here, except insofar as they bear on the main argument.)

Agitation, as planned political strategy, occupied the first two groups throughout the earlier years of the 1880s, especially in relation to the cause of the unemployed. The Social Democratic Federation had attacked such ideas as emigration as a means of solving unemployment, as had the Labour Emancipation League in the late 1870s. Innumerable open-air meetings took place, and it was not long before the police attempted to put a stop to them. In 1883 the Metropolitan Board of Works attempted, without much success, to prohibit meetings in such places as Peckham Rye and Clerkenwell Green; but the first real trouble came in 1885 with the "Dod Street Affair" when the police acted with little restraint against the assembled crowd. This affair did little to suppress William Morris for example; for he was by then a well-known artist and writer, who used his position to embarrass the authorities by making a point of appearing on a "soapbox" with increasing frequency. Within a year, however, he was arrested while speaking in Bell Street, off Edgware Road. Undeterred by this he continued to make speeches in the period between his committal and his trial. At one of these meetings, Morris voiced what was in the minds of many. The middle and upper classes, he said,[17]

> " . . . were enabled to live in luxury and idleness on the poverty and degradation of the workers. There was only one way in which this state of things could be altered – society must be turned upside down."

Morris was under no illusions that this could be easily done. Three years earlier he had written to C. E. Maurice[18]

> "The upper and middle classes as a body will by the very nature of their existence resist the abolition of classes. . . . I have never underestimated the power of the middle class, whom, in spite of individual good nature and banality, I look upon as a most terrible and implacable force."

While Morris was speaking at endless meetings, embarking in fact on the "hard, unremitting toil" that was necessary to build a (working-class) party, the Social Democratic Federation under H. M. Hyndman was "preaching La Revolution" to the unemployed in the East End.

In the early part of 1886 several socialist and social democratic organisations were trying, by one means or another, to organise the unemployed. As is usual in such times, the working class were not only assisted by the organised left towards a resolution of their plight but were constantly assailed by propaganda in one form or another from the right. On this occasion the Tories told them that unemployment was the result of "Free Trade" and unfair foreign competition. The "Tory Fair Traders" (or to give them their proper title on this occasion "The London United Workers Committee")[19] had organised several small demonstrations in

London during January leading up to what they expected to be their longest and most effective protest so far, a mass demonstration in Trafalgar Square on 8 February.

On 1 February the Secretary of the London United Workers Committee wrote to the Commissioner of Police announcing their intention to hold the demonstration and requesting an interview to discuss the arrangements. The police subsequent to the interview, but only after assurances that "the unemployed wished to be perfectly peaceable"[20] had been made, agreed to let the demonstration go ahead. A day later, however, police intelligence reported to the Commissioner that the L.U.W.C. had at their meeting that morning made statements that in all probability the unemployed would be physically attacked by the Social Democratic Federation. In addition to this the L.U.W.C. had said that if the S.D.F. used the "usual violent language of Socialists" they (the L.U.W.C.) intended "to have sufficient force to defy them (the S.D.F.) and if necessary put them in the basins"[21] (Barry's fountains). The S.D.F., on the other hand, had no such plans; no threats were made to either the Fair Traders or of course the unemployed (the police were in fact fully aware of this, as they had agents attending all S.D.F. meetings). Despite this contrary information the police made preparations for a disturbance.

Thus it was that on 8 February in Trafalgar Square, three groups, the Fair Traders, the S.D.F. and a large group of unemployed workers with no particular affiliation to any cause except that of their own cold despair, gathered in the Square to demonstrate their grievances.

The police, caught a little off guard with only sixty-six men present, made attempts to get the leaders to persuade the crowd to disperse. When this did not succeed, they asked for an orderly procession to be led to Hyde Park. This the S.D.F. speakers agreed to do. It was to prove, however, as far as the authorities were concerned, a mixed blessing.

As the demonstration moved off along Pall Mall it was abused by "clubmen" from the safety of their first floor windows, perhaps in response to the earlier remarks of one of the speakers, John Burns:[22]

> "'Look' he (had) cried 'at those clubs,' (pointing towards Pall Mall). What did the members of those clubs care for their (the unemployed) distress? Where were the Members of Parliament that Day? They were sitting comfortably in their clubs, not caring a straw whether the public starved or not."

The demonstrators returned the abuse with stones, the S.D.F. quickly lost control, and riot ensued. Looting began, and breaking of windows

12. Break up of the Black Monday demonstration in the Square. 8 February 1886

13. Demonstrators in St. James's Street outside the New University Club. 8 February 1886

continued up St. James' and into Piccadilly and later Oxford Street where £40 worth of damage was done to Peter Robinson's and £80 worth to Marshall & Snelgrove's. People were assaulted, carriages overturned, and the crowd's activities were relatively unhampered by the police. *The Times*, reporting on the events the following day, had this to say:[23]

> ". . . the West End was for a couple of hours in the hands of the Mob."

For the S.D.F. the immediate upshot of the events was that H. M. Hyndman, John Burns, H. H. Champion and John Williams were prosecuted for sedition. On 17 February they appeared at Bow Street to hear their charges and were released on bail (paid for by William Morris and E. B. Bax) until their trial at the Old Bailey on 8 April. After four days of hearings they were all found, much to their jubilation, not guilty and released.

As subsequent events were to show, the importance of the 8 February was not that a demonstration took place and some property was damaged, but lay in the strength of the middle-class reaction.

The Times leader gave the cue when describing the events the following day:[24]

> "The vagabondage of London, apparently associated by some mysterious sympathy, marched up Pall Mall."

And,

> ". . . the crowd continued under concealed leaders."

Provocative phrases; especially in the light of the growing middle-class fears of "the mob". The next day, a panic akin to that of 1848, encouraged by the presence of dense fog, swept the West End. The police advised the shopkeepers to keep their shops shuttered as they expected renewed attacks. Rumours of "the mob" converging again from all quarters spread like wildfire.[25] At any moment the shopkeepers expected to be attacked. The military were called out, but other than a small congregation of "roughs" that gathered in Trafalgar Square, little trouble transpired. The events of the day before produced a flood of correspondence to the newspapers, in this kind of moralising tone:[26]

> "I had a visit from my tailor this afternoon who came to apologise for not being able to let me have a suit I required this evening, as I intended to go abroad tomorrow morning. He explained that the man giving its finishing touches gave up work at 2.00 to join the demonstration."

Another, criticising the S.D.F. policy, wrote:[27]

> "Now it seems incomprehensible how men who have the credit of being astute members and thinkers of the labouring classes, and who take as their motto, 'Industry is the source or property' can at the same time recommend the shortening of hours of labour – i.e. compulsory idleness."

Ten hours was still the normal working day.

CLEARING THE SQUARE

The panic of 9 February was to pale against that of the following day. Confidence was at first slightly restored in the morning light, and some shops did reopen; but by midday the fog of the day before returned, as did "the disorderly classes" to Trafalgar Square. Rumours once more were rife. "Ten thousand were on the march from Deptford to London, destroying as they came",[28] according to a jeweller in Southwark. More serious was to be the message in a telegram from some residents in the Old Kent Road, to *The Times*:[29]

> "Fearful state all around here in South London. 30,000 men in Spa Road moving to Trafalgar Square. Send special messenger to Home Office to have police in fullest force with fullest military force also to save London."

This, and many other accounts, led to the closing of the banks, and special precautions were taken to ward off sudden attacks on Government buildings. Although most of the rumours were unfounded, and by the middle of the evening no large groups had actually been seen approaching from anywhere, several thousand people did gather in places waiting to join them. This fact, according to Steadman Jones, showed at least that the fear was not entirely unfounded.[30]

A large meeting did in fact take place in Cumberland Market close to Regent's Park on the 10th, but passed off peacefully. That it did so seems not to have been enough for the local police. For in a report to the Chief Commissioner a day later they recommended that all such meetings should be prohibited as it was clear to them that "the greater number of (demonstrators) whom it can at once be seen are bent on disorder whatever the ostensible object of their assembly be".[31]

For William Morris the scare was "the first skirmish of the Revolution".[32] But as many people, Engels among them, have pointed out then and since, a revolutionary situation did not exist;[33] it was not enough just to have raised the red flag ("the cosmopolitan emblem of universal destruction", as one paper put it).[34] A general fear of the poor, as was described earlier, also pervaded many of the letters that appeared in *The Times* in the ensuing days. One, written by a man who proudly stated he had been a special constable in 1848, read:[35]

> "As I passed the War Office entrance . . . a blind fiddler, led by a little girl, came by nearly in the middle of the road, playing some odd tune or other, when a young Guardsman, a sentry, stepped out and said in a commanding tone: 'You stop that noise,' or words to that effect, as well as I could hear. . . . I thought, there is a man of common sense and action. It was a little thing to stop at the time, but when the snowball which a child or a blind fiddler could set rolling at the top of the hill reaches the bottom, it has become in this country an immovable monster, in other countries a destroying avalanche."

Other letters were not so paranoid. Lord Brabazon pointed out that a gift of £1,000 was being used to provide employment in laying the new paving in Trafalgar Square. Perhaps the most constructive, in regard to the unemployed, was a letter from Nathaniel L. Cohen, saying that he had set up a "Labour Exchange" in Eltham and that others should follow his example.

So much for the reaction of the middle class. How did the Metropolitan Police see the affair? Certainly, it is their views which in the end were to be of importance. Fortunately for a researcher, an official enquiry into the police actions on 8 February was instituted,[36] largely, it should be added, in an attempt to find a scapegoat other than the Government in power.[37] The Committee of Inquiry comprised five M.P.s, including the one for Hampstead, Sir Henry Holland, whose seat the S.D.F. had unsuccessfully contested at the election in 1885, and C. T. Ritchie, M.P. for St. George's in the East End, an area the S.D.F. was to contest successfully in local elections in 1891.[38] The Committee met at the Home Office and took evidence from 15–20 February.

The evidence of the first day clearly pointed to the fact that the police expected clashes to develop between the S.D.F. and the Tory Free Traders, but had deliberately not wished to intervene. Although they had 563 policemen in the area, there were only 66 in the Square itself; this fact lends some weight to the often expressed opinion, for instance by Frederick Engels, at the time that the police wanted positively to encourage trouble.[39] The confusion over the sending of Police reinforcements to the Mall to protect the Palace, instead of to Pall Mall where the rioters were, seems to add to this suspicion. The police's instructions seemed to have been twofold: firstly, a small number were employed to keep the traffic moving around the Square; and secondly, the rest[40]

> "were collected round the Nelson Monument, the Superintendent having special instructions to protect the Monument from all damage by the mob."

The Committee were amazed, and rather critical of these instructions:

> "The condition of things described (police arrangements) to us as existing in Trafalgar Square upon the day in question is, under the circumstances, almost inconceivable."

The Chief Commissioner of Police, Sir Edmund Henderson's actions were met with equal incredulity:

> "The Chief Commissioner was in plain clothes, watching the proceedings, but not taking any direct command and issuing no instructions during the day. . . ."

Henderson in his evidence could find no excuse that could satisfy the Committee except that he did not have enough men, and that the "police are not to interfere with persons attending political demonstrations". (As has been remarked above, the police could only act on the obstruction clauses contained in the Police Acts. To the Committee this added to what they saw as a serious need for reform, both of the police and of the legislation that governed the Square.)

The Committee in its final report said nothing about improving the legislation, but did make a seven-point recommendation for reforming the police. The defects listed as needing reform were:

> "1. Insufficient number of officers of superior rank and education.
> 2. Want of a more efficient telegraphic system.
> 3. Absence of an adequate force of mounted police.
> 4. A defective chain of responsibility among the superior officers of the force.
> 5. A want of published police regulations for dealing with large meetings.
> 6. The position and duty of officers in charge of meetings.
> 7. Absence of a proper system of communication with the Home Office in the event of emergency."

On the day following the end of the enquiry the S.D.F. held a meeting in Hyde Park and this time the police were well prepared; 2,072 constables, 184 sergeants, 52 inspectors plus 52 mounted police from all three ranks were at hand. Besides this large civil force – it represented nearly one-fifth of the Metropolitan Police's strength – troops were made ready, as was a magistrate, in Chelsea, Knightsbridge, St. George's and Regent's Park Barracks.[41] The magistrate's job would be to accompany the troops to the disturbances and if need be read out aloud the appropriate dispersing clause of the 1715 Riot Act.

Reform of the police was insufficient for some. Queen Victoria, for instance, believed that "the Home Office was not strong enough".[42] In the event, however, only Sir Edmund Henderson resigned – much, it should be added, to the Queen's displeasure. Henderson may have lost his job, but every effort was made to ease his passage into retirement. He was given the maximum pension – although he retired early; a special banquet was given in his honour at Grosvenor House at which he received "a purse of £1,000" and a portrait of himself by a Royal Academician.[43] Rewards, although not quite so grand, were also forthcoming to the other policemen for their work on "Black Monday" as it had become called. One inspector received a gold watch and chain from a group of Bond Street tradesmen, while the ordinary constables who had "quelled the Oxford Street riot" received gifts paid for out of a fund supported by a hundred of that street's tradesmen.[44]

Sir Edmund Henderson had in fact been the Metropolitan Police's third Chief Commissioner; an appointment which, as was pointed out at the time, was a curious choice. Trained in the Royal Engineers, he had become in 1850 (at the early age of twenty-nine) Comptroller on Convicts in Western Australia, and remained there until 1863. From 1863–9 he was Chairman of Directors of Prisons and Surveyor General at the Home Office, a post he combined with that of Inspector General of Military Prisons. Not a background, it could be argued, that would best fit anyone as head of a civil force such as the Metropolitan Police.

Although there was no shortage of potential successors to Henderson from within the force itself (there were 400 possible contenders all told), a rank outsider, the young Sir Charles Warren, was chosen for the job by Gladstone's Home Secretary, Hugh Childers. As an officer in the Royal Engineers and an archaeologist of sufficient note to have been made a Fellow of the Royal Society on the strength of it in 1884, Warren's background seemed as unlikely a qualification for the job as Henderson's had been. His military experience was far from extensive; he had commanded the Diamond's Field Horse during the "Kafir War" 1877–8 and had been feasted as the "Saviour of Bechuanaland" on his return to England after separating the "natives from the Boers" in 1885. Such activities undoubtedly contributed to his standing, but for Childers two other points were of considerable importance. The first was that Warren was an ardent supporter of Gladstone and the Liberals (and had in fact stood unsuccessfully as a Liberal candidate in Sheffield in 1885).

Secondly, Warren had "proved himself"; for when Childers was Secretary of State for War in 1882, Warren had successfully carried out an important commission for him, that of establishing the fate of the British secret agent (and archaeologist) Edmund Palmer. Palmer, it will be remembered, had been sent by Gladstone to Egypt to "detach Arab tribes (with English gold) from the side of the Egyptian rebels" – the rebels were threatening the Suez Canal. Warren's conduct of the affair, especially the conviction of Palmer's murderers, had brought him considerable praise and publicity.

Warren's appointment was not welcomed by everyone; at least one paper thought he was more used to "dealing with barbarians than the inhabitants of London"; more usually, however, his moving into office was applauded. *The Times*, for instance, thought that he "possessed in no ordinary degree the qualities which would fit him for the post".[45] The *Pall Mall Gazette*, in a reference to the consistent Home Office interference that Henderson had had much difficulty coping with, pronounced Warren to be "of all others left to us . . . the most like General Gordon in conviction, in temper and impatience . . . of being meddled with".[46]

Despite criticism from both inside and outside the police it was generally hoped that the much needed reforms of police procedures would take place with (military) speed and precision.

Warren's publicly expressed views on the unemployed also seemed, to the anxious British middle class, to promise well for his ability to deal effectively with any further disturbances:[47]

> "We all know the history of Rome, that before it fell there were loafers and other bodies who did no work, who were fed by the state. The state first gave them bread, then meat twice a week, then oil, and afterwards gave the liquor free. Soon after that Rome fell, simply because it fed those who were doing nothing."

Fine words from someone who has been described as "a steadfast Christian soldier, fervent in spirit serving the Lord".[48] In the event his appointment did little, during the following year, to prevent large demonstrations from taking place; but it did ensure that those who had sufficient temerity to demonstrate were constantly harassed by police and the occasional appearance of the Life Guards. Many, like the one held on 9 November 1886, Lord Mayor's Day, were forbidden. Residents and shopkeepers of the neighbourhood petitioned unceasingly for the Square to be closed.

By the summer of 1887 there had been little improvement in the economic situation. As a consequence the already high levels of unemployment, especially among London's unskilled and casual workers, continued to rise unabated. For the casual poor their already brutalising conditions were further exacerbated, forcing hundreds of families to make their homes permanently on the street. Much to the growing anger of the middle classes this "camping out" was happening with alarming frequency *in their part of town.* In late July the Vestry of St. Martin's-in-the-Fields wrote in rather uncharitable tones to the Office of Works (with a copy to Sir Charles Warren) complaining of the[49]

> "Unseemly conduct of persons sleeping at night in Trafalgar Square and performing their ablutions in the morning in the basins of the fountains and also the littering of papers and other objects in the Square – by *the people infesting the place*" (my italics – R.M.).

A few days later Sir Charles Warren received another letter[50] on the same subject; but this time its tone was somewhat more sympathetic and less churlish than the one from the Vestrymen. The writer was a Mr. Cavanagh, at one time an inspector in the Metropolitan Police but more lately the Manager of the Oxford Music Hall.

In the letter Cavanagh explains how when he was returning home late one very wet night earlier that week he had come upon several large groups of people "huddled together" on St. Martin's steps, on seats in front of the National Gallery and in Trafalgar Square itself. So appalled was he by what he saw that he tackled a patrolling policeman for an explanation; only to find out that if the night had been dry he would have seen twice the number – in fact at least two hundred. On hearing this Cavanagh says that he resolved to return the next night to see for himself if the constable's statement was true. Sure enough, his letter continues, when he returned the next (and dry) night there was not "only 200 but more were there huddled together on the seats, on the stones round about the fountains and under the lions", making, he thought, "the most terrible sight of open-air human misery in Europe". The letter ends with an urgent request that the public should do what they could to "bring some comfort to these poor creatures, who, it may be in many cases from no fault of their own, have come to this!"

The local police, although they had the power under the Vagrancy Act to clear the Square, had been acting with moderation, caution and even sympathy towards the "nightly campers". The caution stemmed from the period of severe public criticism, some years before, when Sir Edmund Henderson had been extremely heavy-handed in his dealing with a similar problem. The sympathy, judging from police reports, was genuinely felt, particularly at the rank and file level of constables and sergeants.

The presence of the poor in their considerable numbers outraged the middle classes. Was not the "finest site in Europe" becoming a "foul camp for vagrants?"[51] In fact by September the police were getting exasperated with "the meddlesome persons and local busybodies" who assailed them with complaints and yet made no attempt to understand the causes of the problem (let alone to be constructive). For the police, as one of their memorada put it, "it is astonishing to note the orderly conduct of the persons using the Square at night, they appear to simply go there to rest."[52] They also fully understood why even in bad weather many people slept outside. As another memorandum circulated to all local police stations explained:[53]

> " . . . during the Pea and soft fruit season many poor and destitute seek casual work in Covent Garden in the early hours of the morning for small amounts of money they sort fruit and shell peas. They do this in order to have enough money to tide over the dreaded application to a workhouse."

Further to this, the memorandum continued, the people

> "preferred to sleep in the streets rather than go to the casual ward where they run the risk of being detained for three days against their will."

Although the newspapers published accounts or comments daily, and several important people were heard to be indignant, the majority were content to condemn the homeless and unemployed as "depraved and lazy" or to clear their consciences by dispensing charity at a distance.

For the S.D.F. the giving of charity was no answer, and at the end of September 1887 they began to organise the unemployed who assembled in the Square under the banner "Not Charity, But Work".

It was these first signs of an organised movement among the "inhabitants of the Square" that prompted Sir Charles Warren, against the advice of some of his officers, to invoke the relevant clauses in the Vagrancy Act in order to clear the Square. The Act, he said, was to be "enforced more in the spirit of charity than punishment". However, the carrying out of the order was not to be straightforward. For quite soon the daily use of the police began arousing considerable and unfavourable comment from the Press and some of the local inhabitants. This comment, needless to say, was no match for the powerful voices supporting the police's action. On 17 October, Sir Charles Warren gave orders for the clearing and temporary closure of the Square "for the safety of the

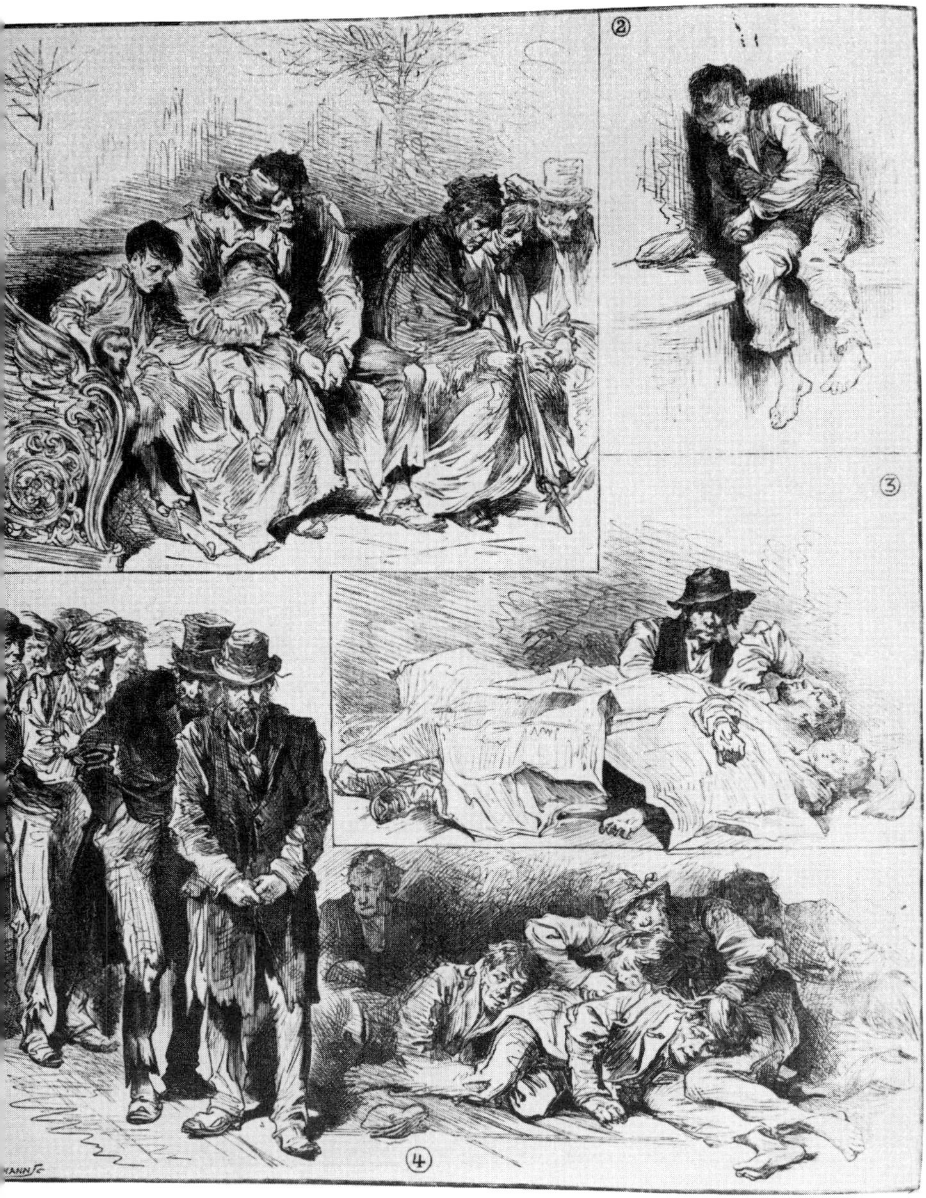

14. Sleeping out in London, Autumn 1887. (1) Thames Embankment (2) London Bridge (3) Trafalgar Square (4) Covent Garden

15. Bread and soup being handed out to the poor at 1 a.m. in the Square, 18 October 1887

16. Meetings and Demonstrations in London, Sunday, 23 October 1887. (1) Trafalgar Square (2) Clerkenwell Green (3) outside Westminster Abbey

Metropolis".[54] Although clear by day the homeless still came back at night and by the 26th a count revealed that the number had risen to four hundred. Up till this time the police had, for reasons noted above, been reticent to engage the help of the local Poor Law Union in providing the Square's homeless with a roof over their heads. Ironically enough, when finally on 26 October they changed this policy, it was only to find that the Strand Union had no vacant accommodation to offer.[55] With some difficulty the police made arrangements, at the Union's request, with many "common lodging houses" in the district. From late October until 9 November between 350 and 450 tickets for such lodgings were issued every night in the Square. Between 11 and 18 November when, as we shall see, everyone was kept out of the Square, the Strand Union continued to issue about 400 tickets a night from outside St. Martin's Church.[56]

The problem of what to do about the whole affair even taxed the mind of the Prime Minister, Lord Salisbury, and he wrote to Queen Victoria suggesting a solution:[57]

> "The difficulty of keeping Trafalgar Square clear is that the police have no legal right to disperse crowds so long as they are orderly. It is your Majesty's property. Would your Majesty object to its being railed in, if the Cabinet advise that step? It would be quite legal.
>
> "I have just walked through Trafalgar Square. There was no sign of disorder; only about 300 dirty people clustering around the column. The streets were in no way obstructed or disturbed, and everything was going on as usual."

Queen Victoria replied with a cypher telegram from Balmoral on 28 October:

> "Whatever would tend to stop these proceedings will have my entire approval. Glad all quiet today. . . ."

No railings were put up, and the police, after Warren's temporary ban was lifted, continued to harass meetings. James Allman recounts what happened at one:[58]

> "The processionists were proceeding towards Stepney Green via Strand and City, when opposite Charing Cross Station, the police suddenly pounced upon them, seized and smashed up their black banners and dispersed the procession."

Sadly, the unemployed did not see that it was Sir Charles Warren's deliberate intention to leave their red flag, for it was their emblem, and as such would be used again, and his tactic was to provoke them into "an insurrectionary temper".[59]

Complaints continued to flood into Sir Charles Warren's office, and the Office of Works.[60] They were unambivalent; the meetings must be stopped. The Royal College of Physicians (like most of the other local complainants) was "in fear of the mob attacking their valuable property". For the college the events outside their windows were however more sinister than just the prelude to theft; it was in their eyes a "chronic revolution which (had) its centre just outside our building".[61]

Sir Charles Warren, too, was greatly concerned about what he saw as a sinister turn in the events of the last few weeks of October. On 31 October he wrote a long letter to Stuart Wortley, an old political adversary (Wortley had won the Hallam Sheffield seat for the Tories in a straight fight with Warren in the 1886 election) and was now Under Secretary of State at the Home Office. The position in the Square, Warren pointed out, was becoming increasingly difficult to deal with, for it seemed that although at first the demonstrations were disorganised they were now[62]

> "beginning to obtain a certain amount of cohesion from constant practice, the roughs are beginning to find out what they can do with impunity . . ."

The cohesion was possible, Warren continued, as it

> "is now the policy of the mob leaders to settle in private their tactics for each day on how to elude the police . . ."

But for the Chief Commissioner the most disgusting thing about the leaders was that

> "by some private signal they appear to be able to get together now to the number of two or three thousand in two or three minutes about the region of Charing Cross."

Besides the meetings in Trafalgar Square and Hyde Park, Warren's and the Home Office's minds were very agitated by the problems of what to do about the "wandering bands" who were "advertising themselves (i.e. forcing their grievances on non-employment on the attention of the well-to-do)". Regretfully for them the Law Officers could see no way within the then present law by which such activities could be stopped.

In the first week of November, meetings were held daily until the 4th, when Warren instructed that the Square be cleared and that his men arrest all speakers using "threatening or dangerous language",[63] and this time the red flag was taken.

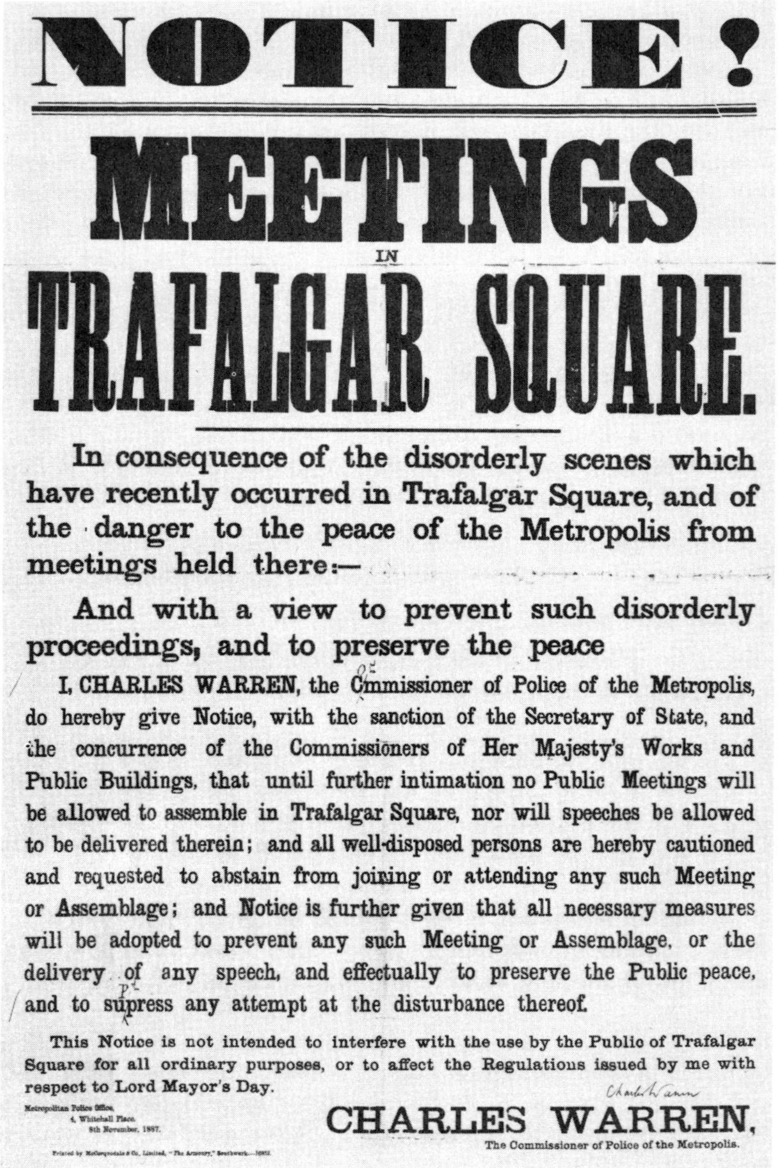

NOTICE!

MEETINGS

IN

TRAFALGAR SQUARE.

In consequence of the disorderly scenes which have recently occurred in Trafalgar Square, and of the danger to the peace of the Metropolis from meetings held there:—

And with a view to prevent such disorderly proceedings, and to preserve the peace

I, CHARLES WARREN, the Commissioner of Police of the Metropolis, do hereby give Notice, with the sanction of the Secretary of State, and the concurrence of the Commissioners of Her Majesty's Works and Public Buildings, that until further intimation no Public Meetings will be allowed to assemble in Trafalgar Square, nor will speeches be allowed to be delivered therein; and all well-disposed persons are hereby cautioned and requested to abstain from joining or attending any such Meeting or Assemblage; and Notice is further given that all necessary measures will be adopted to prevent any such Meeting or Assemblage, or the delivery of any speech, and effectually to preserve the Public peace, and to supress any attempt at the disturbance thereof.

This Notice is not intended to interfere with the use by the Public of Trafalgar Square for all ordinary purposes, or to affect the Regulations issued by me with respect to Lord Mayor's Day.

Metropolitan Police Office,
4, Whitehall Place.
8th November, 1887.

CHARLES WARREN,
The Commissioner of Police of the Metropolis.

17. Notice prohibiting meetings in the Square, 8 November 1887

Three days later, after consultation with the Home Office, the War Office and the Office of Works, Sir Charles Warren issued a Police Order prohibiting meetings or gatherings in the Square altogether. Notices of the Order were pasted up before dawn all over London the following day. As in 1848 the stage seemed set for a final battle.

BLOODY SUNDAY

Outraged by this denial of the freedom of speech, groups such as the Metropolitan Radical Association and the newly formed Law and Liberty League (among the aims of which was the establishment of popular control of the police) came together and drew up hasty plans for joining the demonstration already organised to protest against the imprisonment of William O'Brien in Ireland. It was to be on Sunday, 13 November 1887. Their intention was to make a demonstration in the name of freedom of assembly. Meanwhile on 10 November William Sanders (later to become an M.P.), of the English Land Restoration League, delivered a letter to the Chief Commissioner stating that he intended to hold "a peaceful meeting" to test the legality of the Notice. He was arrested in the Square on the next day and charged at Bow Street; the Treasury Solicitor later undertook the prosecution, so important did the whole affair seem to the ruling class. W. T. Stead, one of the initiators of the Law and Liberty League (and the highly successful editor of the *Pall Mall Gazette*), clearly articulated the principles at stake when he wrote:[64]

> "We have reached a crisis in the political history of the metropolis when something must be done, and that at once, to defend the legal liberties of the Londoner from the insolent usurpations of Scotland Yard. . . . There is no means of defending popular liberties as efficacious as that of resisting at first every encroachment upon their exercise."

The Pall Mall Gazette was in the minority, however. Most of the inhabitants of the West End fully agreed with the ban and with the sentiments expressed in the leading article in *The Times* of 11 November:

> "The notice merely forbids public meetings in one spot in the metropolis, and that the central spot whence the principal thoroughfares radiate, and which is situated close to the House of Parliament, the offices of Government, the Royal residences, the clubs and the richest shops which are to be found. To say that the prohibition to demonstrate in this single piece of ground places the right of public meetings in jeopardy is an absurdity which needs no pains to refute."

18. Police in readiness on the south side of the Square, 13 November 1887

19. The meeting at Clerkenwell Green. The woman addressing the crowd is Annie Besant: the bearded figure beside her, William Morris. 13 November 1887

On the same day also appeared the report of a speech given by Sir Charles Warren at Fishmongers Hall, in which he told his audience of his confidence in dealing with the results of the ban. He did not, he said, believe that[65]

> "there is any body of men in this country or in any other equal to our metropolitan police force for honesty, bravery, truth or any other good quality."

For all his faith in these good qualities, Warren took further precautions against them being put to the test when on 12 November he issued another notice making the following announcement:[66]

> "In exercise of the power vested in me and the Act 2 and 3 Vict. c. 47 I hereby make the following regulation – No organised procession shall be allowed to approach Trafalgar Square on Sunday 13 inst."

20. The police attacking demonstrators in St. Martin's Lane, 13 November 1887

21. Demonstrators from South London crossing Westminster Bridge, 13 November 1887

22. The police attacking demonstrators in the Haymarket, 13 November 1887

23. Police charging demonstrators in the Square, 13 November 1887

24. The arrival of the Magistrate, Mr. Marsham, accompanied by the Life Guards, 13 November 1887

25. The Life Guards parading the Square, 13 November 1887

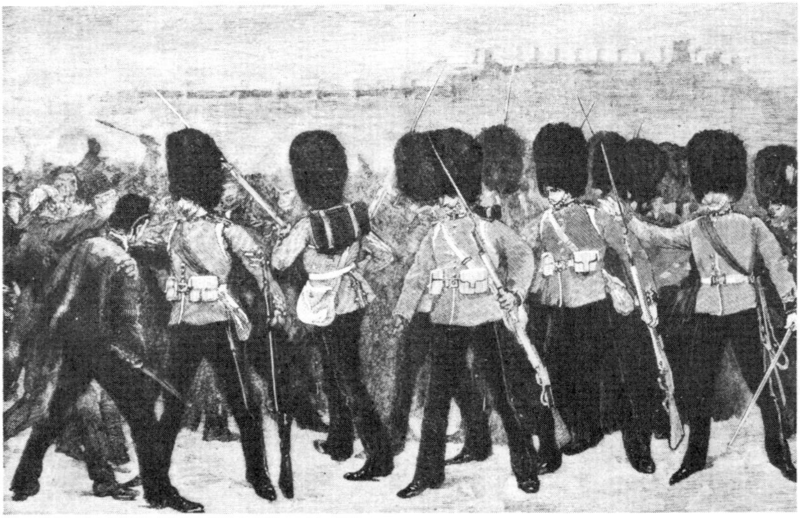

26. The Grenadier Guards attacking demonstrators, 13 November 1887

27. Special constables signing on at the Albany Street Police Station, late November 1887

Just to make doubly sure the order would not be flouted, 2,500 policemen closed off thirty streets to all but buses and cabs, within a mile's radius of the Square.

In the Square itself there was a picket of police by nine o'clock, by eleven it was surrounded, and by just after twelve 1,500 policemen were in position: 100 stood in single file outside the parapets on each side of the Square; 120 stood in double file inside; at the head of the steps at each corner of the north side 100 stood in fours, with an additional fifty for each close by; across the south side 750 stood four deep; 60 mounted police patrolled all sides of the Square in pairs.[67]

Undaunted by this show of "terrible and implacable force" the thousands of demonstrators began assembling at the several starting places all over the city.

At Clerkenwell Green a large crowd of respectable artisans had gathered to hear resolutions and speeches by Annie Besant, Edward Aveling and William Morris. The speeches were of a "determined character", with considerable emphasis, especially by Morris, on the duty of everyone to resist "by every means in their power" any invasion of the rights of free speech. Loud applause accompanied his remarks that in pursuit of their aims it was the business of the day to get to the Square. He himself intended to do so "whatever the consequences might be". The procession some 5,000 strong formed up and, led by the band of East Finsbury Radical Club and St. Peter's, Clerkenwell, and a host of red banners, moved off slowly westward along Clerkenwell Road and Theobalds Road into Bloomsbury. Before the marchers had moved off Morris had had several words of caution to say about the possible reaction of the police; but when the front of the long demonstration turned south into St. Martin's Lane even his worst expectations were surpassed. Out of the side streets rode a detachment of mounted police and plunged wielding staves into the orderly lines of demonstrators. As the people scattered, many fighting back, a large force of foot police, also armed with staves, "struck right and left like what they were, soldiers attacking any enemy". Later Morris was to confess that he "was astounded at the rapidity of the thing and the ease with which military organisation got its victory". The contingents from Peckham, Bermondsey, Deptford and Battersea, all places south of the river, met up at Westminster Bridge and with linked arms marched towards Parliament Square. As they passed under Big Ben the police, headed by mounted constables again wielding their staves, charged into the orderly ranks of demonstrators; many of the marchers fought back as their banners and flags were ripped from their hands, but, as elsewhere, the superior force and organisation of the police forced most into a hasty retreat.[68]

Not more than a mile away in the Haymarket the police were meting out the same treatment to the contingent that had marched peacefully from Notting Hill and Paddington. Although by the middle of the afternoon the organised ranks of the demonstrators had been broken one by one as they came into conflict with Sir Charles Warren's outer cordon; this did not, of course, prevent individuals and small groups from continuing on separately. On arriving at the Square these "helpless units", as William Morris called them, faced an impenetrable mass of 1,500 police. Here, too, the mounted police repeatedly charged upon people on the roads and pavements alike and, as before, the demonstators defended themselves.[69]

At four o'clock "an excited movement was visible among the crowd", for out of the Strand entrance to the Square came a group of four hundred men headed by the radical Socialist M.P. for N.W. Lanark, Cunninghame Graham, and the "Socialist" from Battersea, John Burns. Graham's and Burns' resolute intention was to break through the police cordon and get into the centre of the Square. Their direct assault met with a brutal rebuttal. Both were immediately arrested and Cunninghame Graham in particular was beaten, for no apparent reason, mercilessly round the head with truncheons. Some days later his wife said of the event,[70]

> "Neither my husband nor Burns, who are both strong and active men, resisted in any way, and stood perfectly quiet to be murdered."

This was confirmed by an independent eye witness, Sir E. Reed, M.P., who saw the events from his window in Morley's Hotel.

As Burns and Cunninghame Graham were being dragged away a mixture of cheers and boos went up in the crowd at the top of Whitehall; the 1st Life Guard (200 mounted troopers) were approaching. *The Times* waxed lyrical in describing their progress up Whitehall[71]

> " . . . the prancing horses, the scarlet uniforms, the burnished breast plates and the polished helmets, a long moving streak of brilliant colour among the dense mass of police and of people. It was a striking sight."

At their head rode their Commander, Colonel Talbot, and at his side Mr. Marsham, "a sort of country-looking imbecile", a Metropolitan Police Magistrate from Greenwich who was to read the riot act. As the troops trotted slowly round the police cordon in wide formation, then dividing into two and riding in opposite directions, the 2nd Life Guards (150 mounted troopers) appeared in the middle of Whitehall but did not enter the Square.

Although tightly hemmed in between police and soldiers, the crowd continued to shout abuse at both. When at ten to five a detachment of Grenadier Guards appeared from behind the National Gallery with rifles on their shoulders, their bayonets fixed and twenty rounds of ball cartridge in their pockets cries of "We want free speech" and "Britain shall not be ruled by leaden bayonets" arose from the crowd.[72] As the Grenadiers got in front of the National Gallery they opened their lines and drove the crowd off the road and into the police. Some of those demonstrators who resisted found themselves looking at the point of a bayonet, while others received punches to the face or blows to shins with rifle butts. This show of force by the police and the military could find no match in the demonstrators and by the early evening most of them had made their weary way home. By 7.15 only the regular to and fro of the patrolling Life Guards disturbed the emptiness of the Square.

During the whole day at least 200 people were treated at the local hospitals for injuries received by batons or horses' hooves. Two of them in fact, a W. B. Curner and a man called Cornell, were to die within a couple of weeks as a result of their injuries. Another victim, a man called Harrison, died after a long illness.

For the radicals and socialists it had been a black day – but one which, despite their defeat, had effected a new unity within their ranks. As Morris was to write:[73]

> "The mark is off now, and the real meaning of all the petty persecutions of open air meetings is as clear as may be. No more humbug need be talked about obstruction. . . . The very Radicals have been taught that slaves have no rights."

Needless to say, the middle class saw it all in a very different light:[74]

> "What Sir Charles Warren did yesterday was to crush a deliberate attempt to set aside the elementary safeguards of civilised society and to terrorise London by placing control of the streets in the hands of the criminal classes."

The Times also commented in the same vein the subsequent day:[75]

> "All who have watched the meeting are convinced that they have not been held in the interests of the unemployed – but under the auspices of the red flag. The emblem of communism arouses no fear in the minds of Londoners."

No fear indeed! Writing on the events that followed that Sunday – "Bloody Sunday", as it was to be called – John Burgess stated:[76]

> "For more than a fortnight after Bloody Sunday, Trafalgar Square was in a state of siege. On Friday, the 18th, thousands of special constables were sworn in. On Sunday the 20th the Square was garrisoned by 5,000 constables, 20,000 specials, 1,300 specials in reserve, of whom 500 were posted in Palace Yard and the remainder in Marlborough House."

As in 1848 the local rich and well-to-do offered the police inducements in an attempt to curry police favour (protection), so affeared were they of the "mob"; most of the inducements were in the form of "refreshments". The usual form was for a person to open his house or lay something on in a local church hall. Failing that a large hamper was left at the local police station. One man in Eaton Square sent sixty meat pies to Scotland Yard, another "a van load of cordials"; but perhaps the most extraordinary example was the person who spent £240 in one day feeding 1,100 men.[77]

So many in fact were the offers of help to the police that on 20 November Sir Charles Warren was forced to write a letter of thanks to the press.

The presence of a large number of Special Constables in the Square was, of course, not wholly unnconnected with further fears which the middle class, throughout London, entertained; a police memorandum explains,[78]

> "The concentration of a large number of police in the neighbourhood of Trafalgar Square for the purpose of preventing meetings taking place and preserving order necessarily left the suburbs to a great extent unprotected and the public had become alarmed for the safety of their persons and property as disorder had attracted a large body of men addicted to crime and rowdyism who it was feared would visit the suburbs of the metropolis with evil intent. The inability of the police to sufficiently protect the whole of the metropolis under these extraordinary conditions necessitated the formation of a force of Special Constables, to be drawn from the ranks of law abiding citizens. . . ."

Several ways were used to recruit the Specials, none particularly successful. No difficulty was encountered in obtaining the quantity, it was the quality that seemed the problem. Although the notice that advertised for the Specials had pointed out that "the C.I.D. would attend Court (where Specials were sworn in under 1 & 2 Will. IV, c. 41) to point out objectionable characters", the general feeling among the police was that this "promiscuous" method left much to be desired.[79]

During the later part of November and in December the police began leaving application forms at houses of "suitable persons" (lists having been drawn up by the local Divisional Inspector) or "leaving forms at

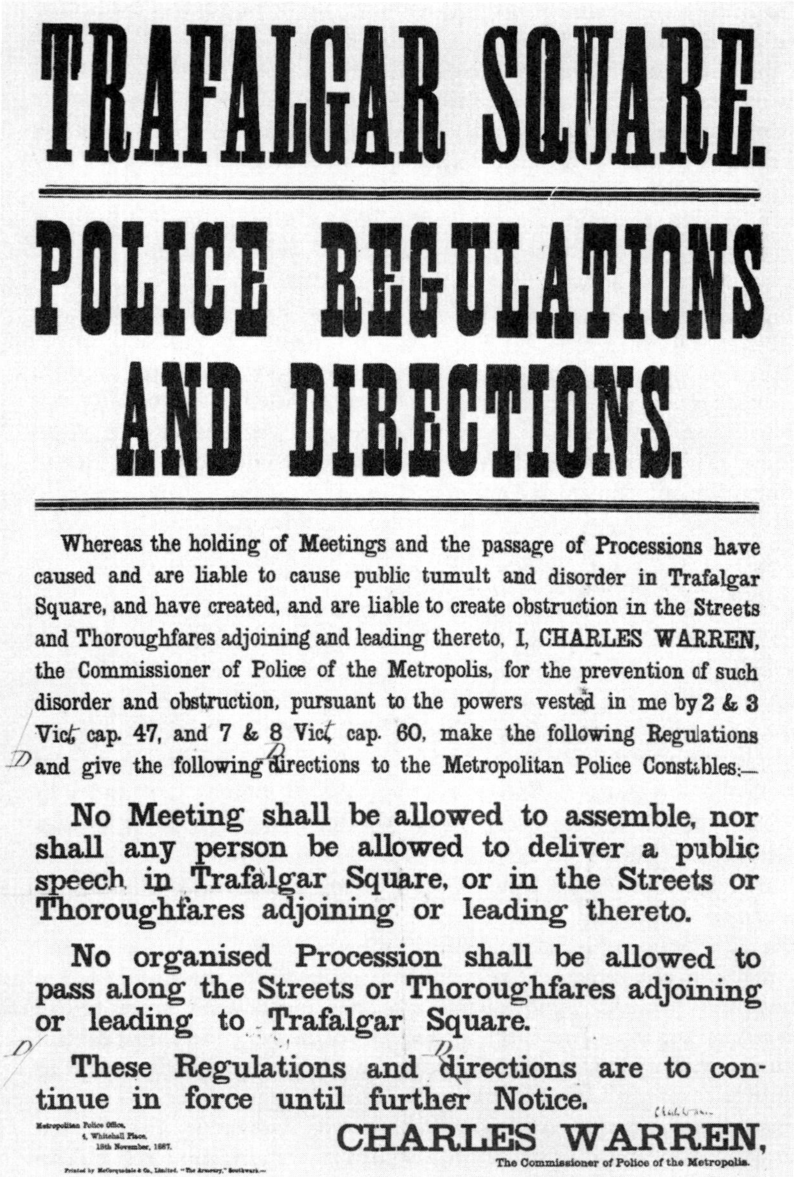

TRAFALGAR SQUARE.

POLICE REGULATIONS AND DIRECTIONS.

Whereas the holding of Meetings and the passage of Processions have caused and are liable to cause public tumult and disorder in Trafalgar Square, and have created, and are liable to create obstruction in the Streets and Thoroughfares adjoining and leading thereto, I, CHARLES WARREN, the Commissioner of Police of the Metropolis, for the prevention of such disorder and obstruction, pursuant to the powers vested in me by 2 & 3 Vict. cap. 47, and 7 & 8 Vict. cap. 60, make the following Regulations and give the following directions to the Metropolitan Police Constables:—

No Meeting shall be allowed to assemble, nor shall any person be allowed to deliver a public speech in Trafalgar Square, or in the Streets or Thoroughfares adjoining or leading thereto.

No organised Procession shall be allowed to pass along the Streets or Thoroughfares adjoining or leading to Trafalgar Square.

These Regulations and directions are to continue in force until further Notice.

Metropolitan Police Office,
4, Whitehall Place,
18th November, 1887.

CHARLES WARREN,
The Commissioner of Police of the Metropolis.

Printed by McCorquodale & Co., Limited, "The Armoury," Southwark.—

28. Notice prohibiting meetings in the Square, 18 November 1887

some of the large places of business and requesting the head of the firm to hand it to employees".[80]

Quality or not, within two days of the first appeal many thousands of "law abiding citizens" were receiving instruction (on the parade grounds of Wellington, St. George's and Knightsbridge Barracks) in how to march and counter march, how to wield a stave and undoubtedly how to identify Socialists and Radicals.

Sunday, 20 November, two days after Sir Charles issued another notice, was to be their first big day out; 2,000 were posted to Trafalgar Square by one o'clock, 1,000 to St. James' Park an hour later, and a further 2,000 were evenly distributed to Russell Square, Lancaster Gate, Hanover Gardens, Berkeley Square, Grosvenor Square and Great Cumberland Place. All this plus a considerable show of both regular foot and horse police just in case there was another attempt by the Radicals and Socialists to repeat the events of the previous weekend. In fact, as the police well knew, these many groups were holding a peaceful "indignation" meeting in Hyde Park.

THE DEATH OF ALFRED LINNELL

After the meeting was over, many, when wandering back home, went via Trafalgar Square, just to see if Sir Charles Warren's display of strength was really as great as rumour had it. As the crowds gathered the mounted police began plunging through them "in a fashion with which London is now so familiar". During one of these "wild charges", which a witness later described as though the police "were trying to imitate the heroes of Balaclava", a young, radical law-writer, Alfred Linnell, fell and was trampled on by a police horse. With his thigh smashed, Linnell "was carried groaning in his agony across the turbulent eddying flood of human life that surged round the Square" to Charing Cross Hospital where he died on 3 December.

Linnell's death was a considerable embarrassment to the police and they made several attempts to explain it away and even hush it up. At the inquest into the death, contradictory evidence caused the coroner to call for a second *post mortem*. This had the effect of delaying the public funeral that was arranged for Sunday, 11 December. It also enabled the police to attempt to discredit Linnell's character. When eventually the inquest was resumed the jury returned an open verdict. The date finally fixed for the funeral was Sunday, 18 December. It was arranged that the hearse should start from the place in the Square where Linnell fell, but at the last minute Sir Charles Warren issued a new decree "forbidding even a funeral cortege to pass the Square or any of the streets adjoining". About this decree Morris bitterly wrote:

> "The Square is a place where the police may kill a man with impunity. It is no longer a place from which we may bury our dead."

Of Sir Charles Warren's actions and those of the Tories over the last few months, Morris saw them for what they were, an unbridled "progress towards despotism" making London for the working class "nothing more than a prison".[81]

However, the funeral did take place and, despite drizzling rain, tens of thousands of people – Socialists, Radicals and Irish – joined its cortege and lined the streets to Bow Cemetery where Linnell was to be interred. The hearse was draped with the Irish, Socialist and Radical flags and a large shield on the front proclaimed the single words "KILLED IN TRAFALGAR SQUARE": beside it walked the six pall-bearers, Annie Besant, Herbert Burrows, Cunninghame Graham, William Morris, Frank Smith of the Salvation Army, and W. T. Stead. At the graveside the crowd was addressed in the failing light by several speakers, including Morris who concluded his passionate but simple speech with a word of caution by begging all present:[82]

> "to do all their best to preserve order in getting to their homes because their enemies would be only too glad to throw a blot upon that most successful celebration,"

for tomorrow they should begin to "organise for the purpose of seeing that such things" as Linnell's death did not happen again. The whole moving ceremony was brought to a close by the crowd singing a "Death Song". The song with words by William Morris and music by Malcolm Lawson appeared on the back pages of a penny pamphlet that had been sold to raise money for Linnell's orphans. On the front page of the pamphlet was a design by Walter Crane showing in unmistakable terms the real significance of Linnell's death.

The attitude of the ruling class during the whole affair can best be summed up by a remark in *The Times*[83]

> "The mounted police were on the spot in the execution of their duties, while LINNELL, to put the matter on the lowest ground, was not."

Charles Bradlaugh, M.P., joined with Morris and other radicals in challenging the legality of Sir Charles Warren's ban on demonstrations

SOLD FOR THE BENEFIT OF LINNELL'S ORPHANS.

ALFRED LINNELL

Killed in Trafalgar Square,

NOVEMBER 20, 1887.

A DEATH SONG,

BY MR. W. MORRIS.

Memorial Design by Mr. Walter Crane.

PRICE ONE PENNY.

29. Walter Crane's design for William Morris's "A Death Song" for Alfred Linnell, December 1887

and processions, especially the one issued on 18 November. This had read:[84]

> "No meeting shall be allowed to assemble or any person allowed to deliver a public speech in Trafalgar Square or in the streets or thoroughfares adjoining it. . . . No organised procession shall be allowed to pass along the streets or thoroughfare adjoining or leading to it. . . . These regulations and directions are to continue until further notice."

The radical group in itself was small in number, and the much needed support from the Liberal Party – then in opposition – was slow to materialise. Several individuals had protested about the ban, but the leader, Gladstone, did little more than urge restraint until a Court ruling on the ban had been established. Constant lobbying by the Radicals throughout the winter months finally persuaded the Liberals openly to challenge the legality of Warren's actions in a debate in the House of Commons at the beginning of March 1888.[85]

PARLIAMENT DEBATES THE RIGHT OF ASSEMBLY

Sir Charles Russell (Liberal M.P. for Hackney South), opening for the Opposition, put the motion

> "That having regard to the importance of preserving and protecting the right of open air meetings for Her Majesty's subjects in the Metropolis and with a view to preventing ill will and disorder, it is desirable that an enquiry should be instituted by a committee of this House into the conditions subject to which such meetings may be held and the limits of the right of interference therewith by the Executive Government."

Sir Charles went on to ask the House to remember some pertinent facts about the then status of the Square and the recent events that had been associated with it. Firstly, he pointed out, if London had been a self-governing community Sir Charles Warren's actions could hardly have arisen. Secondly, the Square was in fact "a no-man's-land", as it did not come within the jurisdiction of the Royal Parks Act of 1872. Thirdly, considering that the Square was "created by public money for public accommodation" (nearly £$\frac{3}{4}$ million plus interest, it will be remembered), the 1844 Act was wrong in assuming that it belonged to the Crown; it in fact belonged to the public. His fourth and final point was a more direct reminder to the Home Secretary, Henry Matthews, that the 1844 Act was in fact a statute for *regulating*, not *preventing*, processions or meetings. In conclusion, Sir Charles remarked (in a tone not likely to endear him to the ranks seated in the Tory benches), that "the right of public meeting has helped form public opinion; it has given voice to public discontent; and I say that public discontent, even if it be unreasonable, ought to have a voice. It has quickened the action of the legislature – aye, and its action has quickened and roused the conscience of Governments."

In reply, Henry Matthews paraded many an old Tory argument about the dangers of seditious speeches, mobs and the substantial danger to the police. In his mind, Sir Charles Russell's argument on the ownership of the Square was a little academic; the Square was held in trust by the Queen, and that, in his view, was that. Consequently, he said, he had acted within the law; and by way of confirmation, as though to push the principle home, declared that

"a meeting convened for the most decorous, prudish, and regular object in the world, conducted the most perfect order, is not unlawful, it it true; but it cannot lawfully come and be held in my garden if I say it is not to be held there".

R. T. Reid, the man who was later to become Gladstone's Solicitor General, speaking next, must have voiced the feelings of many when he caustically remarked of Matthews's speech that it

"had been little less than the funeral oration of the right of the public to meet in the open air in the Metropolis".

Apart from insisting that the Square was private property, the Tories could do little but hurl abuse at both the Liberals and the Radicals. The Attorney General, Sir Richard Webster, extracted the maximum innuendo in quoting to the House the words attributed to John Burns, who on leaving prison was alleged to have said that "Trafalgar Square (was) their revolutionary Square; Pentonville their Bastille". The Government, he concluded, was correct to act as they had done.

Another Tory speaker, A. A. Bauman, M.P. for Peckham, trotted out another allusion to the French Revolution when he claimed that

"the minority who wished to turn Trafalgar Square into a Jacobin Club was a very small minority, and not a very respectable minority at that".

Yet another Tory averred that Trafalgar Square had become a meeting place because "it was in the middle of clubs and plate glass"; another, that it had become unsafe for any woman or child to pass through Trafalgar Square for it had become "the fashion for all that was turbulent, all that was criminal, all that was dangerous in London to congregate in Trafalgar

Square" and afterwards "to disperse themselves through the adjacent streets with the view to terrorising the peaceful inhabitants of the West of London". Newspaper reports after Bloody Sunday had been couched in similar tones.

> "Here and there a group of rough men discussed the events of the preceding Sunday in a snarling tone" (the vocabulary of animals in references to the working class was a common feature of much nineteenth-century reportage, especially in the Tory press).[86]

Cunninghame Graham, on the other hand, remarked bitterly that

> "it was bad taste of the people of London to parade their insolent starvation in the face of the rich and trading portions of the town. They should have starved in their garrets, as he had no doubt members of Her Majesty's Government and most of the upper classes would have wished them to do".

Although the debate enabled the Liberals and Radicals to give the Tories as good as they got by way of abuse, it more importantly gave them the opportunity to give notice of a private members' Bill soon to be presented. James Stuart, M.P. for Shoreditch Hoxton, and five fellow East London M.P.s were preparing a Bill that would provide in their minds proper protection of the Square as a forum for public meetings. The Bill, reprinted in full in Appendix 4A plus Cunninghame Graham's one (reprinted also in Appendix 4B) was finally thrown out – after its second reading had been deferred no less than ten times.[87] Cunninghame Graham's suffered a similar fate, after eight deferrals.[88] James Stuart, however, did not give up, and presented an amended version the following February; but that too failed, at its second reading.[89]

As could be expected, the debate did little to persuade the Tories to change their mind; the Noes to the motion had a majority of 92. The Tories' collective mind had also not been altered by the many attempts in the Courts to challenge the ban. Two of these are important here: the first, the defence of Cunninghame Graham after his arrest on Bloody Sunday by H. H. Asquith; the second, the action brought by E. D. Lewis against Sir Charles Warren and Henry Matthews for using violence and intimidation and for the common law misdemeanour of public nuisance.

H. H. Asquith's choice as defending counsel by Cunninghame Graham was guided more by political than legal strategy. Asquith was a well-known Liberal M.P. His defence failed, and Cunninghame Graham was sentenced to three months' imprisonment. (This was not, however, the last Asquith was to hear of the events of November 1887, as we shall see.) E. D. Lewis' action failed also, but in so doing he demonstrated how a frontal assault on the Courts produced nothing other than a confirmation of the existing Tory policy.[90] Not even the departure in November 1888 of Sir Charles Warren as Metropolitan Police Commissioner succeeded in changing the Government's policy, for Henry Matthews still remained Home Secretary.[91] When the question of the ban was raised again on 20 June 1890 in the House of Commons, Matthews confirmed that the ban of 18 November 1887 remained fully in force.

The situation seemed to have reached an impasse; until, that is, Lord Salisbury's Tory Government suffered defeat at the hands of the Liberals at the General Election in August 1892. Under the new Government the portfolio of Home Secretary was to be taken up by none other than Herbert Henry Asquith. Within two days of Asquith's taking office, the issue of the ban on meetings in Trafalgar Square was being raised in the Press. William Sanders, the Radical M.P. for Streatham, sent him a letter requesting that he do something quickly about the matter. Seeing an opportunity to test the new Liberal Government, the Metropolitan Radical Federation also proposed to hold a meeting in November to commemorate the fifth anniversary of Bloody Sunday.

At first Asquith considered approaching Gladstone for advice on what to do; later, perhaps more cunningly, he sent a barrister friend, W. H. Eldridge, to sound out opinion from the inhabitants and tradespeople in the area of Trafalgar Square (as well as the separate Radical groups) as to whether some compromise solution could be found that would be acceptable to parties both inside and outside Government. The compromise he envisaged, that of a limited right of meeting, was in his opinion the only possible solution, as a total removal of the ban would undermine his hope of a Government of "responsibility and firmness".

At a meeting on 19 October at the Home Office, armed with Eldridge's intelligence that such a compromise would be acceptable to all except the S.D.F., Asquith met a deputation of the Metropolitan Radical Federation and announced his solution – a somewhat modified version of James Stuart's suggested Regulations of three years before. Tragically, as history would have it, James Stuart's Bill never itself became an *Act* – the Liberals, after all, once in power had to retain a few cards up their sleeve to deal with the threat of a burgeoning socialist movement.

Despite the reservations that the Metropolitan Radical Federation may have had on this point, they accepted the compromise, and ten days later, George Shaw-Lefevre, First Commissioner of Her Majesty's Office of Works, issued the first of the Trafalgar Square Regulations (see Appendix

30. The Fifth Anniversary of Bloody Sunday demonstration in the Square, 12 November 1892

4E). The general opinion was that Asquith had acted with "moderation and commonsense".

However, the Tories did not give up easily. In November 1893, using a recent Anarchist demonstration as an excuse, they attempted in a debate in the House of Commons to get Asquith to revoke the Regulations. Asquith fiercely defended his actions and refused to be drawn, despite the fact that during the demonstration an effigy of him had been hanged: an action, he thought, "a little lacking in taste and still more lacking in a sense of humour". The few Socialists in the House also came to the Government's aid. John Burns, now Independent Labour M.P. for Battersea, roundly attacked the Tories for forcing a debate in the first place. In his mind there was no doubt at all that the Tories' real motive was a "desire to fetter the right of public meeting and freedom of discussion" as they had between 1887 and 1892. It was his hope that the House would never countenance such a state of affairs again.

Although the debate concluded in a formal defeat for the Tories' motion, the forces of reaction did not, in retrospect, leave the House totally emptyhanded. It could be argued that without the debate Asquith would never have quite so precisely put the ruling class view on the matter of the Square – the 1892 Regulations notwithstanding. In a reference to the events of 12 November, the Home Secretary said that he regarded these as the [92]

> "outpourings of a very foolish and very ignorant people (and) as having, at any rate, this advantage – that to use a vulgar expression, 'they let off steam' and act as a kind of safety valve to feelings and opinions which are only dangerous as long as they are held in suppression and not properly looked after. . . ."

In the next chapter it will be shown how this view was to become the touchstone for all subsequent Home Secretaries, of whatever political persuasion, in the matter of the Square and its use as a place of demonstration.

Notes to Chapter 7

1. *The Times*, November 1887.
2. 7 and 8 Vic. c. 60: An Act to provide for the Care and Preservation of Trafalgar Square in the City of Westminster.
3. 10 Geo. IV, c. 44 and 2 and 3 Vic. c. 47.
4. *The Times*, 29 June 1855.

5. *Report on the Alleged Disturbances of the Public Peace in Hyde Park on Sunday 1 July 1855, P.P. 1856. XXIII. I.*
6. *ibid.*, p. 71.
7. As with the 1855 meeting several people considered the issuing of such "preventive orders" as having no legal standing.
8. G. M. Trevelyan, *John Bright* (London 1925), p. 82.
9. *PRO WO. 30/81, 11–1 anon.* Barracks in London, memorandum submitted to the Military Secretary 16 July 1875.
10. *ibid.*, Minute paper, dated 28 March 1973.
11. Sir John Burgoyne, *Military Opinions* (London 1800), p. 386.
12. *The Times*, 1 March 1876.
13. Winston Churchill, *Lord Randolph Churchill* (London 1906) vol. 1, p. 268.
14. See Gareth Steadman-Jones, *Outcast London* (Oxford 1971), Part III, "Middle Class London and the Casual Poor", pp. 239–90 for the reasons behind this rediscovery.
15. Samuel Smith, "The Industrial Training of Children", *Contemporary Review*, vol. XLVII, January 1885, p. 108.
16. G. D. H. Cole, *British Working Class Politics*, 1832–1914 (London 1941), p. 92.
17. E. P. Thompson, *William Morris, Romantic to Revolutionary* (London 1955), p. 473.
18. R. Page Arnot, *William Morris, A Vindication* (London 1934), p. 18.
19. One of the activities of this Committee was the supply of scab labour. See T. A. Jackson, *Trials of British Freedom* (London 1945), p. 167–8.
20. *PRO MEPOL. 2/174.*
21. *ibid.*
22. John Burgess, *John Burns; The Rise and Progress of a Right Honourable* (Glasgow 1911), p. 55.
23. *The Times*, 9 February 1886.
24. *ibid.*
25. *The Times*, 10 February 1886.
26. *ibid.*, letter from an Andrew Fairbairn.
27. *ibid.*, letter from V.D.S.
28. *The Times*, 11 February 1886.
29. *ibid.*
30. Steadman-Jones, *op. cit.*, p. 294.
31. *PRO MEPOL. 2/182.*
32. *Commonweal*, vol. 2, no. 14, p. 17.
33. F. Engels, *Correspondence* with *Paul and Laura Lafargue*, (London 1959), vol. 1, pp. 333–5.
34. *The Times*, 11 February 1886, reporting comment in the Paris paper *Le Temps*.
35. *ibid.*, writer anonymous.
36. *Report to Enquire into the Origin and Character of the Disburbance that took place in the metropolis on the 8th Day of February, 1886 and the conduct of the Police Authorities in Relation thereto*, P.P. Report from Commissioners, vol. XXXIV, 1886, pp. 381 *et seq.*; also P.P. Inquiry, Instituted, Accounts and Papers, Law & Crime; Police, vol. LIII, 1886 (c. 4665).
37. See Cole, *op. cit.*, p. 265.
38. Paul Thompson, *Socialists, Liberals and Labour* (London 1967), p. 103, note 4.

39. Frederick Engels, *op. cit.*
40. *Report to Enquire*, etc., pp. 1–2.
41. *PRO MEPOL. 2/182.*
42. A. C. Benson and Viscount Esher (ed.), *Letters of Queen Victoria. 1887–91* (London 1907), vol. II, p. 58.
43. *D.N.B.*
44. *PRO MEPOL. 2/182, op. cit.*
45. Quoted in William Watkins, *The Life of General Sir Charles Warren* (Oxford 1941), p. 194.
46. *ibid.*, p. 196.
47. *The Times*, 22 January 1889, reporting Sir Charles Warren's reply on receiving the freedom of the Guild of Leathersellers.
48. Watkins, *op. cit.*, p. vii.
49. *PRO MEPOL. 2/181.*
50. *ibid.*
51. Steadman-Jones, *op. cit.*, p. 296.
52. *PRO MEPOL. 2/181*, Memorandum dated 30 August 1887.
53. *ibid.*, Memorandum dated 2 August 1887.
54. Watkins, *op. cit.*, p. 210.
55. *PRO MEPOL. 2/181*, Memorandum dated 19 November 1887.
56. *ibid.*
57. G. E. Buckle. *Letters of Queen Victoria. 1886–1890* (London 1930), vol. 1, p. 331.
58. *Commonweal* November 1887: "The Truth about the Unemployed By One of them".
59. Thompson, *op. cit.*, p. 571.
60. *PRO MEPOL. 2/182.*
61. *ibid.*
62. *ibid.*
63. *ibid.*
64. *Pall Mall Gazette*, November 1887.
65. *The Times*, 11 November 1887.
66. Reported in *The Times*, 14 November 1887.
67. Watkins, *op. cit.*, pp. 212–15, quoting *Illustrated London News*, 18 November 1887.
68. *ibid.*; also Thompson, *op. cit.*, p. 575 *et seq.*
69. *ibid.*
70. *The Times*, 16 November 1887.
71. *ibid.*, 14 November 1887.
72. Watkins, *op. cit.*
73. *Commonweal*, 19 November 1887, *London in a State of Siege.*
74. *The Times*, 14 November 1887.
75. *ibid.*, 15 November 1887.
76. John Burgess, *op. cit.*, pp. 101–2.
77. *PRO MEPOL. 2/182.*
78. *PRO MEPOL. 2/174, op. cit.*, Memorandum dated November 1887.
79. *ibid.*
80. *ibid.*

81. William Morris, *Alfred Linnell, killed in Trafalgar Square, November 20th, 1887* (London 1887), pp. 2 *et seq.*
82. *Commonweal*, 24 December 1887.
83. *The Times*, 13 December 1887.
84. *ibid.*, 19 November 1887.
85. *H.C. Debates*, 3rd Series, vol. 322, c. 1879–1974, continued in vol. 323, c. 35–138.
86. See, for instance, *The Times*, 21 November 1887.
87. *House of Commons Journal*, vol. CXLIII, pp. 365, 373, 378, 380, 384, 387, 391, 403, 412, 422, 438.
88. *ibid.*, pp. 365, 373, 378, 391, 395, 403, 412, 422, 438.
89. *ibid.*, vol. CXLIV, pp. 15, 19, 46.
90. See D. G. T. Williams, *Keeping the Peace* (London 1967), p. 81.
91. For details of the reasons behind this see the letter Henry Matthews to Queen Victoria, 10 November 1888 in Buckle, *op. cit.*, pp. 448–9.
92. *H.C. Debs.*, 4th Series, vol. 18, c. 889.

8

IN THE MINISTER'S GIFT

> "Meetings in Trafalgar Square are held in order that public opinion may demonstrate itself. If a meeting is held there which represents the view of only, as I believe, a small minority of the population of London, we might be quite sure that the majority of the population or their representatives would desire to demonstrate conclusively that the views entertained by the people of London are not those advocated by the holders of the meeting."[1]

CELEBRATION – AND GENTLEMANLY VIOLENCE

The promulgation after 1892 of Asquith's regulations not only severely curtailed the availability of the Square to progressive movements, but, more importantly, enabled the State (i.e. the Office of Works and the Home Office through their agents the Metropolitan Police) to decide who should and who should not be allowed to use the Square to advocate their cause. Needless to say, however, the regulations exempted the State itself from any such restrictions. The law on obstruction, as applied to road or pavement, strangely evaporated when large crowds assembled to see a royal personage pass by. The large crowds that filled Trafalgar Square to celebrate Queen Victoria's Diamond Jubilee were left unhindered by the police, as were those that gathered to celebrate the relief of Mafeking in May 1900. Gross expressions of patriotism, especially if attached to the lauding of some imperial hero, were particularly welcomed, not to say positively encouraged.

At the conclusion in 1902 of the Boer War, celebrations of this kind were plentiful, if a little muted. The war cost £217 million and 22,000 lives.[2] This was the price of what was probably from the beginning seen to be a rather regrettable mistake. With hindsight, it was a small outlay to achieve a British monopoly of the gold and diamonds of Kimberley and the Transvaal and the total enslavement of the non-white population to mine them.

At home, the very combination of "third form stupidity and sixth form arrogance"[3] that had stirred up such jingoistic fervour for Chamberlain's and Rhodes' war was, even before it was over, to be turned once again on the traditional enemy of the ruling class, the working class.

Fighting a war so far from home and with so many soldiers (400,000, the largest number Britain had ever sent abroad) was, as already noted, a very costly business. This additional expense to an already enormous arms budget (in 1899–1900 Britain was spending £698 million on defence,[4] which is after all an "unproductive" sector of the economy) could only exacerbate an already burgeoning economic crisis, brought on by the exigencies of free trade. Unemployment began to rise to allay the fall in profits, and the State chose to set back trade union legislation many years by allowing the infamous Taff Vale judgement.

After the war was over imperialist circles attempted to bolster the fallen prestige of the army, the motor of their ambition, by a policy of "scapegoats and heroes". This process, incidentally, was considerably helped along by the constant militaristic rattle-swinging of the Harmsworth Press and the rest.

Women, as can easily be seen from a glance at any novel of this period, figured little in the perspectives of the imperial idea. In the minds of Tories and Liberals alike, the carrying of the imperial standard was the job of a man – and preferably one from a good school. Woman (especially if she was abroad) was there exclusively to provide comfort and relief: the soft edge to the man's grim work of expropriating land, enslaving "natives", thrashing a servant, or lungeing the bayonet. In places like India and Southern Africa, the life of a British government servant's wife was for the most part insulated, especially from any economic crisis back home. As for the possession of the vote, such a change would have altered her situation little if at all. But at home, the militant claim for women's enfranchisement was beginning to shake the nation, and the Tories and Liberals were looking on in alarm.

Increasingly, the normally polite public meetings of these parties were interrupted by persistent demands that the question of women's franchise be no longer ignored. These demands were swiftly answered with gentlemanly violence. Women were thrown out, often brutally, into the street. Later on, many women were denied entrance to Tory and Liberal meetings altogether.

Undeterred by this response by the main parties to their cause, the Suffragettes set out to lobby Parliament in early May 1906. The lobby failed. Although the leadership of the Suffragettes at this time was largely made up of middle-class radicals, the movement as a whole was not without its strong links with the organised working class. Such links undoubtedly prompted the movement to organise, following the rebuttal of the lobby, their first mass outdoor public meeting in Trafalgar Square on 19 May of the same year.

Meeting in the "forum of London democracy", as Hyndman had called it a few years before, was a significant event to many Suffragettes. Sylvia Pankhurst,[5] for one, felt proud to be proclaiming the rights of women "on this ground, consecrate to the discontented and the oppressed". She felt part of their struggle as she stood side by side with Keir Hardy, "in his rough homespun jacket". But uppermost in her mind, that day, was the thought that on the very spot where they stood, forty years before on the "historic 23rd July 1866. . . . Edmund Beales and the other leaders of the Reform movement had spoken from the plinth in favour of the vote for working men in towns". When she described her fellow Suffragette Annie Kenney speaking that day as a

> "striking, almost startling figure against the blackened stone work of the plinth, (speaking) with a voice that cries out for the lost childhood, blighted hopes, and weary, overburdened lives of the women workers she knows so well",

she could hardly have foreseen how deaf the ears of male hegemony would be to such sentiments.

Two years later, on 11 October 1908, another attempt was made to make Parliament listen. Again a rally was held in Trafalgar Square. This time the Suffragettes threatened to "rush" Parliament, rather than lobby quietly.[6] The police shorthand writers took copious notes. Next day, several of the leading Suffragettes were arrested and later sentenced to a one month term of imprisonment. On the day of their release, much to the Government's annoyance – but there was little they could do about it – a carriage drawn by four white horses and emblazoned with a banner "To Victory" carried the ex-prisoners slowly and ceremoniously round Trafalgar Square.

The Suffragette meeting in the Square, as well as the almost weekly ones on unemployment held by the Social Democratic Federation put an enormous burden, the police complained, on their already undermanned force. So, too, did the enormous increase in arrests and convictions for begging and sleeping out.[7] The rise in unemployment was to continue as the conditions of the working class nationally deteriorated; conditions which liberalism was unable to change or improve.

In February 1908 shipyard workers and engineers struck in the North-east. Eight months later, it was the turn of the cotton operatives. Between July 1909 and April 1910, hardly a week went by without a group of miners striking against their appalling conditions. In June 1911 there was a country-wide strike by seamen and dockers, followed two months later by a similar one by the railwaymen. All this organised working-class activity was too much for some sections of the bourgeoisie, who were beginning to feel that their lives and their property were in serious danger.

So it was that on Trafalgar Day (21 October) 1911, in Trafalgar Square, their self-appointed leader, a William Mailes Power, art dealer and critic, founded the Volunteer Civil Force, with the aim of preparing and defending the country against the imminent onslaught from within. The liberal Government, far from looking askance at the formation of a para-military and armed group, treated Power with some favour. The Home Secretary at the time, it will be remembered, was that well-known antagonist of the working-class, Winston Churchill. He thoroughly approved of the formation of this force of "mature men" (he himself was just thirty-seven years of age). The identification with Churchill of Power's force was sufficient for it to be known for some years by the title "Winston's Bobbies".[8] (The Volunteer Civil Force continued to exist up to the outbreak of war in 1914, when it contributed to the formation of the Artists Rifle Regiment. There is a certain historic irony in this, for the Artists Rifles once counted William Morris among its members.)[9]

FIRST WORLD WAR

When war broke out in 1914, it should have surprised no one. After all, the European ruling class (including the British Liberal Party) had been preparing the ground for it for all of twenty years. And European Socialists had long been warning that the arms race between the Great Powers would inevitably lead to war. Four years before, in 1910, at the Second International's meeting in Basle, all the Socialist parties had passed a resolution that, in the event of war breaking out,[10]

> "their duty (was) to intervene in favour of its speedy termination and with all their powers to utilise the political and economic crisis created by the war to arouse the people and thereby hasten the downfall of capitalist class rule".

Sadly, there was only a token reaffirmation by the leaders of the Labour Party of this pledge at a large rally in Trafalgar Square on the eve of the war. For within a month, both the Labour Party and the T.U.C. had fallen in completely with the Government's plans for recruitment. Worse, before the year was out, the T.U.C. surrendered all the safeguards against employers that they had won after so many years of bitter struggle.

By declaring war against Germany on 4 August 1914, Britain brought into the conflict, with scarcely any consultation, the populations of her

Empire. The white populations rallied readily enough to the cause; but as one commentator pointed out,[11] "50 million Africans and 250 million Indians were involved . . . in a war of which they understood nothing, against an enemy who was almost unknown to them."

At home, bewilderment beset much of the working class, as their leaders continued to show little resistance to the erosion of many traditional liberties. The Labour Party and the T.U.C. were almost completely silent over the introduction of the Defence of the Realm Act ("DORA") which throughout the duration of the war was especially useful to the government when it wished to suppress left-wing literature, propaganda, or meetings.

The Trafalgar Square Regulations were not to escape the effects of "DORA". In anticipation of the Square becoming a focus of recurrent anti-government sentiments, the First Commissioner of Works, Lord Emmott, revised Clause 2b of the Regulations in October 1914 to read[12] (see Appendix 4F):

> "A second notice from the same promoters will not be regarded as valid until their first meeting has actually taken place or been abandoned."

In the event, few demonstrations did take place, and almost without exception they were pro-government. However, during the time of the introduction of the Military Service Act at the end of 1915 and the beginning of 1916, things began to change.

Throughout the early part of 1915 the war still seemed a long way off. Rosy pictures of young heroes were painted in the *Illustrated London News* and the *Daily Mail*; little notice was taken of losses sustained. But the early lull in industrial disputes was coming to an end, and in February "new signs of life appeared in the great engineering centre of the Clyde under the leadership of the Shop Stewards movement".[13] The strike which followed gained one penny an hour for the engineers. In June, the miners in South Wales successfully struck against the introduction of the Munitions Act, introduced as a direct result of the engineers' success four months previously. This Act made it illegal for workers in a number of war industries to strike.

Strikers were identified with 'slackers' (of whom there were said to be 650,000 somewhere),[14] and the clarion call went out in the popular press for compulsory service. Even some Unionist ministers threatened to resign if it was not introduced. The purpose of conscription at that time was almost openly admitted, by some high-ranking government officials, to be political, and had no origin in an expressed need by the Army or the

Navy. Some time later, Auckland Geddes, who became Director of National Service in 1917, admitted that[15] "the position of military conscription added little, if anything, to the effective sum of our war efforts".

The Military Service Act was for many groups yet another step towards the total militarisation of the country; a step which they were not going to allow to go unchallenged. Four of these groups, the London Stop the War Committee, the Workers Suffrage Federation, the Independent Labour Party and the No Conscription Fellowship, planned to hold an anti-war demonstration in Trafalgar Square in late April 1916.

No Conscription Fellowship had been busy for months holding meetings and issuing leaflets (5 million were produced during January 1916) calling for the repeal of the Act. Conscription was for them "the climax of militarism . . . it means the subordination of civil life and liberty to military authority".[16] Their campaign culminated in an Emergency National Convention of 8 April.

In anticipation of the meeting Sylvia Pankhurst prepared an article entitled "The execution of an East London Boy" for *Woman's Dreadnought*. The article, reprinted as a leaflet also for the meeting,[17] described how a young boy, Private Aby, had been shot for desertion on 20 March. The events leading up to and including his arrest were described by reprinting his letters to his mother. Of his execution, Sylvia Pankhurst wrote:

> "This is Militarism! The rank and file in the world's war are but pawns in a great game; they are lightly cast aside when they have served their turn."

On 18 April, the Independent Labour Party put a notice of the meeting in their paper *The Labour Leader*. It read:[18]

> "A peaceful demonstration will be held in Trafalgar Square on the 23rd April at 3.30 when the following resolution will be submitted: that this meeting calls upon the Government to take steps to stop the war by opening up negotiations at once for an immediate and righteous peace."

It was signed by all four groups.

The response by the militarists was immediate; the Home Secretary, Sir Herbert Samuel, was bombarded with questions in the House. The Tory Robert McNeil asked whether "such meetings (should) be allowed in the Capital of the British Empire", for were not the organisers being "deliberately seditious in their propaganda"? With evident approval from most of his listeners, he concluded that the meeting was "hostile to Great

Britain . . . pro-German . . . disloyal . . . and would encourage the King's enemies".[19]

The Home Secretary in his reply was able to report that as the police feared disturbances, the meeting would be prohibited under "DORA", and that in any case "the views (to be expressed at the meeting) represent an insignificant minority in this country". As the murmurs of agreement died down round the Chamber, Philip Snowden, the Labour M.P., was heard to say: "Do not make that mistake."[20]

Less than three months later, on 1 July, thirteen divisions of British troops went "over the top" in the Somme. By the end of that day, German machine guns had killed 19,000 and injured 57,000 men – the greatest loss sustained in a single day by any army in the whole of World War I. Lord Kitchener, unmoved by such decimation, continued to battle through until the November. The whole ghastly operation was forced to a lurching halt by the third and unconquerable enemy, mud.

The final losses for the four month campaign (which, even if it had resulted in a decisive victory, would have been of small strategic advantage to either side) was more than one million dead; Britain, 420,000; France, 194,000; Germany 465,000.[21] War, however, that ever present worm in the gut of imperialism, remained unsatiated. By the time the armistice was signed with Germany on 11 November 1918, another half million British soldiers were dead. (The total casualties, counting all sides, for the whole war, was in the region of $8\frac{1}{2}$ million killed and 21 million wounded.)[22]

As the battle on the Somme was coming to its bloody conclusion, the Office of Works were busily trying to find some means more permanent than legislation for preventing demonstrations in Trafalgar Square. The answer, on the face of it, was quite simple: build on it. That, however, could only be a temporary expedient; for in many people's minds the Square was already practically an ancient monument. Something, perhaps, to house one of the war supply departments?

A scheme was drawn up for a single storey building of 29,800 square feet to occupy almost the whole of the Square between Nelson's column and the north wall.[23] The design of the building, in the view of the Office of Works,

> "would drastically restrict the area available for public meetings, if not render them altogether impossible".

This proposal was seen by Sir Edward Henry, the Chief Commissioner of the Metropolitan Police (who was consulted on the matter), to be without

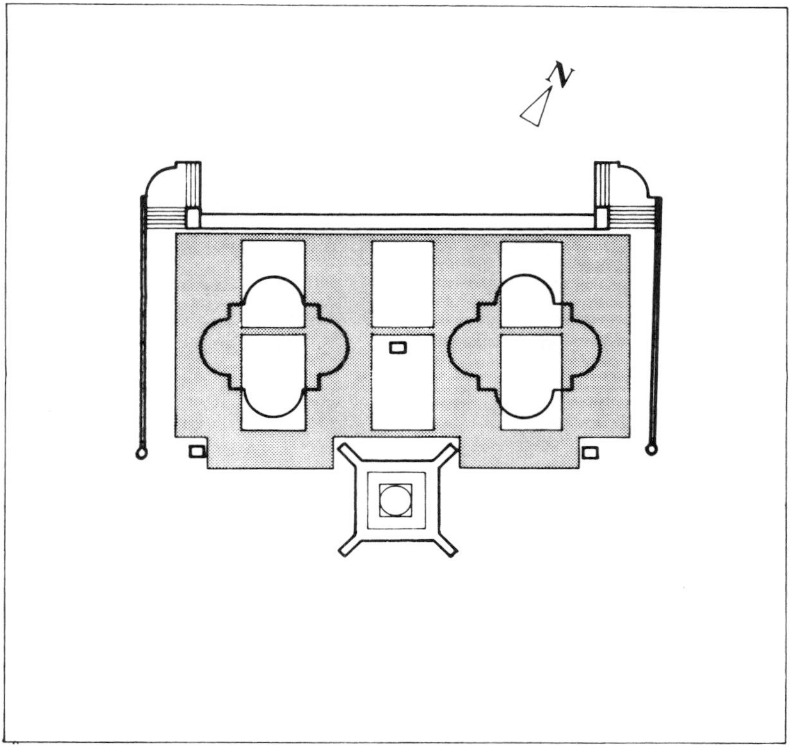

31. Plan for a temporary building (shaded area) on the Square, 1916

doubt "in the public interest". Such a radical step could not be taken by the Office of Works alone; the Cabinet's advice was sought, and it readily agreed. In the event, however, for reasons which are not clear, the building was not proceeded with.

At about the same time a "temporary hut"[24] was erected on the east side near the Havelock statue, for the sole object of

> "arranging parties of soldier sightseers to go round London under the leadership of well known connoisseurs";

not only to look at the sights, but to

> "give the men instruction and keep them amused, thereby preventing them falling into the many traps that await them in London".

A similar hut was put up by the Ministry of Labour on the west side a year later during the recruiting drive for the Women's Army Auxiliary Corps.[25]

Demolition of these huts was postponed in the summer of 1920, thanks to an Office of Works memorandum, which said:[26]

> "In view of the possible emergency requirements with the present industrial unrest, I think the removal of the hut should be deferred."

Perhaps a recruiting office for special constables or a revived Volunteer Civil Force was in mind. Anyway, as soon as the strike was over, the unoccupied huts were demolished – not, it should be noted, until after the Armistice Day celebrations were over.

HUNGER MARCHERS

During the next twenty years, demonstrations in Trafalgar Square reflected the two dominant issues that faced the Labour movement: unemployment, and the fight against fascism. By 1920, Government promises of full employment in a land fit for heroes had turned suddenly sour. Unemployment rose sharply, till it was well over the one million mark. Hundreds of thousands of working-class families, already burdened by the losses of war, were faced with near starvation. A year later, the number registered as wholly unemployed reached over two million.

Given such numbers, it was not long before the unemployed began to organise themselves into groups and committees, in an attempt to press the Government into some form of action. April 1921 saw the formation of the most important of these, the National Unemployed Workers' Committee Movement. All too soon the Movement, and more precisely the London District Council of the Unemployed, came into confrontation with the police over their wish to demonstrate in Trafalgar Square.

The Council's demands were threefold: work, or full maintenance; immediate restoration of cuts in benefits; and the release of the Poplar borough councillors (George Lansbury and several other Poplar councillors had been jailed for refusing to pay sums from their Council to the L.C.C. until something was done about unemployment benefit). The date chosen, 4 October 1921, was a weekday, in contravention of the 1892 regulations. The police duly banned the demonstration. On hearing of this ban Wal Hannington, the demonstration organiser, remarked that he had not forgotten[27] "that during the war such police regulations had been waived, and that Horatio Bottomley and others had held big recruiting meetings during a weekday. . . ."

The meeting was held instead in Hyde Park; but after many insistent demands by the large crowd, it was decided to test the police ban. Having processed in a most orderly manner along Oxford Street, the demonstrators broke up into small groups to make their way south down Charing Cross Road to the Square. The police were waiting. A brief but brutal battle followed, during which Hannington and several other members managed to gain the plinth of Nelson's Column and unfurl a big red flag. The police mercilessly used their truncheons, striking out at anyone not in a blue uniform. Unfortunately for them, their zeal also extended to some rather well-to-do onlookers who had come to watch the fun.

The violence of the police on that day only confirmed once again, as it had a year before when they attacked the unemployed in Whitehall, that the comradeship of the trenches was well and truly over. In Wal Hannington's words,[28]

"Ex-soldiers in blue uniforms were now ready to club down ex-soldiers in rags at the bidding of the only class that had profited by the war."

Almost exactly a year later, the N.U.W.C.M. organised what became known as The Great National Hunger March of the Unemployed on London; the climax of which was to be a deputation to the Prime Minister. With the aim of arriving in London on 17 November, contingents of unemployed workers set out from Scotland, Tyneside, Cumberland, Lancashire, the Midlands, South Wales and the South of England. After a massive welcoming demonstration in Hyde Park, the various contingents held daily meetings until the 22nd, the day fixed for the deputation of the unemployed to see the Prime Minister, Bonar Law.

On the day, the capitalist press went into hysterics (reminiscent of 1848 and 1887). The *Daily Express* envisioned that[29]

"A hundred thousand armed men are going to march on Downing Street which they intend to take by storm. Telegrams have already been prepared for sending to Moscow, stating that the unemployed rebels had captured the Government offices and had compelled the Government to capitulate."

Some papers even claimed that machine guns were being mounted on the roofs of several Government buildings. The actions of the police were leading many others, like Hannington, to a different view:[30]

> "Never before (had) London witnessed such a glaring display of the Iron Heel of Capitalism, ready to crush the appeal of the workers for food, and to drown their cries in rivers of blood."

Bonar Law refused to see the unemployed, even after being petitioned. His attitude was unequivocal.[31]

> "I am sick and tired of hearing about the Unemployed Marchers, and I do not want to have anything more to do with them."

But the unemployed did not go away. In late December the N.U.W.C.M. began its preparations for the "Great Day of National Demonstration" to be held on 7 January 1923. The venue in London for this "Unemployed Sunday" was to be Trafalgar Square. Hannington later described the event:[32]

> "That day will be recorded in history as the greatest day of national demonstration ever witnessed in Great Britain until then. Never before had Trafalgar Square presented such a sight. Thousands of the last contingents to arrive never succeeded in getting into the Square at all, the crowd was so enormous, and the unsuccessful among the demonstrators had to be content to remain in the Strand, Charing Cross Road, Whitehall, and Northumberland Avenue. It was a sight of a lifetime that will long be remembered by those who participated."

A month and a half later, the Square was the site of a Farewell Demonstration to all those who had taken part in the Great National Hunger March. The West End breathed again; and the "gay young things" could promenade the streets once more without the fear that reality would brush their short skirts or baggy trousers.

The Chief Commissioner of the Metropolitan Police expressed his view of these meetings of the unemployed in no uncertain manner:[33]

> "The Square is being misused in a most flagrant manner by a negligible number of agitators who can lay no claim to speak for any representative body of public opinion. . . .
>
> . . . the meetings are started by half a dozen men generally of a low type and holding Communistic views . . .
>
> (they are) vendors of Communistic and pernicious literature . . . collections taken . . . for propaganda purposes by Communistic societies."

Added to all this, he objected to the fact that it required his police "having to work on Sundays". The Commissioner's suggested remedy to this "scandalous state of affairs" was not unsubtle. Briefly, it was reasoned as follows.

At each N.U.W.C.M. mass meeting in Trafalgar an appeal was made by the speakers for donations to the movement's funds. On many occasions this had brought in as much as £100 – a useful contribution to a growing national organisation. The police knew this. Their plan was simple: prohibit the collection of money and the sale of pamphlets altogether, and thus cancel one of the main attractions for the unemployed of holding their meetings in the Square. Sadly for the police, the Office of Works and the Home Office could not wholly oblige, for to prevent collections would also mean that the Government itself would be prevented from launching campaigns like the "Victory Loans" one of 1919. Selling literature presented little problem; sellers would have to have permits, and the number issued for any meeting could be strictly limited.

Before any mass meeting in the Square, it was often a problem for the police to decide how many constables, sergeants and the rest should be present. To over-supply could be tantamount to provocation; to under-supply might indicate a lack of vigilance. On the whole, the police preferred to under-supply, but on several occasions this policy seriously backfired when they found themselves unable to bring up reinforcements quickly enough to deal with trouble.

In 1919 some attempt was made to overcome these difficulties by stationing a constable with a direct telephone link to Scotland Yard in a small police box near Havelock's statue. From this vantage point the constable could call for help or seek advice as soon as trouble started. The box being only a wooden one, however, was felt by many of the constables who used it to be rather vulnerable. There had, after all, been a longish history of small wooden huts being burnt down in the Square. During the winter of 1922–3, indeed, several unemployed meetings had included mischievous elements in the crowd who had threatened to turn it into "a coffin", by turning it on its side.

Finding a site for a more permanent box presented considerable difficulties. Nobody, it seemed, wanted to put up yet another obstruction in the Square, and the search for a suitable place in all the surrounding buildings had failed to produce anything suitable.[34] It was not until the end of 1926 that someone in the Office of Works had a "brainwave . . . take down the old drum (of one of the Bude lights) and cut out the inside . . . making a 3 foot 9 inch diameter police observation point". The design of the box has a narrow door on the square side "filled with triplex glass . . . in the event of stonethrowing", and tall thin slits on the Northumberland

Avenue and Strand sides. "Ventilation" could also be "secured with the door and window closed".[35] (Incidentally, as far as can be ascertained, the floor of the box is not, as popular belief would have it, the exit of a tunnel direct from Scotland Yard, out of which a constant stream of men in blue could emerge at a moment's notice.) The new granite box was finished, complete with flashing light on top, in March 1928.

But the old wooden one had to suffice, perilous as it may have been for the constable inside, during the massive miners' demonstration five months before on 20 November 1927. Since the General Strike of May 1926 the miners had continued their struggle against the mineowners. The owners' policy of enforcing lower wages and longer hours had the inevitable consequence of throwing more and more miners out of work. Between January and July 1927 the percentage of miners registered as unemployed (this excludes the number who had already exhausted their right to benefit) rose from 16·3 to 21.[36] The situation in South Wales was particularly bad, and it was from the many small villages in the Rhondda that most of the marchers came. The march's purpose was clear: to draw attention to the chronic destitution affecting the unemployed and employed miners, arising out of the failure of private enterprise in the mining industry; to demand that the Government prevent more pits being closed, and that a thorough overhaul be made to the unemployed benefit system.

The march, comprising 270 men, set out from Newport on 9 November. Within two days it had reached Bath, where to the surprise and consternation of some local townspeople it marched through the crowd-lined streets just ahead of the town's Armistice Day parade. It must have been an ironic sight. Nine days later in the pouring rain a huge crowd welcomed the marchers into Trafalgar Square. Of the march, A. J. Cook, the miners' leader, was later to remark:[37]

> "The great miners' march of 1927 will be remembered as a historic landmark in the struggles of the workers; a warning to Toryism and capitalism. The reverberations of that tramp, tramp, tramp from South Wales to London will live for ever. It echoes the defiant call of men being sacrificed on the altar of capitalism. It was a last warning of the great multitude of unemployed who refuse to quietly suffer and die that capitalism may live. That great Trafalgar Square demonstration on November 20th is the forerunner of victory greater than 'Trafalgar' for the workers."

Within fifteen months, faced with a continued high level of unemployment and the unwillingness of the Government to provide proper benefits, the N.U.W.C.M. organised another march. It commenced in Scotland on 22 January 1929 and, with contingents joining up all along the way it finished up with a triumphant entry into Trafalgar Square on 24 February. Across the plinth of Nelson's column a huge banner simply read: "Welcome to the Hunger Marchers".

Tom Mann was one of the many speakers who stood at intervals round the whole plinth and addressed the enormous crowd. (At that time it was quite usual – there being no loudspeakers – for several speakers to be addressing the assembly at the same time; the most important speaker normally took the north facing side.)

The enormity of the march and the demonstration – some estimates suggest there were at least 50,000 people in the Square and the surrounding streets – persuaded the Government to change its mind over the "30 stamps qualification" for unemployment benefit. But hunger and unemployment still thrived, and in April 1930 the marchers were back on the road again. This time their target was a Labour Government. Ramsay MacDonald turned out to be no more receptive than his Tory predecessor.

By 1932 the Labour Government was out of power; in its place came the so-called National Government: a hotch-potch of Tories and Liberals, seasoned with a token sprinkling of "national" Labourites. Although MacDonald was Prime Minister, more than 60 per cent of his Cabinet were Tories; including, as far as the unemployed were concerned, the Minister of Health.

Since 1929 unemployment had nearly doubled, to reach $2\frac{1}{4}$ million. In a feeble attempt to reduce the huge financial drain this made on Exchequer funds, the Government brought in a means test and reduced existing benefits even further. Clashes between police and the demonstrating hungry unemployed became a frequent occurrence in nearly every city throughout the country. In October 1932 another massive hunger march on London was organised. Violence, largely provoked by the police, broke out again, when as a prelude to the mass meeting to be held in Hyde Park on 27 October, thousands of London demonstrators converged on the headquarters of the London County Council at County Hall.

The Hyde Park meeting, too, came in for its share of violence, especially by the mounted police. Three days later, in the midst of loud cries from the Tory press that it should be banned, the unemployed held their largest (one estimate put the numbers at 150,000) meeting in Trafalgar Square. The police made very little attempt to interfere with the main meeting, but continually harassed demonstrators round its edges. In some places the fighting was fierce, the police making numerous baton and horse charges. At times the crowd had difficulty hearing the many speakers for the sound of the small police aeroplanes that circled overhead (the planes were connected by radio to the officer commanding below).

By 1934 the number of unemployed was still above two million. The hunger marches continued. To the National Government and certain "capitalist elements", the marches, and their culmination – if they were directed towards London – in those heartlands of the ruling class, Trafalgar Square and Hyde Park, were seen as a threat which could not be ignored. The Home Secretary was asked by the Duchess of Atholl if he would take steps to prevent the meetings, especially the ones in Trafalgar Square. So fierce were the warnings by the Home Secretary and the Attorney General that the big march due in London in February 1934 was peopled by unruly and disorderly persons, that a recently formed group calling itself the Council for Civil Liberties wrote to the press to point out that[38]

> ". . . certain features of the police preparations for the present march – for example, instructions to shopkeepers to barricade their windows – cannot but create an atmosphere of misgiving, not only dangerous but unjustified by the facts".

As there was a "general and alarming tendency to encroachment on the liberty of the citizen", the letter continued, the Council would "maintain a vigilant observation of the proceedings of the next few days". The procession and meeting passed off quietly, as did the massive one held in Trafalgar Square on 4 March.

Despite resistance to the mass demonstrations both from Tories (inside and outside Government) and the Labour Party, the well-disciplined marches and petitions of the National Unemployed Workers' Movement (by now the word "Committee" was dropped) finally forced the National Government to restore the 10 per cent cuts it had introduced as an economy measure in 1931.

THE FIGHT AGAINST FASCISM

During the period 1932–9 the British Union of Fascists (which the "New Party" formed by Sir Oswald Mosley as a breakaway from Labour rapidly became) held few political meetings in Trafalgar Square, being engaged on the whole with "Jews" and "reds" in the East End of London. It was only after being prevented by the police from these activities that they organised a march directed at Trafalgar Square (4 July 1937).[39] Here, as in the East End, and despite the efforts of the police to protect them, the fascists met considerable popular resistance. Once again, however, as had so often been the case in the preceding years, it was not the mouthers of anti-Jewish slogans, nor the outright exponents of Hitlerian political violence that the police arrested: it was those naughty left-wingers bent, as ever, on the destruction of public order, and by implication, British democracy.

Although "DORA" ceased to exist in 1920, she had spawned several ugly offspring. Among these could be counted the Police Act, 1919, the Emergency Powers Act, 1920, the Official Secrets Act, 1920, the Trades Disputes Act, 1927, the Incitement to Disaffection Act, 1934, and the Public Order Act, 1936. (Not, it should be emphasised, that each and every section of these Acts were objectionable; but common to all of them, as indicated several times already, was the general tendency greatly to increase the powers of the police in some important areas of civil liberties.) The most important of these, in its effect on the use of Trafalgar Square as a meeting place, was of course the last: the Public Order Act.

The origins of this Act, briefly, derived from the intensification of pressure by the Labour movement (following especially on the "Battle of Cable Street" when the people blocked a fascist march to the East End) for the Government to take positive action against fascist activities. The banning of uniforms was thought to be of particular importance. The 1936 Edinburgh Labour Party Conference that started the day after Cable Street tabled an emergency resolution calling for anti-fascist legislation. A special conference was held in London attended by the Executive Committee of the London Labour Party, members of the L.C.C., several Labour M.P.s and Mayors from Labour boroughs. Even the King's Speech in November made special mention of the need to strengthen the law on public meetings and processions.

The Bill, when the Government did finally introduce it, was found to go much further than the intentions of many of its supporters (that is, the banning of political uniforms and the prevention of militarisation of politics). It contained, as Ronald Kidd has pointed out, provisions "which were capable of being used for repressive purposes against democratic organisations".[40] This was particularly true of the freedom to organise a procession without having to obtain the previous consent of the executive (the police or the Home Secretary). Section 3, subsection (i) of the Act, headed 'Powers for the preservation of public order on the occasion of processions", reads as follows:[41]

> "If the chief officer of police, having regard to time or place at which the circumstances in which any public procession is taking place or is intended to

take place, and to the route taken or proposed to be taken by the procession, has reasonable grounds for apprehending that the procession may occasion serious public disorder, he may give directions imposing upon the persons organising or taking part in the procession such conditions as appear to him necessary for the preservation of public order, including conditions proscribing the route to be taken by the procession and conditions prohibiting the procession from entering any public place specified in the directions.

"Provided that no conditions restricting the display of flags, banners or emblems shall be imposed under this subsection except as are reasonably necessary to prevent risk of a breach of the peace."

The serious implication of this section is that it "placed discretionary – and, virtually, dictatorial powers in the hands of the chief officer of police over all processions".[42] It also places in his hands the power to ban the carrying of a trade union banner proclaiming "Unity is Strength", should he deem these words to be inflammatory.

In case these powers should be insufficient, a further subsection of the Act enabled the Chief Commissioner to apply direct to the Home Secretary for an order prohibiting any public processions for a period not exceeding three months.

(The State's attitude to demonstrations has hardly changed since then, except to become, if anything, still more illiberal. Only recently (1975) the Chief Commissioner of the Metropolitan Police, Sir Robert Mark, called for a statutory seven days' notice of any demonstration. It is noteworthy that these remarks were made after the police had clashed with a large crowd of anti-fascist demonstrators in Red Lion Square – a clash at which one demonstrator, Kevin Gately, died.)

In London the police already had the power, under the 1839 Police Act (which they had used on countless occasions) to prevent demonstrations of any kind whatsoever. Technically a demonstration obstructs the highway, and as such can be dispersed. Sir John Simon, the Home Secretary responsible for the Public Order Bill, defended himself against criticism on this point by claiming that the 1839 Act was written "in archaic language" and that there was the need to insert "a plain provision on the subject".[43]

During 1939–45 Section 3 of the Public Order Act was supplemented by Regulation 39E (i) of the Emergency Powers (Defence) Act, 1939. This endowed the Home Secretary with particular powers to ban any procession or meeting that was deemed likely to promote disaffection among any section of the armed forces.

Thus the beginning of World War II saw "the forum of London

Democracy" still further hedged about by regulations of one sort or another. Even if an organisation succeeded (and several did) in breaking through these paper obstacles and getting approval for a meeting, still more obstructions would await them within the space of the Square itself. Such were these physical obstacles that on more than one occasion complaints were made that disrespect was being shown to one of the country's finest heroes by the building of concrete air-raid shelters, ventilation ducts and the like, on his shrine.

The meetings that were held in the latter years of the war concentrated on two issues: one, the need to support the Soviet Union by opening a second front (an issue which for a brief moment found the left peeping over the sheets with such bed-fellows as Lord Beaverbrook); and two – a topic that was to be the subject of many demonstrations for the remainder of the war and for several years after it – India's need to throw off its colonial yoke and become independent. The first was not realised until 1943, and the fulfilment of the second had to wait until 1947; even then, India's independence was to be conditional on her membership of the Commonwealth and continuing domination by British capital.

Although by 1945 the apparatus of German and Italian fascism had been defeated, the monopoly capitalism which had bred it was being carefully nurtured back to life by the victors in those areas under their control, and especially by the United States.

> "... there is no doubt which powers derived most advantage from the way the war worked out . . . Soviet Russia did most of the fighting against Germany, sustained nine tenths of the casualties and suffered catastrophic economic losses. The British suffered considerable economic loss and sustained comparatively few casualties. The Americans made great economic gains and had a trifling number of casualties. . . . In short, the British and Americans sat back . . . while Russia defeated Germany for them. Of the three great men at the top, Roosevelt was the only one who knew what he was doing; he made the United States the greatest power in the world at virtually no cost."[44]

But what of fascism at home? Surely with the coming to power of a Labour Government (with a majority of 146 in the House of Commons) in 1945, coming as it did, on top of the revelations about the indescribable fascist horrors of Belsen and Buchenwald, the ghost of fascism would finally be laid. Sadly, it was not to be so; and a Labour Home Secretary, Chuter Ede, stood by with averted eyes while it crawled back out of the woodwork.

Within six months of Germany's capitulation, Mosley (who had been interned from 1940–3) was announcing his comeback at an "Xmas Dance" at the Royalty Hotel in London. The fascists' leader, with the help of many of his old B.U.F. cronies, began to organise – though as yet not in public – a network of local groups around so-called "book clubs". One book that was of course to be avidly read by members of these clubs was Mosley's own *My Answer*, published under his own imprint in 1946. Several organisations, not explicitly fascist, like the Union of British Freedom, the Sons of St. George, the Imperial Defence League, and the British Workers Party for National Unity, sprang up around the country. In London one of these, the British League of Ex-Service Men and Women, was soon marching the streets and holding out-door meetings in a way that was indistinguishable in style and content from the B.U.F. of the early thirties. Their slogans and propaganda were unashamedly anti-semitic, and like Mosley before them, they marched in military fashion to the beat of a drum often through predominantly Jewish areas such as Hackney, in East London. These marches inevitably provoked disorder as anti-fascists attempted to prevent their progress. The police, once again, provided the fascists with all the necessary protection, arresting on the whole only their opponents. At the time, Marcus Lipton, M.P., wrote:[45]

> "Great Britain is the only European country engaged in the last war where undisguised Fascist propaganda is not only permitted, but even granted police protection. This is a fantastic and intolerable situation."

The summer of 1947 saw a considerable upsurge of fascist anti-semitic activity. The prominence given by newspapers like the *Daily Mail* and *Daily Express* to the activities of Zionist terrorists in Palestine added considerable fuel to the fascists' already viscious campaign in East London and in the Jewish quarters in other large cities. So provocative became their marches and meetings that innumerable organisations called upon the Home Secretary, Chuter Ede, to ban them. The London County Council put the feelings of most people when, in a statement on 7 October, it said:[46]

> "That the Council . . . views with concern disturbances provoked by recent meetings of the British League of Ex-Service Men and Women by the provocative and insulting words and behaviour of certain speakers and their supporters, and deplores the publicity given to such disturbances and persons; . . . while reaffirming the rights of the public to freedom of speech and assembly, sees recent occurrences as a serious threat to the preservation of those rights and therefore calls upon the Home Secretary to use to the full in

regard to such meetings the powers vested in him to deal with seditious utterances and with conduct conducive to breaches of the peace."

Undeterred (some would say aroused) by the campaign that was building up against him and all that he and his adherents stood for, Mosley published his "full blown Fascist programme for Britain", *The Alternative*, also in October, again under his own imprint. This book, as with his *My Answer* of a year before, received full publicity in the *Times Literary Supplement*[47] and elsewhere. A month later, on 15 November at a meeting in Farringdon Hall, London, Mosley brought together all the separate fascist groups into one organisation, the Union Movement, with himself at the head.

Just before Christmas 1947 a deputation made up of several M.P.s and members of the N.C.C.L. went to see the Home Secretary, Chuter Ede, with the hope of persuading him to prohibit by legislation all fascist activities. Chuter Ede was unmoved by their pleadings. Perhaps, he indicated, he might do something about the fascists' anti-semitic utterances, or perhaps prohibit the use of loudspeakers in certain public spaces. (Loudspeakers had only been allowed in Trafalgar Square since March 1943.) When a little later it became known that Chuter Ede was contemplating, besides the prohibition of the use of loudspeakers, a blanket ban on *all* demonstrations irrespective of their purpose, the N.C.C.L. in particular, and the labour movement in general, were horrified. In a letter to the Home Secretary at the end of January the N.C.C.L. laid out the simple points of the case:[48]

"We are strongly against the principle of such an overall ban on the use of loudspeakers. . . . We feel that the effect of such a ban would constitute a serious limitation of the democratic rights of *all* organisations, in an attempt to deal with what have undoubtedly been serious local abuses of the use of loudspeakers by a Fascist organisation. (In our view, the policy of such organisations depends very largely upon capitalising their disruptive 'nuisance value' in order to attempt to secure a general viewpoint with regard to the prohibition of bodies thus providing themselves with a more fertile soil for the dissemination of their poisonous anti-Semitic provocations.) . . . Very much the same considerations dictate our general viewpoint with regard to the prohibition of public meetings."

The Home Secretary was again unmoved.

The N.C.C.L., and many other bodies, continued their anti-fascist campaign. A large petition was organised requesting the L.C.C. to refuse to let school halls to the Union Movement, who were now being forced, because of bans elsewhere, into using them. Many large public meetings were organised under the banner of "End Race Hatred".

To many in the Labour movement Chuter Ede's slowness to act against the fascists was a little bewildering. He was, after all, the Home Secretary in a Labour Government committed, some its members claimed, to socialism. The bewilderment increased when, as the demands for concerted action against the fascists became more widespread, the Government announced on 15 March 1948, that there would be a campaign against the main opponents of the fascists, the Communist Party; and especially any of its members in the civil service.

Britain, it appeared, was preparing to ally itself to the Truman Doctrine, in identifying the enemy both within and without as Communism. The purge of the civil service, the B.B.C., and many other organisations and industries, of Communists and pro-Communists, following Attlee's announcement was, it would seem, a precondition of Britain joining the Brussels Pact. This Pact, which was a grouping of France, Belgium, the Netherlands and Luxembourg, was itself to be subsumed, a year or so later, into the American-dominated Atlantic Pact. Anti-Communism in Europe had come to stay.

Meanwhile, at home, fascism remained unchecked. Its well-orchestrated campaign of provocation continued. A few days before the traditional London Trades Council May Day march, Mosley announced his intention to hold a "May Day Rally" at Hertford Road in Hackney. Worse; rumours were circulating that he intended to march his supporters from the same starting point as the London Trades Council march – the Victoria Embankment. The Home Secretary was besieged with demands that the march of the Union Movement should be banned altogether. Once again, Chuter Ede declined to act. He did, however, indicate that if the Metropolitan Police wished to stop Mosley they would have his full consent to do so. In the event, the police provided an escort of 834 men for the march, and arranged for it to take a different route to avoid any clash with the London Trades Council. Inevitably, though, clashes did take place, and about thirty anti-fascists were arrested. Moseley in contrast remained untouched, and contented himself with the extremely provocative action of taking the "fascist salute" outside his "home" of some five years before, Holloway Prison. The next day the newspapers were full of reports of the disorder.

A few days later, in answer to a question in the House of Commons on the fascists' activities, Chuter Ede announced that he had given his consent to the Chief Commissioner of the Metropolitan Police to ban, for three months, all political processions in his district. Fortunately the ban did not extend to *meetings* in Trafalgar Square, and on 23 May the London Trades Council were able to hold a protest meeting against the Commissioner's actions. Their objections, sadly, had little effect. The Commissioner extended the ban even further until February 1949.

Within a few days of the order being cancelled, the fascists were out in force again, marching and singing their Horst Wessel song. Unprovoked attacks on Jews were renewed. A month later, on 20 March, despite pleadings from M.P.s and representations from the Mayors of the boroughs concerned, the Home Secretary allowed the fascists to hold another march through parts of the East End. The disorder anticipated by all except Chuter Ede inevitably took place.[50] Yet again, he responded as he had done the year before, and through the Chief Commissioner of Police had the three month ban on political processions reimposed. This time it looked as though his intransigence would put in jeopardy altogether London's traditional May Day procession. Questions were asked; but the answers only confirmed the worst fears of London's Labour Movement. The Home Secretary viewed the London Trades Council's procession as "political" – and it was therefore banned.

A Labour Government banning a May Day procession! The news was met with incredulity. In only two other places in Europe had a May Day demonstration been forbidden by law: Athens and Madrid (in pro-fascist and fascist countries).

> "1949 – THE LABOUR GOVERNMENT STRIKES A BLOW AGAINST THE WORKERS . . . But the workers of London have other ideas."[50]

Indeed they had. Marches were organised, and not surprisingly, were met with police resistance. Despite what amounted to very provocative actions by the police, many orderly groups of marchers made their way to the London Trades Council's May Day rally in Trafalgar Square. By the time the meeting began, nearly 30,000 people had assembled in the Square. (Many daily papers reported that there were only 6,000 present; but photographs of the event and other witnesses seriously contradict this.) Aware that the meeting was a triumph for the Trades Council, the police (some would say out of spite), continued to harass demonstrators as they left at the conclusion of the speeches.[51] Most speakers had of course added to their remarks on the need to fight for peace, full employment and the continuing defeat of the Tories a strongly expressed determination that the ban on processions should be lifted by next May Day.

To many people the complete ban was totally unnecessary. The N.C.C.L. felt that the fascists' provocations could easily be dealt with under Section 3 of the Public Order Act. Precedent already existed for this in the cases of Wise v. Dunning and Duncan v. Jones.[53] The central objection to the Home Secretary's action was, of course, that it gave precedence to any small group who could just by a *threat* prevent any form of public demonstration whatsoever. In fact, it seemed that this was the very tactic of the Union Movement – evidenced, six months later, when, after the Union Movement had announced their intention to march once again through the East End, the ban was extended for a further period. By the end of 1949 Chuter Ede not only had extended the ban for a further three months, but was also giving no sign of the slightest intention to act separately against the fasicists. It was impossible to see him as doing anything but support their activities; his role as their agent seemed to have become clear. For Mosley and his supporters – and for some sections of the Tory Party – the sight of a Labour Home Secretary so clumsily alienating large sections of his Government's support must have gladdened their hearts.

The latest ban was due to expire on Tuesday, 2 May 1950. In anticipation (and in part in celebration) the London Trades Council set about organising a May Day procession ending in a rally at Trafalgar Square for Sunday, 7 May. Suddenly and without warning, on 28 April, Chuter Ede announced that the ban was to be reimposed for a further three months.

The London Trades Council was determined, despite this setback, that at least the rally itself should not be cancelled; and calls for support went round to all trade unionists. On the day, thousands of demonstrators assembled at several points around London, and on the clear instructions of the Trades Council's stewards made their way in small groups or separately to the Square. Banners were to be furled and tied, and posters and placards held down. Under no circumstances, urged the stewards at the start of the gatherings, should any action be taken to provoke the police or infringe the regulations laid down by the Commissioner of Police's order.

But the Police had different ideas.

"As people were moving in an orderly fashion along the pavements a group of twenty or thirty police would collect and slow down their progress by pushing the crowd in some direction. Mounted police then came upon the pavement to speed up the people, creating anger and confusion. . . . Individuals were then arrested in the melee and thrown with some vigour into the police vans."[54] "As the contingent from South East London formed into marching ranks across the Strand just before they reached Trafalgar Square the police drew their batons and set about breaking up the procession."[55]

In and around the Square itself mounted police wheeled and charged, crushing women and children alike against the wall beside the pavement. Photographers, too, were deliberately ridden at. By the end of the afternoon, seventy people had been arrested.[55]

For many, a grim day was made yet more bleak on the discovery of two related events. Firstly, of those arrested, several were sent to prison on charges of inciting others to take part in a banned procession (this in fact was the first time that such charges under the Public Order Act had been preferred since its coming into law in 1936). Secondly, and in strict contrast to the police actions in an around Trafalgar Square, Mosley had been provided with a large and passive police escort at his demonstration in Hackney on the same day.

The public outcry at the events of 7 May, in addition to the nearly weekly deputations, at last seemed to penetrate Chuter Ede's obduracy; for when the three month ban was up, he did not renew it. Whether the Chief Commissioner of Police asked for it and it was denied, it is not, of course, possible yet to say. It may be that with another general election not very far away, the Labour Government was attempting to regain some of its erstwhile supporters. With respect to the police, the N.C.C.L. had this to say in their 1950–1 Annual Report:[56]

> "As far as can be ascertained, London is the only city where political processions are not permitted. It would be interesting to know how far this is due to the fact that other cities have some form of democratic control over the police force through the Watch Committees. The Metropolitan Police are under the direct control of the Home Office; there is our local control."

Despite this absence of any formal control over the Metropolitan Police, the Labour movement had again shown that mass pressure can induce the Executive to change its mind. In addition to this regaining of an important civil liberty, another small victory should perhaps be registered. Under Section 2 of the 1892 Trafalgar Square Regulations the promoters of meetings in the Square had to give notice of their meeting to the Metropolitan Police. The implication behind this requirement was clearly that public meetings in the Square were synonymous with public disorder, not civil liberty (a view, understandable enough, remembering the circumstances in which the Regulations were originally drafted). In the eyes of the Government this was rather untimely emphasis. The words *Commissioner of Police of the Metropolis* in Section 2 of the Regulations were replaced by *Minister of Works*.[57] This did not imply that the traditional role of the Metropolitan Police, that of giving advice on public order, was to be in any way curtailed. It obviously was not. Sadly, this small advance for the cause of free speech was to be shortlived. In October 1951 the Labour Government was defeated at the general election; the Tories under Winston Churchill hastily sought to change the Regulations.

THE POWER TO BAN DEMONSTRATIONS

While in opposition the Tories had voiced, both inside and outside the House of Commons, their age-old dislike of demonstrations – especially those of the working class – in Trafalgar Square. But at the same time, they had little need in the main to press the Labour Government into proscription when the situation required it. However, once back in government, things of necessity changed; the sniping from the wings had to be transformed into some form of concrete political action.

Unhappily, as the source of the advice for this action is still far from clear, some important points need to be raised. Previous experience would suggest that the opinions of the Metropolitan Police, the officials in the Home Office and, to a lesser degree, the Ministry of Works, were fundamental in the making of policy in this matter. The extent to which these opinions took root in legislation of course depended on the political moment at which they were allowed to surface. The police, for instance, had been with very few exceptions hostile to both the idea and the practice of demonstrations in the Square. The Home Office and the Ministry of Works, on balance, had been far less so. Two, perhaps obvious, questions need, then, to be asked, in the absence of firm evidence. Both are conditional on the fact that the new Regulations appeared within three months of a new Government taking office.

Firstly, were the new Regulations already under discussion while Labour was still in office, and if so, would they have been implemented had Labour remained in government? In short, was David Eccles, the Tory Minister of Works, merely rubber stamping a Labour policy he largely agreed with?

Secondly, or did the administration (including the police,) take advantage of the Tories' known antipathy towards demonstrations to encourage the Ministry to take the action he, and they, preferred in any case?

The evidence seems to point to the former. It is hard, otherwise, to explain the new Opposition's total silence during the forty days[58] that the draft of the new Regulations lay before both Houses of Parliament (19 February–8 April). It seems probable that the new Regulations, along with the similar ones for Parliament Square[59] that came into operation at the same time, were but one further effort by a Labour Government to restrict, harass and even proscribe the activities of any person or organisation to their political left. Of course no Tory in his right mind, whether in or out of office, would attempt to discourage such a state of affairs.

It is also interesting to note that, although the Square had come within the scope of the Parks Regulations (Amendment) Act twenty-six years before, nothing had been done by way of issuing new regulations then. Also, that the new Regulations did not, as practice has shown since, revoke the old ones – even as amended in April 1951. In fact all the Sections (see Appendix 4G) *except* number (2) still apply.

Let us now look in detail at the way in which these new Regulations did substantially interfere with the right to free speech and assembly that had existed for sixty years under the old 1892 Regulations. Without the slightest doubt, the most important change is contained in the preamble of Section 3 and its paragraphs (1), (4) and (5) which read:

> "Within the Square the following Acts are prohibited unless *written permission* of the Minister has first been obtained" (my italics – R.M.).

Among these "Acts" were

> "(1) selling or distributing anything or offering anything for hire. . . .
> (4) organising, conducting or taking part in any assembly, parade or procession . . .
> (5) making or giving a public speech or address."

In 1892 and 1914 the comparable paragraph had read:

> "No public meeting shall be held unless *written notice* shall have been sent four clear days beforehand by the promoters" (my italics – R.M.).

The new Regulations not only extended the scope of the old, but fundamentally changed their meaning. Between 1892 and 1952 organisations wishing to use the Square were only required to give *notice* of their intention to do so; after 1952 any organisation similarly wishing to use the Square had to *seek and be granted official permission.*

The substance of paragraph (1), relating to the sale of literature, although not referred to at all in the earlier Regulations, was already subject to licensing, as has already been mentioned. Although restrictive, this licensing did not prevent anyone selling any explicitly political literature to anyone else during a meeting or demonstration. A Socialist, for example, would not be prevented from selling or distributing a pamphlet on unemployment to people attending a meeting on the need for increased temperance. The new measures sought to change this, for in practice under[60]

> "the new Regulations, application for permission to sell (literature) would have to be made at the same time as application for permission to hold the meeting, and no difficulty would arise provided that the literature was concerned with the subject of the meeting or the objects of the organisation holding it."

Clearly David Eccles (or his Labour predecessors) did not believe in the free and democratic exchange of ideas that literacy allows.

This paragraph, however, was not to go unchallenged. Several organisations, prominent among which was the N.C.C.L., pressed immediately for its amendment. In response, the Minister granted a small concession, not in the wording of the paragraph but in its interpretation. He stated that he was, for the time being, willing to issue up to eight general letters of authorisation to bodies desiring to sell political literature at any meeting, provided it was understood that such permission[61]

> "exists in consequence only for as long as the Minister wishes, and may be withdrawn at any time without a change in the Regulations or any consultation with Parliament".

The Minister's "wish" lasted six years. In 1958 the emergence of the Campaign for Nuclear Disarmament stimulated the Minister suddenly to revert to the original spirit of the 1952 Regulations. This piece of repression was short-lived; protests, from three members of the House of Lords, among others, got a temporary reversal of his decision.[62] Three years later it was revived again, and remains in force to this day.

For twenty years both Labour and Tory Governments used the Regulations in one way or another to restrict or even ban individual demonstrations and meetings. On some occasions when it was thought that the ban in itself was an insufficient deterrent to the would-be holders of meetings, extra powers, usually under sub-section 3 of Section 3 of the Public Order Act, have been invoked. Such a major step has nearly always brought about a serious clash between the police and the public.

The most famous incident in this respect is probably the Committee of 100's demonstration in the Square on the night of Sunday, 17 September 1961.[63]

These occasional bans, connected most often with the activities of the Campaign for Nuclear Disarmament or the Committee of 100, have followed a pattern; clearly, the Government, as often before, has equated a threat to their own security with a threat to the security of the State. The ban on demonstrations calling for nuclear disarmament were in this sense blatantly political in nature. The Tory Government obviously wished to prevent the advocacy of views contrary to its own by being alarmist about the occasions on which they were to be given public expression. Despite this, as the record shows, not all demonstrations connected with this major issue of common concern were banned.

Sadly, this could not be said to be the case latterly with the issue of Northern Ireland. Throughout the period since the War, the Square has been used innumerable times as a forum by various progressive organisations to discuss and debate the issue of the partition of Ireland. And during this time there is not one recorded occasion on which disorder took place. Yet in 1972, three years after the most recent troubles began, the Tory Secretary of State for the Environment, Peter Walker, advised by the Home Secretary, Reginald Maudling, placed an absolute ban, not on one meeting whose subject was Ireland (they had done that to Sinn Fein on 26 September 1971), but on all such meetings. The proposed demonstration by the Anti-Internment League on 23 March was the first to suffer.[64]

The official explanation for the Government's action was that after the bomb at Aldershot Barracks a few weeks before, any demonstrations which appeared to be pro-Republican in sympathy might lead to disorder. There exists no means of appealing directly against the ruling. In spite of this, several attempts have been made recently (1975) to declare the ban illegal; none, so far, has succeeded.

On the day before the planned demonstration was to take place, Jock Stallard, Labour M.P. for St. Pancras, asked the Under Secretary of State for the Environment, Paul Channon, for a further explanation of the ban.[65] "These are highly exceptional times in Ireland", Channon vaguely replied. In Britain, too, the times are "highly" exceptional – when it is not possible to discuss publicly the question of imprisonment without trial, or the most bloody crisis in our recent history.

As this book goes to press, the ban continues to be enforced. Labour, since it came to office in October 1974, has done nothing to change the situation created by their Tory predecessors. To use the words of the last official statement on the matter, the position is still "under review".

What, then, can be concluded from all this? Surely only one thing. As long as a demonstration in Trafalgar Square could be seen to be, in the eyes of the State, merely an "encouraged public spectacle", it would be permitted. If, on the other hand, it could be suspected of being a "rehearsal of revolutionary awareness", it would quickly and resolutely be put down.

Notes to Chapter 8

1. Sir Herbert Samuel, the Home Secretary, on the occasion of the banning of an anti-war demonstration. *H. C. Debs.*, 5th Series vol. 81, c. 31.
2. David Butler and Jennie Freeman, *British Political Facts* (London 1963), p. 160.
3. A. P. Thornton, *The Imperial Idea and its Enemies* (London 1959), p. 90.
4. Butler and Freeman, *op. cit.*, p. 159.
5. E. Sylvia Pankhurst, *The Suffragette – The History of the Woman's Militant Suffrage Movement 1905–10* (New York 1911), pp. 79–80.
6. *ibid.*, pp. 262 *et seq.*
7. *Report of the Commissioners of the Metropolitan Police for the Year 1906*, Cd. 3771. *P.P. 1908 (Cd. 3771) L1. 765.* The number convicted for begging rose from 1,260 in 1886 to 4,308 in 1906, number convicted for sleeping out rose from 150 in 1886 to 257 in 1906.
8. Information supplied by Metropolitan Police Musuem, Bow Street (this fascinating museum sadly is not open to the public).
9. H. A. R. May, *Memoirs of the Artists Rifles* (London 1929), p. 4.
10. Quoted in A. L. Morton, *A Peoples' History of England* (London 1968), p. 531.
11. A. J. P. Taylor, *English History, 1914–1945* (Oxford 1966), p. 3.
12. *London Gazette*, 23 October 1914.
13. Norton, *op. cit.*, p. 333.
14. Taylor, *op. cit.*, p. 53.
15. *ibid.*
16. No Conscription Fellowship, *Why we object* (London 1915).
17. Workers' Suffrage Federation, *The Execution of an East London Boy* (London 1916).
18. *The Labour Leader*, 18 April 1916.
19. *H.C. Debs.*, 5th Series, vol. 81, c. 31. Robert J. McNeill, later Baron Cushendon, once hurled a Blue Book at Winston Churchill's head during a debate on tariff reform.
20. Philip Snowden was a known supporter of the No Conscription Fellowship, see *The No Conscription Fellowship – A Record of its Activities* (London 1916).
21. Taylor, *op. cit.*, p. 61.
22. See World War I entry, *Chambers's Encyclopaedia* (1966).
23. *PRO WORKS 20/3–4*, November 1916.
24. *PRO WORKS 20/3/5.*
25. *PRO WORKS 20/3/6.*

26. *ibid.*
27. Wal Hannington, *Unemployed Struggles, 1919–1936* (London 1936), p. 16.
28. *ibid.*, p. 17.
29. *The Daily Express*, 22 November 1922.
30. Wal Hannington, *The Insurgents of London* (N.U.W.C.M. pamphlet) (London 1923).
31. *ibid.*,
32. *ibid.*,
33. *PRO WORKS 20/111.*
34. *PRO WORKS 20/180.*
35. *ibid.*
36. Wal Hannington, *The March of the Miners* (N.U.W.C.M. pamphlet) (London 1927).
37. See A. J. Cook's Introduction (entitled *Miners March Forward*) to Hannington's pamphlet.
38. Quoted by Hannington *op. cit.*, p. 283. The letter was signed by, among others, Harold Laski, C. R. Attlee, A. P. Herbert, Kingsley Martin, D. N. Pritt, H. G. Wells and Ronald Kidd.
39. Robert Benewick, *The Fascist Movement in Britain* (London 1972), pp. 249–50.
40. Ronald Kidd, *British Liberty in Danger* (London 1940), p. 72.
41. For an extended explanation of this Act see Albert Crew, *The Law Relating to Public Meetings and Processions* (London 1937), pp. 60 *et. seq.*
42. Kidd, *op. cit.*, p. 73.
43. Benewick, *op. cit.*, p. 242.
44. Taylor, *op. cit.*, p. 577.
45. Quoted in *Civil Liberties*, October 1947.
46. *Civil Liberties*, November 1947.
47. See *T.L.S.* review of *My Answer*, 14 September, 1946, p. 435.
48. *Civil Liberties*, April 1948.
49. *Civil Liberties*, April/May 1949.
50. Communist Party of Great Britain, *Day of Struggle for Peace and Socialism – Souvenir of London May Day 1949* (London 1949).
51. Stuart Bowes, *The Police and Civil Liberties* (London 1966), p. 59.
52. Harry Street, *Freedom, the Individual and the Law* (London 1972), pp. 51 *et seq.*
53. *Civil Liberties*, Summer 1950.
54. *Daily Worker*, 8 May 1950.
55. For an excellent view of these events see *The Maintenance of Law and Order on May Day*, a film issued by New Era Films in association with the London Trades Council (London 1951).
56. *Civil Liberties*, April 1951.
57. Information supplied by the Department of the Environment.
58. As the new Regulations were issued as a *Statutory Instrument, 1952, No. 776*, the forty days were demanded by Section 6 of the *Statutory Instruments Act, 1946*. See footnote to Appendix 3.
59. *S.I. 1952 No. 775.*
60. *Civil Liberties*, Spring 1953.
61. *ibid.*

62. National Council for Civil Liberties, *Annual Report, 1958–59.*
63. *ibid. Public Order and the Police – a report on the events in Trafalgar Square, Sunday 17th to Monday 18th September, 1961.*
64. *The Observer*, 18 March 1972.
65. *H. C. Debs.*, 5th Series, vol. 833, c. 1497–8.

1. Aerial view of Whitehall looking north towards Trafalgar Square with Horse Guards Parade on the left and the Ministry of Defence bottom right. The National Gallery stands behind Nelson's Column.

2. The Duke of York's Column, Waterloo Steps.

3. Statue of Charles I standing on the site of Charing Cross.

4. The Imperial Standards of Length in the north wall of Trafalgar Square.

5. John Goldicutt's proposal for a London Ampitheatre to stand in the Square; the building was modelled on the Coliseum in Rome. The view is taken from just north of St. Martin's-in-the-Fields, the building beyond topped by a lion is Northumberland House. To the right of the Amphitheatre is the Royal College of Physicians (1832).

6. The new opening to St. Martin's Church from Pall Mall East (*c.* 1825).

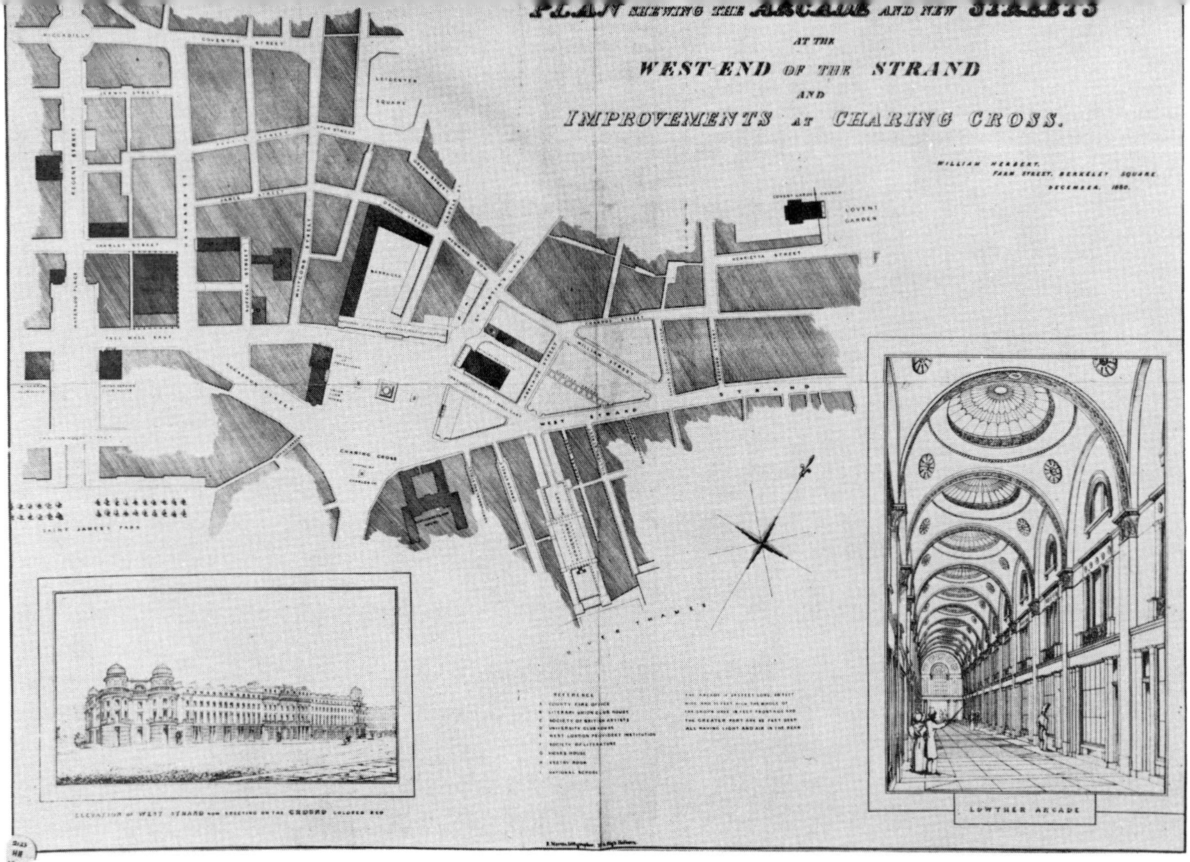

7. Lowther's Arcade by William Herbert (1830). One of the effects of John Nash's "improvements" was the replacement of

8. Morley's Hotel by George Ledwell Taylor. This building survived for a hundred years until it was replaced by South Africa House in the 1930s (photo *c*. 1850).

9. William Wilkins's National Gallery and proposed layout for the Square (*c*. 1838).

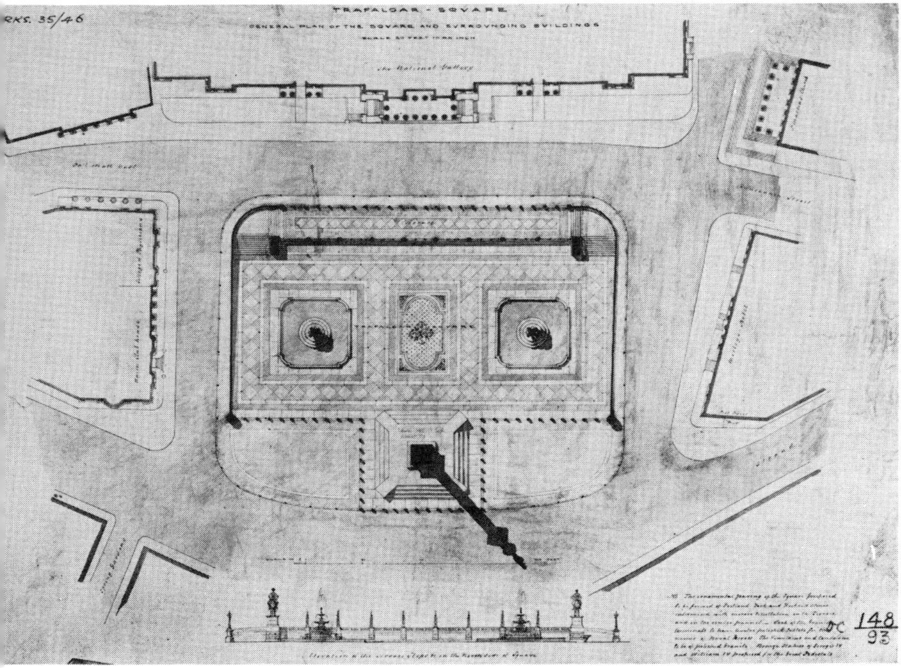

10. Charles Barry's plan for the layout of the Square (*c*. 1840).

11. M. C. Wyatt. Drawing of a model devoted to the memory of Lord Nelson (1808).

12. Nelson's Pillar, Dublin (1808). Demolished in 1966 on the fiftieth anniversary of the Easter Rising.

13. Wellington Monument, Hyde Park Corner (1848).

14. William Wilkins's Nelson Monument, Great Yarmouth, Norfolk (1817–20).

15. John Goldicutt. Design for a Naval Monument in Trafalgar Square (1833).

16. Thomas Bellamy. Design for a National Naval Monument in Trafalgar Square (*c.* 1837).

17. William Railton's winning design for Nelson Memorial (1839).

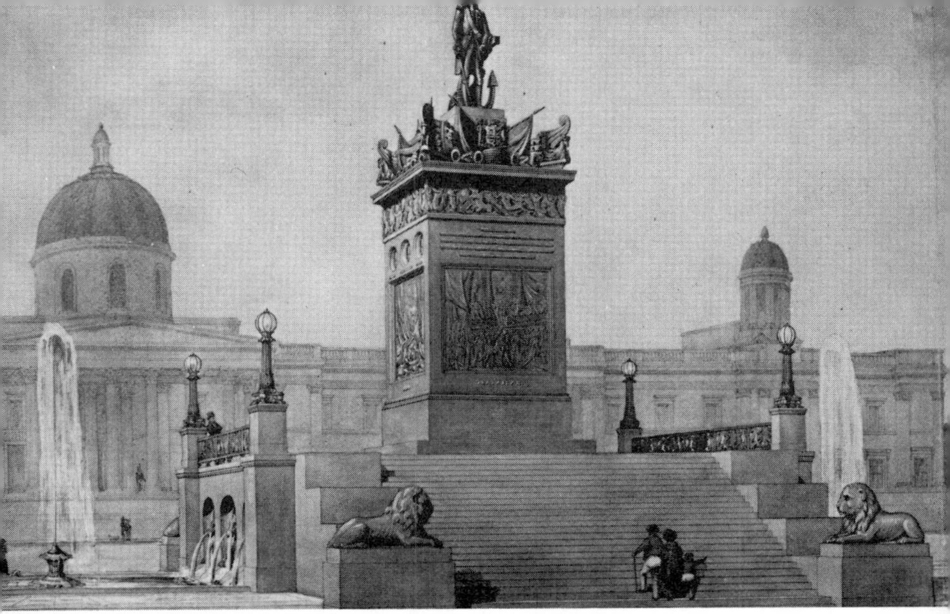

20. Leonard W. Collmann's entry (1839).

21. John Goldicutt's entry (1839).

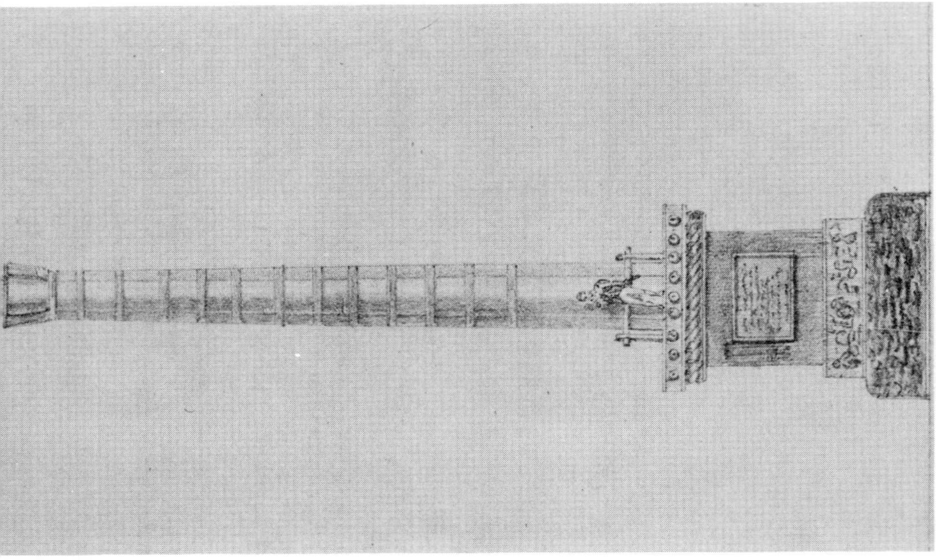

24. William Railton. Nelson's Column. This engraving shows clearly the podium as changed by Lord Lincoln (*c.* 1845). Compare with plate 17.

25. William Railton. View of proposed layout for the Square (*c.* 1840).

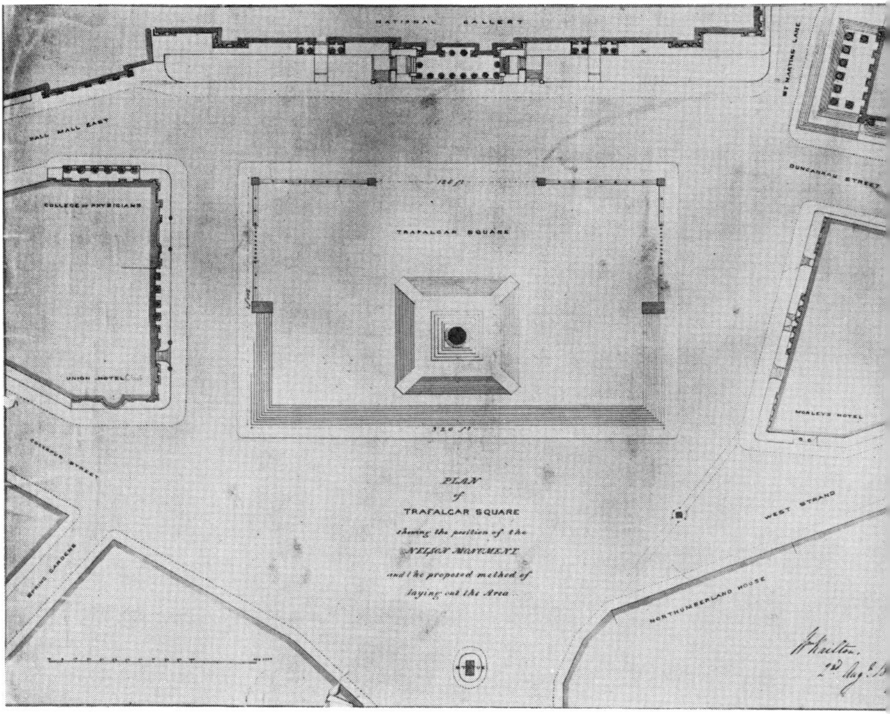

26. William Railton. One of his several designs for the layout of the Square (1839).

27. Nelson's Column under construction (photographed by W. H. Fox Talbot 1844).

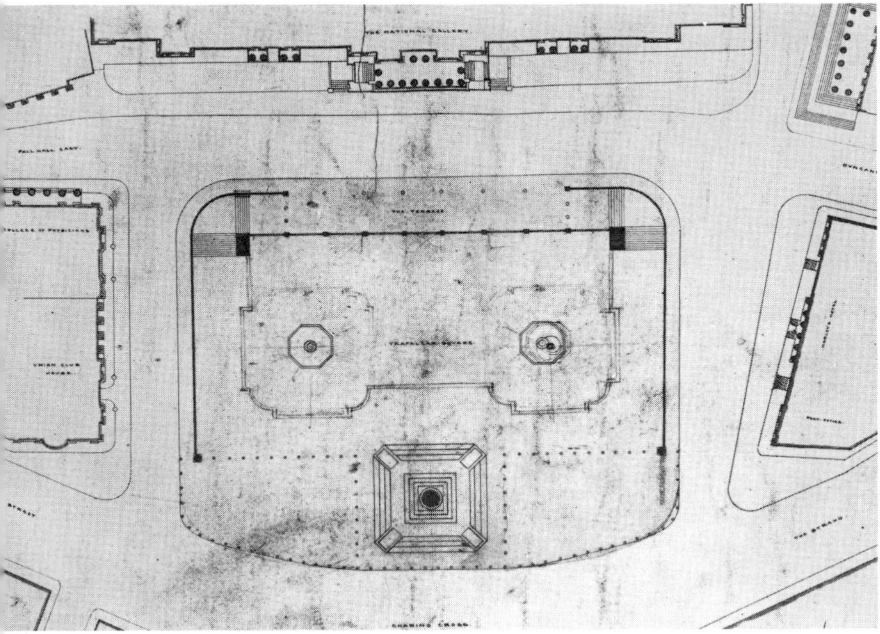

28. Charles Barry's proposal for a single basin in the Square (1841).

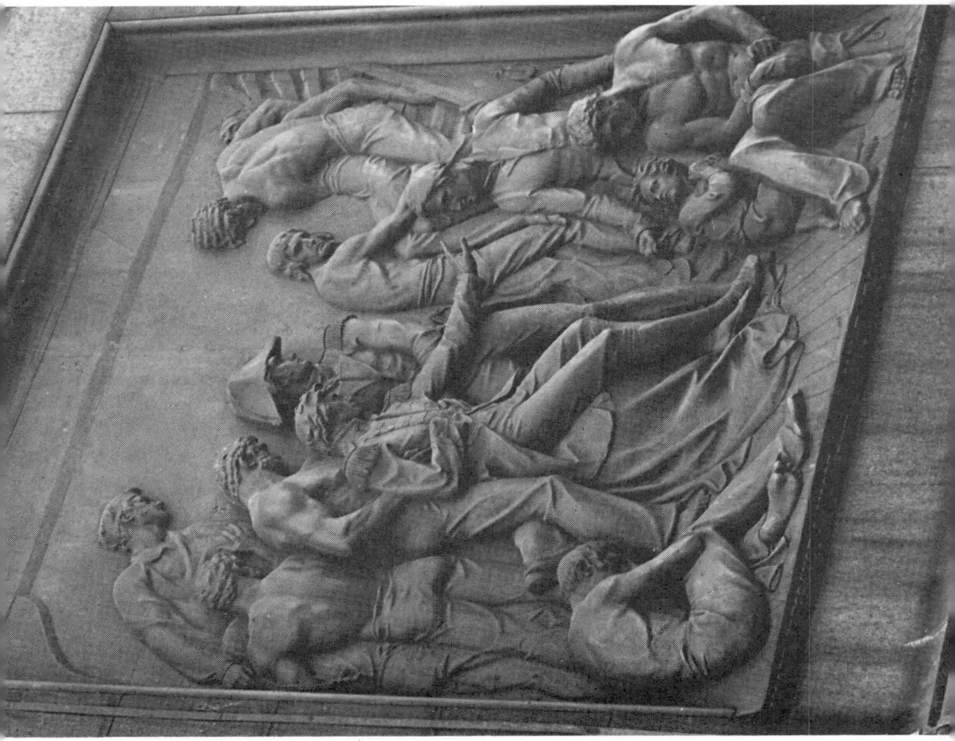

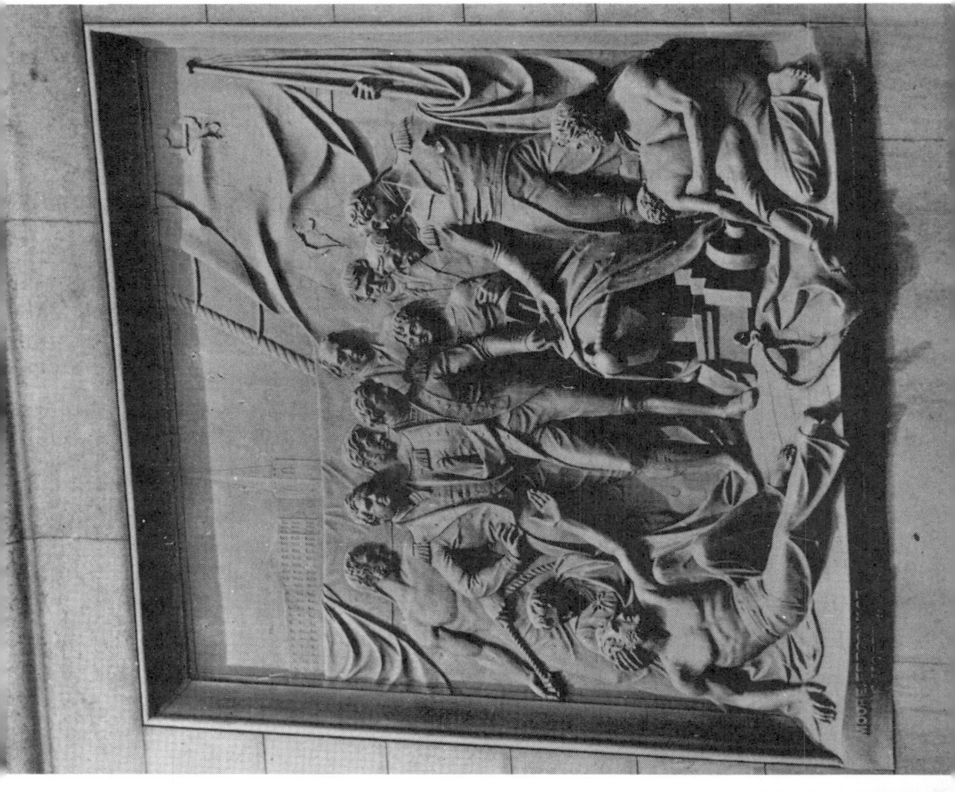

31. West side bas relief "St. Vincent"

32. South side bas relief "Trafalgar".

33. Edward Baily's statue of Nelson (photographed when the Column was cleaned in 1968).

34. A policeman emerging from the Bude Light Drum police box in the south-east corner of the Square.

35. The North Wall of the Square, showing busts of (left to right) Cunningham, Jellicoe, and Beatty. To the right are Lutyens's flower-beds. In the background is the equestrian statue of George IV.

CHARLES JAMES NAPIER
GENERAL
BORN
MDCCLXXXII
DIED
MDCCCLIII

TO
MAJOR GENERAL
SIR HENRY HAVELOCK
K.C.B.
AND HIS BRAVE COMPANIONS
IN ARMS
DURING THE CAMPAIGN IN INDIA
1857
"SOLDIERS! YOUR LABOURS
YOUR PRIVATIONS YOUR SUFFERINGS
AND YOUR VALOUR
WILL NOT BE FORGOTTEN BY
A GRATEFUL COUNTRY"

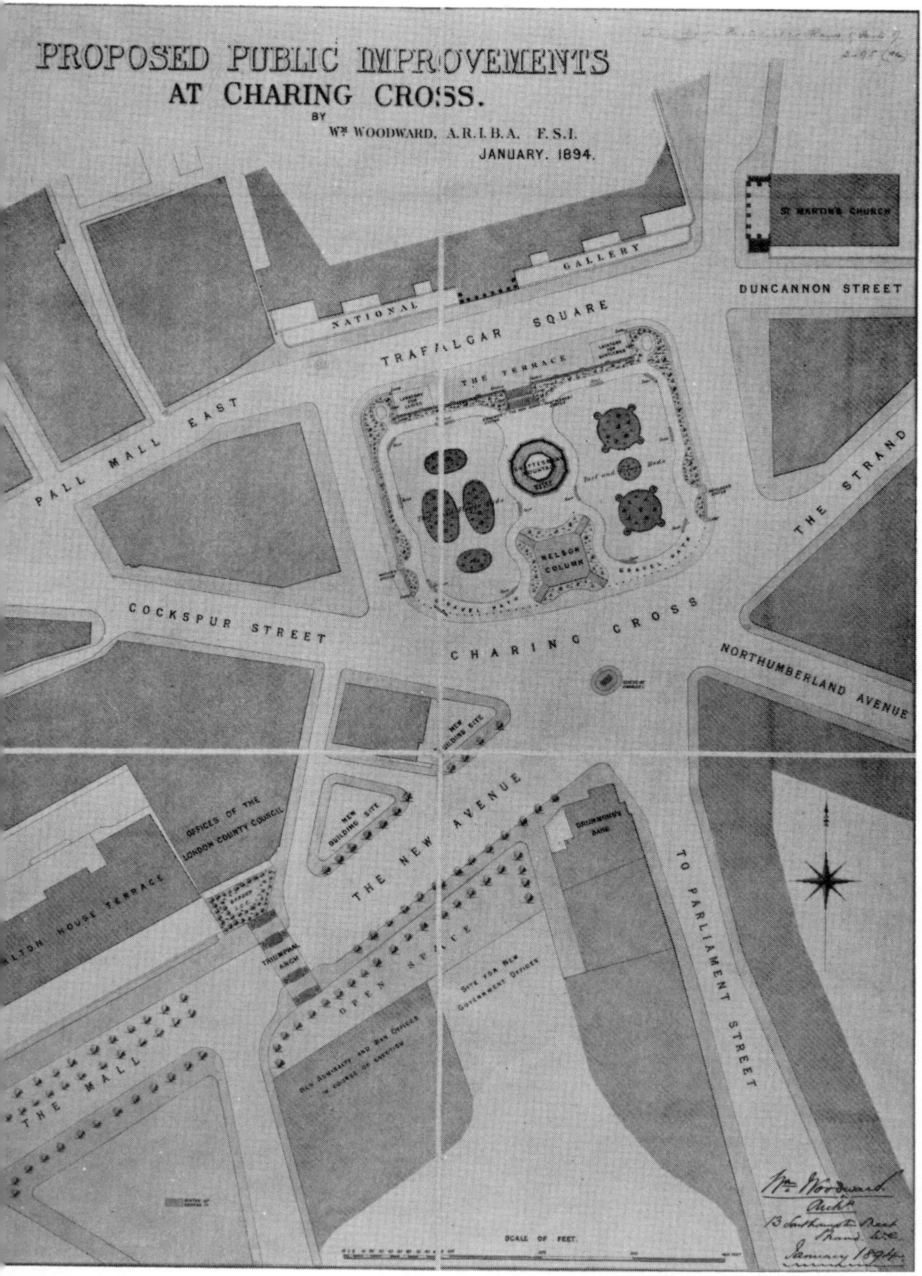

38. One suggestion that would have effectively prevented demonstrations in the Square. A scheme by William Woodward for turning the space into a garden (1894).

39. H. Heathcote-Statham's project of 1912 suggests redesigning the Square (and the National Gallery). The steps in the Square Statham thought would facilitate more orderly meetings.

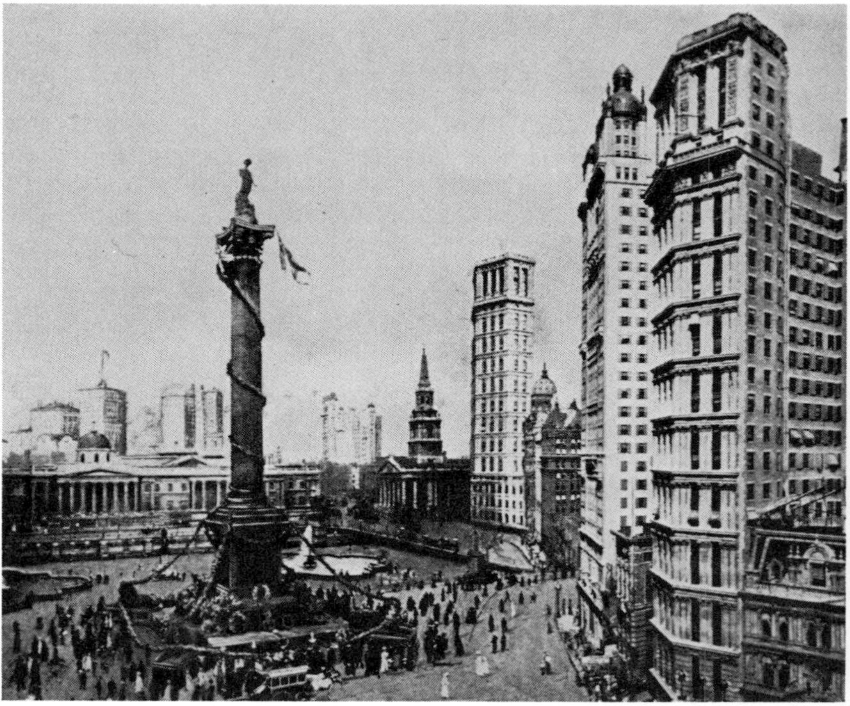

40. A mildly prophetic photo-montage of 1902 that suggested that Trafalgar Square would in time be renamed Washington Square, and Nelson's Column The Washington Monument.

41. Mounted police clearing a Suffragette meeting in the Square.

42. Launching of the "Peace and Joy Loan", June 1919. The temporary hut can be seen just behind Napier's statue.

43. Meeting in the Square to press for the release of Irish prisoners, February 1922.

44. Part of the huge crowd that welcomed the group of Welsh miners who had walked all the way from South Wales, 20 November 1927.

45. A. J. Cook addressing the Welsh miners from the plinth of Nelson's Column 20 November 1927.

46. Unemployed assembling in the Square, 29 October 1932.

TO-LET

48. Mounted police on their way to harass the unemployed in the Square, 30 October 1932.

49. Great mass meeting of the unemployed in the Square, 4 March 1934.

50. "National Service – it's up to YOU." Placard associating "England expects every man, etc." with Military Service: a theme that was to be constantly repeated during World War II.

51. Second Front demonstration, 25 October 1942.

52. "Wings for Victory Week" 1943 (from a painting by Frank E. Beresford). Gordon's statue was moved to make way for the Lancaster Bomber. Note how the bas reliefs on Nelson's Column have been covered by pictures of fighter planes.

53. Statue of Charles George Gordon (from the rear). Photo taken during a meeting

54. Suez Crisis. Meeting to protest against British invasion of Suez in early November 1956. This view clearly shows how the basins divide up the crowd.

KEEP BRITAIN WHITE
WHITE DEFENCE LEAGUE

56. Suez Crisis. "Law not War" demonstration, 5 November 1956. Later that day, mounted and foot police attacked demonstrators, causing several injuries.

57. Campaign for Nuclear Disarmament. Crowd listening to Canon Collins before starting four-day march to Aldermaston, Good Friday, 1958.

58. Campaign for Nuclear Disarmament, Easter Monday, 1961.

59. Police carrying off a demonstrator during the Committee of 100 sit-down in the Square, 17 September 1961.

60. "Ban the Bomb" demonstrators approaching the Square up Whitehall, 15 April 1963.

61. Vietnam Solidarity Campaign demonstration, 17 March 1968. During the cleaning of Nelson's Column meetings were addressed from the North Terrace over the foliage of Lutyens's flower-beds.

62. "Attack Injustice" demonstration. Trades Union Congress protest against the Industrial Relations Act, 2 February 1971. The photograph also shows the clear space in front of the podium created by a steel barrier erected in the early 1960s. This barrier ensures that the crowd is kept at a distance from any speakers.

63. Lapel sticker for National Union of Students demonstration, 23 January 1972. The demonstrators were protesting against the attempts of the Minister of Education (Margaret Thatcher) to interfere with Student Unions.

64. Senora Salvador Allende speaking before a mass rally in support of Chilean resistance, 15 September 1974. The large banner hanging behind the platform is by John Dugger.

65 Protest in front of the National Gallery on the ban on meetings in the Square on Irish Questions, 5 October 1975

66. GLC leader Ken Livingstone as Nelson. Lee Robinson's front cover cartoon on a book that formed part of the 1983-85 campaign to save the Labour run Greater London Council from being abolished by the Thatcher government (Rodney Mace)

67. The day that finished Thatcherism. Poll tax riot March 1990 (David Hoffman Picture Library)

68. *Alison Lapper 8 Months Pregnant*. Marc Quinn's winning design for the 2003 Fourth Plinth competition (Marc Quinn)

69. After 150 years of celebrating death the Square is transformed in 2003 by the new Greater London Authority into a place of popular celebration (Hayley Madden, courtesy GLA)

APPENDICES

APPENDIX 1

A list of architects and artists who are known to have contributed an entry for the Nelson Memorial Competition for Trafalgar Square.

AN ARCHITECT FROM MIDDLESEX
EVELYN W. ASHTON, sculptor
EDWARD HODGES BAILY, sculptor (1788–1867)
WILLIAM BEATTIE, sculptor (fl. 1829–1864)
ALFRED BEAUMONT
JOHN BELL, sculptor (1812–1895)
THOMAS BELLAMY, architect (1798–1896)
RAPHAEL BRANDON, architect (1817–1877)
JOHN BRITTON, antiquarian (1771–1857)
TIMOTHY BUTLER, sculptor (1806–?)
HENRY CASE
H. COFFEE, sculptor (fl. 1819–1845)
LEONARD W. COLLMANN, architect (1816–1881)
THOMAS DONALDSON, architect (1795–1885)
GEORGE FOGGO, sculptor (1791–1867)
CHARLES FOWLER, architect (1791–1867)
R. E. GAVEY
JOHN GOLDICUTT, architect (1793–1842)
WALTER GRANVILLE
W. P. GRIFFITHS
WILLIAM GROVES, sculptor (1809–18?)
JAMES HAKEWILL, architect (1778–1843)
J. HARRISON
PETER HOLLINS, sculptor (1800–1886)
THOMAS HOPPER, architect (1776–1856)
W. HOSKINS
RICHARD KELSEY, architect (1791–18?)
THOMAS LEWIS, architect
JOHN G. LOUGH, sculptor (1798–1876)
S. MANNING, sculptor (1816–1865)
M. M.
G. B. MOORE, architect (1777–1859)
THOMAS MOULE, antiquarian (1784–1851)
GEORGE NELSON, sculptor (1810–1888)

JAMES H. NIXON, architect
SAMUEL NIXON, sculptor (1803–1854)
EDGAR G. PAPWORTH, sculptor (1809–1866)
PATRICK PARK, sculptor (1811–1956)
FREDERICK C. J. PARKINSON, architect
BENEDETTO PISTRUCCI, sculptor (1784–1855)
WILLIAM PITTS
WILLIAM RAILTON, architect (1801–1877)
C. A. REEVES, sculptor (1778–1860)
GEORGE RENNIE, sculptor (1802–1860)
ROBERT W. S. SIEVIER, sculptor (1794–1865)
SYDNEY SMIRKE, architect (1798–1877)
CHARLES H. SMITH, sculptor (1792–1864)
J. TARRING, architect (1806–1875)
V. TAYLOR
JAMES THRUPP, architect
CARL TOTTIE
MUSGRAVE L. WATSON, sculptor (1804–1847)
(SIR) RICHARD WESTMACOTT, sculptor (1775–1856)
ROBERT F. WETTEN
WILLIAM F. WOODINGTON, sculptor (1806–1893)

APPENDIX 2

NELSON MEMORIAL COMPETITION ENTRIES

The following are some of the architects' and artists' descriptions that accompanied their entries. They are taken from several sources as no complete list was ever published.
From, the *Civil Engineer and Architects Journal*, August, 1839 pp. 290–7. (As was the normal practice in competitions authorship was identified by number until the final judgement was made.)

MODEL NO. 2, *Thomas Hopper*. – The custom of mankind has been to elevate those characters who have distinguished themselves, by investing them with power and titles, and to transmit those names to posterity who have been pre-eminently exalted, by erecting temples to their memory. – Such was the practice of the great nations, whose example other nations have endeavoured to imitate. The Jews had a divine command to erect a temple for the Ark of the Covenant, and Christian nations have dedicated churches to honour the memory of men of eminent piety. Even Trajan's pillar was part of a temple.

Believing that the highest honour which can be bestowed in commemoration of great actions by a nation, is the dedication of a temple to immortalize the character of the hero: and as no difference of opinion exists, as to the immense superiority of Lord Nelson, over the multitude of naval heroes whose names adorn the British history, he, above all men, has deserved the noblest tribute that a nation can bestow. – Such being the conviction of my mind, I have endeavoured to design a naval temple, commemorative of Nelson, and founded on the principles of ancient art. I have adopted a circular open temple for many considerations, but above all, because I think it best adapted to the site, and calculated to improve the grouping of the other buildings in Trafalgar-square.

The upper part of the temple and the steps only are exhibited: the crypt and basso relievos want of time compelled me to omit, as well as the painting of the dome. – The crypt I propose to surround the granite pedestal which supports the statue, on which Nelson's motto should be inscribed: the columns of the crypt to have the names of the ships and the commanders delineated on them, and the niches to contain the statues of the commanders who fell in the battles; and also paintings of Nelson's various personal encounters. – The pedestals which divide the steps are intended to contain the entrances to the crypt, and the statues of the three seconds in command. – The divisions on the frieze to contain, in sculpture, the history of a naval fight: the architrave within to contain a procession of naval triumph, and also a lamentation for the loss of the hero in the moment of victory. The dome to be painted with three stars as an allegory, descriptive of the three great battles, in all of which Nelson had triumphed. The centre to be lighted from the crown, in imitation of a star, with Nelson's last glorious command, the light from which would descend full upon the statue. – The capitals of the columns are composed of oak, thistle, and shamrock: and all the mouldings and architectural ornaments are taken from parts of naval architecture, as the ornaments of the Erectheium were taken from the nautilus. – The design is formed to admit of a great fountain to play on the anniversaries of Nelson's birth, – and the three battles: and at night the whole building could be illuminated.

This is all that would be required in the dedication of the temple of Nelson.

P.S. The flag ships of the naval crown are intended to represent the navy; the commanders to represent the officers of the service; the sailors who support Nelson's statue, to represent the foremost men; and the naval crown, which surmounts the building, is intended as the emblem of power and authority, and the immortality of Nelson.

MODEL, NO. 3, *T. Butler*. – In the model which I offer to the consideration of the committee, I have laboured to embody those points of character upon which is founded the naval greatness of England, and which in my humble opinion, (in whatever way they may be expressed) ought not to be forgotten, in association with a monument consecrated to the memory of a hero, whose achievements are among the most renowned of the only nation upon earth that has claimed and maintained the wide dominion of the seas.

The extreme elevation of the monument would be 84 feet, and, as materials, I propose granite and bronze, as being best adapted to withstand the deteriorating effects of this climate. The statue of Nelson, and the graduated shaft upon which it is placed, together with the subordinate figures, and the rest of the effective part of the monument in which the story is told, would consist of metal; and the massive base I propose to construct of granite.

The projected height of the statue of Nelson is 19 feet, that of the figure of Britannia 20 feet, and that of the Sailor of the like dimensions. Britannia is represented as resting with her left hand on the anchor, her hope, glory, and strength, and with her right hand she points at once to Nelson, and the first word of his ever-memorable signal, "England expects every man to do his duty", which appears inscribed round the column.

Behind Britannia and above her head waves triumphantly the British Flag, grasped by the sailor, in the rear of the monument. This figure of a seaman stripped for action, represented the unshrinking front and unquailing heart, with which England has ever met her enemies. The top of the column is enriched by a chaplet of laurel, and on the pannels of the base are inscribed Nelson's three grand victories – Nile – Copenhagen – Trafalgar. The four lions would be of granite, the same material as the base, and the whole encircled by a chain cable supported by globes of granite.

The *estimate* of the monument is calculated according to the proposed sum, 30,000*l.*

In this design, it has been as much as possible my wish to avoid remote allegorical allusion, by adhering to an alphabet of symbols, so familiar as to be legible to the plainest understanding, and to impart to the whole a naval and a British character. It has also been my study to observe somewhat of a pyramidal form, as best calculated to lead the eye upwards to the hero of the story.

MODEL, NO. 7, and DESIGNS NOS. 73 & 74, *John Goldicutt, F.R.I.B.A.* – Addison, in his work upon medals, produces one of Britannia seated on a winged globe, holding in her right hand a Roman standard, (S.P.Q.R.) This medal was struck in honour of Antoninus Pius, who extended the boundaries of the Roman province in Britain.

There is also in Addison's work a medal of Marcus Aurelius Antoninus, successor to A. Pius, representing Italia seated on a celestial globe; for it exhibits a section of the zodiac, and is studded with stars, probably struck in honour of the Quadi, Parthians, &c.

Allegorical figures standing on spheres, or holding a ball in the palm of the hand, are of the most ancient date; perhaps the medal Eternitas struck by Ant. Pius, is one of the finest: it represents a matron holding in her right hand a globe surmounted by a bird having a radiating crest.

From the Romans having placed Britannia and Italia reposing on spheres, there is classical authority for choosing such a basis for a statue of Nelson, the hero of an hundred battles.

The sphere, which is posited so as to bring Britain on its zenith, is 30 feet diameter; the statue of Nelson 13 feet high; the entire base 25 feet. From the base line to the crown of Nelson's head the whole is about 70 feet. This altitude will be in accordance with the adjacent buildings, and especially the National Gallery, which measures 50 feet from the base line to the apex of the pediment. The diameter of the monument across the bastions which support the allegorical figures measures 40 feet.

An elevation such as this possesses the advantage of bringing the colossal figures fully into view to the public eye, and every feature can be traced. Moreover, upon a sphere the figure is thrown out in a manner not to be achieved were it placed upon a column, in which, from the continuity of the shaft, and the figure terminating that continuity, there is less of attraction and imposing grandeur than in a massive globe, a geometrical figure characteristic of stability and strength; and therefore, in every respect, if we may be governed by the taste of the Antonini, indicative of victory and peace, and of the power of that country whose "flag for a thousand years has braved the battle and the breeze." From the National Gallery to the statue of King Charles, the ground slopes about 16 feet. It is proposed to lower this ground from the National Gallery, to such a level as would give perspective elevation to that building, the Church of St. Martin, and the College of Physicians. This would be accomplished by a terrace on the south side of the road skirting the front of the National Gallery, and which would be carried partially along the east and west flanks of the square southwards. The quadrangle thus levelled would confer perspective elevation also on the monument, and be better adapted to its adjuncts and accessories. The base on which the sphere rests is surmounted by allegorical figures. Fame, Neptune, Victory, and Britannia, occupy the east, north, west, and south points of the base; on the lower section of which tablets appear in these cardinal points inscribed with the words Nile, Copenhagen, Trafalgar, and "England expects every man to do his duty." Thus, beneath Fame, to the east, the Nile; beneath Neptune, to the north, Copenhagen; under Victory, to the west, Trafalgar; and Britannia, after the medal or national coin, sits over the last words of the hero. Beneath these entablatures the masonry of the base indicates stability, and allows the eye to rise gradually, first to the allegorical figures, in the midst of which the sphere rests in its own simple grandeur, leaving the colossal figure of the hero disengaged and entire. A circular area extends 60 feet from the base, which, being paved and surrounded by a ballustrade, may serve the purpose of private promenade to view the monument, or be made a permanent sheet of water which the adjacent mains may supply. This water would be in character with the profession of Nelson and of his country, giving besides to Trafalgar Square, a great degree of municipal comfort; for whether we view this water as an ornament, or physical agent conferring salubrity on the atmosphere of a city, there can be but one opinion respecting its adaptation to the design it surrounds. It is proposed to construct the sphere of polished granite or bronze, and the whole to be polished to resist the effects of smoke and atmosphere; and that access be had to the interior of the monument, where a chamber and other depositories should be constructed, to contain the busts of illustrious persons distinguished by acts of valour, and where thousands who visit this great metropolis may be admitted to inspect the same, – drawn to the object by the display of a building of massive grandeur, unique in character, and interesting in effect.

MODEL NO. 13, *M. L. Watson.* – The design is an oblong pedestal supporting a statue of Nelson, and surrounded at the base by allegorical groups of figures. The first group represents a nymph rising from the ocean at the command of Neptune, with a wreath of laurel, whilst Britannia directs the attention to the hero for whom it is destined. On either side are the victories of the Nile and Copenhagen. The fourth group is designed for the victory of Trafalgar, with peace and power. The whole subject is raised on a platform, on the four angles of which are placed the different oceans in which Nelson distinguished himself. Throughout the composition I have endeavoured to convey boldness, energy and grandeur, and to impress on the mind the stirring character of the British navy. My original sketch for this design, will be found among the water-colour drawings, unaltered since the first competition.

The architectural parts of the design are proposed to be executed in granite, the sculpture in bronze. Height 120 feet; width 64 feet.

MODEL NO. 17, *Frederick Claudius J. Parkinson.* – The height of the obelisk, with pedestal and substructure to the surface of the ground, to be 145 feet. – The extreme length of the monument, 120 feet. The height of Nelson to be 12 feet, and the other figures in proportion, as shewn in the model. One one side of Nelson stands Britannia; on the other, Victory. In the semi-circular recesses are deposited the arms of the subdued nations, in commemoration of the victories achieved; the captives being guarded by the British lion. – On the opposite front of the monument, is placed a sarcophagus, with angels protecting the tomb of Nelson; above the sarcophagus are affixed the arms and mantle of the hero.– The sides represent the prows of ships, with various other nautical emblems. – The obelisk is surmounted by the shield of Britannia and the British ensigns. – Various other emblematical figures and trophies are shown in the model.

The sculpture executed in bronze, will amount to the sum of	16,000	0	0
The monument, composed of the best granite, will cost	12,600	0	0
	£28,600	0	0

MODEL NO. 19, *William Groves.* – In the rudely embodied idea, bearing my name, I have endeavoured to place before the nobelmen and gentlemen of the committee, a composition which should appear at once triumphal and monumental, and therefore presenting the character which an Englishman attributes to a sacred edifice – while, from its simplicity of outline it should not clash with the surrounding buildings.

The monument is surmounted by a group representing Strength rearing, and Wisdom and Justice supporting the Admiral's flag. Immediately beneath at the angles are the four winds, Zephyrus, Notus, Apeliotes and Boreas, with their respective attributes, publishing to the four quarters of the globe, the glory of the hero, who stands on an elevated pedestal beneath, in front. On his right is Britannia, who has just embossed the name of her favourite on her shield, thus converting it into a Ægis for future war. On his left is the wingless victory of the Athenian, which I have selected as the most applicable to the hero, whom she never quitted. – At the back in the centre, is commerce seated, her right hand resting on a trident, her left on a sphere, (indicative of her influence over sea and land,) and her foot on a rudder. On one side of her is the genius of the Torrid Zone, and on the other the genius of the Temperate Zone, surrounded by the emblems of commerce, and depositing the produce of their respective climes at her feet. On the pedestals at the sides, I propose putting the hero's arms, and above them inscribing the names of the officers, his companions in victory. In the front and two side panels in the base, are reliefs commemorative of his great victories. *Copenhagen.* – Neptune ordering the British Flag to be reared in triumph on the ocean. *The Nile.* – On the left the Nile; behind, the genius of

Alexandria advancing with extended arms to welcome Britannia, who, accompanied by the lion, is standing on the broken and prostrate eagle of France. *Trafalgar.* – A sarcophagus bearing the hero's name; the genius of death about to deposit thereon a wreath of laurels; a weeping warrior is seated at the base of the sarcophagus, and at the sides are the flags of France and Spain. In the back panel would be particulars of the erection of the monument. On the four projecting portions of the base, four lions. The figures to be 15 feet high, and executed in bronze; the building in granite, and the total height of the monument from the ground line to the top of the flag staff to be 120 feet. The whole cost would be 30,000*l.*

MODEL NO. 21, *Charles Fowler, Architect, and R. W. Sievier, Sculptor.* – The composition presented by the accompanying model is intended to combine architecture with sculpture; in order to obtain a more striking effect from their union, than either is calculated to produce separately: the one by its form and mass being calculated to arrest the attention and make a general impression, which may be heightened and perfected by the more refined and interesting details of the other. With respect to the first it may be observed, as the result of existing instances, that a mere structure cannot properly convey the feeling, or produce the effect required in the erection of a mounument to commemorate any celebrated character or event; whilst, on the other hand, a statue or group of sculpture is ineffective for want of mass, and distinctness of form and outline: the former is appreciated only as a distant object, and the latter on close inspection. The object therefore has been to combine the advantages peculiar to each art, so that the many who pass along may be struck with the general aspect of the monument; and the few who may pause to examine its details, may find their first impressions carried forward and perfected by the beauty and significance of its historical illustrations.

With respect to the design now submitted, the endeavour has been to render it characteristic and appropriate; avoiding plagiarism, but without affecting novelty. The rostrated angles of the pedestals and the accompanying decorations determine its character as a naval trophy; whilst the basso relievo and other parts of the sculpture plainly tell of the hero and his achievements.

In regard to the structure it will be seen that the basement is distinguished by plainness and solidity; and it is proposed to be formed entirely of granite in very bold masses. The couchant lions on the angular pedestals are to be of the same material, but of a different colour.

The colossal figures seated against the four fronts of the pedestal represent Britannia, Caledonia, Hibernia, and Neptune; Britannia accompanied by couchant lions, and Neptune reclining on a sea-horse, 23 feet in length; under which is the entrance to a winding staircase, by which parties can have access to the gallery.

The die of the pedestal contains on its south front an inscription, briefly recording the fame and achievements of Nelson; and on the north front a few simple historical facts relating to him, and the erection of the monument.

On one side is a medallion containing the head of Nelson; in order that the lineaments of his countenance might be brought more distinctly within view, the statue being so much elevated: and on the other side are his armorial bearings.

The central compartment of the elevation has the dado or lower part inscribed with the names and dates of his four principal actions; and in the panel over each is a representation in basso relievo of some striking incident in each battle:

First. – Cape St. Vincent. When "on the quarter-deck of an enemy's first-rate he received the swords of the officers, giving them one by one to William Fearney, one of his old Agamemnon's, who, with the utmost coolness, put them under his arm."

Second. – At the Nile. "After his wound was dressed he was now left alone, when suddenly a cry was heard on the deck that the Orient was on fire. In the confusion he found his way up, unassisted and unnoticed; and, to the astonishment of everyone, appeared on the quarter-deck, where he immediately gave orders that boats should be sent to the relief of the enemy."

Third. – Copenhagen. – "A wafer was given to him; but he ordered a candle to be brought from the cockpit, and sealed the letter with wax, affixing a larger seal than he ordinarily used. 'This,' said he, 'is no time to be hurried and informal.'"

Fourth. – Trafalgar. "Hardy, who was a few steps from him, turning round, saw three men raising him up. – 'They have done for me at last, Hardy!' said he. – 'I hope not!' cried Hardy. – 'Yes,' he replied; 'my backbone is shot through,'"

The latter occupies the front, and displays at once the climax of his achievements, and the termination of his brilliant career.

The gallery above is supported on cannons, in lieu of the usual architectural consoles, and the intervals in the soflite are enriched with bombs and grenades instead of rosettes. The railing of the gallery is composed of decorations and emblems having reference to the object of the monument, thus combining ornament with characteristic expression.

The upper compartment changes into the circular form, and is more fully charged with decoration illustrative of the honours which Nelson achieved. The four large wreaths encircling the pedestal contain repectively the naval and mural crowns, the viscount's and ducal coronets; beneath which are suspended the decorations of the four orders conferred upon him by their respective sovereigns.

The frieze of this pedestal is entirely occupied by the heraldic motto, which is peculiarly expressive and appropriate. The ornaments surmounting the cornice, which are analogous to the Grecian antefixæ, are composed of escallop shells; and the cupola is to be of copper gilt.

The statue of Nelson crowns the whole, and is to be executed in bronze, about 16 feet in height. The entire height of the monument, including the statue, will be 128 feet from the area of the square, being 19 feet more than the York column.

The structure, with all its decorations and accessories, to be completed in the most perfect style for the sum of 25,000*l.*; and ample security will be given for the due accomplishment of the undertaking for that amount.

MODEL NO. 29, *Patric Park.* – Allegory, and particularly the old allegory of Neptune, Tritons, nymphs and sea-horses, can only be used in commemorating a man, whose virtues are unknown, or problematical. In a monument to a man like Nelson, such cannot be tolerated. – The character of man, is *stamped* on his countenance, and proved by his form. – On this just principle, which is the vitality of true sculpture, I have based this design. I illustrate, by form and expression, in single statues and groups, the characteristics of Nelson, as thus: – his ardent youth – his hopeful contest in the West Indies – his daring manhood under Sir John Jervis – his heroic struggle at the Nile – his piety after that glorious victory – the applause of the world – his resolved character at Copenhagen – his death at Trafalgar – the sorrow of his country. – These characteristics claim our veneration, and sculpture hails with enthusiasm a character so congenial to her pure and sublime genius. – The obelisk is used as a sign post to attract attention to the sculpture.

The height is 95 feet; the statue of Nelson is 16 feet; the illustrative statues are 11 feet; and the groups of the proportion of 7 feet. All the sculpture to be executed in Ravaccione marble; the obelisk, &c. in freestone; for 30,000*l.*

MODELS NO. 32 and 168, *S. Manning, Sculptor.* – A column representing the British state, founded on a rock; on one side of the base Nelson is receiving the trident from Neptune, accompanied by other sea divinities; on the other, he is dying in the lap of victory. The column is surmounted by a figure of peace.

Statue of Nelson 12 feet, monument 100 feet high. To be executed in bronze, marble, and granite, &c. Probable estimate under 30,000*l.*

MODEL NO. 37, *William Pitts.* – Grandeur and simplicity have been the objects of attainment in this model. As a colossal statue he is raised overlooking the city which his judgment and valour have preserved, and his immortal memory is a glory to its prosperity.

The statue of Nelson is proposed to be 30 feet, the pedestal and steps about 60 feet, the entire height of statue, pedestal, and steps, 90 feet. The statue, lions, and subjects, in the panels, to be executed in bronze, the pedestal and steps in solid blocks of granite; to be completed in the best style of art, for the sum of 30,000*l.*

MODEL NO. 38, *J. G. Lough.* – In the model I now have the honour of submitting to your inspection, my great aim has been to render it perfectly simple, and at the same time purely Nelsonic; with this view the four subordinate figures I have kept four feet smaller than the statue of Nelson, and have so interwoven them with the form of the pedestal, that is to say, adapted them to the curve of the pedestal, that the eye is carried to Nelson at once. I trust you will find that in this design architecture and sculpture are completely blended, an effect which could never be produced by a number of scattered figures; and in the monuments we have handed down to us of the best ages of the Egyptians and Greeks, we universally find this point has been strictly attended to.

I propose that the monument should stand 40 feet high, the pedestal to the base on which Nelson stands being 24 feet, and Nelson 16 feet, whom I have represented in a boat cloak, holding a telescope, as emblematic of his constant vigilance. I have chosen the above-mentioned height as one at which the features of Nelson may be clearly recognized, and also as being peculiarly adapted to the intended site. The four lower figures are intended to be 12 feet in length, raised $6\frac{1}{2}$ feet from the ground; they are meant to represent sailors – and I have adopted the costume at the moment of action, it being more sculptural. My idea of a monument being to make it national and intelligible to all classes. I have studiously avoided allegory; I have introduced such attributes as I thought would not interfere with the general outline. The two sailors in front are holding flags, supposed to have been taken in battle; the pensive one to the right holding that of Trafalgar, and the one on the left that of the Nile. The bassi relievi on the pedestal are intended to be cut in intaglio in the granite in the Egyptian manner, as my great object has been to produce a great whole and to preserve the general outline. The whole to be built of granite, except the five figures, which, with their attributes, would be in bronze – materials which would last as long as time; and with a view to its duration I have carefully avoided all paltry ornament and trifling mouldings; I have also abstained from the introduction of fluid – a thing always guarded against by the ancients, as a violation of the laws of sculpture. As it regards the cost, I have confined myself within the limits named by the committee.

MODEL NO. 39, *E. H. Baily, R.A.* – An obelisk raised to the memory of Nelson by his grateful country. At the base, our great naval commander is represented supporting the imperial standard; on his left stands the genius of Britain, hailing with affection the hero of Trafalgar; his attendant, Victory, being seated on his right. At the back of the obelisk rests the Nile – Neptune with the subordinate deities of the ocean, form a triumphal procession round the rock on which the monument is placed, thereby indicating that the victories of Nelson were as extensive as the element on which he fought.

The height of the monument is intended to be 80 feet; the diameter of the steps the same extent, and the height of Nelson to be 9 feet; the other figures in proportion as in the sketch. To execute the whole monument in Ravaccioni marble (the same as the arch before Buckingham Palace is built of), 22,000*l.* If executed in bronze, 30,000*l.*

MODEL NO. 40, *E. H. Baily, R.A.* – On four projecting parts of the base are four sea-horses, indicative of the element on which the hero's battles were fought. On three sides of the base are three colossal emblemetical figures of the Atlantic, the Mediterranean, the Baltic; and on the fourth, that of the genius of Britain.

Above these figures are four projecting antique prows, and still higher, four figures of victory linked hand-in-hand and facing the four quarters of the globe. On the summit stands the statue of the immortal hero.

The cost of erecting this monument would be from 25,000*l.* to 30,000*l.*, according to the magnitude of the figures.

MODEL No. 41, *Patric Park.* – In this design, I devote one group of a victorious hero, 20 feet high, in honour of Nelson's deeds. The statue is 30 feet high; on one side of which, Manhood mourns the death of Nelson; on the other, Honour is consoled by the glory and triumphs of Nelson. Executed

MODEL No. 45, *J. Harrison, of Chester.* – In designing a memorial to Nelson, I have at the same time endeavoured to arrange a temple to the navy, suitable in its style to the general architecture of Trafalgar-square; and from its mass, or elevation, not appearing to take from the importance of the Gallery, or attempting to rival St. Martin's spire.

In the centre of the interior is erected a colossal statue of Nelson, around which are receptacles for the statues of future naval heroes as they arise. The 16 statues under the porticos are of the admirals of England, with the panel above each of them filled with bas-relief, illustrating the principal feature of their professional career. The sculptures in the tympanums of the pediments, and in the compartments of the base of the obelisk, are intended to carry out a biography of Nelson. And (if the funds permitted) to complete the design, the metopes in the frieze should be filled with sculpture, conveying a history of the navy (after the manner of the Parthenon). The whole surmounted by the obelisk, bearing in letters of gold on its imperishable sides to the four winds, the future watch-word to naval greatness. The four colossal figures, at the angles of the middle terrace, are symbolical of the Nile, Copenhagen, and Trafalgar subdued, and Thames triumphant. The crocodiles and lions are to be fitted up as fountains, to play on the anniversaries of naval victories, having the name of the victory hung in the panel over the four doorways. The space under the terraces are intended as vaults for any useful purpose, to be approached by doorways in the breast walls at the lower side of the square, which will admit of another flight of steps to make up for the dip of the ground.

The height to the apex of the obelisk is 100 feet; and, consequently, about 20 feet higher than the centre dome of the National Gallery. The height of the pediments is about 17 feet lower than that of the gallery; and the extreme width, from outside of columns, is about 17 feet wider than the centre portico of the gallery. The building, with its relievi's and statues of the admirals, it is proposed should be executed in one of the approved freestones of the country: the statue of Nelson in marble, and the symbolical figures, with the crocodiles and lions, in iron. The cost of the whole will be 50,000*l.* The model is worked to a-fourth of an inch scale.

Model No. 46, *Henry Case.* – In composing such a monument, to be placed in Trafalgar-square, there are many difficulties to be surmounted, in addition to that, of doing justice to the achievements of so great a man.

The large space to be filled, demands considerable extent and importance, in the design itself, while the general effect equally requires, that this shall be obtained, with as little obstruction as may be possible, to the view of the surrounding buildings. These objects combined, seem more easy of attainment, by adopting, as the characteristic of the design, the graceful and towering, rather than the massive and severe, taking care that the solidity and repose, so indispensable to greatness, be not lost.

The character of the place, (one of the gayest thoroughfares in London), also suggests a similar design. Art will be more effective when it avails itself of feelings already half formed, and strives to direct them to noble ends, than when it attempts to force them into other channels: – and in the temple, on the mountain, or the sea-shore, a hero's monument, should induce reflection, and impress by solemnity, but in the more busy and crowded parts of a city, where a thousand hurry past, for one who stops to think, it should address itself to emulation, at once, without the intervention of thought, possessing however, that which shall satisfy the mind of the more attentive beholder.

Again, – whatever the mental character of the man, gaity cannot surely be misplaced, in a "Memorial of the Achievements" of one whose life was a succession of victories. If these ideas be correct, that design will be best adapted to the circumstances, which is most calculated, to excite, at a glance, in the thoughtless idler, or hurrying man of business, the desire, by a life like Nelson's, active and honourable, to win honours like his, from a grateful country; – which by its sculptures and inscriptions, shall tell, to the observant, more striking features of his life and character; – which shall leave on the minds of all the impression of a monument appropriate to a naval hero, and worthy of a Nelson; – and shall combine with these qualities, the indispensable conditions, that it shall assist the effect, of the surrounding buildings, and be in its dimensions of sufficient importance to occupy the most magnificent site in the metropolis.

This is the arduous task which has been attempted in the design now submitted to the committee, and for the accomplishment of which a Corinthian column appeared to me to offer the greatest facilities.

The column, with its pedestal, stands on a platform of an elevation of 14 feet 6 inches, at the angles of which are triumphal stelæ, 5 feet 6 inches in diameter, and rising 16 feet from the platform: they support the naval and mural crowns, the ducal and viscounts' coronets, proposed to be in metal gilded.

This is placed on a terrace 140 feet square, 6 inches higher than the ground immediately opposite the centre portico of the National Gallery. At each angle of the terrace is a trophy of sea-horses and flags, (proposed to be executed in bronzed metal, or black marble,) on a cippus surrounded with wreaths, inscribed with the dates of the numerous minor engagements in which Nelson was concerned; the pedestal of the column being reserved for the great actions. In each front are two lions, flanking a flight of steps 60 feet wide. The cippi are 12 feet 6 inches in diameter, and the lions are 7 feet high, from the blocks on which they are placed.

The pedestal of the column is rectangular on plan, its sides slightly inclined and panelled for the reception of relievi; over which are inscribed the names of the victories celebrated and Nelson's flag-ships: St. Vincent, Captain; – Nile, Vanguard; – Copenhagen, Elephant; – Trafalgar, Victory: these and the other inscriptions, are shown in the perspective view.

The podium of the platform bears on one side, – "England expects every man to do his duty;" – on another, – "Westminster Abbey or Victory;" – on the third, – "I have done my duty, I thank God for it;" – and the fourth is reserved for an historical inscription.

The column rises over four prows, issuing from a frieze, 3 feet in height, (emblematic of the sea,) and a plynth bearing the motto, "Palmam Qui Meruit Ferat." The base of the column is cabled. The capital was composed after a minute study of four of the most beautiful capitals Greek and Roman art has left us; I have endeavoured to collect their beauties and produce a whole more adapted to an isolated position than the ordinary Corinthian capital, and at the same time more easily executed on a large scale.

Over the column four Tritons support a Tholus, on which stands the statue of the hero, 17 feet 6 inches in height: in construction the support of the figure is independent of the Tritons. This part forms a lantern of observation, and from it the surrounding scenery may be viewed in every direction. The figure does not stand on a point, but on a circle whose diameter is more than one-third the height of the statue

It is proposed that on the south, east, and west of the monument, the site should be reduced to a level, three feet higher than the ground at its lowest part, to form an extended base to the whole monument. This would make the levels, which at first appeared a disadvantage, a means of obtaining a considerable effect: on the south there would be two steps, each 1 foot 6 inches in height, broken at proper distances with blocks for candelabra, and with a flight of steps in the centre; on the north, a retaining and low parapet wall would place the National Gallery on a terrace; while on the east and west of the monument from an area 180 feet by 80, a flight of steps 30 feet wide, would give access to the upper level immediately opposite to each of the wing porticoes of that building; producing unity and the idea of purpose; and the repose on either side would heighten the effect of the monument. This is illustrated, and its effect shown in the general plan and perspective view.

If it should be thought desirable, a gallery, (a plan and section of which is shown,) for the reception of paintings, models and sculpture, (with a room for a keeper), may be obtained under the platform of the column. The gallery would be 12 feet high, and 16 wide, and have a total extent of 120 feet; larger dimensions might be obtained, but the keeping the platform within the smallest possible limits, seems of paramount importance; it would be lighted by skylights unseen from without. The entrance to the monument is also entirely screened from sight.

PRINCIPAL DIMENSIONS	Ft.	In.
Height to the upper platform	14	6
base of column	50	6
Height of column including base and capital	118	0
Entire height	207	0
Entire height of the London Momument	202	0
Entire height of the Duke of York's Monument	137	9
Diameter of the proposed column	13	0
Extent of terrace	140	0

The entire cost of the monument, the masonry of granite, and of the best workmanship, would be 30,000*l.* It is proposed to introduce gilding in parts, as shown in the perspective view. In the drawing I have omitted the victories on the prows, as they appeared somewhat to detract from simplicity in the design; they are however retained in the model.

The time and labour I have bestowed on this design, to obviate the objections urged against a column as a monument, will I hope, offer sufficient apology for the length at which I have found it necessary to describe it.

MODEL NO. 50, *Samuel Nixon.* – In monuments, it appears to be extremely desirable that the individual in honour of whom it is erected should be conspicuously pointed out; that his figure should in fact be the monument, and that all else should be merely accessory to that main object. The artist has therefore so composed this design, as that the eye shall almost involuntarily fix itself at once upon the statue; and he has endeavoured to represent the hero in that calm and dignified attitude, which appears to be best fitted for a monumental structure.

To denote his country, a group of statues representing Britannia exultingly rising from the waves, supported by Freedom and Order, is placed in front; to mark the scenes of his triumphs, the Atlantic with the Tagus and the Gulf of Bothnia, and the Mediterranean with the Nile and the Tiber, enrich either side; and, especially to point out that deep sense which he entertained, of having been raised by Providence to scourge and to subdue the enemies of his country and of social order, the Fates are represented as weaving the tissued thread of his career. The plinth course is proposed to be decorated with bassi-relievi of his achievements.

MODEL NO. 51, *Richard Kelsey and Samuel Nixon.* – It appearing to be very desirable that the monument, and its accessories, should be made to appear a component part of the original design for the National Gallery; in the general arrangement of the whole area, this object is kept in view, and it is proposed that the ground should be excavated to the point of lowest level, that the retaining wall on the north side should form one terrace line, and the centre be occupied by a wide ascent, or scala regia to the National Gallery.

It is suggested that the steps should be bounded on either side, by a tier of colossal lions only, or of monuments to distinguished naval commanders, in which colossal lions should bear a prominent part; and it is anticipated that such an avenue would not only, in itself, be magnificent, but lead the eye gradually forward to rest upon the portico of the Gallery, and bring it into the picture. It is proposed that in the centre of this avenue, an enlarged, but exact model of Pompey's Pillar at Alexandria, should be erected; that the statue of Nelson should be placed in front of it, so as to be distinctly visible; that his achievements and those of his brother officers should be sculptured in basso relievo upon the sub-plinths which support the column; that the pillar should be surmounted either by a Victory or a Britannia; and that the whole should be made to form one majestic trophy, in that style of simple grandeur which best accords with the character of all great men.

It is conceived that not only do the simplicity of its composition, the gracefulness of its proportion, and the artist-like breadth of its foliage, render it peculiarly applicable for such a purpose; but that the circumstances of his first great victory having been achieved almost at its very foot, of his title being indissolubly united with Egypt, of the familiar acquaintance which mariners of all European nations have with it, and of the facility with which they might recognize and hail it as an old friend; appear to point it out as more appropriate for a memorial of "Nelson of the Nile", than any other example of ancient art, or any column composed by a modern architect could possibly be.

DESIGNS NOS. 57 and 60, *Walter L. B. Granville.* – The triumphal column I propose as a memorial to Nelson is of the Corinthian order, after the ancient remains of the Temple of *Jupiter Stator* at Rome, which Palladio considered to be superior to any work he had ever seen, and anterior to the temple of *Mars Ultor.* It rises on a sub-basement to the height of 218 feet, including the statue.

The entire shaft is of cast-iron, composed of 26 courses of a proper thickness, and 111 ft. 3 in. high. It rests on a square pedestal, the die of which is 23 feet wide and 19 feet high; and this again upon an octagonal sub-basement, 19 feet above the ground, covering an area of nearly 32,000 square feet. The base of the shaft and the capital are cast in brass. The former is 6 ft. 9 in. high, the latter, 14 ft. 9 in. From the top of the capital, a round pedestal 15 feet high, made of cast-iron, and ornamented with brass festoons, supports the statue of Britannia Tonans standing on a globe, hurling the thunder-bolts as emblems of naval power with her right hand, and holding in her left hand the sceptre of the sea. This figure, typical of the pre-eminence of Great Britain on the ocean, has been deemed a more appropriate termination to a lofty column raised to the glory of the first naval commander that ever lived, than the statue of the hero himself, whose lineaments could not be perceived at such an elevation. It was consequently substituted for the latter. It will be 25 feet high, and it is proposed to make it of cast-iron gilt, or of yellow bronze, like some of the most recent monuments erected on the continent.

The pedestal of the column, 36 feet in height, is of masonry and solid stone, cased in by statuary marble; of the latter material are the four sides of the die, at the angles of which four colossal cariatids, in marble, stand to support the massive cornice and ornaments of the pedestal. They represent, by appropriate emblems, the figures of Spain and Denmark weeping over the defeat of their navies, and of the genius of Cape St. Vincent and of the Nile, as witnesses of the two great naval fights bearing those names. Resting on each angle of the cornice of the pedestal is an ancient rostrum, to give character to this great naval column, and rich hanging festoons link the four rostra together; all which ornaments are to be of brass. On the south face of the die the hero himself, seated in the triumphal chair of state, holding the truncheon of command, and having just received from his country the imperishable laurel, occupies the centre. He is clad in classical costume, and by the well-known lineaments of his countenance, carefully preserved by the sculptor, and placed within reach of the eye, will remind the beholder of the cherished object of this monument. On the broad plinth of the pedestal, however, and within a wreath supported by Victories, the name of Nelson is inscribed. The east and west faces of the die will represent, in alto relievo, the battles of the Nile and Copenhagen: while on that of the north side, over the entrance door, the closing scene of Nelson's immortal career, will present its naked and impressive truth to the multitude that daily passes in front of the National Gallery. The sub-basement, of an octagonal form, is enriched with 24 projected blocks close to the ground, intended to serve as plinths, to receive, hereafter, the statues of those naval commanders who most distinguished themselves during the last protracted war; or short pedestals, with the colossal busts only of such commanders, might be substituted for the statues on the blocks in question. A space is left between each statue on the faces of the octagon, whereon to inscribe the name and a short epitome of the deeds of those commanders. In its interior, this octagonal sub-basement offers four spacious rooms 41 by 25 feet each, and 19 feet high (besides smaller apartments for the accommodation of keepers), which being well lighted from the top present an excellent opportunity for forming a naval library, and gallery of pictures. The shaft of cast-iron is 13 feet 6 inches in diameter close to its base, and under the astragal 11 feet 4 inches. A band 4 feet wide, beginning at the base of the shaft, rises spirally to the height of 62 feet, developing a superficial length of 724 feet of cast-iron bas-reliefs, representing the Fasti of Nelson: and those of the naval history of Great Britain connected with his career. The figures will be 3 feet high. The flutings of the shaft descend from below the astragal to where the spiral terminates. A light geometrical staircase of wrought iron, 3 feet wide, runs all the way from the ground up to a door in the round pedestal which supports the statue. The door opens into the upper part of the capital, so arranged as to form a gallery for the visitor, – thus avoiding the usual unsightly appendage to insulated columns of a top railing which disfigures the abacus in most of those monuments. The staircase will consist of 365 steps of very light construction, and be lighted by loop-holes, or *soupirails*, placed in different parts of the spiral band as well as among the flutings. The great entrance door, at the north side of the octagonal sub-basement, will be seven feet high by three feet and a half wide; and will afford immediate access to the staircase, through a spacious waiting-room.

To this description I have only to add that I have selected iron as the material for my column because it is the emblem of strength – because it may be supposed to proceed from the iron cannon captured by the hero to whom, the column is erected – because it is not only the most abundant metal found in Great Britain, but also that in the working of which the English has outstripped every other nation – lastly, because the use of iron for so gigantic a structure, offers the character of originality, and the more important quality of economy. The Prussian and the French governments have felt the truth of this, and while the former raises pyramids and obelisks in cast iron, the latter is now occupied in erecting colossal fountains in the *Place de la Concorde*, with the figures made of cast iron.

Since my first proposition of a cast iron column, objections have been started against the employment of that material, on the grounds, first, of its being of an easily oxydizable nature; second, of its being likely to be struck and damaged by lightning. The latter ground, I am happy to state, is considered by some of the first philosophers in this country, who have been consulted on the subject, to be purely imaginary. On the contrary, as the iron shaft from its apex will be continuous down to the ground, – should the electrical fluid be at all attracted by the column, the fluid will be transmitted, as in the case of the ordinary protecting rod on the top of houses, to the earth, and there dispersed in silence. As to the first ground of objection, that of the easily oxydizable nature of iron, it is happily done away with by the most recent discoveries of chemistry. Many are the processes now in use for protecting the surface of iron in the most effectual manner; and without entering into the most scientific of these manipulations, it may be stated that the preparation employed by the Prussians in all their public monuments of cast iron, has hitherto preserved them most completely.

RECAPITULATION OF THE SEVERAL MEASUREMENTS OF THE NELSON COLUMN

	Feet.	In.
Sub-basement	19	0
Pedestal	36	0
Base	6	9
Shaft	111	3

Capital	14	9
Meta	15	0
Statue with the globe	25	0
Total	217	9

ESTIMATE

I was proposed to erect the former column for the sum of 25,000*l*.; but in consequence of the increased quantity of sculptured marble in the pedestal, and the addition of the sub-basement in the present column, the sum required will be 29,500*l*.

COMPARATIVE ALTITUDE OF TEN TRIUMPHAL COLUMNS IN EUROPE, INCLUDING THE INTENDED ONE TO NELSON

	Feet.	In.
1. Duke of York (London)	123	6
2. Earl Grey's Column (Newcastle)	134	0
3. Place Vendome (Paris)	136	0
4. Alexander Column (St. Petersburg)	144	0
5. Trajan Column (Rome)	145	0
6. Colonne de Juillet (Paris)	148	6
7. Antonine Column (Rome)	150	0
8. Melville Column (Edinburgh)	150	5
9. City Monument (London)	202	0
10. Nelson Memorial (London)	217	9

MODEL NO. 62, *James Hakewill*. – Before attempting to design a Nelson memorial adapted to the locality of Trafalgar-square, I have asked myself, and others upon whose judgment I placed reliance, the following questions, which, with the replies, I subjoin.

Must it not be desirable that the National Gallery be as little masked as possible?– Undoubtedly.

What form of monument would best ensure that object? – A column.

As there are several points of view from which the monument would be seen, what form will give, on so many angles, the best outline? – A column: its contour being always the same from whatever points it is viewed.

Is it correct in principle or feeling that the statue of a subject be placed looking down upon royalty, as the statue of Nelson would be, if placed on the summit of the column immediately over that of Charles the First? – Certainly not.

Would it not be better, then, to place the statue of the hero on the base of the column, following out the example of Sir Christopher Wren? – I think so; for that altitude would allow the interesting contemplation of the features and person of the hero, and *render a secondary statue unnecessary*. The height would preserve it from accidental injury, and the projection of the cornice protect it from the weather.

Of what material would you recommend its construction? – Of stone; for of the tens of thousands of bronze statues which embellished ancient Greece and Italy, ACCIDENT alone has preserved to our time scarcely half a dozen. The statues which adorned the summits of the columns of Antonine and Trajan, are probably now circulating among the populace of Rome, under the degrading form of Roman baiocchi; we know that that of Henry the Fourth from the Pont Neuf, transformed into pieces of two sous and stamped with the emblems of revolutionary France, forms the common medium of traffic of the Parisian vulgar. No memorial intended to convey information to posterity, should be formed of a valuable and convertible material; – and, with such examples before him, who will be bold enough to say the Pitts and the Foxes, the Wellingtons and Nelsons, of our time, will arrest what seems to be the course of nature.

Upon this basis I have formed my design.

"Si quæris descroptionem, aspice."

DESIGN NO. 64, *Thomas Bellamy*. – The erection of a memorial to the hero of Trafalgar being at length determined upon, the country will doubtless ere long be enabled to look upon a monument worthy alike of Nelson and of the arts; and honourable to that national feeling which, after the lapse of 33 years, is now awakened to record imperishably his brilliant exploits.

The columnar form from the time of Duillius (the first naval hero to whom the Romans decreed a monument), through those of Trajan and Antonine down to our own day, has generally been adopted whenever a monument has been required of colossal dimensions, and is consequently most favourably associated in the public mind; but, notwithstanding this association, and the intrinsic beauty of the column when of good proportion, its fitness is questionable when applied as the isolated pedestal of a statue.

The proximity of Trafalgar-square to the York column renders it highly important that any monument to be erected there, should be essentially distinctive in design from that monument. That monotony may be avoided, and something new in art produced.

Much has been said on the injurious effect which any object erected near the National Gallery would have upon that edifice, if the parts of which that object might be composed were to be larger than those of the Gallery itself, but this could only apply if the parts of the Gallery possessed magnitude, or approximated to that quality, which is clearly not the case. Its facade would in truth be benefited by any monumental object that should present a marked contrast to it in scale and character.

The simple form of the obelisk when magnitude is taken into account, renders it, next to the pyramid, perhaps the most imposing of all forms; and it would be difficult to point out a situation better suited for its adoption than Trafalgar-square, where contrast with existing forms, masses and materials is most necessary.

The obelisk of the accompanying design is 96 feet high, and 12 feet square at its base, being larger than that before the Lateran church at Rome. The author had conceived the idea of procuring it of one block from the granite quarries of Hayter, but the funds announced as available for the memorial are too limited to allow of more than mention being made of the idea. The memory of Nelson would perhaps not be unfitly recorded by a form which had its origin on the banks of that far-famed river, at the mouth of which he won one of the brightest of his laurels. The tridents, ships, and victories on the bases of the obelisk, and on the obelisk itself, are sunk below the surface of the granite, as are also the words – Nile, – Copenhagen, – Trafalgar, – and, the signal to the fleet on the day of the last quoted battle, "England expects every man to do his duty;" with which each face of the uppermost base of the obelisk is respectively charged. This design might be executed for 28,000*l.*

Design No. 67, *George Foggo.* – Round the mainmast of a man-of-war are piled trophies of Nelson's valour – mute ponderous cannon, silent musketry, &c. In front the hero receives additional tokens of success – the swords and banners of humbled France and Spain; but beneath, in the base of the monument, a bas-relief, in form of a ship's hull, represents the Conqueror of Trafalgar death-struck – passing to immortality. The word "*Victory*" inscribed over the scene of triumph, and against that of death "*Westminster Abbey*," remind us of his vigorous – almost prophetic – eloquence and enthusiasm. At the mast-head (decorated with three crowns of sea-weed) a British Tar proclaims the glorious victory. On either side is seen a figure in action, intended to represent some renowned companion of Nelson's prowess; and reliefs of the Nile and Copenhagen will complete the exterior.

The ornaments consist entirely of objects obtainable at sea, and characteristic of our navy and its illustrious leader, who dared beyond the rules of art. Objects that savour of preparation, and partake not of enthusiastic impulse, and likewise the mystic visions of antiquity, have been discarded for the more terrible features of modern warfare.

The interior of the basement will afford well-lighted space for fifteen or twenty bas-reliefs or pictures, commemorative of our navy's gallantry.

The height proposed is about 160 feet, which from its prominent position, and the effect of perspective, will appear lofty among surrounding objects; the principal figures about 12 feet. At that proportion the monument can be well executed in stone far more durable than Italian marble, under 25,000*l.* A real mast of a line-of-battle ship would be most suitable for the upper shaft, and bronze may with propriety be applied to various decorations.

Design No. 68, *Carl Tottie.* – The colossal statue of the hero (27 feet 9 inches), is placed on the apex of the column, which signifies Britain, and is supported by England, Scotland and Ireland, represented by the three counterforts, each carrying their respective genius (with appropriate emblems, the Rose, Thistle and Shamrock) in inclined position, contemplating the great services of Lord Nelson. The divided composition is redeemed or brought to unity below the basement by the three steps or gradius. The platform with the three second counterforts, supporting the lions as symbols of strength and power, comes next; below these the steps are spreading to an amazing circular extent, according to the immensity of British connexion and influence, as likewise the great firmness of the united kingdoms. Underneath one of the lions is the entrance to a circular gallery, decorated with naval trophies, connected with the spiral staircase, which by 320 steps brings the visitor on the balcony to enjoy a magnificent prospect. The whole height from the pavement to the top of the statue is 217 feet 3 inches. All the sculptures of Scotch granite. Erected of granite and Portland stone, estimate, 28,000*l.*; and entirely of Aberdeen granite, 40,000*l.*

DESIGN NO. 72, *Thomas Bellamy.* – The design consists of a platform 150 feet square, charged at the angles with marine and naval emblems; the base of the pedestal is sculptured with colossal models of first rates and victories, and bears the following inscription ranging round its four faces:

TO ADMIRAL HORATIO VISCOUNT NELSON, DUKE OF BRONTE,
This memorial is erected by public subscription,
A. D. MDCCCXXXIX.
Thirty-four years after his death, to commemorate his unparalleled achievements

The plinth bears the names of Nelson's three great victories, Nile – Copenhagen – Trafalgar – and the memorable signal to the fleet, "England expects every man to do his duty." – The circular portions of the pedestal are sculptured with a dance of Tritons and dolphins, oaken bands, prows of ships, shells of the nautilus, and with the palm. – This design might be executed for 27,000*l.*

DESIGN NO. 89, *Frederick Claudius J. Parkinson.* – A triumphal archway 100 feet square, enclosing a circular temple formed of 12 Corinthian columns supporting a richly panelled dome; under the centre of which is placed the statue of Nelson, with various emblematical figures.

The height of the building to be 70 feet. The length of each front including the steps and landings, 140 feet.

The cost of the building would be 18,300*l.* The statue and emblematical figures would not exceed the amount of 8,000*l.*

DESIGNS NOS. 90 and 91, *Richard Kelsey.* – Agreeing with Mr. Nixon that, if a column be deemed an inappropriate memorial of Nelson, there is but one other kind of monument which, under the circumstances of the proposed site and the money to be expended upon it, can well be considered applicable to the purpose; the artist has, in both his sculptural designs, made the statue the most conspicuous feature. In one composition it has been his object to place before posterity all the distinguishing characteristics of the man and the hero; and to render it fitted to illustrate the poet's idea, "This story shall the good man teach his son."

It is proposed that each face of the basis shall significantly teach one great lesson. In this elevation, his *mercy* is chiefly shewn. The inscribed quotations of his own words, "May humanity, after victory, be the predominant characteristic of the British fleet," and "The moment an enemy submits, from that moment I become his protector," breathe that angelic feeling. The sculptured group of a beautiful female pleading for a fallen warrior, reiterates the charge: and it is impressed more deeply by the basso-relievo of the wounded Nelson rushing from a bed of anguish to save his drowning enemies.

On the remaining sides it is proposed, in like manner, to depict his courage, his perseverance, and his integrity.

In the other design, the proportions of the masonry are altered, and the groups at the foot of the centre block are intended to point out the immediate results of his exertions; as, the protection of the East and West Indies, the saving of Egypt and the Turkish empire, the general assistance of Europe, the dissolution of the Northern Confederacy, the exaltation of the British empire, and the humiliation of our enemies.

The bassi-relievi in this front include the incidents of his death, his funeral, and the general regret; which is also further shown by the mourning figures in the centre.

The drawing of Pompey's pillar is merely intended to show the effect of placing the statue of Nelson on the summit. The substructure is also altered, and the revolutionary dragon writhing under its deadly wounds is intended to point out the attainment of the great object of his life.

In the three sculptural designs, the statue being considered as distinctly the chief feature, all else, however colossal it may be in itself, is kept subordinate and unobtrusive. It is anticipated that, from a distant point of view, the mere mass of each would be perfectly expressive of that strength and simplicty of character which marked the man; that, on a nearer approach, the groups and statues would detach themselves and attract attention; and that, upon closer inspection of bassi-relievi, composed in the quiet but expressive style of Grecian art, the interest would be full kept up, and all the beautiful lessons of his life form a pictorial history, at once adapted to impress the uneducated and to gratify the most refined. The artists who submit them beg very respectfully to remark, that they are only sent in as sketches; they feel them to be capable of many and great improvements, and regret that time has not admitted of more than one being modelled; but should the leading idea of the composition point out either of them as adapted for the monument in memorial of Nelson, it would give them the greatest pleasure so to improve it, as to be creditable to themselves and to their country. – With respect to the scale upon which they should be erected, that must much depend upon the money which will be really applicable to the purpose, but they conceive that the statues should be about 30 feet in height.

Samuel Nixon proposes that as to his design the statue of Nelson should be in bronze, the masonry in granite, and the accessory sculpture in the best of our native stone.

Richard Kelsey proposes that no portion of his designs should be in bronze, but that the finest grained granite should be used in all the colossal work and the reliefs, but thinks it may be necessary to adopt other material for the main groups of statues.

Richard Kelsey would wish to model of Pompey's pillar to be ten feet in diameter, and has no doubt of being able to give the shaft the appearance of being hewn out of one stone, and thus to obtain all that imposing effect which appertains to monolithal monuments.

Design No. 97, *James Henry Nixon.* – This design is a monument of colossal dimensions calculated for duration, in which the form is simple, the material imperishable. The statue of Nelson in a calm and dignified attitude, is intended to be 30 feet in height; and being placed on an elevated pedestal and basement, would prove a commanding object from Parliament-street, shewing the figure distinct from the surrounding buildings; and not so high, but from its colossal size, the features would be plainly distinguishable when viewed from below: the total height of the monument to the top of the figure, would be 90 feet. On the basement is intended to be scuptured in bas-relief, a representation of the most remarkable actions; showing the gallant conduct which ever marked the daring career of the illustrious hero. On the four projecting blocks of the basement are represented emblematical figures of those virtues which Nelson is acknowledged to have possessed in an iminent degree. – Courage and Mercy, Fortitude and Justice. The whole of this design, carefully executed in red and white granite, can be erected for the sum proposed by the honourable committee.

Design No. 110, *R. E. Gavey.* – A partially enclosed column, surmounted by a statue, with a mausoleum interior; altogether forming a sculptural architective monumental pile, commemorative of the hero. Height 170 feet.

Beneath the azure vault of nature's vast architrative dome, of collossean form, (visible to myriads of lesser breathing mortals, scattered around o'er hill and dale) stands the sculptured representative to unborn ages of the person, – the most glorious of the greatest maritime nation's naval heroes, Nelson. The statue, with naval trophies, surmounts a column, around which twirl antagonist dolphins, emblematic of sea war.

Beneath a gallery are embodied a series of four allegoric bas-relievoes, hypothetical of the hero's attributes, enterprise, valour, victory, and immortality.

Enterprise, a youth of fiery mien, with heart swollen with enthusiasm, over-canopied by the perils of stormy danger; he sees, through the vista of breaking thunder-clouds, starry rays encircling the hero's wreath of laurell'd glory; emulations incentive: with eager haste to win the prize he throws off the habiliments of inglorious inactivity, and, with heroism armed, dashes to the immortal goal, in vain withheld by the syrens, Luxury, Effeminacy, and Fear.

Valour, with destructive weapon, rushes to the pinnacle of danger's rock, followed by his brave compeers with victory's pennon streaming: there, with energy heroic, they engage with invasion's monster and its usurping legion, – scattering with destruction the foe to oblivious death and darkness.

Victory. – The conquering victor, lion-skin habilimented sits on the throne of conquest, crowned with laurel by radiant glory and the sire renown, in whose historic tome the hero's achievement stands recorded: amid captured prizes, that lay scattered at the hero's feet, the captive leaders of the foe upon bended knee, deliver to the conqueror their inglorious arms; whilst, with soaring flight aloft, on wings of swiftness, Fame with trumpet blast to the world the victor's triumph proclaims.

Immortality. – The hero's bust, laurel wreathed, rests on fame's pedestal in glory's altar, enshrined; lighted by the censor light of imperishable immortality; thus, through the darkness of obscurity, and through all time, his resplendent fame is rendered manifest to man, woman and infancy; who approach the altar with their choicest gifts as offerings, dedicative to the hero's memory; the man with implements laborial; the woman with sweet fruits; and infancy with lovely flowers and gentle innocence; whilst, with united voice, Europe, Asia, Africa and America, acknowledge the hero's greatness.

Descending from the allegorically *ideal* to the typically *real*, is presented a second series of bas-relievoes, illustrative of the memorable events that occurred during the hero's victorious achievements; the battles of St. Vincent, the Nile, Copenhagen, and Trafalgar.

Between the lower bas-relievoes are placed personifications of Genius, Fame, Victory, and the Sea.

The structure at various parts is graced with naval trophies and emblematic devices of the sea and war.

From four double flights of steps a circular collonade is approached, in which are arches; thus, through their gates is viewed the interior, a mausoleum.

Beneath fame's monumental pile, as by a nation's joint acclaim enshrined, on pedestal the sculptured sea hero lies in sepulchral rest; though mantled in death's pall, he is wreathed with fame's laurel glory; laved in the gorgeous golden rays of day's effulgent orb, or bathed in the silvery gleam of the gentle, calm, sepulchral beams of the silent queen of night.

Over the front arch is placed the Nelson heraldic arms.

Surmounting pedestals (at the summit of four semi-flights of steps) are placed sculptural groups of naval characters, engaged in the various occupations on board a British ship of war; thus, steering the ship, taking the observation, weighing the anchor, and firing the gun.

Around the structure are placed 8 British lions on pedestals. – The object of the erection of the galleries is to afford a near inspection of the sculptures. – The entrance to the galleries staircase is by a door in the side of one of the archways. – The monument to be encircled by an ornamental stone promenade; and the whole enclosed with an iron palisade and gas lamps of a naval design.

DESIGN NO. 117, *James Thrupp.* – Britannia's great naval hero, and the upholder of her maritime supremacy, receiving from his country the laurel crown, and from the nations, whose fleets were subdued by his genius and daring, tokens of their submission, is the idea intended to be expressed in this design.

A few words in explanation, and more particularly of the emblematical representations of France, Spain and Denmark, may not perhaps be deemed irrelevant.

The subject seems to require that they should be represented as warriors. The act of lowering their banners has been chosen, as being the actual mode of expressing submission adopted in naval warfare; and also because it neither implies arrogance on the one part, nor abjectness on the other; for it might be that of the bravest warrior when unable longer to contend against his foe.

The eagle France has long appropriated to herself as an emblem, as may be seen on the monumental records of her own victories. Ancient coins have been the authority for the indicative of Spain; and to Denmark has been given the raven of the north. This lesser kingdom has also been represented under a more youthful form than the others. The medallions of the respective reigning sovereigns on the shields mark the era.

In portraying the hero it has been the aim to avoid any expression of ostentation; for Nelson's illustrious deeds were ever accompanied by a simple dignity of character. The principal basso relievo tells his fate: the colours of the hostile fleets are struck – the hour-glass is broken – Nelson has fallen – and the flag of his country enshrouds him. The rays of a setting sun betoken that he terminated his career in glory. The other bassi relievi are to represent some of the noble traits of the hero's character; such, for example, as that which he exhibited when wounded at the battle of the Nile.

While desirous to retain the proportions and the general features of those examples in art that have been sanctioned by ages, the architect has attempted to engraft upon them the characteristics of a triumphal pillar. The shaft is enriched with laurel leaves, and the names of the principal battles; and the capital is formed of four figures of victories, bearing wreaths entwined with Nelson's heraldic motto: – Palmam – Qui – Meruit – Ferat: – words which seem alike appropriate to the act of Britannia and to the hero himself.

The letters it is proposed to cut through the stone: – thus formed, they will not readily be obliterated, nor affect the outline of the shaft, whilst they will serve to light the staircase within.

The inner side of the abacus may be sunk sufficiently low to render a gallery-railing unnecessary as a protections.

Nelson's last immortal signal encircles the pedestal.

The whole height of the design, with the crowning figure, is 168 feet; and its cost, provided the figures of Nelson and Britannia only are executed in bronze, will not exceed 30,000*l.* The present inequality of surface in the intended site, it is proposed to alter by lowering the upper portion.

DESIGN NO. 128, *An Architect of Middlesex.* – A monument to the honour of the greatest hero that ever adorned the annals of a maritime nation, worthy of the genius, valour, and ambition of his country, is an undertaking very difficult to effect successfully. Nevertheless the author flatters himself that he has solved this important problem in a fitting, clear, and distinct manner.

The author's first point is to represent the history of the hero in a language at once technical, expressive, and comprehensive, to all classes of the nation. – His second point is, to express this technical language in a clear and elegant style, united to historical truth. – His third point (which, until now, has been neglected by every one,) is to build the monument to harmonize with the buildings which surround it, especially St. Martin's Church, and the National Gallery. – The author has endeavoured to effect this object as completely as possible, and thinks the monument, when finished, will give the National Gallery a more elegant, imposing, and materially improved appearance, as a public edifice. – This epico-technico poem is to be thus realized:

"After the victory of Trafalgar, sanctified by the hero's own blood, the spoils and trophies are brought on the Admiral's ship to the capital of the British empire, to be exposed to the admiration of the nation."

Trafalgar-square having been selected for such an exhibition, will be made to represent a port at the entrance of a canal in the metropolis. This port is protected by four moles. The two moles towards the south will be surmounted by two rostral towers, on which are represented the capture of the enemy's vessels: the other two moles towards the north, will be surmounted by trophies gained in his various battles.

The four principal victories of the hero, viz. St. Vincent, the Nile, Copenhagen, and Trafalgar, will be represented by four great bas-reliefs placed round the moles, and explained by inscription in Mosaic asphalte on the pavement. Above the towers and trophies are placed four great globes, indicating the tropical parts of the world over which England reigns, viz. Asia, Africa, America, and Australia; and over each globe is set the British crown. In the midst of the port is seen the ship Victory, that has brought home the spoils and trophies gained by Nelson. In the centre of the deck, on a pedestal raised upon a large die, is placed a colossal statue of Nelson, in the dress of an Admiral, leaning on his sword. On the four sides of the die are placed an inscription and 3 bas-reliefs, viz., towards the south, or grand entrance, is inscribed a summary of the history of the hero, with the dedication. On the east side is a bas-relief descriptive of his nativity. On the north, his inauguration; and on the west, his apotheosis. Two lateral basins supply the port with water. The port is surrounded by a balustrade, and the four moles by a railing. The die is protected by four large, and eight small bar stones, with chains hung in festoons. At each entrance are two pillars, on which are placed two lions. The pavement and deck will be inlaid with inscriptions and ornaments of Mosaic asphalte. In the interior of the ship are apartments for one or two porters, who will have the care of the keys of the towers, and whose duty will be to keep the monument perfectly clean, and likewise to preserve it from wanton injury.

It is almost impossible to give an exact *estimate of the expenses* of a monument which may be constructed so differently with regard to the artists, and materials employed, and of which the cost of the statue and bas-reliefs may differ so considerably. Nevertheless, the author believes that it would not exceed the sum of 30,000*l*. The expense would be easily diminished by building the two towers lower and without rost, rendering the south moles similar to the north, viz. surmounted by trophies only, and sacrificing the two lateral basins.

The author hopes that the committee will condescend to observe that his plan can undergo such modifications as they may deem fit, under any circumstances. If the original idea is preserved, the author does not doubt but that it might be made the most classical and important monument of the age, and worthy of the national honour.

DESIGN NO. 132, *Raphael Brandon*. – I have adopted the form of a circular temple to commemorate the deeds of the illustrious hero, as it at once offers a complete protection for his statue, however beautifully executed, and forms a magnificent object when seen from the various avenues to the square.

The temple is divided by ornamental pilasters into four compartments: the one towards the south being left open, affords an ample view of the statue, which is placed on a pedestal in the middle of the building, and receives a direct light from the centre of the dome – for this purpose covered with stout glass; the other three compartments are closed up with bas-reliefs of his principal victories – A faithful resemblance of the heroic victor would thus be handed down unimpaired to posterity, enshrined within those glorious achievements, which shed lustre on the annals of our country, and immortalize his name.

The height of the monument is 60 feet, that of the statue 15 feet.

The entire work can be executed in the most perfect and elaborate manner for the sum specified, in the following materials. – the base of grey granite, the temple of Anglesea marble, the statue and bas-reliefs of statuary marble, the lions of red granite, and the trophies of bronze.

DESIGN NO. 134, *Thomas H. Lewis*. – The design consists of an enriched octangular obelisk 150 feet high, surmounted by a figure of Britannia, and having a statue of Nelson 12 feet high, on a pedestal about 30 feet from the ground. Bas-reliefs of his victories adorn the faces of the obelisk, which rises from a double platform occupying the centre of the given space.

DESIGN NO. 144, *J. Taylor, jun.* – A triumphal pillar 172 feet high, surmounted with a statue of Nelson, 18 feet high, ascended by a spiral staircase inside, having a gallery on the top sunk out of the capital of the column, and a short railing almost inperceptible.

On the front of the pedestal the hero is represented as falling, while defending Britain, who is seated on the column above; victory descends and sustains him in death, while he grasps to the last moment the standard of his country. A British vessel is seen in the back-ground, and on that side the column a weeping willow is introduced, referring to the universal feeling which deplored the loss of this greatest of all naval commanders.

The figures in the foreground are entire, the back-ground in bold relief.

On the other three sides of the pedestal may be represented the three principal naval actions in which he was engaged.

N.B. It is submitted, that a sculptural group, commemorating Nelson, should represent his dying moments, as he expired in action, and in the midst of the greatest of all his victorious naval engagements.

With a Wellington, and other heroes who have survived the conflicts in which they were engaged, an animated statue alone is appropriate; not equally so with those who fell in action, which event it is considered should stand recorded as well as their bravery and prowess.

DESIGN NO. 148, *G. B. Moore.* – In designing the memorial, attention ought to be directed to the period at which it is proposed to erect it. In the excitement of victory, trophies are allowable; but after twenty-four years of peace, to revive the exultation of triumph, would be unworthy the generosity of a great civilized Christian nation. The ancients never restored their trophies, when destroyed by time or accident, considering that old enmities ought not to be perpetuated. The present memorial should be rather a testimonial of gratitude, to one who died to obtain an honourable peace, than a record of national glory; and all allusions to victories should be introduced as illustrations of the actions of the hero, and not as triumphant emblems. Under this train of feeling, this design has been composed.

The subjects of the bassi relievi have been selected to illustrate the various virtues of Nelson. – No. 1, Duty: Nelson proceeding to his vessel during a storm near the Goodwin Sands. – 2, Intrepidity: Cape St. Vincent: Nelson boarding the San Joseph. – 3, Mercy: the Nile: Nelson saving the enemy from drowning. – 4, Piety: the Nile: Nelson and his sailors returning thanks to the Deity after the battle. – 5, Justice: Nelson in the Senate claiming attention to the services of his compatriots. – 6, Magnanimity: Copenhagen: Nelson rendering justice to the brave defence of the Danes. – 7, Solicitude: Nelson, on his arrival in England, visiting his wounded seamen. – 8, Heroism: Trafalgar: the death of Nelson.

Above the bassi relievi are medallions of George III., George IV., and William IV., the sovereigns he was honoured by; and Victoria I., marking the reign in which the memorial is erected. At the angles are lions and boys denoting courage combined with gentleness. The statue of Nelson is in front of a pillar, supporting the heraldic banners of England, Scotland, Ireland, and Wales: and terminated by an angel bearing the olive-branch of peace, emblematical of the end for which he struggled and fell; for if any man could say with truth he fought for peace, – it was Nelson.

Design No. 150, *Thomas Moule*. – This design, presenting a union of architecture and sculpture, sufficiently announces its destination by its leading forms. The statue of Lord Nelson is represented on an enriched pedestal; which, with the basement and its graduated foundation, makes the total height of the monument 65 feet. Its greatest diameter is 140 feet.

Nelson, the principal object, is intended to be represented at the moment of perceiving a decided advantage obtained over the enemy. The admiral is attended by a captain, and near him is a boatswain, ready to communicate orders. Without diminishing the importance of the principal figure, this group would show the different grades of the navy, and form a just tribute to their successful co-operation.

The figure of Lord Nelson, 15 feet in height, might easily be discerned from the extremities of the large square in which the monument is required to form the centre object. To place a lofty column in such a situation is objectionable in point of taste, as its height would overpower the facade of the building erected as a National Gallery, in front of which the monument of Nelson is intended to be placed. That building presenting a lengthened elevation of Greek architecture, this design is made with corresponding reference to its prescribed site.

The pedestal bears, on its principal front, a bas-relief of King George III. receiving the Admiral as Viscount Nelson – a title granted to the brave seaman, in 1801, for his services in the Baltic; together with the appropriate motto – "*Pabnam qui meruit ferat.*" On the reverse of the pedestal is intended a bas-relief representation of the public funeral decreed to Nelson; the car bearing his body, approaching St. Paul's; and with the inscription of his last words – "England expects every man to do his duty."

Between these bas-reliefs, on one side, is intended to be placed the arms of Nelson of Burnhamthorp, with the crest of his family; on the other side, the heraldic augmentations, as Lord Viscount Nelson, K.B., Duke of Bronte in Sicily, Knight of Saint Ferdinand, &c. &c. &c., badges of military honour.

The basement of the pedestal is square, having upon its angles massive naval trophies of victory over the French, the Dutch, the Spaniards, and the Danes. To give breadth and quantity to the design, correspondent with the very large space for which the monument is required, the basement is extended on its western and eastern sides by an architectural elevation, terminated by rostral columns, each of which is surmounted by a classical figure of victory, making a height of 45 feet: the lower part of the shafts of these columns is environed by boarding-pikes used in the navy. The whole basement, divided into three compartments, is enriched with sculpture in bas-relief, representing the consequences of the battles of the Nile, Copenhagen, and Trafalgar: dismantled ships of war, prizes from the enemy, are shown on their way to British ports.

The monument is intended to be placed within an enriched enclosure, elliptical on its ground plan, and 140 feet in length, rising to the height of about 9 feet. A part only of this inclosure is shown in the architectural elevation, as it was deemed necessary to exhibit the graduated and broad foundation of the basement, which could not actually be seen in a general view. The pedestals on the enclosure are surmounted by female figures, bearing alternately palm branches, naval crowns, laurel wreaths, and the funereal torch. The fronts of the pedestals to be charged with emblems of the sea, and the trophies between them to record separately the successive victories in which the gallant Nelson was engaged.

Including the ornamental decoration, the author of this design feels convinced that, under careful management, the whole may be carried into execution (in Portland stone) with the means proposed, viz. 30,000*l*.

DESIGN NO. 160, *Thomas Bellamy*. – It is proposed by this design to form a semi-circular platform in the centre of Trafalgar-square, elevated one step above the paving of the road next the National Gallery, and continued of the same level to the line of paving connecting the Strand with Cockspur-street, along which line it acquires a height which is ascended to by steps. This platform is enclosed by a metal railing, except at the steps and opposite the National Gallery, which are reserved as approaches to the platform and monument.

The base of the monument is circular, 100 feet in diameter, having six radial blocks sustaining colossal couchant and dormant lions, significant of the result to which the achievements of Nelson mainly contributed. The pedestal which rises from this base is also circular, having three radial masses sustaining colossal seated figures, personifications of the Nile, Copenhagen, and Trafalgar, his three great victories, over which are characteristic trophies in bronze. The three intermediate faces of the pedestal are each charged with an alto-relievo illustration of some striking incident in each of the said battles. The three minor pedestals bearing sea-horses are charged with the names of the most important of Nelson's lesser victories. The columnar portion of the pedestal is 12 feet in diameter, and has a wide gallery supported by corbals decorated with Tritons, underneath which in relief is the motto, "Palmam qui meruit ferat." The terminating portion of the pedestal is encircled by an arrangement of tridents and festoons of laurel, and has a palmated capping. A naval crown receives the statue of the hero 16 feet high. The whole height of the structure from the paving to the top of the statue is 153 feet. The material of the substructure is proposed to be of granite; that of the superstructure free-stone, well selected as to durability and colour. The parts proposed to be of bronze are distinguished by its colour.

From, *Description of a Drawn Model (No. 113) proposed for the Monument intended to be erected in Trafalgar Square to The Memory of Lord Nelson with some collateral remarks, by M.M.* London 1839.

As prefatory to the Description of my own Model, as well as to account for my rashness in thus attempting, as a Layman, to compete with Professors of the Art, – I will make a few Remarks on the Subject generally, including a glance at some of the Models or Designs that have already been before the Public in the late Exhibition for that purpose.

In doing this – I beg here, once for all, to apologise for any seeming presumptuousness in whatever part of my attempt; and to deprecate any the least offence being taken thereat in whatsoever quarter, as nothing can be farther from my intention than such, but only desiring a fair discussion of the merits of the case. And it may at all events serve to show that I am of good faith in hoping that he may wear the palm who deserves it, by wishing to see chosen that Model – whatever it be – which shall be considered most suitable for the purpose, however "*Mast*-high" I should "jump" at the adoption of my own.

I was led to turn my thoughts to some idea of my own for the thing, from not being entirely satified with any one of the exhibited Models or Designs, that is – with reference to the specific purpose intended. As to their general merit in an Architectural point of view – whether for learning invention or design, it would not become me – a Philistine in the matter – to speak, if even I could differ from the general opinion, which was, I believe, but one in their favour. But this was not sufficient where a single – special – and important object was in view.

Much dissatisfaction has been attributed to the Artists who lately competed for this purpose – for what they are said to have considered the dilatory or irresolute measures of the Committee in not sooner coming to a decision upon the matter, and their consequent expense of time and labour to no purpose. As to this – it is quite clear that all the Competitors could not obtain the prizes. But, not at all to assume the fact of their complaint, they would certainly very much have misunderstood their own interests to make it: for, on the contrary, and notwithstanding the criticism that must have been expected, it cannot be denied that an opportunity was thus given for exhibiting to all but the merely gaping part of the Public an assemblage of very high and various architectural talent, short only of that displayed the year before last in the competition for the Houses of Parliament, that did those Gentlemen and the Country very high credit, and that no doubt must have been very useful to themselves – and thus reflectedly on their Art – by putting their respective works in antagonism and enabling them to communicate as well as receive improvement by the comparison.

As to expedition in the matter, of course setting aside the case of any individual being injured by delay, it seems that this is the very last point at all necessary to press. The object is to do the thing – not quickly – but well: if both can be effected – all the better: but this conjunction, always difficult, may here be doubtful. The thing has been suspended or delayed for more than thirty years: it has now all Time – Eternity before it: and surely there can be no possible reason for hurrying it in any way that may tend to prevent its being done in a manner that shall give the fullest satisfaction to all parties concerned – to the Subscribers – to the Country – and, one may say, to the World at large. What, then, is the matter of a few Weeks or Months, or even a Year – or more, given to this object, when we consider it intended to last as long as its materials can endure?

Moreover – a little protraction would give time for the receipt of more subscriptions, which could hardly be expected to come in when once the choice should be made and the accounts closed. And there is little doubt that, in so national an object as this, when a determinate sum should be fixed upon for the purpose, – if much exceeding that already received, an appeal to the Public – to the Country – could not fail of being attended to. And surely the Government, to whom The Crown has already set so handsome an example, would not refuse to make up the necessary sum.

A Monument, then, is about to be erected by Public Subscription, headed in the most munificent manner by The Sovereign, and that it cannot be doubted will be assisted by the Government – by the Nation at large in Parliament, if need be – to one of the most illustrious Men England ever produced, unquestionably her greatest Naval Hero, of a fame – a military renown – only shared by One Cotemporary, – One even still more illustrious in the Field than he was on the Quarter-Deck, and whom let us hope it will yet be very long before his Memory comes before us to ask for a such, tho we have already rejoiced to raise some – however indequate ones – to his glory – in his life time.

This Monument will be raised in the Metropolis – in London, in its centre, in a spot, considering the unavoidable rarity of such, admirably adapted for the purpose; in a space sufficiently large, and where it will be both countenanced and – so to say – emulated by Public Buildings of no mean extent and beauty. England, the Great Naval Power – The Mistress of the Seas, – this will be the first thing that Foreigners will come to see in her Capital – to see how England has honoured that NELSON whom they all know, who did so much to raise her Naval Fame to its late – yea not less present pinnacle of greatness: and which, by the way, let us hope She will ever maintain, in spite of "Bulls" or "*Bears*" – of hollow friends or of open foes!

Things may have been raised to Nelson elsewhere: Portsmouth, or Edinburgh, or Dublin, may talk of theirs: but this will be emphatically *The* NELSON MONUMENT. This will stand the imperishable record of the admiration – the applause – and the gratitude of England to her great Naval Chief; to gratify his brother Seamen of all grades of this and future generations, and to encourage them to emulate his glorious deeds. Should it not also combine and hand down to Posterity the – however minor – record of knowledge and good taste in the Arts, as of judgment and liberality in their application? And one might here add that this particular – the character and style of the Monument, tho but secondary and subordinate, will certainly help the principal one to the degree in which those points of detail are combined.

It behoves, then, those, in whom the execution of this project is vested, to proceed about it with caution and deliberation – as with spirit, in order that its important ends may not in any way be defeated, nor that the great hopes it has raised in its encouragers be disappointed.

In such an interesting if not great cause as this – the Government indeed might well, not only but negatively patronise it, but take its charge and direction. It has, however, already given the *local*, and may therefor be considered as pledged to co-operate with the Projectors. It will, therefor, now behove it, upon every ground, to take care that nothing be erected there unworthy of either – The public dignity of a Great Nation, or the glory of one of its most illustrious Commanders, or of the honour of the Arts – to which it should always be supposed to give its countenance and support.

In the late Exhibition there were Models and Designs of every possible variety, Monuments in the abstract – Temples – Cenotaphs – Sarcophagi – Fountains – Pillars or Columns – Obelisks, and more indeed than there are distinguishing names for. Of all but the two last mentioned it will be unnecessary here to take any particular notice; because, with the exception of one more – Messrs. Fowler and Sivier's No. 37 that obtained the third prize, none of them, however much to be admired in general respects, seemed to have appeared to the Committee as desirable for the intended purpose: This, probably, besides whatever other reasons, from their occupying more room than would be expedient either with reference to the limited extent of the Spot or the proper display of the Things themselves. To this last objection, assuming it to be one, the latter two mentioned structures – The Column and The Obelisk – do not seem to be obnoxious; and, unless with highly ornamental adjuncts, would also no doubt be much less expensive. We must suppose that it was a combination of these considerations, not less than a regard to the actual beauty of the Things themselves, that determined The Committee in their adjudication of the Prizes and the anticipative Nomination – so to say – of the future Monument, the First having been given to Mr. Railton's Column No. 81 and the Second to Mr. Baily's Obelisk No. 10.

Assuming then A Column, or An Obelisk, one or the other, to be the kind of Structure that The Committee are most likely to adopt, I shall confine my Observations to those.

The thing being gone by, – tho quite prepared to give reasons for not conceding to them the merit of perfection (which indeed seems to have been denied them by The Committee, as it sent them home to mend their manners – however already so good) I will not here permit myself any criticism on either of the successful Models, two of which were of that description, but treat the subject wholly in the abstract.

It is not necessary here to repeat that, – generally speaking, and with reference to the Rules of Art in Architecture, The Column is only a Member of an Edifice, and not originally intended to stand alone; because it was only invented to support – in conjunction with others – a superincumbent weight, and was never conceived of as a separate Structure and existing only for itself. This, however, is only a general rule; to which, as everybody knows, there are – tho after all only a very few – some splendid exceptions, namely – Pompey's Pillar in Egypt, the Trajan and Antonine Columns at Rome, the Napoleon Column at Paris, and our own magnificent MONUMENT in London. These are instances of overleaping the bounds of rule, "snatching a grace beyond the reach of art", that Genius in most departments of it is sometimes given to exhibit; and which justify themselves; but are fatal to less gifted imitators, who soar that flight on only Icarian wings to meet with the consequent failure and fall.

The above named Exceptions are truly splendid; all partaking of those qualities of either, – vast dimensions – combined with a just proportion of parts, or great beauty of details – which make up for the absence of great extent, and thus, where not both, either sublime or beautiful: the First in its vast size, of admirable proportions; and not a little aided by the beauty of the material, red granite, coupled with that of being a single block, which fills both the mind and the eye with astonishment and admiration: the Others, occupying the eye with a still greater magnitude – while satisfying it with an outline of the severest classical proportion of its parts, delight it with a profusion of beauties of detail in the *bas-reliefs* with which their whole surfaces are covered, that entirely employ it; leaving nothing to be desired, nor making any other impression but that this Form was intended for the very and no other purpose than that to which it is here applied. Indeed this is so perfectly the case as to entitle The MONUMENTAL COLUMN to be considered as a separate Member of Architecture of itself, and not having any relation to the Auxiliary Supporting Column that yet no doubt first suggested it.

It is, then, fully legitimate for its purpose. The only question here is – how far it is suitable in the present case with reference to the Site it would occupy. That Site is very limited in the absolute disposable ground; and still more confined, except on the South side, by the proximity of the neighbouring Houses and Buildings, especially the National Gallery on the North side which is only about fifty yards from its centre.

A COLUMN, then, would have the advantage of occupying little room, and of being less killed (or, as the French call it, choked – smothered – *etranglé*) only "kilt" by its circumadjacents than would a more diffuse Structure.

The OBELISK, again, appears a thing particularly suited for the present purpose. And the fact of there having been several, besides Mr. Baily's, among the offered Models in the Exhibition would seem to show that there is a general feeling, at all events among the Artists, in favour of this Column as at least suited generally for the ornament of a Public Square. And so it certainly is, for it combines several of the points most essential thereto. – In the first place, Great beauty of form, combining unity – simplicity – and elegance – with that appearance of stability, in spite of its height and slenderness, which is always given by the pyramidal form. Nextly, its connection with the remotest antiqutiy, calling up in the mind a number of pleasing images and recollections independent of those with which it would here be associated. And lastly – While entirely filling the eye in the vista of space, the very little ground-room it actually takes up, and the very little by which it can be interfered with – and inversely – by neighbouring objects: Thus uniting beauty and grandeur with simplicity, and producing – with the least possible – all that can be effected by the combination of the greatest means. And, if that sordid item is to be regarded, it certainly would have the advantage of "cheapness."

Not having any thing of the kind that deserves the name in this Country – we are comparatively strangers and unaccustomed to this elegant Structure; but those who have seen the Obelisks of Rome, tho there marred and disfigured by the religious symbols with which they are surmounted, and still more the beautiful one from Luxor lately erected in the Place Louis Quinze at Paris, will not consider this view of it overcharged.

The reason I consider an Obelisk* (always with the exception of my own MAST) most particularly suited for the present purpose is, In the first place – Its general recommendations just above stated, that are peculiarly applicable to a space so limited as ours: And, in the next, – as considering it with reference to the Country of its origin in connection with the scene of one of our greatest Naval Battles – of our Hero's finest achievement – *The Nile*, it would accord particularly well with a Monument destined to commemorate his fame.

Altho so behind hand with our virtu*osi* Neighbours here – It is too late? – are they all gone? – might not a such be got from Egypt, for love or money, for this great purpose? If not past hope – it is surely worth the trial. Or, as an alternative, might not this be considered a sufficient occasion to see what our own Quarries might produce; and what our own mechanical skill, urged – not to say shamed – by our own Salisbury Plain, might effect in transport and erection? would not perhaps the Druids *lend* us a stone for him whose like their Scalds never had to sing? For it need not be remarked that an Obelisk, for perfect beauty, must not be *built*: it must be, at least, from its Pedestal, a single block, shooting up to the Sky like the branchless Pine or Tree whatever by which it was perhaps suggested.

A Column, as already said, is generally understood to be the kind of Structure The Committee are most likely to adopt. At the same time it is possible that this is only with reference to the other Models and Designs hitherto offered, and that new ones may now induce a change in Their views. It may also be presumed that Their leading motive for preferring that – had especial reference to its intended situation, as compared with those that would have occupied either a greater area of ground or more space in the vista – both which of course have their limits.

The Monument here proposed, however different in its details from a Column, is of exactly the same nature with reference to the above assumed reasons for its preference, besides very much resembling it in its principal points. It may therefor be considered as in the same category. The following further reasons for its adoption are deferentially submitted.

When, in a Structure that necessarily admits but of little variety, there are already existing types of acknowledged beauty, that have called forth the approval and admiration of ages – successive and numerous generations, it may be admitted that, – when it is desired to erect a thing of just the same sort, there is no occasion to seek further for a Model nor to resort to invention for one different, but merely to copy what is thus acknowledged as perfect and excellent. But this consideration only applies to just the premised case; and does by no means exclude the adoption of a new – a specifically different – thing, tho of the same general kind, when the circumstances that call for it are different and there is a legitimate and sufficient occasion to make that diversity be marked.

The Monumental Column is of itself a very beautiful thing. It was first imagined by the Romans, to record their military triumphs: and combining it, as they did, with a graphical description of the events it was designed to commemorate, at once simple – grand – and highly ornamented, seemed peculiarly appropriate to its object, and almost as if – instead of being borrowed from Architecture – it had been first invented for this particular purpose. This, as we have seen, has been imitated – or rather adopted – and with considerable success by some modern Nations.

If it were desired in this Country to raise a Monument for a precisely similar purpose, perhaps nothing could be better than to do precisely the same – to copy exactly that Model, to adapt the feelings and the taste of the Antients to our own times and events; and thus at least avoid the risk of not commanding from succeeding generations that admiration for the Architecture of our Monument which they most certainly would not refuse to the great deeds for whose commemoration it was erected.

But the object here in view is – in one principal respect – widely different. It is to raise a Monument – not to record military triumphs achieved on land – but for great Naval Victories; raised to a Warrior whose field of battle was the Ocean, an element on which, from the necessity of circumstances, the feats of the Antients as compared with those of modern days – with our own – sink into absolute insignificance. The Sea-fights of the Greeks and the Romans were in real fact mere Small-Craft or Boat businesses; and could not therefor – at least out of their own elements – produce any more extensively descriptive Monument for their record than A Rostral Column – a small Pillar, perhaps standing for a Galley's Mast, ornamented with the beaks or prows* – the heads – of other captured Barges. The necessary smallness of the object made it – however interesting – quite unsuitable for the purpose of a great arechitectural ornament. In short the Romans had no exclusively nautical *implement* sufficiently large to serve for the type of such a Structure: They could have no great Monument specifically Naval. –

We have that implement – in the *Masts* of our ships, those floating Castles that would have carried – not some few Companies – but Cohorts – a Legion of their Soldiers, and for whose colossal spars all their forests could not have supplied a tree sufficiently large. The MAIN-MAST of an English First Rate Man of War – The VICTORY's own, upon whose towering head, when erect in all the pride of simulated life, flew the burning signal that reminded – not told – her Sons that "*England expected all would do their Duty*," is the Monument here proposed to be raised to Him who bade it fly and under which He fell.

It is contended that, combining (as I hope this will be found to do) a peculiarly technical appositeness with simplicity – grandeur – and beauty, nothing whatever could be so appropriate to the occasion. As an Architectural Structure it would be new – bold – and striking, and most eloquently speaking to its object: it is also graceful and elegant in its form: and – I repeat it – from its entire novelty, while in nothing shocking the received opinions and feelings as to archtectonic propriety, and calling up ideas so entirely different to any connected with ordinary Structures and so closely allied with its purpose, would be singularly impressive and I think not less pleasing. Neither, tho something shorter than some of the Monumental Columns above spoken of, would it be at all too low to have a full effect even in the particular of height. It would in its life – or natural – dimensions be 109 feet from the ground; which is 10 feet higher than Pompey's Pillar, about the height of the highest Obelisks with their Pedestals, and only 12 feet less than the Trajan Column at Rome not including its Statue about 11 more: while, if thought adviseable, it could be increased to what might be considered an "heroic" height; and which, indeed, as the Statue of the Hero would be 25 feet from the ground and therefor require a size larger than life, the relative proportions of the Monument for perspectival accuracy would perhaps demand to be proportionably encreased, which would bring it very little – if anything – below the Classical Column.

The Plan of the Monument is – A *Pedestal*, the cap or upper surface of which represents so much of the Quarter-Deck of the Ship. From this springs The MAST; with its *Bitts* around it, and against which – their "after" part – the Hero is standing, in the attitude of repose while in condensed thought. The front face of the Pedestal – the Die – to be occupied by a suitable Inscription; and the other three to represent respectively in relief his three great victories of the Nile, Copenhagen, and Trafalgar. The Cornice is moulded with gun-mouths in low relief, and *cabled* (if the word may be allowed) in the form of rope. The Base is sculptured with emblematical figures and designs: And the Plinth rusticated – so to call it – in imitation of water. A Sub-Base of half a dozen steps might be introduced; which would give it greater elevation and insulateness, and tend to throw it out in better relief.

It will at once be noticed that, – tho so wholly dissimilar in their natures, there is a singular affinity and resemblance between the parts of the Architectural COLUMN and the MAST, and in very nearly the same proportions: the Pedestal standing for so much of the *Mast* as is "housed" down to the water-line of the ship – corresponding with the ground: the Shaft with its body from the Deck up to the *Hounds:* and the Entablature with its *Head.* While preserving to the lower part in its general character the strictly classical form of the Pedestal – I have aimed at combining with it an outline that should not be dissimilar to that of a Ship's side, and which the eye of at least a Seaman would please itself to fancy if not to recognise; thus making it, tho so different, to harmonise with the rest and keep up the leading idea.

As to the *Sub-Base*, or in general the details of the Pedestal, I do not at all insist upon any of them; but leave them to the determination of the more competent judgement of The Committee; only holding to my general idea of The MAST.

As for the Material, that of the Shaft part – the *Mast* proper (for of course the Pedestal must be of stone) – it must be matter for consideration whether, for still greater stability, it should not be of massive iron. This would exclude a staircase – access to its top from within: but which I am very decidedly of opinion would be no objection at all, but on the contrary, for reasons not necessary here to state, very much otherwise. Its top, if need be, can always be reached, even were there no gunpowder and one should resort to Jack's Kite for Pompey's Pillar.

There is one point, however, about my MAST, that I am aware may be liable to objection, namely – its bulk, as being perhaps something too small for stability with reference to its height. But this may easily be obviated by encreasing it: which I think may be done without producing any deformity whatever: at all events its so-appearance may easily be tried to the sight. The usual Diameter of a Column is one tenth of its whole height: while this is only about half that proportion: If then this is really a just objection, I would propose – the Diameter to be doubled at the foot, with a little less encrease at the head: which would fully meet the point. In order to test this, as well as may be done on so small a scale, – I have exhibited – The true bulk or diameter of the MAST by the darker drawing within the other, and the proposed encreased one by the lighter shaded one withoutside that. The *Bitts*, of course, to corespond with this enlargement, are removed a little beyond their proper place, with only a very little encrease of dimension. I confess also not to have satisfied myself about its colour: As every body knows – the Lower Masts of large ships are *painted*, as well for preservation as ornament: And, however it might shock received opinions as classical taste, there really seems no reason why such a column should not be painted, as represented in the Drawing. If it were so determined, and the State should take it in its custody like other Public Buildings (and be more liberal of pigments than heretofore – at least in certain Arsenals) a fund (and which would not require to be more than very litte) might be formed, even out of the Subscription, to keep it in good kelter by periodical renewals of its coat. At all events, should this Form be adopted, it would be well worth while to try the effect.

This last point particularly leads to the suggestion I had already intended to make on general grounds, that – Whatever Model may be chosen, or more than one, if likely to be suitable, should, before its final erection, be tried by raising it of temporary materials in absolute *fac simile* as to appearance; so as to enable a judgement to be formed of its effect; and so have the means of making any requisite modifications, or to reject the thing altogether, before it should be too late. This very obvious and sensible plan is now commonly pursued abroad, as lately in the erection of that beautiful object (already here alluded to) the Luxor Obelisk in the Place Louis Quinze at Paris.

This, of course, could not always be done without an inordinate expense. But, in how many cases – even of recent Erections – could it not have been used, and no doubt with the best results? To go futher back, and not look beyond Trafalgar Square, – Is it to be supposed that the Public opinion could have tolerated the anomalous and hideous excrescences that deform so many of our Churches under the name – not in the shape – of *Steeples*, if an opportunity had been allowed for judging of their effect by this means of – at least in some measure – a Life-Size Model?* But, on this latter subject, the greater wonder and reproach is – That *they are still allowed to stand!* – to be a just subject of ridicule and contempt to all of the least good taste among ourselves and – still worse – to Foreigners. It is a national stigma.

It not being necessarily incidental to the adoption of this Model that any suggestion should here be made as to the laying out of the ground generally of Trafalgar Square, – I will not permit myself to offer any suggestion about it, other than that – the Monument, or whatever other be erected, should be properly protected from either wanton or accidental injury; a precaution which, as to the former, is, whether from our want of familiarity with objects of Art – which has not yet made us feel a proper fondness and respect for them, or that, as free-born Englishmen," we feel ourselves justified in destroying or defacing any thing – in which we have no personal interest, is unfortunately indispensable in this Country.

In recapitulation – A Monument is intended to be raised – not of a general military nature – but one purely *Naval*, with reference to nothing but our achievements by sea – in our *Ships*, to the memory of England's first Seaman –

her great naval Chief – the illustrious and immortal NELSON. A Model is here proposed for one; that, with all the accessories of architectural and sculptural ornament, shall represent him in his general character – and where he may be supposed to have fallen – at the foot of his VICTORY'S MAST.

"Palmam qui meruit ferat."

From, *A Descriptive Account of the Literary Works of John Britton, F.S.A. being the Second Part of his Auto-Biography* by T. E. Jones, London, 1849, pp. 55–58.

BRIEF ACCOUNT OF A DESIGN
for

The Nelson Cenotaph, and British Naval Museum

BY JOHN BRITTON, F.S.A., &c.
AS SUBMITTED TO THE COMMITTEE FOR THE NELSON TESTIMONIAL;
JANUARY, 1839

"In Perpetuam Memoriam"

"IN COMPLIMENTING ANY GREAT CHARACTER, EXPENSE IS A SECONDARY CONSIDERATION. ALL WORKS OF ART PLEASE OR DISPLEASE IN PROPORTION AS TASTE OR JUDGMENT PREVAILS."

Marquess of Lansdowne, on Howard's Monument, 1794.

To commemorate the "great and good deeds" of the Hero of Trafalgar, by a building which shall make an instant impression on the passenger, – which will irresistibly excite inquiry, awaken curiosity, and keep up a continued stimulus of gratification, – which is calculated to arouse at once an intense reverence for, and admiration of, the dauntless British Admiral, and further, call forth that emulation in the incipeint hero which may lead to a perpetual succession of Nelsons, it is presumed and hoped may be effected by such an edifice as the accompanying design suggests.

After long deliberation, and a critical investigation of the monumental memorials raised by different nations, and in various parts of the civilized world, I am impressed with the conviction that no one species of design is so completely adapted to honour and immortalize an eminent person as a BUILDING, combining the elements of *Architecture, Sculpture, Painting,* and *Literature.* These, judiciously collected and united, will administer to each other's preservation, – to each other's influence, – to each other's attractions and beauties.

A building, a piece of sculpture, a picture, or even a book, is not alone sufficient to tell the whole history, – to emblazon all the exploits, – to illustrate the many memorable deeds and characteristics of a Nelson: but the whole concentrated into a focus, and displaying their respective powers and fascinations, would amply and forcibly portray and record the leading incidents of professional skill and heroism which belonged to the man, and to the era he adorned.

Never was patriotism more pure – never was courage more ardent – never was example more animating, than were inherited and exercised by Nelson. These prompted the spirit-stirring admonition which he addressed to his comrades on commencing his last memorable battle:

"ENGLAND EXPECTS THAT EVERY MAN WILL DO HIS DUTY."

Nothing that was ever written or uttered by sages of the ancient or modern world surpasses this sentence and sentiment in appositeness and impressiveness. It is truly English in every particle, and should be a motto, and a public monition written in all the naval and military schools of the kingdom. His emphatic prediction was fulfilled, – every man was ambitious and eager to surpass rather than be deficient in his duty.

Never was hero more honoured in life and lamented in death than *Nelson:* but the lamentations have subsided; the fleeting honours of his day have nearly faded away; nor is the monumental trophy in St. Paul's Cathedral, the Column at Yarmouth (in his native county), or the other memorials in Liverpool, Dublin, and Edinburgh, enough to mark the national feeling and gratitude for such a man and such an Admiral.

To raise a trophy more commensurate with his intrinsic worth and unflinching intrepidity than either of those alluded to, is at once a duty and an honour which every true-born Englishman, who duly appreciates his character, must feel to be a desideratum. In calling into competition and exertion the abilities of English artists for such a subject, the Committee have acted laudably and wisely: and it cannot be doubted that several designs, of varied merit and beauty, will be produced. The most appropriate, the most effective, the *best*, it is hoped and presumed, will be selected; and happy and fortunate will that artist be whose name may thereby be associated with that of Nelson in a grand national monument.*

For the complete understanding of the accompanying Design, I venture to claim the attention of the Committee to the following considerations, which gave rise to its composition, arrangement, and application. Impressed with the conviction that the slight and quickly mouldering monuments hitherto placed over the graves of eminent men have been too trivial and unsubstantial, – that they have generally decayed or entirely perished after a few years, or, at the most, after one or two centuries, – and that the only efficient way to guard against such occurrence will be the creation or investment of a fund adequate to keep in perpetual repair any monument, however expensive, or however stable; it is proposed that the *Nelson Cenotaph* shall also be a *British Naval Museum.* In this vast and still increasing metropolis, there are thousands of persons who continually frequent places of public exhibition, which are usually to be seen on the payment of one shilling for each admission. By a much smaller fee for entrance, and by the display of a building unique in character and interesting in effect; by bringing within its walls many and various objects of popular curiosity, and the whole dissimilar to any other museum, it may be assumed that a revenue will be raised sufficiently ample to uphold the integrity and entirety of the edifice, gradually augment its attractions, and pay annual stipends to such officers, &c. as may be required. These should be *naval men* who have served their country, but who, from wounds or other causes, may be unfitted for active service, and to whom an honourable asylum and home, with a moderate income, would be objects of solicitude to the receiver and of honour to the giver.

Convinced of the eligibility and permanent utility of this plan, I would willingly enter upon a full explanation of these suggestions, but from a persuasion that the Committee will have so many beautiful designs to engross their attention, and fascinate their imaginations, that they will not be able to give it that full consideration which the novelty of the scheme requires.

The accompanying *Plan and View*, are intended to illustrate the general form, as well as the arrangement and disposition of the proposed Cenotaph; but from the smallness of the scale they cannot fully shew the numerous naval and Nelsonic details, nor the varied features which are suggested to form parts of the finished edifice. Every aspect, and almost every sub-division, may have forms and insignia, bearing direct reference to those memorable scenes, and to that peculiar service, in which the hero won his glory. If this design be adopted, his figure and personal features will be preserved and perpetuated in stone, bronze, marble, and enamel: his eventful life and its vicissitudes, his courageous and dauntless conflicts, will be fully detailed in the writings of the historian and the biographer, deposited in this building: the gratitude and adoration of sovereigns, statesmen, and contemporary officers, will be registered in the diplomas and other official documents addressed to him on different occasions; whilst Literature, Sculpture, Painting, and Engraving, will all find appropriate places in such an edifice to display their respective offerings at the shrine of British Heroism. This quadruple alliance of the arts and literature to honour and emblazon the fame of the most distinguished naval officer of the world, will, it is believed, be more apposite than a mere column, or a statue, and therefore secure the preference which the design aspires to obtain.

The *Entrance Porch*, approached from the south by a flight of twenty-four steps, is to be adorned with architectural decorations and sculptural enrichments. A statue of *King William the Fourth*, the personal friend and companion of Nelson, crowns the gable, whilst another of the Hero will occupy a central niche; and the armorial bearings of the Monarch, and of the Admiral, are architecturally attached to each. The memorable injunction of the Commander to his intrepid comrades to be displayed architecturally around the building, with other apposite inscriptions.

For the purpose of giving an unequivocal demonstration of the purport of the building, this porch will be adorned with numerous sculptured objects of a naval character; and will be under the care of a seaman-porter, provided with a berth in the same part of the building.

Beyond the inner doorway of this porch is a lofty, light, and highly enriched octagonal apartment, having eight clustered columns and lofty arches, separating the central area from an ambulatory. Whilst the latter is destined to receive a great variety of basso-relievos, busts, statues, windows of painted glass, &c., and is adorned with a series of arcades and other architectural dressings, forming frames and panels for pictures and basso-relievos; the former will enshrine a large and skilfully executed *Statue of the Hero.* This will stand on a pedestal rising within the basement story, and surrounded by an architectural screen, on which will be eight smaller pedestals, with busts of as many of his associate admirals and officers.

Branching from three sides of the octagon are three apartments, or divisions of the building, intended respectively for libraries, and for the residence of a Curator. In the libraries are to be collected and preserved all the books and other documents published in Great Britain, and in other countries, relating to naval tactics, history, and biography. One of these wings may be called the *Nelson*, and the other the *Naval Library.*

THE MUSEUM is the main building, in which all objects connected with naval affairs can be distributed and classed. In the porch, the central area, the ambulatory, the crypt, or ground apartment, and in the triforium, will be ample space, and a variety of places adapted to display a large collection of objects.

It is well known that the "United Service Museum", at Whitehall, and the Admiralty, possess numerous naval relics and curiosities; which, it may be fairly presumed, would be transferred to, and form part of, the proposed great National Museum.

It is suggested that the government or management of the British Naval Museum be vested in Trustees, who shall become such by virtue of their public appointments.

It is proposed that on the Anniversaries of the Battle of the Nile, and of the Birth-day of Nelson, and on other days of great rejoicing, the flag, which Nelson won at Trafalgar, be hoisted to the top of the spire; and that the lantern be illuminated by a jet of gas, which, by means of coloured lenses in the windows, might be rendered visible from distant points in and around London.

A building conformably to this design may be raised, with good materials, and a liberal amount of decoration, for THIRTY THOUSAND POUNDS. But such are the capabilities of this species of architecture, that its decorations may be reduced or augmented to any extent.

Should the Committee entertain a favourable opinion of the design, many variations and improvements can be made; and the author would gladly enter more fully into particulars.

* Alas! how vain and futile are the most reasonable hopes and anticipations of our nature in the lottery of life. The wisdom and justice of requiring competition in works of art, and other productions of mind, have long been questioned: and it is now very generally admitted that it should never be required unless the tribunal can be composed of men of strict impariality, of sound judgment, and good taste. That these qualities were lamentably deficient in the Committees who decided on the York Column, the National Gallery, the London University College, the Nelson Columns, and many other public works, is now universally admitted. These designs are more disreputable to the parties who selected, than to the artists who designed them; for they impeach the national mind and character. Committees should never be self-elected, or, rather, self-appointed: they should be chosen from the whole body of persons who may associate for a specific public object; if, among such bodies, the necessary qualifications can be found. [April, 1849.]

*** In the above design, I availed myself of the professional advice and skill of my esteemed friend, Mr. W. Hosking; and, had the plan been accepted, it was agreed that the execution of the edifice was to have been under his direction.

APPENDIX 3

ON THE MEASURES TO BE ADOPTED IN LONDON AGAINST POPULAR TUMULTS

London is peculiarly liable to danger from internal commotions.

The population is enormous, and among them are to be found many thousands out of work, suffering and discontented, with numbers of political enthusiasts ready for the most violent attacks on the Powers that be.

These spring at once into activity on occasion of excitement, fit for any act of violence against the State with great danger of being accompanied by indiscriminate plunder and destruction.

The forms of the Constitution admit of these risings and of the preparations for them gaining a great head before they can be resisted; while the Government has no sufficiently numerous body of Troops for the repression of any extensive movement.

The public safety in such emergencies therefore must be dependent upon the feelings of the Class which by numbers and property have the greatest stake in the Country; and who it should be presumed, would not be inclined to allow of changes which they may think even desirable or necessary, if to be enforced by violent popular commotion, attended as it must necessarily be, by great social evils, – well knowing that what is decidedly the will of that body which has a right to be called "the Country" must be carried out eventually by a gradual and less injurious process.

In these disturbances however the circumstances of the initiative being taken by the turbulent admits of their being under a certain degree of preparation and organization that may lead to great misfortunes if not immediately checked, which they can only be by some degree of constant preparation and understanding on the part of the authorities and the well disposed.

It is submitted that these precautionary measures are in a great degree wanting.

It is true that we have a powerful Police admirably adapted for the security of the Metropolis on all ordinary occasions who would form an excellent nucleus to any temporary force of Citizens that may be embodied for preserving the Peace, but are insufficient of themselves to put down extensive commotions.

The enrolling of the Civic mass (on whom eventually in our present situation the power of repression must depend) takes under most favorable circumstances, some little consideration and time, and may require more in proportion as these natural guardians of the public peace, may have imbibed sentiments in common with those on which the popular demonstration is founded; and even when enrolled they are greatly in want of a combined system of action, in which respect they would be even inferior to the Rioters.

Each body of "Special Constables" attending exclusively to its own locality (as usually regulated) is every where weak against congregated masses and yet if not numerous they may be so employed with great advantage, to perform the ordinary duty of the Police, while these are made generally available; and it may be worthy of consideration whether when in great numbers, some selection of Volunteers from them might not be placed at the disposition of the Officers of the Police for exterior combined action with that body, with which they would then form a supplementary force.

If the alarms are continuous, some system will be required for calling out portions for duty at a time, with arrangements for collecting the remainder if the emergency became serious.

It would however be very unadvisable to give to even the best order of Citizens any permanent organization that would constitute a species of National Guard.

Such a force however plausible the system may be *theoretically*, being found liable *practically* to operate in effecting sudden permanent changes on temporary popular delusions, and thus injuriously jumping at conclusions before time is given for deliberation.

The most difficult case with which a Government will have to deal will be when these popular tumults shall have the plausible protest of supporting measures which a very large number of the more influential classes may be endeavouring to force upon a reluctant Government and Parliament.

It may be considered good policy by those who desire the changes, (and who ought to be looked to for the preservation of the peace) not to discourage this species of pressure, overlooking in their warmth of their desire to carry their point, that there is a risk of the movement gaining a head which may prove beyond their control, or that at least very great mischief may be occasioned during the process.

In such cases every power and effort of the Government may be needed to prevent excesses in London that might effect great and permanent injury to the Country.

That we are more liable to these attacks now than hitherto, and that we shall be so for some time to come, may be confidently inferred from the impulse that has been given to such attempts, by the success that has recently attended them in so many Countries on the Continent.

Accordingly we have a formidable association under the denomination of Chartists only waiting its opportunity and ready to connect themselves with any other malcontents of high or low station, hints having already been thrown out of a combination of efforts between them and the advocates for a renewed reform agitation.

Every circumstance therefore indicates the urgency of entering into well regulated preparation for sudden outbreaks.

Considering that occasions of public disturbances may be very sudden, and that the absolute force at the disposition of Government is small, I would submit that it would be very desirable to make every possible arrangement for the permanent security of the Government Offices and Public Establishments that can be effected without creating jealousy or exciting much attention.

In the early part of April of this year (1848) when the threats of the great Chartist demonstration to carry out Revolution in this Country induced the Government to take energetic precautions, Officers of Royal Engineers were employed at many of the Public Establishments, to place them in the best state of defence that circumstances would allow.

In no case had they any record for their guidance of such measures as must have been adopted on former occasions, nor did they find that any precautions had been taken in the construction or arrangement of the premises to meet such emergencies. They had in consequence to examine every part, and to consider and to apply the most ready means that could be employed for the purpose.

These consisted of temporary barricades to particular entrances, the opening of internal communications, the construction of loop-holes, sand bag covering, temporary obstacles, the arrangement of arms, ammunition and stores, the posting and general disposition of parties allotted for defence, etc.

As a similar contingency may at any time occur, and with very little warning, it is suggested that many of these arrangements should be made permanent, and that a description of each Building should be kept on record with a detail of the measures previously adopted and recommended for their protection.

It is not proposed to make any display of these preparations but to apply only such (and they are very many) as can be adopted without attracting notice, and without disfiguring the building, or in any degree interfering with its internal conveniences and arrangements.

As a measure of apparent ordinary precaution, or proceeding, very strong barricading bars might be adapted to doors, iron bars to lower windows, and musquet proof iron shutters with loop holes fixed or at hand for immediate application when necessary; internal communications might be arranged, and appropriate collection of arms and ammunition deposited under some charge in an apartment where it may be secured from deterioration, depredation or accident, and even (which is most important) some external projections might be added, where necessary, for flanking in the way of turrets or balconies, with the sanction of the Architect, and according to his own design.

When the buildings already possess flanking lines, but without openings, they can usually be made with all the appearance of windows, large or small, and may be used as such if convenient, or if otherwise they may be habitually closed internally, and only have their strong shutters and Loopholes applied in times of need.

A degree of perpetual organization of the Officers and servants of the several Establishments may be maintained.

However general or violent any political discontent may become, the persons in Government employ will always have strong inducements to resist sudden great changes, and may therefore be depended upon. Some well understood system for their action will add greatly to the power of protection and will reduce the demand for Police or Soldiers in each locality; and consequently leave the latter more efficient bodies to act in greater force as general reserves.

The requisite organization would consist of the arming, and the allotment to specific duties or posts of each Individual according to his known capabilities or previous habits, with Instructions how and when to proceed with certain measures etc.

Although it may not be desirable to drill and practice the whole body in these matters, a description should be kept on paper, and a few of those who would direct the operations should be made to understand them thoroughly and be ready to allot each to his several charge.

It would be very desirable that some one or more Officer in each Establishment should be a Magistrate sufficiently conversant with the law, to decide when the Defenders may be duly authorized to act with vigour, for there is not any thing more embarrassing or more likely to lead to disastrous results, than a want of knowledge of the degree of provocation which may justify the use of all the available means of opposition.

Among the measures for the prevention of evil, the stock of firearms at the several Gunsmiths and Manufacturers should be secured. It is calculated that not much less than 100,000 stands of different kinds, but all in a state fit for use might be found in London in these Depots.

As it would be impossible for Government to protect each of the premises, in order to prevent these arms falling into the hands of the Rioters these Tradesmen at periods of alarm, should be requested to deposit as many as possible in the Tower or other place of security, those that cannot be so provided for might have their locks separated from their Pieces, and deposited for the time elsewhere.

The leading public Establishments that are here contemplated as requiring attention, and to which it may be possible to apply more or less of permanent arrangement, comprehend

The Royal Palace
The Houses of Parliament
The Treasury

and other Offices and official residences of Ministers in Downing Street and Whitehall

The Horse Guards
Admiralty
Somerset House
Ordnance Office

The Bank
Mint
Custom House
British Museum and Post Office

These are all absolutely Government Establishments except the Bank, and that is so connected with the interests of the Country at large, and presents so much temptation to plunder, that the Government will always consider itself bound to provide specially for its safety.

There are many others of importance that are quite independent of Government and will have to make their own arrangements; but it might be well if each of these also, in proportion to its liability to call the attention of the populace in times of disturbance were to be somewhat prepared and organized for self-protection.

Of the Premises above mentioned the Bank, British Museum and Post Office may be considered as insulated and without support, with the exception of such as can be obtained by penetrating from a distance through the Streets.

The remainder however may be combined into one or more systems of mutual or concentrated support. A most valuable line of communication may be obtained along the Thames connecting the Tower with the Custom House, Somerset House and the Houses of Parliament, by small Steamers from the Dockyards of Woolwich and Deptford, or taken up for the purpose on the emergency; thus securing a line for receiving reinforcements, and support from each other, from the Lower Thames, the Medway and the Sea.

A command of the Bridges would be necessary for the continued maintenance of this advantage, and is otherwise most desirable, as an interruption to any combined action on the part of the Insurrectionists on the two sides of the River.

Another advantageous circumstance of Position is to be derived from the number of public Establishments that are round St. James's Park, comprising,

Buckingham Palace
St. James's Palace
Queen Dowager's Palace
Ordnance Office
Admiralty
Horse Guards
Treasury

Offices and Residences of the principal Ministers at Whitehall and in Downing Street, Irish Office and Wellington Barrack.

This would enable a general Reserve Force, which should occupy St. James's and Hyde Parks (and might be of Cavalry, Infantry and Artillery in these open spaces) not only to support powerfully any point that might be threatened or attacked but to debouche from any part of that Circuit to attack the Rioters in front or flank.

By the occupation also of Whitehall and Gwydir House, this position might be easily connected with the Thames, and thus complete command obtained of an entire internal line, between the River and Kensington Palace, including the communication along Parliament Street and Whitehall to Charing Cross.

Westminster Bridge, the Parliament Houses and Palace Yard would be supported from this position on one side, and by the occupation of Charing Cross and Trafalgar Square on the other, another very leading line of communication would be commanded between the East and West Ends; and the great advantage gained of cramping considerably the movements of the rioters, with the power of bringing masses to bear on any part of a very extensive range from one central line of position well adapted to the more organized forces of the Government.

In all future constructions and alterations in the great public Buildings that are connected with this arrangement it may be well to consider what might be done not only for their distinct self protection, but that advantage may be taken of this general view especially by secure and available communications towards the rear for mutual support; and among them if it could be combined with any useful purpose, it would be desirable to establish some small Building or Tower on the top of the Garden of Buckingham Palace, which might combine the purpose of ornament with the capability of defence, as an additional security to the Palace premises, and to assist in commanding the communications between the Parks, and along the roads approaching to Hyde Park Corner.

In cases of formidable riots, all private residences are usually secured as well as circumstances will permit, and according to the temptation they may afford to attack either for the purpose of plunder or from the circumstance of their being the property of Parties obnoxious to the Rioters.

Some Clubs would probably be included among the latter; and amongst these, no doubt those belonging to the Navy and Army.

One of these that of the Senior United Service in Waterloo Place, may take a useful place in the general system connected with St. James's Park; it may be made very strong for self defence by some small means applied to the Balconies, while by its position, it would command and protect the great communication in or out of the Park by the Duke of York's stairs, and a debouche to the great avenue of Regent Street.

The Officers of Royal Engineers engaged on the 10th April last, in preparing for the protection of many of the public Establishments, viz, the Public Offices about Whitehall and Downing Street, the Bank, British Museum and Mint, have drawn up Reports of the nature of their proceedings on that occasion with suggestions for some Government arrangements that it would be desirable to make, these Reports will afford useful guides for the future.

The Bank has already authorized their Architect to make the permanent alterations that have been suggested; and the Treasury have sanctioned similar undertakings for some of the Government Premises, and will probably allow of the whole.

These views for protective measures for London may be considered too large for the object; and perhaps despised as being only applicable to such occasions and dangers as are not likely to occur. It is to be hoped that such may be the case, but by the contemplation of the worst state of circumstances we shall be the better prepared to meet the lesser emergencies, which may only require the application of a portion of the prepared measures, these however might still be on the same previously understood system.

There is the less reason to object to the consideration of the principle of preparation for an extraordinary occasion as it is not proposed to increase the means for protection, but only that they should be applied towards one given end.

It may also be remarked that the successful issue of some Revolutions altering the fate of Nations, appears to have been mainly attributable to the want of a due consideration of the importance of such preparations on a sufficiently extended view.

J.F.B.
June 1848

Major General Sir J. F. Burgoyne, K.E.

Source: *PRO MEPOL: 2/59.*

APPENDIX 4

A.

A

BILL

FOR

The regulation of Meetings in Trafalgar Square A.D. 1888.

WHEREAS it is expedient that regulations should be made with respect to public meetings in Trafalgar Square:

Be it therefore enacted by the Queen's most Excellent Majesty, by and with the advice and consent of the Lords Spiritual and Temporal, and Commons, in this present Parliament assembled, and by the authority of the same, as follows:

Short title.

1. This Act may be cited for all purposes as the Trafalgar Square Regulation Act, 1888.

Regulations for meetings.

2. No person shall deliver or invite any person to deliver any public address in Trafalgar Square except in accordance with the regulations contained in the schedule to this Act, or such other regulations as may hereafter be made in virtue of powers conferred by this Act.

Making of new regulations.

3. The Commissioners of Her Majesty's Works and Public Buildings, herein-after called the Commissioners of Works, are hereby empowered to make regulations in substitution for those in the schedule to this Act, provided that any regulations made in pursuance of this section shall be forthwith laid before both Houses of Parliament if Parliament be sitting, or if not, then within three weeks after the beginning of the then next ensuing session of Parliament, and if any such regulations shall be disapproved of by either House of Parliament within one month after the same shall have been so laid before Parliament, such regulations shall not be substituted for those in the schedule to this Act.

Penalty on violating regulations.

4. If any person does any Act in contravention of any regulation contained in the schedule annexed hereto, he shall, on conviction by a court of summary jurisdiction, be liable to a penalty not exceeding *five pounds*.

Publication of regulations.

5. Copies of regulations to be observed in pursuance of this Act shall be put up in Trafalgar Square in such conspicuous manner as the Commissioners of Works may deem best calculated to give information to the persons frequenting Trafalgar Square.

Saving of certain rights.

6. Nothing in this Act shall authorise any interference with the rights of way, or any right whatever to which any person or persons may be by law entitled.

Act to be cumulative.

7. All powers conferred by this Act shall be deemed to be in addition to and not in derogation of any powers conferred by any other Act of Parliament, and any such powers may be exercised as if this Act had not been made.

Saving of the rights of the Crown.

8. Nothing in this Act contained shall be deemed to prejudice or affect any prerogative or right of Her Majesty, or any powers or duties of any officers, clerks, or servants appointed by Her Majesty or by the Commissioners of Works.

Saving of 30 & 31 Vict. c. 134.

9. Nothing in this Act contained shall affect the Metropolitan Streets Act, 1867, or the application thereof to Trafalgar Square or to any part thereof to which it is by law applicable.

Saving of 57 Geo. 3. c. 19.

10. Nothing in this Act contained shall affect the provisions of an Act passed in the fifty-seventh year of George the Third, chapter nineteen.

Summary proceedings for offences.

11. Any offence against this Act may be prosecuted before a court of summary jurisdiction in manner directed by the Act of the session of the eleventh and twelfth years of the reign of Her present Majesty, chapter forty-three, intituled "an Act to facilitate the "performance of the duties of justices of the peace out of sessions "within England and Wales with respect to summary convictions "and orders," and any Act amending the last-mentioned Act.

"Court of summary jurisdiction" shall in this Act mean and include any justice or justices of the peace, metropolitan police magistrate, stipendiary or other magistrate or officer by whatever name called, to whom jurisdiction in respect of offences arising under this Act is given by this section or any Acts therein referred to.

SCHEDULE

Regulations for Public Addresses in Trafalgar Square

1. No public address of an unlawful character or for an unlawful purpose may be delivered.

2. No public address may be delivered unless a written notice of intention to deliver the same signed with the names and addresses of

two householders residing in the metropolis be left at the offices of the Commissioners of Her Majesty's Works and Public Buildings at least two clear days before. Such notice must state the day and hour of intended delivery. After such a notice has been received no other notice for the delivery of any other address on the same day will be valid.

3. No public address may be delivered except after sunrise and before sunset.

4. No public address may be delivered except in that portion of the paved part of Trafalgar Square which is bounded on the north and south by the granite posts, and on the east and west by the boundary wall of the roadway; and no such address shall be delivered where the assemblage of persons to hear the same causes obstruction to the use of any road or walk by the public outside of the boundaries herein mentioned, and no such obstruction shall be wilfully caused by any person forming part of any assemblage which may have met to hear any such address.

B.

A

BILL

TO

Declare and regulate the Right of Public Meeting in Open Spaces A.D. 1888.

WHEREAS it is expedient to declare the law in relation to the right of open public meeting and to give to public authorities certain powers to regulate the same for the public interest and convenience:

Be it therefore enacted by the Queen's most Excellent Majesty, by and with the advice and consent of the Lords Spiritual and Temporal, and Commons, in this present Parliament assembled, and by the authority of the same, as follows:

Right of user of open spaces for public meetings.

1. In all cases where the public have at any time heretofore from time to time during a period of not less than twenty years used or enjoyed, or shall in like manner hereafter use or enjoy, any open space for the purpose of meeting and delivering or listening to public addresses, the public are hereby declared and shall be deemed for all purposes to have acquired an absolute and inalienable right to the user thereof for the said purposes.

Rules may be made by public authority.

2.—(*a.*) It shall be lawful for any public authority as hereby defined to make in respect of any public open space within their several jurisdiction or control rules for the purpose of regulating, in the public interest and convenience, the holding of such meetings for the purposes aforesaid: Provided that no such rule shall have any force or effect unless and until the same has been sanctioned, under his hand and seal, by Her Majesty's Principal Secretary of State for the Home Department.

Rules to be sanctioned by the Secretary of State.

No rule shall prohibit public meetings.

(*b.*) No such rule shall be repugnant to the law of England, nor shall any rule purporting to be made under the provisions of this Act be allowed or be valid if the same be in restraint or prohibition of the general right of public meeting or freedom of speech, or otherwise than for the purpose of regulating the same in the public interest and convenience.

Rules to be laid before Parliament.

(*c.*) Every rule made in pursuance of this section shall be forthwith laid before both Houses of Parliament, if Parliament be sitting, or if not, then within one week after the beginning of the then next ensuing session of Parliament; and if any such rule or any part thereof shall be disapproved by either House of Parliament, such rules, or such part thereof as shall be so disapproved, shall not be enforced.

Definition of "public authority."

(*d.*) For the purposes of this section the expression "public authority" shall mean:—

1. In any case where the open space is vested in Her Majesty, Her heirs and successors in right of Her Crown, or as part and parcel of the hereditary possessions and revenues of the Crown, or in the Commissioners for the time being of Her Majesty's Woods, Forests, and Land Revenues, or the Commissioners of Her Majesty's Works and Public Buildings, "the said Commissioners of Her Majesty's Works and Public Buildings":
2. When the open space is vested in the Metropolitan Board of Works, the said Metropolitan Board of Works or any other public body which may be substituted for the said Board by parliamentary authority; and in any other case the corporation, municipal or otherwise, local board, or other public authority in or by whom the particular open space is vested or controlled.

Penalty for breach of regulations.

3. If any person shall do any act in contravention of any rule made or published under the authority of this Act, he shall, on conviction by a court of summary jurisdiction, be liable to a penalty not exceeding *five pounds*, to be recovered in manner provided by law in the case of a summary conviction.

Unlawful interference with public meetings.

4. Any person who shall wrongfully and without lawful authority molest, disturb, or interfere with any public meeting held under the authority or provisions of this Act, with a view to prevent the same

being held, or shall unlawfully use violence or intimidation to any procession, persons, or person proceeding or on the way to any such meeting, with a view to compel them or him to abstain from proceeding to or attending the same, shall be guilty of a misdemeanor, and liable on conviction thereof, on indictment, to imprisonment for a term not exceeding *one year*, or to a fine, in the discretion of the Court.

This Act not to affect the law as to unlawful assemblies.

5. Nothing in this Act shall in any way affect the law as to meetings held for an unlawful purpose or in breach of the public peace.

Saving as to existing rights.

6. Nothing in this Act contained shall be deemed to be in derogation of, or otherwise prejudice, any right, title, or privilege enjoyed by the public, or any section of the public, to which they may be by law entitled.

Short title.

7. This Act may be cited for all purposes as the Public Meetings in Open Spaces Act, 1888.

C.

7° & 8° VICTORIÆ, Cap. 60.

An Act to provide for the Care and Preservation of *Trafalgar Square* in the City of *Westminster*.

[6th *August* 1844.]

WHEREAS the Queen's most Excellent Majesty, in right of Her Crown, is seised to Herself, Her Heirs and Successors, of the Place or Square called *Trafalgar Square*, in the Parish of *Saint Martin-in-the-Fields* in the City of *Westminster* and County of *Middlesex*: And whereas such Place or Square has recently been formed, laid out, embellished, and ornamented, at the public Expence: And whereas upwards of Twenty thousand Pounds have been collected by private Subscription, and expended towards the Erection of a Column in the said Square to commemorate the public Services of the late Vice Admiral Lord Viscount *Nelson*; and it is expedient that Provision should be made for the Care and Preservation thereof, and for the ornamental and other Works, Matters, and Things erected upon or around the same, as hereinafter mentioned: May it therefore please Your Majesty that it may be enacted; and be it enacted by the Queen's most Excellent Majesty, by and with the Advice and Consent of the Lords Spiritual and Temporal, and Commons, in this present Parliament assembled, and by the Authority of the same, That the said Place or Square called *Trafalgar Square*, and all the ornamental and other Works, Matters, and Things now being or which may hereafter be placed or erected in, upon, about, or around the same, shall be and the same are by this Act vested in the Queen's

Trafalgar Square, and the Works thereon, vested in Her Majesty.

most Excellent Majesty, Her Heirs and Successors, as Part and Parcel of the Hereditary Possessions and Revenues of Her Majesty in right of Her Crown, within the ordering and Survey of the Court of Exchequer.

Care and Management of the Square, and of all Works thereon, vested in the Commissioners of Woods, &c.

II. And be it enacted, That the Care, Control, Management, and Regulation of the said Place or Square, and of all ornamental and other Works, Matters, and Things now being or which may hereafter be placed or erected in, upon, or about or around the same, shall be and the same are by this Act vested in the Commissioners for the Time being of Her Majesty's Woods, Forests, Land Revenues, Works, and Buildings; and the said Commissioners shall and they are hereby required, by and out of such Monies as may from Time to Time be placed at Her Majesty's Disposal for that Purpose by Authority of Parliament, to well and sufficiently pave, light, cleanse, water, repair, and keep in good Order and Condition the said Place or Square, and all ornamental and other Works, Matters, and Things now being or which may hereafter be placed or erected in, upon, about, or around the same, any Law, Statute, Custom, or Usage to the contrary in anywise notwithstanding.

Powers of 10 G. 4. c. 44. and 2 & 3 Vict. c. 47. extended to this Act.

III. And be it enacted, That all the Clauses and Provisions of an Act passed in the Tenth Year of the Reign of His late Majesty *George* the Fourth, intituled *An Act for improving the Police in and near the Metropolis*, and of another Act passed in the Second and Third Year of the Reign of Her Majesty, intituled *An Act for further improving the Police in and near the Metropolis*, shall extend and apply to this Act, and to the said Place or Square, and to the Works, Matters, or Things for the Time being in, upon, about, or around the same, so far as such Clauses and Provisions are not repugnant to or inconsistent with the Provisions of this Act.

Act may be amended this Session.

IV. And be it enacted, That this Act may be amended or repealed by any Act to be passed in this present Session of Parliament.

Public Act.

V. And be it enacted, That this Act shall be deemed to be a Public Act, and shall be judically taken notice of as such by all Judges, Justices, and others.

D.

ORDER OF THE COMMISSIONER OF POLICE OF THE METROPOLIS, DATED OCTOBER 26, 1892, REVOKING THE REGULATIONS OF NOVEMBER 18, 1887, AS TO MEETINGS IN TRAFALGAR SQUARE.

WHEREAS on the 18th day of November 1887, regulations were issued by the Commissioner of Police of the Metropolis, under the powers conferred on him by the Metropolitan Police Acts, as follows:—

"No meeting shall be allowed to assemble, nor shall any person be allowed to deliver a public speech in Trafalgar Square, or in the streets or thoroughfares adjoining or leading thereto. No organised procession shall be allowed to pass along the streets or thoroughfares adjoining or leading to Trafalgar Square," which regulations were to continue in force until further notice.

Now I, Edward Ridley Colborne Bradford, the Commissioner of Police of the Metropolis, hereby revoke the foregoing regulations as from 31st day of October, 1892.

E. R. C. Bradford,
The Commissioner of Police of the Metropolis.

Metropolitan Police Office,
New Scotland Yard,
October 26th, 1892.

E.

REGULATIONS BY THE COMMISSIONERS OF WORKS, DATED OCTOBER 26, 1892, AS TO MEETINGS IN TRAFALGAR SQUARE.

WHEREAS by the Trafalgar Square Act, 1844,* and by the Crown Lands Act, 1851,† the care, control, management, and regulation of Trafalgar Square is vested in the Commissioners of Her Majesty's Works and Public Buildings;

And whereas it is expedient that public meeting should be permitted to be held in Trafalgar Square, subject to such regulations as may be necessary with a view to the public convenience and safety and to the due observance of order;

Now I, on behalf of the Commissioners of Her Majesty's Works and Public Buildings, in exercise of the powers vested in in them as aforesaid, do hereby make the following regulations with regard to the holding of meetings in Trafalgar Square:—

1. No public meeting shall be held except between 2 p.m. and sunset on Saturday, or between sunrise and sunset on Bank Holidays or Sunday.
2. No public meeting shall be held unless written notice shall have been sent four clear days beforehand by the promoters to the Commissioner of Police of the Metropolis, specifying the object of the meeting, and the day and hour when it is proposed to be held.
3. Speeches shall not be delivered except from places authorised by the Commissioners of Her Majesty's Works and Public Buildings.
4. Not more than one meeting will be allowed at the same time; and if notices of two or more meetings are given for the same day, preference shall be given to that meeting of which notice shall have been first received.

These regulations shall come into force on the 31st day of October, 1892.

G. Shaw Lefevre,
First Commissioner of Works.

H.M. Office of Works, &c.,
October 26, 1892.

F.

Whereas by the Trafalgar Square Act, 1844, and by the Crown Lands Act, 1851, the care, control, management, and regulation of Trafalgar-square are vested in the Commissioners of His Majesty's Works and Public Buildings;

And whereas it is expedient that public meetings should be permitted to be held in Trafalgar-square, subject to such regulations as may be necessary with a view to the public convenience and safety and to the due observance of order.

Now I, on behalf of the Commissioners of His Majesty's Works and Public Buildings, in exercise of the powers vested in them as aforesaid, do hereby make the following regulations with regard to the holding of meetings in Trafalgar-square:—

1. No public meeting shall be held except between 2 p.m. and sunset on Saturdays, or between sunrise and sunset on Bank Holidays or Sundays.

2. (a) No public meeting shall be held unless written notice shall have been sent four clear days beforehand by the promoters to the Commissioner of Police of the Metropolis, specifying the object of the meeting, and the day and hour when it is proposed to be held.

(b) A second notice from the same promoters will not be regarded as valid until their first meeting has actually taken place or been abandoned.

3. Speeches shall not be delivered except from places authorized by the Commissioners of His Majesty's Works and Public Buildings.

4. Not more than one meeting will be allowed *on the same day*; and if notices of two or more meetings are given for the same day preference shall be given to that meeting of which notice shall have been first received.

5. These regulations shall come into force on the 1st day of November, 1914, and the regulations of the 26th of October, 1892, are hereby cancelled as from that date.

(Signed) *Emmott*,
First Commissioner of Works.

H.M. Office of Works, &c.,
5th day of October, 1914.

G.

The Trafalgar Square Regulations, 1952*

Draft Laid before Parliament	19*th February,* 1952
Made	8*th April,* 1952
Coming into Operation	8*th June,* 1952

The Minister of Works, in exercise of the powers conferred upon him by the Trafalgar Square Act, 1844(a), and the Parks Regulation Acts, 1872(b) and 1926(c), and of all other powers enabling him in that behalf, hereby makes the following Regulations:—

Interpretation

1.—(1) In these Regulations—

"the Minister" means Minister of Works:

"the Square" means so much of Trafalgar Square in the City of Westminster as is within the area enclosed by the public carriage ways on each side of Trafalgar Square.

(2) The Interpretation Act, 1889(d), shall apply to these Regulations as it applies to an Act of Parliament.

(3) These Regulations may be cited as the Trafalgar Square Regulations, 1952.

Prohibited Acts

2. Within the Square the following acts are prohibited:—

(1) wilfully interfering with the comfort or convenience of any person in the Square;

(2) dropping or leaving litter or refuse except in a receptacle provided for the purpose;

(3) polluting any water;

(4) walking on any shrubbery or flower bed;

(5) damaging, cutting or picking any tree or plant;

(6) damaging, defacing or climbing on any structure, seat or other Government property;

(7) bathing or paddling.

Acts for which Written Permission is Required

3. Within the Square the following acts are prohibited unless the written permission of the Minister has first been obtained:—

(1) selling or distributing anything or offering anything for sale or hire;

* In accordance with Section 2 of the Parks Regulation (Amendment) Act, 1926, and Section 6 of the Statutory Instruments Act, 1946, these Regulations, before being made, have lain in draft for forty days before each House of Parliament, during which time no Address has been presented to Her Majesty against the draft or any part thereof.

(a) 7 & 8 Vict. c. 60. (b) 35 & 36 Vict. c. 15. (c) 16 & 17 Geo. 5. c. 36.
(d) 52 & 53 Vict. c. 63.

(2) carrying on any trade or business;
(3) using artificial light or a tripod or stand for photography;
(4) organising, conducting or taking part in any assembly, parade or procession;
(5) making or giving a public speech or address;
(6) placing or exhibiting any display or representation;
(7) erecting or using any apparatus for the transmission, reception, reproduction or amplification of sound or speech by electrical or mechanical means unless the sound emitted is audible to the user only;
(8) causing any obstruction to free passage;
(9) singing or playing a musical instrument.

Commencement

4. These Regulations shall come into operation on the expiry of two months after the day on which they are made.

Dated this 8th day of April, 1952.

Given under the Official Seal of the Minister of Works.

David Eccles,
Minister of Works.

APPENDIX 5

Applicants for use of Trafalgar Square for Political Meetings

1867	
11.2	Reform Demonstration
2.3	Reform League
9.3	Reform League
11.3	Reform League
1869	
26.3	Ernest Jones Demonstration
20.9	Release of Political Prisoners
1870	
19.9	Sympathy with French Republic
18.12	Recognition of French Republic
1871	
28.1	Indignation at Bombardment of Paris
1972	
5.2	Freedom of Speech
17.3	Early Closing Movement
29.3	Land and Labour League
9.9	Price of Provisions
18.11	Hyde Park Prosecution
1878	
28.2	Tichborne Demonstration
1880	
5.6	Address to Mr. Parnell
1881	
2.8	Bradlaugh Meeting
3.8	Bradlaugh Meeting
1883	
15.2	Bradlaugh Demonstration
1885	
13.5	Increased Duties on Beer

APPENDIX 5—*continued*

1886		
8.2		Unemployed
1887		
13.11	*	Unemployed
1892		
12.11		Anarchists
1892		
Trafalgar Square Regulations (H. Shaw Lefevre)		
1904		
28.8		Social Democratic Federation
1905		
14.5		Social Democratic Federation
3.10	*	Woman's Suffrage
1906		
19.5		Woman's Suffrage
1908		
4.10		Social Democratic Federation
11.10		Woman's Suffrage
13.10		Woman's Suffrage
1911		
21.10		Volunteer Civil Force
1914		
2.8		Anti-War Demonstration
Regulations revised (Lord Emmott)		
1915		
7.11		Voluntary System of Military and Naval Service against Military Service Act
1916		
23.4	*	London Stop the War Committee Workers' Suffrage Federation Independent Labour Party No Conscription Fellowship
1919		
3.5		National Union of Police and Prison Officers

* Application refused.

APPENDIX 5—*continued*

1920	
October	National Unemployed Workers' Committee Movement
1921	
4.10	National Unemployed Workers' Committee Movement
1922	
occasional Sundays	National Unemployed Workers' Committee Movement
30.12	National Hunger March
1923	
occasional Sundays	National Unemployed Workers' Committee Movement
7.1	"Unemployed Sunday"
17.2	Farewell demonstration for Hunger Marchers
1924	
occasional Sundays	Farewell demonstration for Hunger Marchers
16.10	Unionist Central Office
1925	
occasional Sundays	National Unemployed Workers' Committee Movement
1926	
occasional Sundays	National Unemployed Workers' Committee Movement
1927	
12.2	Independent Labour Party
20.11	National Unemployed Workers' Committee Movement (The Miners' March)
27.11	National Unemployed Workers' Committee Movement
1928	
occasional Sundays	National Unemployed Workers' Committee Movement
1929	
occasional Sundays	National Unemployed Workers' Committee Movement
24.2	National Hunger March

APPENDIX 5—*continued*

1930	
occasional Sundays	National Unemployed Workers' Committee Movement
1931	
occasional Sundays	National Unemployed Workers' Committee Movement
1932	
occasional Sundays	National Unemployed Workers' Committee Movement
1933	
occasional Sundays	National Unemployed Workers' Committee Movement
1934	
24.6	Against Incitement of Disaffection Bill
1935	
occasional Sundays	National Unemployed Workers' Committee Movement
1.9	British Union of Fascists
1936	
occasional Sundays	National Unemployed Workers' Committee Movement
1937	
occasional Sundays	National Unemployed Workers' Committee Movement
1938	
17.7	National Conference on Spain
1939	
25.6	Friends of the Irish Republic
1940	
	Use of amplifiers permitted for music. Restricted to London County Council bands, official and semi-official bodies
1941	
	* London Labour Party

* Application refused.

APPENDIX 5—*continued*

1942	
29.3	Communist Party
24.5	Communist Party
27.7	Daily Worker League
18.10	Democratic Alliance
25.10	Communist Party
1943	
7.3	Amplifiers permitted to be used, placed on northern platform of plinth of Nelson's Column pointing downwards and in a northerly direction towards centre of square and incorporating an efficient volume control device.
7.5	Amplifiers permitted on Havelock and Napier statues, not more than four on each. Equipment to be attached to legs of figures. Speakers must point north to National Gallery. Efficient control of sound level.
3.4	Communist Party
14.3	Communist Party
25.3	Salute the Soldier Week
17.4	Indian Freedom Committee
2.5	London Labour Party
29.5	Indian Freedom Campaign
4.7	London District Communist Party
19.9	Communist Party
28.11	Communist Party
1944	
30.4	First of May Demonstration Committee
7.5	London Labour Party
4.6	Fire Brigades Union
14.6	London Co-op.
2.7	London Co-op.
1945	
27.1	India League
6.5	London Labour League
1.7	Amalgamated Union of Engineering Works
8.11	* National League of British Parents
24.11	Pan African Federation
2.12	National Dock Strikers Committee
9.12	Pan African Federation

* Application refused.

APPENDIX 5—*continued*

1946	
17.3	Amplifiers permitted on lions or Havelock or Napier statues
27.1	Indian league
10.2	Face the Facts (pro Fascist)
10.3	Emergency Committee for Democratic Spain
17.3	Face the Facts
23.3	All India Muslim League
14.4	All India Muslim League
26.5	British Soviet Society
2.6	All India Muslim League
23.6	Peace Pledge Union
14.7	Face the Facts
21.7	Communist Party
18.8	Liberal Candidates Association
25.8	London Trades Council
1.9 or 26.9	Communist Party
21.9	Liberal Candidates Association
22.9	Communist Party
1947	
27.4	Communist Party
1.6	Student Movement for World Government
7.6	British Housewives League
13.7	Peoples Common Law Parliament
13.7	Young Communist League
27.7	International Brigade Association
27.7	International Brigade Association
7.9	Communist Party
14.9	Nigerian Union of Great Britain and Ireland
27.9	Equal Pay Demonstration Committee (Equal Pay Campaign Committee) (Status of Women Committee)
from 23.6.1947	Greater portion of Square fenced off for work on Beatty and Jellicoe statues. Area south of bollards available for meetings
7.12	Communist Party
1948	
9.5	Commonwealth Party
23.5	London Trade Council
6.6	Commonwealth Party
20.6	Young Communist League

APPENDIX 5—*continued*

18.7		Port Workers' Strikes Committee
24.7		Old Age Pensions Association London Area Council
5.9		International Woman's Day
14.11		Peoples Press Printing Society Ltd.
14.11	*	British Soviet Society
1949		
30.1		Communist Party
3.4		Peace Pledge Union
10.4		Communist Party
17.4		Anti-Partition of Ireland League
19.6		Communist Party
10.7		Anti-Partition of Ireland League
14.8		African League
18.9		National League of Young Liberals
2.10		United Irishmen
9.10		Communist Party
16.10		Anti-Partition of Ireland League
23.10		Building Workers Wage Campaign Committee
13.11		Congress of Peoples Against Imperialism
1950		
19.2		Cities of London & Westminster Labour Parties
19.3		African League
26.3		Coloured Workers Association of Great Britain and Ireland
2.4		Young Communist League
9.4		Anti-Partition of Ireland League
30.4	*	African League
7.5		London Trades Council
14.5		Coloured Workers' Association
25.6		London Trades Council
9.7		London Trades Council
23.7		British Peace Committee
30.7		Coloured Workers' Association
6.8		Peace Pledge Union
20.8		British Empire Party
27.8		British Empire Party
3.9		London Peace Council
17.9		Anti-Partition of Ireland League

* Application refused.

APPENDIX 5—*continued*

24.9	The British and the Tottenham Nationalists
1.10	Britain China Friendship Association
8.10	Union Movement
5.11	Communist Party
24.12	London Youth Peace Council
31.12	Communist Party
1951	
25.2	Ex-Service Movement for Peace
25.2	British Peace Committee
25.2	Coloured Workers' Association
4.3	Joint Trade Union Defence Committee
18.3	Coloured Workers' Association
25.3	Anti-Partition of Ireland League
1.4	Caribbean Labour Congress
15.4	United Irishmen
22.4	Young Communist League
6.5	Cities of London & Westminster Labour Parties
6.5	London Trades Council
27.5	Coloured Workers' Association
3.6	United Irishmen
10.6	British Peace Committee
17.6	Sinn Fein
17.6	Peace Pledge Union
17.6	United Irishmen
1.7	Union Movement
7.7	Equal Pay Campaign Committee
8.7	Union Movement
15.7	Communist Party
22.7	Peace Pledge Union
28.7	Freedom Defence Committee
29.7	United Irishmen
5.8	British Empire Party
19.8	Coloured Workers' Association
8.9	London Liberal Party
16.9	Anti-Partition of Ireland League

1952

S.I. 1952 No. 776

Trafalgar Square Regulations 1952

Draft before Parliament:	19.2.1952
made	8.4.1952
Coming into operation	8.6.1952

APPENDIX 5—*continued*

27.1		African League
10.2		Sinn Fein
17.2		African League
24.2		Sinn Fein
2.3		London Trades Council
8.3		National Committee for Celebration of Woman's Day
13.4		Sinn Fein
27.4		British Empire Party
3.5		London Trades Council
4.5		London Labour Party
11.5		Connolly Association
18.5		Coloured Workers' Association
8.6		London League of Young Liberals
15.6		Coloured Workers' Association
22.6		Sinn Fein
20.7		Christian and Gentile Front against Communism
16.8		National Federation of Old Age Pensioners
17.8		London League of Young Liberals
31.8	*	Union Movement
7.9		London Peace Council
14.9		London League of Young Liberals
21.9		Anti-Partition of Ireland League
12.10		Cities of London & Westminster Labour Parties
23.11		African and Afro Descent Progressive Movement
1953		
18.1		Nationalised Road Transport Shop Stewards Association – London area
22.3		African league
5.4		Anti-Partition of Ireland League
19.4		Scottish National Party
26.4		Ex-Service Movement for Peace – London Area Committee
3.5		London Liberal Party
17.5		Coloured Workers' Welfare Association of Great Britain and Ireland
30.5		KEPT FREE OF MEETINGS
31.5		KEPT FREE OF MEETINGS
4.7		Peace Pledge Union
4.7	*	No Conscription Council
12.7		Communist Party

* Application refused.

APPENDIX 5—*continued*

2.8	Coloured Workers' Welfare Association of Great Britain and Ireland
23.8	Kenya Committee for Democratic Rights for Kenyan Africans
20.9	Anti-Partition of Ireland League
17.10	Peace Pledge Union
18.10	Confederation of Ship Builders and Engineering Union
1.11	African Association Congress
1954	
18.4	Anti-Partition of Ireland League
1.5	London Trades Council
9.5	Ex-Service Movement for Peace
23.5	No Conscription Council
13.6	Sinn Fein
27.6	African League
17.7	No Conscription Council
18.7	Coloured Workers' Welfare Association of Great Britain and Ireland
4.9	Peace Pledge Union
5.9	National Council of Tenants' & Residents' Associations
12.9	Anti-Partition of Ireland League
3.10	Communist Party
7.11	Confederation of Ship Builders and Engineering Union
21.11	Ex-Service Movement for Peace
1955	
20.3	British Peace Committee
10.4	Anti-Partition of Ireland League
11.4	Home Rule for Scotland and Wales
22.5	Communist Party
30.5	Home Rule for Scotland and Wales
4.6	Peace Pledge Union
12.6	Sinn Fein
10.7	Young Communist League
23.7	National Federation of Old Age Pensioners' Association
6.8	British Peace Committee
4.9	Cyprus Turkish Association
13.11	Movement for Colonial Freedom
20.11	Ex-Service Movement for Peace

APPENDIX 5—*continued*

1956	
15.1	Confederation of Shipbuilders and Engineering Union
25.3	Malcolm Muggeridge
31.3	Commonwealth
1.4	Anti-Partition of Ireland League
15.4	Helen Jarvis
6.5	London Joint May Day Committee
13.5	Movement for Colonial Freedom
2.6	Peace Pledge Union
3.6	African League
17.6	Sinn Fein
30.6	Peace Pledge Union
1.7	Union Movement
15.7	Communist Party
28.7	National Federation of Old Age Pensioners' Association
5.8	Coloured Workers' Welfare Association
2.9	Coloured Workers' Welfare Association
16.9	Movement for Colonial Freedom
4.11	London Labour Party (against Suez)
1957	
27.1	Confederation of Ship Building and Engineering Union
17.3	National Association of Tenants and Residents
21.4	Anti-Partition of Ireland League
28.4	Hungary & Egypt Pilgrimage and Relief Association
12.5	Movement of Colonial Freedom
18.5	Liberal Central Association
25.5	Young Conservatives
16.6	Movement for Colonial Freedom
30.6	Sinn Fein
7.7	Union Movement
14.7	Communist Party
21.7	Victory for Socialism
11.8	Transport and General Workers' Union (Covent Garden Dispute Committee)
15.9	National Association of Tenants' and Residents'
22.9	Movement for Colonial Freedom
29.9	Movement for Colonial Freedom
20.10	London Labour Party
24.11	Ex-Service Movement for Peace

APPENDIX 5—*continued*

1958	
23.2	Cyprus Turkish Association
23.3	Sinn Fein
4.4	Direct Action Committee Campaign for Nuclear Disarmament (after refusal because Good Friday – Emmott rules amended to make Good Friday a Bank Holiday)
6.4	Anti-Partition of Ireland League
13.4	London Labour Party
20.4	National Cypriot Committee
11.5	Victory for Socialism
17.5	Peace Pledge Union
18.5	Movement of Colonial Freedom
24.5	Young Conservatives
25.5	Young Communist League
1.6	Transport and General Workers' Union
8.6	London Trades Council and Old Age Pensioners' Joint Committee
7.6	Liberal Party
15.6	Sinn Fein
22.6	Campaign for Nuclear Disarmament
29.6	Communist Party
6.7	Union Movement
27.7	Movement of Colonial Freedom
21.9	Movement of Colonial Freedom
28.9	Communist Party
2.11	Ex-Service Movement for Peace
1959	
22.2	National Union of Kamarun Students
15.3	National Union of Students
29.3	Anti-Partition of Ireland League
30.3	Campaign for Nuclear Disarmament
18.4	Committee of African Organisations
3.5	Union Movement
10.5	Union Movement
23.5	Young Conservatives
24.5	National Labour Party
7.6	African Association Congress
14.6	Sinn Fein
21.6	Connolly Association
28.6	British Peace Committee

APPENDIX 5—*continued*

19.7	Movement of Colonial Freedom
26.7	Union Movement
30.8	Committee of African Organisations
6.9	National Labour Party
20.9	Campaign for Nuclear Disarmament
1.11	Ex-Service Movement for Peace
1960	
31.1	Communist Party
14.2	National Union of Railwaymen
27.3	Labour Party
3.4	Socialist Labour League
17.4	Anti-Partition of Ireland League
18.4	Campaign for Nuclear Disarmament
24.4	Connolly Association
8.5	Union Movement
15.5	British Peace Committee
22.5	Campaign for Nuclear Disarmament
29.5	British National Party
4.6	British National Party
12.6	Sinn Fein
26.6	Committee of African Organisations
3.7	Connolly Association
10.7	Labour Party
4.9	Union Movement
11.9	British National Party
18.9	Movement for Colonial Freedom
24.9	Campaign for Nuclear Disarmament
25.9	Committee of African Organisations
9.10	Sinn Fein
6.11	Ex-Service Movement for Peace
14.11	London Peace Campaign
27.11	Anti-Apartheid Movement
4.12	Movement for Colonial Freedom
1961	
1.1	Anti-Apartheid Movement
15.1	Movement for Colonial Freedom
18.2	Committee of 100
19.2	Movement for Colonial Freedom
26.2	Christian Socialists
12.3	African Associations Congress

APPENDIX 5—*continued*

19.3		Anti-Apartheid Movement
2.4		Anti-Partition of Ireland League
3.4		Campaign for Nuclear Disarmament
23.4		Sinn Fein
24.4		Committee of 100
30.4		British National Party
14.5		Union Movement
27.5		Young Conservatives
28.5		Movement for Colonial Freedom
4.6		Direct Action Committee against Nuclear War
10.6		Anti-Apartheid Movement
18.6		Sinn Fein
25.6		Connolly Association
1.7		Peace Pledge Union
2.7		Communist Party
8.7		Movement for Colonial Freedom
16.7		British National Party
30.7		Union Movement
6.8		Committee of 100
13.8		Kenya Students' Association
10.9		Campaign for Nuclear Disarmament
17.9	*	Committee of 100
23.9		Committee of 100
23.9		Union Movement
24.9		British National Party
8.10		Union Movement
21.10		Young Liberals
22.10		Sinn Fein
29.10		Committee of 100
5.11		Ex-Service Movement for Peace
11.11		Society of Friends' Peace Committee
12.11		Christian Action
16.12		Stepney Tenants' Association
16.12		National Association of Tenants and Residents
1962		
7.1		Listeners for Peace
14.1		Movement for Colonial Freedom
11.2		African Association Congress
25.2		Committee of 100
11.3		Campaign for Nuclear Disarmanent

* Application refused.

APPENDIX 5—*continued*

22.4		Anti-Partition of Ireland League
23.4		Keep Britain Great Committee
29.4		British National Party
6.5		European Union of Fascists (withdrawn)
13.5		Union Movement
19.5		Algeria Committee
3.6		Anti-Apartheid Movement
10.6		Young Communist League
17.6		Connolly Association
1.7		National Socialist Movement
7.7		London Committee of 100
15.7		Sinn Fein
21.7		London Trades Union Old Age Pensioners' Joint Committee
22.7		Union Movement
30.7		Daily Peace Picket and Parliamentary Lobby
19.8		National Socialist Movement (refused on grounds that proposal might lead to grave inconvenience to public)
1.9		Yellow Star Organisation
2.9		British National Party
9.9		Forward Britain Movement
16.9		Common Market – Keep Britain out Campaign
14.10		Irish Political Prisoners' Release Committee
14.10		Committee of Six for Social Credit
27.10	*	London Committee of 100
28.10		Common Market
28.10		Union of Democratic Control
4.11		National Union of Railwaymen
17.11		Campaign for Nuclear Disarmament
1963		
6.1		Christopher Payne
17.3		Anti-Apartheid Movement
23.3		Common Market
14.4		Anti-Partition of Ireland League
15.4		Greater Britain Movement
15.4		Campaign for Nuclear Disarmament
27.4		Labour Party
28.4		Irish Political Prisoners' Release Committee
12.5	*	Union Movement

* Application refused.

APPENDIX 5—*continued*

19.5	Pakistan League
19.5	* National Socialist Movement
9.6	* British National Party
16.6	Connolly Association
31.6	Sinn Fein
6.7	* "Save Greece Now"
21.7	Movement for Colonial Freedom
28.7	Campaign for Nuclear Disarmament
15.9	Socialist Party of Great Britain
22.9	Friends of Spain
29.9	Communist Party
27.10	* National Socialist Movement
3.11	Anti-Apartheid Movement
17.11	Society for Improved Conditions in British Gaols
24.11	Post Office Workers
16.12 to 24.12	* London Committee of 100
1964	
29.3	United Ireland Association
30.3	Union Movement
30.3	Campaign for Nuclear Disarmament
5.4	Liberal Party
19.4	Clann na h'Eireann
3.5	Union Movement
3.5	Socialist Party of Great Britain
7.6	Anti-Apartheid Movement
14.6	Movement for Colonial Freedom
14.6	Anti-Apartheid Movement
21.6	Connolly Association
28.6	Sinn Fein
12.7	Cyprus Turkish Association
19.7	Cyprus Turkish Association
19.7	* National Socialist Movement
5.9	Christie-Carballo Defence Committee
13.9	Socialist Party of Great Britain
19.9	* Greater Britain Movement
27.9	Keep Left
27.9	British-United States Elections Committee
5.10	British-United States Elections Committee
10.10	Anarchist Federation of Britain
11.10	National Socialist Movement

* Application refused.

APPENDIX 5—*continued*

24.10	Americans Abroad for Senator Goldwater Commitee
25.10	Alexander Defence Committee
31.10	* Anti-Apartheid Movement
8.11	Friends of South Africa
1965	
29.2	Movement for Colonial Freedom
21.3	Anti-Apartheid Movement
4.4	British Peace Committee
4.4	Christian Action
18.4	Clann na h'Eireann
19.4	Campaign for Nuclear Disarmament
2.5	* Socialist Party of Great Britain
29.5	Campaign for Nuclear Disarmament
13.6	Challenge (Young Communist League)
20.6	* Clann na h'Eireann
20.6	Connolly Association
27.6	Anti-Apartheid Movement
4.7	Campaign for Nuclear Disarmament
11.7	Clann na h'Eireann
25.7	British Council for Peace in Vietnam
1.8	Cyprus Turkish Association
11.9	Kashmiris in London
25.9	Hindustani Nationalist Party
3.10	British National Party
16.10	Committee of 100
13.11	Monday Club
1966	
5.2	British Council for Peace in Vietnam
6.2	* National Youth Movement
10.4	United Ireland Association
10.4	* Clann na h'Eireann
11.4	Campaign for Nuclear Disarmament
1.5	Independent Labour Party
8.5	Ex-Servicemen's Movement for Peace
14.5	Campaign for Nuclear Disarmament
5.6	National Union of Seamen
12.6	Clann na h'Eireann
19.6	Connolly Association
26.6	Anti-Apartheid Movement

* Application refused.

APPENDIX 5—*continued*

3.7		Communist Party
10.7	*	National Socialist Movement
11.9		Independent Labour Party
18.9		United Anti-Communist League
28.9	*	Vietnam Solidarity Campaign
2.10		National Council for Abolition of Factory Farming
16.10		Loyal Orange Institution of England
16.10	*	Campaign for Nuclear Disarmament
12.11		Movement for Colonial Freedom
13.11		Young Liberals
1967		
8.1		Independent Labour Party
15.1		Duncan Sandys M.P.
12.2		Ukrainian National Committee
18.2		Young Conservatives
4.3		Amnesty International
12.3		Liaison Committee for Defence of Trade Unions
19.3		Young Liberals
24.3		Radical Students' Alliance
27.3		Campaign for Nuclear Disarmament
9.4		Racial Adjustment Action Society
22.4		The Week
23.4		Zimbabwe African National Union
30.4		Committee of 100
1.5		The Democratic Party
13.5		London Young Conservatives Campaign for Commercial Radio
21.5		Youth for Peace in Vietnam
10.6		Old Calabar People's Connection of Great Britain and Ireland
11.6		British Peace Committee
18.6		Connolly Association
24.6		British Council for Peace in Vietnam
1.7		Radical Students
2.7		British Committee for Peace in Vietnam
9.7		League for Democracy in Greece
16.7		Independent Labour Party
30.7		Disablement Income Group
19.8		British Committee for Peace in Vietnam
3.9		Socialist Party of Great Britain

* Application refused.

APPENDIX 5—*continued*

17.9	National Council for Abolition of Factory Farming
8.10	United Anti-Communist League
15.10	Young Communist League
21.10	Committee of 100
22.10	Vietnam Solidarity Campaign
5.11	Nigerian Union of Great Britain and Ireland
11.11	* Rhodesian Rally Organising Committee
12.11	* Movement for Colonial Freedom
12.11	Irish National Union
1968	
3.3	National Union of Students
10.3	Youth for Peace in Vietnam
17.3	Vietnam Solidarity Campaign
31.3	United Kingdom Committee for Human Rights Year 1968
7.4	Duncan Sandys M.P.
14.4	United Anti-Communist League
15.4	Campaign for Nuclear Disarmament
21.4	North London Group for the Restoration of Democracy in Greece
5.5	London Joint May Day Committee
12.5	Connolly Association
1.6	Common Front
9.6	Jordan Refugee Committee
23.6	Anti-Apartheid Movement
30.6	Clann na h'Eireann
7.7	Save Biafra Committee
20.7	Radical Students Alliance
21.7	Young Communist League
4.8	National Front (withdrawn)
11.8	Save Biafra Committee
24.8	Black Panther Movement
1.9	Community Action Groups
15.9	National Campaign for the Homeless
22.9	Joint Greater London Council Estates Tenants' Committee
229.9	* Campaign for Democracy in Ulster
29.9	Save Biafra Committee
13.10	* Young Communist League
20.10	Movement for Colonial Freedom

* Application refused.

APPENDIX 5—*continued*

21.10	Confederation of Shipbuilders and Engineering Union
26.10	Vietnam Solidarity Campaign
27.10	October 27 Committee for Solidarity with Vietnam
10.11	British Committee for Peace in Vietnam
16.11	National Union of Agriculture and Allied Workers
1969	
12.1	Movement for Racial Unity
1.2	Friends of China
2.2	Czech Students
9.3	British Vietnam Solidarity Front
16.3	The March Vietnam Mobilization Committee
23.3	Movement for Colonial Freedom
30.3	Ad Hoc Committee for Solidarity with Vietnam
6.4	Clann na h'Eireann
7.4	Campaign for Nuclear Disarmament
20.4	Connolly Association
4.5	Duncan Sandys M.P.
11.5	Arab Students' Union and Solidarity with Palestinian People
18.5	National Action Campaign for Women's Equal Rights
26.5	Ruskin College Kitson Committee
1.6	Ulster Solidarity Campaign
8.6	National Association of Tenants and Residents
15.6	Irish Republican Party
22.6	Ulster Civil Rights Supporters
29.6	Ulster Civil Rights Supporters
13.7	Connolly Association
19.7	Campaign for Nuclear Disarmament
27.7	Friends of South Vietnam
7.9	Northern Ireland Civil Rights Association
5.10	Young Communist League
26.10	Save Biafra
11.11	Rhodesian Rally Organising Committee
11.11	Movement for Colonial Freedom
12.11	Irish National Union
1970	
14.3	Policemen's Wives' Committee
15.3	The Irish National Liberation Solidarity Front
21.3	Anti-Apartheid Movement

APPENDIX 5—*continued*

28.3	Campaign for Nuclear Disarmament
29.3	Clann na h'Eireann
30.3	British Campaign for Peace in Vietnam
19.4	Vietnam Solidarity Campaign
	Ad Hoc Committee
3.5	Monday Club
9.5	Committee for Peace in Vietnam
10.5	Northern Ireland Civil Rights Association
17.5	Palestine Solidarity Campaign
23.5	Iranic Students' Society
25.5	Ruskin College Kitson Committee
30.5	The Red Mole
7.6	Clann na h'Eireann
12.7	Connolly Association
25.7	Britain-Cuba Association
26.7	Northern Ireland Civil Rights Association
22.8	Civil Rights Action Committee
6.9	Labour Party
13.9	The Socialist Party
20.9	London Trade Unions and Old Age Pensioners
4.10	Irish National Liberation
25.10	Anti-Apartheid Movement
22.11	Northern Ireland Civil Rights Association
28.11	Campaign for Nuclear Disarmament
1971	
17.1	Cambridge Students' Union
21.2	Trades Union Congress
21.2	Front for the National Liberation of Great Britain
29.2	Union Committee for Soviet Jewry
6.3	Women's Liberation (National Co-ordination Committee)
14.3	Women Against the Common Market
4.4	Bangla Desh Action Committee
11.4	Sinn Fein
12.4	Campaign for Nuclear Disarmament
18.4	Bangla Desh Action Committee
24.4	Vietnam Solidarity Campaign
25.4	Young Liberals
15.5	Free Palestine
23.5	Universities Committee on Soviet Jewry

APPENDIX 5—*continued*

30.5		Clann na h'Eireann
6.6		Young Conservatives
13.6		Communist Party
20.6		Connolly Association
3.7		Trade Unions against the Common Market
11.7		Northern Ireland Civil Rights Association
17.7		The Zimbabwe National Union
18.7		International Society for World Government
1.8		Action Bangla Desh
15.8		Pakistan Solidarity Front
30.8		Friends of Soledad
5.9		Communist Party
12.9		London Co-op. Political Committee
12.9		British Movement
26.9		Sinn Fein
16.10		National Union of Agricultural and Allied Workers
17.10		Freedom Press
24.10		National Anti-Common Market Demonstration Committee
7.11		Labour Party
1972		
23.1		National Union of Students
6.2		National Union of Mine Workers
13.2		Anti-Apartheid Movement
26.3	*	Anti-Internment League
31.3		Campaign for Nuclear Disarmament
2.4	*	Sinn Fein
2.4	*	Clann na h'Eireann
29.4		British Constitution Defence Committee
30.4		Labour Party
14.5		General Union of Arab Students
4.6		British Committee for Peace in Vietnam
11.6		Angela Davis Defence Committee
18.6	*	Connolly Association
1.7		Gay Liberation Front
9.7	*	Northern Ireland Civil Rights Association
9.7		Association of London Housing Estates
15.7		World Development Movement
23.7	*	Union Movement
19.8		Bangla Desh Concert

* Application refused.

APPENDIX 5—*continued*

17.9	Association of all London Tenants' Associations
28.10	Labour Party
12.11	* Anti-Internment League
19.11	British Workers against Immigration
1973	
20.1	British Committee for Peace in Vietnam
10.3	Women's Liberation Workshop
17.3	Indo-China Solidarity Conference
1.4	Covent Garden Community Association
22.4	* Clann na h'Eireann
28.4	Indo-China Solidarity Committee
5.5	Indo-China Solidarity Committee
19.5	* Grand Orange Lodge of England
15.7	Canvey Island Protest
15.7	* Irish Civil Rights Association
29.7	Campaign for Nuclear Disarmament
12.8	Pakistan Solidarity Front
1.9	Homeless Action Campaign
23.9	Socialist Party of Great Britain
13.10	Pakistan Solidarity Front
14.10	The Zionist Federation
4.11	Indo-China Solidarity Committee
4.11	Chile Solidarity Campaign
25.11	National Union of Railwaymen
1974	
27.1	* Clann na h'Eireann
27.1	Young Socialists
3.2	Trades Union Congress
24.2	Labour Party
31.3	Covent Garden Community Association
7.4	Simon Community
15.4	Campaign for Nuclear Disarmament
28.4	Society for the Protection of Unborn Children
5.5	Zimbabwe African National Union
12.5	National Union of Students
16.6	Committee for Freedom in Mozambique, Angola and Guinne
13.7	* Troops Out Movement
11.8	* Clann na h'Eireann

* Application refused.

APPENDIX 5—*continued*

11.8		Pakistan Solidarity Front
18.8		Cyprus Turkish Association
25.8		National Co-ordinating Committee of Cypriots in Britain
8.9		Chile Solidarity Committee
22.9		Socialist Party of Great Britain
6.10		Pakistan Solidarity Front
27.10	*	British Peace Committee and Troops Out Movement
2.11		Campaign for Homosexual Equality

* Application refused.

Source: Department of the Environment

SELECT BIBLIOGRAPHY

A. ARCHIVES: in the Public Record Office

PRO ADMIRALTY 1/727
PRO CREST 26/53
PRO CREST 26/54
PRO CREST 26/75
PRO CREST 26/152
PRO CREST 26/178
PRO CREST 26/1816
PRO CREST 26/187
PRO CREST 26/188
PRO CREST 40/83
PRO HO 40/59
PRO HO 41/26
PRO LRRO 37/42
PRO L.R. 1/255 et seq.
PRO MEPOL. 2/64
PRO MEPOL. 2/174
PRO MEPOL. 2/181
PRO MEPOL. 2/182
PRO WO. 30/81
PRO WORKS 2/2
PRO WORKS 6/119
PRO WORKS 20/2–1
PRO WORKS 20/3–1
PRO WORKS 20/3–2
PRO WORKS 20/3–3
PRO WORKS 20/3–4
PRO WORKS 20/3/5
PRO WORKS 20/3/6
PRO WORKS 20/27
PRO WORKS 20/32
PRO WORKS 20/34
PRO WORKS 20/50
PRO WORKS 20/111
PRO WORKS 20/180
PRO WORKS 20/229
PRO WORKS 20/5/1

B. PARLIAMENTARY PAPERS

PP. 1812 (357), XII, 347: *First Report to His Majesty's Commissioners for Woods, Forests and Land Revenues*

PP. 1817 (79), III, 83: *Report from the Committee on the Petition of the Tradesmen and Inhabitants of Norris Street and Market Terrace . . .*

PP. 1826 (368), XIV, 1: *Fifth Report to His Majesty's Commissioners of Woods, Forests and Land Revenues*

PP. 1829 (343), III, 37: *Report from the Select Committee on Crown Leases*

PP. 1840 (381), XXIX, 753: *Arrangements entered into between the Commissioners of Woods Forests and Committee for erecting the Nelson Monument; also, a Statement of the Plan approved and sanctioned by the Commissioners for laying out the vacant space in front of the National Gallery*

PP. 1840 (434–I), XXX, 885: *Estimate of the Amount required to complete the laying out of the Area of Trafalgar Square*

PP. 1840 (548), XII, 387: *Report from Select Committee on Trafalgar Square, together with Minutes of Evidence taken before them and Appendix. 27.7.1840*

PP. 1843 (91–I), XXXI, 393: *Estimate of the Amount required on account of Trafalgar Square*

PP. 1844 (484), XXXIII, 6: *Estimate of the Sum required towards defraying the Expense of completing the Monument erected in Trafalgar Square to the Memory of Lord Nelson*

PP. 1856, XXIII, I: *Report on the Alleged Disturbances of the Public Peace in Hyde Park on Sunday 1st July 1855*

PP. 1861, L 779: *Correspondence with First Commissioner of Works as to placing Statue in Trafalgar Square to Memory of Sir Henry Havelock*

PP. 1886, XXXIV, 381 et seq., PP. 1886 LIII (Cd 4665): *Report to Enquiry into the Origin and Character of the Disturbances . . . 8th day Feb.*

PP. 1908 (Cd. 3771), LI, 765: *Report from Commissioner Metropolitan Police for the Year 1906*

C. ACTS AND BILLS

1 Geo. I, c. 5

5 Geo. IV, c. 100

6 Geo. IV, c. 38

7 Geo. IV, c. 77

7 Geo. IV, c. 78

7 & 8 Vic., c. 60

Statutory Instrument no. 775, 1952

Statutory Instrument no. 776, 1952

A Bill for the Regulation of Meetings in Trafalgar Square (1888)
A Bill to Declare the Right of Public Meeting in Open Spaces (1888)

D. NEWSPAPERS AND PERIODICALS

Arena
Art Union
The Builder
Civil Engineer and Architects Journal
Civil Liberties
Commonweal
Contemporary Review
Cork Historical and Architectural Journal
The *Daily Worker*
The *Daily Express*
Dublin Historical Record
Edinburgh Review
Illustrated London News
The Labour Leader
London Gazette
The *Morning Chronicle*
The *Observer*
Pall Mall Gazette
Punch
The Times
Transactions of the Royal Historical Society

E. PRINTED BOOKS, REPORTS, PAMPHLETS, etc.

Published in London, unless otherwise stated.

ANONYMOUS, *To Horatio Viscount and Baron Nelson* (1810)
—— *Who and What is Havelock?* (1857)
ARNOT, R. PAGE, *William Morris – A Vindication* (1934)
ASPINALL, A. I., *The Correspondence of Charles Arbuthnot* (1941)
AYLEN, W. H., *The Soldier and the Saint: or Two Heroes in One* (1858)
BACON, REGINALD, *The Life of John Rushworth Earl Jellicoe* (1936)
BAMFORD, SAMUEL, *Life of a Radical* (1859)
BENEWICK, ROBERT, *The Fascist Movement in Britain* (1972)
BENSON, A. C. and ESHER, VISCOUNT, *The Letters of Queen Victoria 1837–61* (1908)
BOETIUS, AXEL and PERKINS, J. P. W., *Etruscan and Roman Architecture* (Harmondsworth, 1970)
BOWES, STUART, *The Police and Civil Liberties* (1966)
BRIGGS, ASA (ed.), *Chartist Studies* (1959)
BUCHAN, S., *The Water Supply of the County of London* (1938)

BUCKLE, G. E., *Letters of Queen Victoria 1886–1890* (1930)

BURGESS, JOHN, *John Burns: The Rise and Progress of a Right Honourable* (Glasgow, 1911)

BURGOYNE, SIR JOHN, *Military Opinions* (1859)

BUTLER, DAVID and FREEMAN, J., *British Political Facts* (1963)

(CAMB.), *The Cambridge History of India* (1929)

(CHAMB.) *Chambers's Encyclopaedia* (1966)

CHURCHILL, WINSTON, *Lord Randolph Churchill* (1906)

COLE, G. D. H., *British Working Class Politics, 1832–1914* (1946)

COLE, G. D. H. and POSTGATE, RAYMOND, *The Common People, 1746–1946* (1971)

COLEMAN, TERRY, *The Railway Navvies* (1965)

COLLINS, R. O., 'Egypt and the Sudan', *The Historiography of the British Empire & Commonwealth* (Durham N.C., 1966)

COLVIN, H. M., *Biographical Dictionary of English Architects, 1660–1840* (1954)

COLVIN, H. M. and CROOKE, M., *The History of the Kings Works*, vol. VI (1973)

COMMUNIST PARTY OF GREAT BRITAIN, *Day of Struggle for Peace and Socialism – A souvenir of London May Day 1949* (1949)

CREW, ALBERT, *The Law Relating to Public Meetings and Processions* (1937)

CUNNINGHAM, PETER, *A Handbook for London* (1849)

(DICT.) *Dictionary of National Biography*

DONNELLY, IGNATIUS, *Caesar's Column* (Chicago, 1890)

EDWARDS, STEWART, *The Paris Commune, 1871* (Newton Abbot, 1972)

ENGELS, F. and LAFARGUE, P. & L., *Correspondence*, Vol. 1 (Moscow, 1959)

FARRADAY, PETER, *Victorian Architecture* (1963)

(GEOL.) *Memoirs of Geological Survey* (1889)

GUNNIS, RUPERT, *Dictionary of British Sculptors* (1953)

HAKE, A. C., *Events in the Taiping Rebellion* (1891)

HALEVY, E., *Victorian Years, 1841–1895* (1951)

HAMMOND, J. L. and B., *The Bleak Age* (1934)

HANNINGTON, WAL, *The Insurgents of London* (1923)

—— *The March of the Miners* (1927)

—— *Unemployed Struggles, 1919–1936* (1936)

HIBBERT, CHRISTOPHER, *George IV, Prince of Wales, 1762–1811* (Newton Abbot, 1973)

HILTON, W. S., *Foes to Tyranny* (1963)

HOLMAN, DENNIS (ed.), *Earlier Nineteenth Century Portraits and Documents* (1965)

HOLMES, T. R. E., *Four Famous Soldiers* (1889)

HORRABIN, J. F., *A Short History of the British Empire* (1946)

HU SHÊNG, *Imperialism and Chinese Politics* (Peking 1955)

HUTCHINS, FRANCIS G., *The Illusion of Permanence* (Princeton, 1967)

JACKSON, T. A., *Trials of British Freedom* (1945)

JACOB, JOHN, *Remarks on the Native Troopers of the Indian Army* (Bombay, 1854)

JAMES, WILLIAM, *Naval History of Great Britain* (1902)

JELLINEK, FRANK, *The Paris Commune of 1871* (1937)

JENKINS, ROY, *Asquith* (1964)

JENNINGS, D. L. J. (ed.), *The Croker Papers* (1944)

JONES, T. E., *A Descriptive Account of the Literary Works of John Britton F.S.A., being the Second Part of his Auto-Biography* (1849)

KEIRNAN, V. G., *Marxism and Imperialism* (1974)

KIDD, RONALD, *British Liberty in Danger* (1940)

LAMPE, DAVID, *The Last Ditch* (1968)

(LOND.) *London County Council Statistics*

LONGMATE, NORMAN, *If Britain Had Fallen* (1972)

LUDLOW, LIEUTENANT-GENERAL, *Memoirs* (1690)

MACAULAY, T. B., *History of England* (1849)

MACMICHAEL, J. H., *The Story of Charing Cross* (1906)

MAJUMDAR, R. C., *An Advanced History of India* (1960)

MARX, KARL, *On China* (1968)

MASEFIELD, JOHN, *Sea Life in Nelson's Time* (1971)

MAY, H. A. R., *Memoirs of the Artists Rifles* (1929)

M. M., *Description of a Drawn Model (no. 113) proposed for the Monument . . .* (1839)

MORRIS, WILLIAM, *Alfred Linnell, Killed in Trafalgar Square, November 20th 1887* (1887)

—— *News from Nowhere* (1968)

MORTON, A. L., *A People's History of England* (1968)

—— *The English Utopia* (1969)

NAISH, GEORGE P. B., *Nelson and Bronte (1958)*

NAPIER, CHARLES J., *Defects, Civil and Military of the Indian Government* (1853)

—— *Remarks on Military Law and the Punishment of Flogging* (1837)

NAPIER, PRISCILLA, *Revolution and the Napier Brothers, 1820–1840* (1973)

NATIONAL COUNCIL FOR CIVIL LIBERTIES, *Annual Report* (1958–59)

—— *Public Order and the Police – A Report on the Events in Trafalgar Square, Sunday 17th to Monday 18th September 1961* (1961)

NELSON MEMORIAL COMMITTEE, *Statement of Subscriptions to the Memorial of the Achievements of the late Admiral Lord Viscount Nelson* (1841)

NO CONSCRIPTION FELLOWSHIP, *Why we Object* (1915)

OMAN, CAROLA, *Nelson* (1947)

PANKHURST, E. SYLVIA, *The Suffragette – The History of the Woman's Militant Suffrage Movement, 1905–10* (New York, 1911)

PEVSNER, N., *Some Architectural Writers in the Nineteenth Century* (1972)

PHYSICK, JOHN. *Design for English Sculpture 1680–1860* (1969)

—— *The Wellington Monument* (1970)

POLLOCK, W. C., *Way to Glory* (1957)
PURCELL, V., *The Boxer Rebellion* (Cambridge, 1963)
RAWSON, GEOFFREY, *Beatty* (1936)
REED, D., *Peterloo* (Manchester 1958)
ROTHSTEIN, TH., *From Chartism to Labourism* (1929)
RUSSELL, W. H., *My Indian Mutiny Diary* (1957)
SMITH, V. A. (ed.), *The Oxford History of India* (1970)
SNOWDEN, PHILIP, *et al., The No Conscription Fellowship – A Record of its Activities* (1916)
STEADMAN-JONES, GARETH, *Outcast London* (Oxford, 1971)
SUMMERSON, JOHN, *John Nash – Architect to George IV* (1949)
SWAFFER, HANNEN, *What Would Nelson Do?* (1946)
SYME, RONALD, *The Roman Revolution* (Oxford, 1966)
TAYLOR, A. J. P., *English History 1914–1945* (Oxford, 1966)
TAYLOR, GEORGE L. *Autobiography* (1870)
THOMPSON, E. J., *The Other Side of the Medal* (1925)
THOMPSON, E. P., *William Morris, Romantic to Revolutionary* (1955)
—— *The Making of the English Working Class* (1963)
THOMPSON, PAUL, *Specialists, Liberals and Labour* (1967)
THORNTON, A. P., *The Imperial Idea and Its Enemies – A Study in British Power* (1959)
TREVELYAN, G. M., *John Bright* (1925)
WATKINS, WILLIAM, *The Life of General Sir Charles Warren* (Oxford, 1941)
WILLIAMS, D. G. T., *Keeping the Peace* (1967)
WARNER, OLIVER M. H., *Cunningham of Hyndhope* (1967)
WHEATLEY, R. A. A., *Operation Sea Lion* (1958)
WHINNEY, MARGARET, *Sculpture in Britain, 1530–1830* (1964)
WILLIAMS, DAVID, *The Rebecca Riots: a Study in Rural Discontent* (Cardiff, 1955)
WOOD, WILLIAM, *An Essay on National and Sepulchral Monuments* (1808)
WORKERS SUFFRAGE FEDERATION, *The Execution of an East London Boy* (1916)
WRIOSTHESLEY'S *Chronicle* (1575–7)
WYATT, M. C., *Prospectus of a Model to the Memory of Lord Nelson* (1808)

INDEX

Aberdeen, Earl of, 62
Aboukir, Battle of, 49
  naval pillar, 49
Afghanistan, 115
Agitation, 160
Albertin Academy, Turin, 108
A letter on the Defence of England by Corp of Volunteers and Militia, 116
Alexander, Grand Duke of Russia, 93
Allen, George, 95–6
Allman, James, 176
An Essay on National and Sepulchral Monuments, 52
Anti-Communism, 224
Anti-Internment League, 231
Anti-Jacobinism, 54, 57
Antoninus, Column of, 83
Arbuthnot, Charles, 35, 36–7, 39, 40, 151
Arbuthnot, Harriet, 57
Armistice Day celebrations, 212
Art Journal, 107
Art patronage, 48
Art Union, 63, 80, 108
Artists Rifles, 207
Asquith, H. H., 197–8
Athenaeum, 125
Atholl, Duchess of, 218
Atlantic Fleet, 127
Atlantic Pact, 224
Augustus, Forum of, 16
Auckland, Lord, 115
Aveling, Edward, 187

Bailey, E. H., sculptor, 62, 65, 89–90, 98
Bank of England, 93
Barracks and disturbance, 158–9
Barrackpore rising, 118–19
Barry, Alfred, 45
Barry, E. M., 23
Barry, Charles, architect,
  appointed to design Trafalgar Square, 45
  attitude to National Gallery, 46, 78
  attitude to Nelson's Column, 45, 74
  attitude to strikers, 96
  designs for Trafalgar Square, 70, 73, 74, 75, 76, 87–8, 111
  evidence to Select Committee, 75–9
  relations with William Wilkins, 76
  other references, 87, 89, 95, 100
Bas reliefs, Nelson's Column, 100–7
Bax, E. B., 165
Beatty, David, Admiral, 126–31
Bedford, Duke of, 40
Behnes, W., sculptor, 122
Bell Street, 161
Bellamy, Thomas, architect, 56
Bengal mutinies, 119
Beresford, Lord, 56
Berhampore rising, 118
Besant, Annie, 187
Bethnal Green, 152
Bethlehem Hospital, 40, 149
Betjeman, John, 44
Billeting of soldiers, 113–14
Blacklegs, 96
Blanketeers, 139
Bloody Sunday, 179–89
Bloomsbury, poor in relation to, 31
Blore, Edward, architect, 74, 80–1, 82
Boccius and Co., 89
Boer War, 204
Bonar Law, Andrew, 213, 214
Bottomley, Horatio, 213
Boxer Rebellion, 127
Bradlaugh, Charles, 193
Bramah, Presage and Ball, 89, 97
Bridges, use by Army, 159
Bridgetown, Barbados, 82
Bright, John, 157
British Army, 16, 119–20, 155

British Empire Service League, 128
British League of Ex-Service Men and Women, 222
British Legion, 128
British Navy, 17, 19
British Seamen, portrayed in sculpture, 55
British Union of Fascists, 218, 222
British Workers Party of National Unity, 222
Brittania, portrayed in sculpture, 50, 55
Brotherhood of Destruction, 18
Brussels Pact, 224
Buccleuch, Duke of, 58, 59, 89
Buckingham Palace, 35, 111
Bude Light Co., 89
Builder (The), 88
Building contractors and Unions, 95
Burgess, John, 189–90
Burgoyne, Major-General Sir John F., 151–2, 159
Burke, Edmund, 39
Burleigh Street, 40
Burns, John, 162, 165, 188, 196, 200
Burton, Decimus, architect, 74, 80, 81, 82, 86–7

Cable Street, 219
Cadogan, Earl of, 62
Caesar's Column, 18–19
Campaign for Nuclear Disarmament, 230, 231
Campbell, J., sculptor, 100
Canning, George, 16
Carew, J. E., sculptor, 100, 101, 104
Caribbean, British wars with French, 49
Carlton House, 44
Carlton Mews, 152
Cavenagh, Mr., Manager Oxford Music Hall, 171
Cawnpore, 120
Champion, H. H., 165
Channon, Paul, 231
Chantrey, Sir Francis, sculptor, 57, 74, 80–4, 111–12
Charing Cross,
  Great Mews at, 29
  Green Mews at, 29
  hangings, etc., at, 24, 25
  House of Commons debate Improvements, 36–9
  Improvements at, 31, 33, 36, 74
  leases, cost of, 40
  leaseholders, 40
  site for Antiquarian Society, 31
  site for Royal Academy, 31
  site for Royal Society, 31
  temporary barracks at, 29
  other references, 15, 23, 24, 26, 31, 37, 143
Charing Cross Fields, 26
Charing Cross Hospital, 192
Charing Cross Road, 31, 213
Charles I, statue of, 26
Chartism, 112, 137, 146, 148, 151, 153
Chaucer, Geoffrey, 26
Chauvinism, 52, 93
China, 118, 126–7
Christian Duty, 121–2
Christianity, in China, 127; in India, 121
Churchill, Winston, 127, 129, 159
City of London, 24, 55, 61
Clarke, George and Sons, 97
Clarke, Tierney, engineer, 65
Clerkenwell Green, 152, 187
Cochrane, C., 135
Cockburn, Admiral Sir George, 58, 62, 64, 98
Cockerell, C. R., architect, 16, 43, 74, 80, 82, 83
Cockspur Street, 46, 73
Cohen, N. L., 167
Cole, G. D. H., 160
Committee of Artists, 63
Committee for National Monuments, 52
Committee of 100, 231
Conscription, 209
Crimean Monument, London, 125
Crimean War, 118
Croker, J. W., 65
Cross's Menagerie, 29
Crown lands, exchange of, 39
Crown Stables, 29
Cubitt, Thomas, builder, 100
Cumberland Gate, 112

Cumberland Market, 34
Cunningham, Andrew, Admiral, 21, 131

Daily Advertiser, 25
Daily Express, 213
Daily Mail, 208
Dalhousie, Lord, 117–18
Davies, Colonel, 39
Death, portrayed in sculpture, 55
Defects, Civil and Military in the Indian Government, 116–17
Defence of the Realm Act, 1914 (D.O.R.A.), 208, 210, 219
Defence, Ministry of, 126
Defoe, Daniel, 26
Delhi, 119
Demonstrations, in Trafalgar Square,
  Anarchist, 200
  Anti-war, 209–10
  Black Monday, 162–4
  Bloody Sunday, 179–89
  Chartist, 135–7
  Committee of 100, 231
  Fascist, 218
  Indian questions, 221
  Irish questions, 231–2
  Lord Mayor's Day 1886, 170
  May Day 1949, 225; 1950, 226–7
  Miners, 216–17
  Patriotic, 204, 215
  Reform League, 158, 206
  Second Front, 221
  Social Democratic Federation, 162, 172, 206
  Socialist, 207
  Suffragette, 205–6
  Tory Free Traders, 161–2
  Unemployed, 212–13, 214, 217, 218
    Other,
    Clerkenwell Green, 152, 161
    Cumberland Market, 166
    Hyde Park, 156–7
  Kennington Common, 138, 148–51
  Peckham Rye, 161
Deptford, 166
"Dod Street Affair", 161
Donaldson, Thomas, architect, 75, 80–1, 82, 83
Donnelly, Ignatius, 18
Dover, Lord, 122
Dowager, Queen, 93
Dual Alliance, 127
Dublin,
  Easter Rising, 52
  Nelson's Pillar, 51–2
  O'Connell Street, 51–2
Duke of York, Memorial, 16
Duke Street, St. James's, 40
Duncannon, Lord, 37, 43
Duncannon Street, 76

East India Company, 93, 117, 123
Eastlake, Charles, 100, 101
Easton and Amos, engineers, 88
Eccles, David, 228, 229
Ede, Chuter, 221, 222, 223, 224, 225, 226, 227
Edinburgh, 89
Eleanor of Castille, Cross of, 23
Elgin, Lord, 123
Elizabeth, Queen, 26
Ellenborough, Earl of, 115, 117
Ellice, Sir E., 159
Emergency Powers Act, 1920, 219
Emergency Powers (Defence) Act, 1939, 220
Emmott, Lord, 208
Empire, idea of, 19
Equitable Society Assurance Company, 41
Euston Road, 37
"Ever Victorious Army", 124
Exeter Change, 40
Exeter, Marquis of, 40

Fascism, 218–19, 221–2, 223, 224
Feudalism, 155
Flashman, John, 40
Flaxman, John, sculptor, 50, 55, 56
Fleet Street, 24
Fowler, Charles, architect, 62
Fox, C. J., 31
France, 155

French expansionism, 49
French Revolution, 49, 155
Frith Street, 40

Gage, Sir John, 24
"Gagging Acts", 139, 140–4
Gately, Kevin, 220
Gautier, Theophile, 17
Geddes, Auckland, 209
Geddes, Sir Eric, 128
Gentleman's Magazine, 52
George II, 29
George IV, 35, 56, 111, 112, 129
German Invasion of England, 17
Germany, 221
Gibbons, Grinling, sculptor, 26
Gibbs, James, architect, 26
Gladstone, W. E., 169, 195
Goldicutt, John, architect, 37, 56
Gordon, Charles G., 122–6, 170
Gordon Riots, 143
Graham, R. B. Cunninghame, 188, 197
Granton Quarry, 89
Graphic, 125
Great Mews at Charing Cross, 29
Great National Hunger March, 213
Great Yarmouth, 81
Green Mews at Charing Cross, 29
Greenwich Hill, 50
Greenwich Observatory, 50
Greenwich Naval Hospital, 50, 77
Grenadier Guards, 189
Grey, Earl, 45
Grey, Sir George, 138, 148
Grissell and Peto, builders, 67, 88, 94, 95, 96
Guildhall, London, 55
Gwilt, Joseph, 75, 80, 82, 83

Habeas Corpus, 139
Habsburgs, 128
Hackney, 222
Halifax, Viscount, 129
Hamilton, Lady, 101
Hannington, Wal, 212, 213
Hardwick, Philip, architect, 74, 80, 81, 82
Hardy, Vice-Admiral Sir Thomas, 42, 57
Harmsworth Press, 205
Havelock, General Sir Henry, 117–22, 129
Hay Market, 34
Haymarket, 188
Health, Minister of, 217
Henderson, Sir Edmund, 168–9
Henry VIII, 24, 26
Hill, Lord, 113
Hitler, Adolf, 17
Hohenzollerns, 128
Holland, Sir Henry, 167
Homeless in Trafalgar Square, 171–2, 176
Home Office, 113, 156, 158, 177, 179, 228
Home Secretary, 138
Houses of Parliament, protection of, 159
Howard, William, 40
Hughes, Superintendent, 157
Hungry Forties, 147
Hyde Park, 24, 31, 112, 156, 157, 213
Hyndman, H., 161, 165, 206

Illustrated London News, 208
Imperial Defence League, 222
Incitement to Disaffection Act, (1934), 219
Income Tax, 135
Independent Labour Party, 209
India, 114–15, 221
Indian Mutinies, 117, 119, 121
Indian Soldiers, 118–19
Inglis, Sir R. H., 62, 64, 70
Institute of Architects, 63, 81
Ireland, 51, 52

Jacobites, 25
James, C. H., sculptor, 130
Jellicoe, Admiral John R., 126–31
Jellicoe, Lady, 130–1
Jermyn Street, 40
Jingoism, 204
Johnson, Francis, architect, 51
Jones, Ernest, 150, 152

Kenney, Annie, 206
Kennington Common, 138, 148–9, 150
Kent, William, architect, 29

Khartoum, 125
Kidd, Ronald, 219
Kirk, Thomas, sculptor, 51
Kitchener, Lord, 125, 210
Knight, Galley, 79
Knightsbridge Barracks, 31, 159

Labour Emancipation League, 161
Labour Leader, The, 209
Labour, Ministry of, 212
Labour Party, 219
Laissez-faire, 160
Lansbury, George, 212
Lansdowne, Lord, 45
Lansdowne, Marquis of, 151
Landseer, Sir Edwin, 107–8
Law and Liberty League, 179
Leeds, Duke of, 34
Lewis, E. D., 197
Liberal Party, 125
Life Guards, 188–9
Lincoln, Lord, 95, 99, 101
Linnell, Alfred, 192–3
Lions, symbolic use of, 53
Lipton, Marcus, 222
Liverpool, Lord, 35, 55
Lodging Houses, 176
Lomellini, Caesar, 18
London Assurance Company, 41
London County Council, 212, 217, 222
London District Council of the Unemployed, 212
London Gas Company, 88–9
London Labour Party, 219
London Stop the War Committee, 209
London Trades Council, 224
London United Workers Committee, 161–2
London, City of, 55, 57, 61
  East End of, 218
  Fortification of, 149
  other references, 17, 88, 153
Lough, J. G., sculptor, 65, 67, 107
Lucknow, 120
Luddites, 139
Lutyens, Sir Edwin, architect, 88, 130

MacDonald, Ramsay, 217
Mahdists, 125
Malcolm, Admiral Sir Pulteney, 57
Malta, 49
Mann, Tom, 217
Mansion House, 57
Marathon, 53
Marble Arch, 82, 112
Marochetti, Baron, sculptor, 108
Mars Ultor, Temple of, 16
Marshall, Joshua, sculptor, 26
Mark, Sir Robert, 220
Marx, Karl, 160
Mary, Queen, 24
Masefield, John, 21
Master of Fortification, 29
Matthews, Henry, 195–6, 198
Maudling, Reginald, 231
May Day Processions, 225
McLagen, Eric, 129
McMillan, William, sculptor, 130
McNeil, Robert, 209–10
Mediaeval Churches, sculpture in, 48
Mediterranean, Napoleon's control of, 49
Meerut, 119
Melbourne, Lord, 56, 58
Memorials, didactic use of, 49
Metropolitan Board of Works, 161
Metropolitan Police,
  banning of demonstrations, 137, 179
  and Chartism, 152
  Committee of Inquiry into, 167
  and demonstrators, 167, 168, 187, 188, 220, 227
  and fascists, 222, 224
  and homeless, 172, 176
  and political processions, 225
  reform of, 169
  and socialists, 214, 226
  and Trafalgar Square Regulations, (1952), 227–8
  and unemployed, 162, 167, 169, 171–2, 176–7, 212–15, 217, 219
Metropolitan Radical Association, 179, 198
Middle Classes, attitude to Bloody Sunday, 189–90

Military discipline, 117
Military Opinions, 159
Millbank, 159
Military Service Act, 1915, 208–9
Milne, Alexander, 29, 42, 74
Milnes, Thomas, sculptor, 107
Minto, Earl of, 62
Mob, fears of, 165, 166, 167
Monopoly Capitalism, 18, 221
Moore, Fressage and Moore, founders, 105–7
Morley's Hotel, 42, 43, 188
Morning Post, 125
Morpeth, Lord, 101
Morris, William, 21, 160, 161, 165, 166, 187
Mosley, Sir Oswald, 218, 221–2, 223, 224
Mutinies in India, 118
Munitions Act, (1915), 208

Napier, Major-General Charles, 113–17, 129, 147
Napoleon, 17, 57
Napoleonic Wars and sculpture, 48–9
Nash, John, architect,
accused of fraud, 39
appointed as Surveyor-General, 35
attitude to classes, 31
design for Marble Arch, 111
estimates for Charing Cross Improvements, 41
First Report to H.M.W.F.L.R., 29, 31, 33, 34
plan for square at Charing Cross, 35–6, 37
project for National Gallery, 43
proposed street to Bloomsbury, 33
relations with other architects, 81
National Charter Association, 146
National Council for Civil Liberties, 218, 223, 226, 227
National Gallery, 43, 65, 73, 75, 82, 149, 159
National Government, 218
National Monuments, money for, 52
National Unemployed Workers Committee Movement, 212, 214, 215
Naval battles, 101–2, 103
Naval traditions, 126
Nazis, 17
Neo-Classicism, 15
Nelson, Horatio,
and British Empire, 49
attitude of City of London towards, 48
attitude to Prince of Wales, 111
and British Fleet, 49
death, 51, 103–4
fame of, 56
as hero, 49
and lesser heroes, 53–4
monuments to, 51, 55, 82, 130
portrayal in sculpture, 55
proposed marble statue of, 62
proposal of monument in London to, 58
sailors conditions under, 21
sculpture on Marble Arch, 82
subscription for memorial 1805, 58
Nelson Column Emeute, 134
Nelson Memorial (Column) Trafalgar Square,
bas reliefs, 98, 101–7
capital design of, 97
classical references, 16, 17
Competition results, 62
completion of, 109
concern over height, 62
cost of, 65
crowds attack, 137
effect on National Gallery, 70–1, 75–6
exhibition of designs for, 63
Government approval of, 59
height of, 72
highest Corinthian column, 66
hoisting of Nelson statue, 90–3
lions, 98, 107, 108, 109
and Select Committee on Trafalgar Square, 69
subscriptions for, 57, 67
tenders for building, 67
Nelson Memorial Committee (N.M.C.), 56, 57, 59, 89, 93, 98, 99
Nelson Memorial Sub-Committee, 62, 64

New Street (Regent Street)
Commissioners, 29, 40–1
New Street, 34, 41, 42
News from Nowhere, 21
No Conscription Fellowship, 209
Nore, Mutiny on the, 19
Northampton, Marquis of, 151
Northumberland, Duke of, 40, 62, 64
Northern Ireland, 231
Nurse, William, 43

O'Brien, William, 179
O'Connor, Fergus, 147, 150
Old Kent Road, 166
Old Round Court, 40
Operative Stonemasons Union, 94, 9
Opium trade, 123
Opium Wars, 123
Ottawa, 88
Oxford Circus, 77
Oxford Street, 213

Paddington Road, 88
Paget, Sir Edward, 119
Pall Mall, 162
Pall Mall East, 76
Pall Mall Gazette, 170, 179
Palmerston, Lord, 16, 104, 151
Pankhurst, Sylvia, 206, 209
Paris, 17, 83
Paris Commune, 17
Park Crescent, 77
Park, Patrick, sculptor, 60, 62
Parliament Square, 156
Patriotic Fund, 58
Paving Board, 87
Peking, 123, 127
Peel, Sir Robert, 16, 43, 62, 100, 104
Persia, 118
Peshawar, 121
Peterloo, 142
Peters, Hugh, 24
Philip, King of Spain, 24
Philippe, Louis, 137
Physicians, College of, 37
Piccadilly, 34, 40
Pick, Frank, 131
Pitt, William, 49
Place Vendôme, 17
Police Act, (1919), 219
Political processions, banning of, 226
Poor, conditions of, 31
Poor Law, 146
Poplar, Borough of, 212
Porridge Island, 31
Poverty, rediscovery of, 160
Power, William Mailes, 207
Poynter, Ambrose, architect, 60
Prendergast, Mr., 40
Prospectus of a Model devoted to the Memory of Lord Nelson, 54, 55
Public Order, 219
Public Order Act, (1936), 219–20, 226–7, 230
Public Service (the Army), 34
Punch, 77, 135

Railton, William, architect,
and bas reliefs, 101
as classicist, 16
design of capital, 97
and Grissell and Peto, 94
and Lord Lincoln, 101
design of lions, 107
site for Nelson Monument, 65
wins Nelson Memorial Competition, 62
and Select Committee, 72, 83–4
plans for Trafalgar Square, 73
Railway builders, 94
Rainy, Alexander, 61, 62
Red Lion Square, 220
Reform Bill (1831), 145; (1867), 145
Reform Club, 137
Reform League, 157
Reformers Wall, Geneva, 131
Regent's Park, 39, 41
Regent Street, 41, 137
Reichstag, 17
Reid, R. J., 196
Republicanism, Irish, 231
Reynolds, G. W. M., 135
Rhodes, Cecil, 129
Rice, T. Spring, 58, 59, 62, 64, 79
Richards, George, 40

Ridley, Sir M. W., 39
Riots, 31, 139, 145, 147, 148
Ripon, Bishop of, 93
Roman Empire, 16
Roman legions, 54
Romanovs, 128
Romantics, 53
Rome, 16, 83
Rosebery, Lord, 126
Rothschilds, bankers, 35
Royal Academy, 63
Royal College of Physicians, 86, 177
Royal Commission (1855), 157
Royal Exchange Assurance Company, 41
Royal Fine Arts Commission, 129–30, 131
Royal George, 97
Royal Mews at Charing Cross, 26, 34, 149
Royal Palaces, 149
Royal Parks, 152, 159
Royal Parks and Gardens Act, (1872), 158
Rudé, George, 31
Russia, Emperor of, 99
Russell, Sir Charles, 195
Rutland, Duke of, 57

St. Anne's, Soho, 34
St. George's Barracks, 40, 149, 159
St. George's-in-the-East, 167
St. Giles, rookery, 31
St. James's Market, 34
St. James's Park, 25, 137
St. James, poor in relation to, 31
St. James's Square, 77
St. Margaret's, Westminster, 26
St. Martin's-in-the-Fields, 26, 34, 36, 37, 44, 73–4, 171, 176
St. Martin's Lane, 26, 37, 40, 187
St. Martin's Workhouse, 42
St. Petersburg, 83
St. Paul's Cathedral, 48, 56, 125, 128
Salisbury, Lord, 176, 198
Saltaire, 107
Samuel, Sir Herbert, 209
Sanders, William, 179
Scab labour, 97
Scott, Charles D., 58, 59, 62, 67, 79, 89–90
Scott, John, 58
Seamen, conditions of, 19, 20, 21
  impressment of, 20
  injured, 19, 58
  killed, 58
Second International, 207
Select Committee on Trafalgar Square, 69–85
Seven Dials, 31
Seymour, Admiral Sir E., 127
Shaftesbury, Lord, 16
Shaw-Lefevre, George, 198
Sheddon, George, 58, 59
Sheddon, W. G., 59
Shopkeepers and Police, 169
Shortt, Thomas, 95–6
Sievier, Robert W. S., sculptor, 62, 100
Simon, Sir John, 220
"Six Acts", 144–5
Skeat, Walter, 23
Smirke, Sir Robert, architect, 66, 73, 75, 86
Smirke, Sydney, architect, 80, 81, 82
Smith, Abel, 59
Smith, C. H., and Company, 89
Smith, G. R., 59
Smith, James, sculptor, 55
Smith, Samuel, 160
Smollet, Tobias, 25
Soane, Sir John, architect, 35
Social Democratic Federation, 161, 162, 165–7, 172, 198, 206
Soeur, Hubert le, sculptor, 26
Soldiers, flogging of, 19
Sons of St. George, 222
Soviet Union, 221
Special Constables, 138, 151, 190, 192
Speer, Albert, 17
Spring Gardens, 25
Stallard, Jock, 231
Standard Imperial Measures, 17
Stead, W. T., 179
Strand, 36, 73, 152
Street lighting, 88

Strikes,
on Westminster Abbey, 95
on Trafalgar Square and Nelson's Column, 96
Stuart, James, 197–8
Sudan, 124
Suffragettes, 205–6
Summerson, Sir John, 31
Syme, Ronald, 16

Taiping, 124
Taiping Rebellion, 123
Taylor, George Ledwell, architect, 42
Ternouth, John, sculptor, 100, 101
Tennyson, Lord, 116
Thames Embankment, 126
Thames, River, 23, 40, 159
Thatched House Tavern, 57
Thermopylea, 53
Thornycroft, Hammo, sculptor, 125
Tientsin, 127
Times, The, 137–8, 152, 165, 170, 179, 188, 189, 193
Tory Fair Traders, 161
Tower of London, 149
Trades Dispute Act, 1927, 219
Traders, 34
Trade Unionism, 21
Trafalgar, Battle of, 50, 56
Trafalgar Day, 98, 207
Trafalgar Square,
Armistice Day celebrations, 212
Anti-war rally, 207, 209
and Beatty bust, 129–31
Black Monday, 162
Bloody Sunday, 188–9
and Cunningham bust, 131
demonstrations, *see* Demonstrations
effects of laying out, 87–8
Emmott Rules, 208
fountains and water supply, 88, 130
George IV statue, 112
and Gordon statue, 125
Government fears of, 87
and Havelock statue, 117
homeless sleeping in, 171–2
Hunger Marchers, 217
and Jellicoe bust, 129
loans for building, 41
and loudspeakers, 217
May Day Rally 1949, 225
and miners, 216
and Napier statue, 117
open and unenclosed, 88
Parliamentary debates on, 195–200
Police Box, 215–16
relationship to National Gallery, 75
residents attitude to demonstrations, 170
sale of literature, 215
shopkeepers, 170
site for Naval monuments, 56
Standard Imperial Measures, 50
and State Celebrations, 204
Suffragette meetings, 206–7
temporary buildings on, 210–11
and unemployed, 213–18
Wings for Victory Week, 126
other references, 15, 17, 19, 21, 23, 26, 58, 64, 165, 166
Trafalgar Square, Acts and Regulations,
57 George III c. 19, 143
7 and 8 Victoria c. 60., 155–6, 195
Regulations 1892, 198
Regulations 1914, 208
Regulations 1952, 228–30
Trafalgar Square, Select Committee on,
appointment of, 69
attitude to Barry's plan, 70
attitude to Nelson Memorial Committee, 71–2
attitude to Railton, 71
expert witnesses, 70, 80, 84
members of, 69
Trajan's Column, 16, 83
Treasury, H.M., 45, 65, 66, 87, 99
Triple Alliance, 127
Troops in London, 152
Trowbridge, Sir Thomas, 59
Truman Doctrine, 224
Tyburn, 25

Unemployed, 170, 171, 205, 212, 213
"Unemployed Sunday", 214

Union Club House, 37
Union Movement, 223, 226
Union of British Freedom, 222
United Services Club, 125
United States of America, 221
Uttar Pradesh, 119

Vagrancy Acts, 171
Vendôme, Place, Paris, 17
Victoria and Albert Museum, 129
Victoria Park, 152
Victoria, Queen, 56, 93, 176
Victoria Street, 159
Victory as portrayed in sculpture, 55
Vine Street, 40
Vivian, Sir Hussey, 63, 93
Volunteer Civil Force, 207
Voysey, Charles, architect, 130

Walker, Peter, 231
Walker, T., engineer, 66, 73
War Memorials, government finance for, 49
War Office, 158, 179
Warren, Sir Charles, 169–70, 171, 172, 176, 177, 181, 190, 192, 193, 195, 198
Watch Boxes, 88
Waterloo, Battle of, 139
Waterloo Place, 16, 125
Watson, Captain, 51
Watson, M. L., sculptor, 100, 101
Webster, Sir Richard, 196
Wellington City Committee, 97
Wellington, Duke of,
  Chairman of N.M.C., 61
  Chairman of N.M.C. Sub-Committee, 62
  and civil disturbances, 159
  contributes to N.M. subscriptions, 93
  duel with Winchelsea, 57
  and Duke of York Memorial Committee, 16
  as hero, 17
  as Member of N.M.C., 59
  military preparations for 1848, 149, 150, 151, 152
  and Philip Hardwick, 81
  as Prime Minister, 57
  and Reform Bill, 145
  attitude of Select Committee towards, 84
Wellington Memorial Committee, 57
Welstein, Gabriel, 18
Westmacott, Sir Richard, sculptor, 55, 75, 80, 81, 82, 100
Westminster Abbey, 48, 125
Westminster, City of, 17
Westminster Hall, 29
Wheeler, Charles, sculptor, 130
Whig Government, 57
Whitcombe Street, 26
Whitehall, 17, 23, 188
Whitehall Palace, 23, 24, 25
Wilkins, William, architect, 43, 44, 45, 51, 78, 82
William IV, 42–3, 49, 56
Williams, John, 165
Wilson's Court, 40
Wings for Victory Week, 126
Wood, William, 52–4
Woods, Forests and Land Revenues, Office of, 44, 64, 65, 87, 100, 101, 107, 111
Woodington, William F., sculptor, 100, 101, 104, 105, 107
Workers Suffrage Federation, 209
Works, Ministry of, 126, 228
Works, Office of, 112, 117, 122, 125, 129, 177, 212, 215
World War I, 17, 104, 126, 207–11
World War II, 131, 220–1
Wortley, Stuart, 177
Wren, Sir Christopher, architect, 25, 82
Wyatt, Benjamin, architect, 16
Wyatt, James, architect, 55
Wyatt, M. C., 54, 55, 57, 82
Wyatt, Sir Thomas, 24

Yeats, W. B., poet, 51